SCIENCE FICTION AND FANTASY SERIES AND SEQUELS

GARLAND REFERENCE LIBRARY
OF THE HUMANITIES
(Vol. 611)

SCIENCE FICTION AND FANTASY SERIES AND SEQUELS
A Bibliography

Volume 1: Books

Tim Cottrill
Martin H. Greenberg
Charles G. Waugh

GARLAND PUBLISHING, INC. • NEW YORK & LONDON
1986

© 1986 Tim Cottrill, Martin H. Greenberg,
and Charles G. Waugh
All rights reserved

Library of Congress Cataloging-in-Publication Data

Cottrill, Tim, 1958–
  Science fiction and fantasy series and sequels.

  (Garland reference library of the humanities ;
vol. 611–)
  Bibliography: p.
  Includes index.
  Contents: v. 1. Books.
  1. Science fiction—Bibliography. 2. Fantastic
fiction—Bibliography. 3. Series (Publications)—
Bibliography. 4. Sequels (Literature)—Bibliography.
I. Greenberg, Martin Harry. II. Waugh, Charles.
III. Title. IV. Series: Garland reference library of the
humanities ; v. 611, etc.
Z5917.S36C67   1986   016.80883'876   85-45121
[PN3433.8]
ISBN 0-8240-8671-6 (v. 1 : alk. paper)

Cover Design by Alison Lew

Printed on acid-free, 250-year-life paper
Manufactured in the United States of America

CONTENTS

Foreword	vii
Publisher Abbreviations	ix
Special Acknowledgments	xix
Series and Sequels	1
Anthology Series	241
Addenda	276
Sequence Index	285
Book Title Index	307
Bibliography	395

FOREWORD

WHAT THIS INDEX CONTAINS

Science Fiction & Fantasy Series & Sequels is a comprehensive checklist of publications comprising extended series, two-volume sequences, sequels to an author's original work by other authors, and other multi-volume book formats which possess elements of the science-fiction, fantasy, and horror genres published between 1700 and 1985. Though most of the works listed are novels, collected stories by an author are also included when the collections clearly comprise part of the sequence. In a few instances collections have been included which may only contain one or a few stories pertaining to a series, and these are so identified.

Series classification can be a somewhat subjective determination, but in general we have included those sequences which contain common characters, locations, societies, or in some cases share a common created history or closely connected theme. Notes or subject information are included with some of the more complex series which we felt required additional explanation.

HOW TO USE THIS GUIDE

Entries are arranged alphabetically by author. In the case of multiple-author series, the series will be listed under its overall title, with each contributing author cross-referenced throughout the index as well. Each sequence is given a title, with the individual works of the series listed beneath. The date of the original first book publication follows the title, as does the name or abbreviation of the original publisher. In some cases, where original magazine or pulp publication preceded book form by a considerable number of years, two dates are given— the first being the pulp appearance.

If a book is known by two or more titles, the original title is listed first, followed on the next line by "aka" and the later variation with its publisher and date in parenthesis. The author's name in multiple-author series is located in parenthesis immediately following the title. Additional information indicated by an asterisk (*) beside a series title follows at the end of that individual series. Series which have been collected in a single volume under the series title are identified by the abbreviation "coll" followed by the omnibus copyright and publisher.

The Anthology section of listings at the end of the guide is arranged alphabetically by editor, and is cross-referenced within the Anthology division. However, the two sections of this guide are not cross-referenced between each other.

When possible, titles are arranged in the order of their internal chronology of events when such chronology is significant. Otherwise, listings are in order of publication.

In some instances, late additions to this index may be lacking publisher identification. We hope to amend these omissions in future editions, and also solicit information on any series, titles, etc., which the reader feels we have overlooked.

PUBLISHER ABBREVIATIONS
(pb= paperback; L= London)

A&B	Allison & Busby (L)
A&CBk	Adam & Charles Black (L)
ABC	American Book Company
Abeld	Abelard-Schuman
Abram	Ben Abramson (Chicago)
Ace	Ace Books (pb) (NY)
Adver	Advertiser (Hawaii)
Aeon	Aeonian
ALane	Allen Lane (NY)
Altem	Henry Altemus (Philadelphia)
Ang&R	Angus & Robertson (Australia)
Apoll	Apollo (pb) (Woodbridge, Connecticut)
Apple	Appleton; or Appleton-Century-Crofts (NY)
Aquar	Aquarium Press
Arbor	Arbor House (NY)
Ariel	Ariel (NY)
ArkH	Arkham House (Sauk City, Wisconsin)
Arlin	Arlington Books (L)
Armad	Armada (L)
Arrow	J.W. Arrowsmith (L)
Athen	Atheneum Publishers (NY)
Atom	Atomic Books (NY)
Avalo	Avalon Books (NY)
Avon	Avon Books (pb) (NY)
Award	Award (NY)
Badgr	Badger (pb) (L)
Baen	Baen Books (pb) (NY)
Ball	Ballantine Books (NY)
Bant	Bantam Books (pb) (NY)
BantL	Bantam (pb) (Los Angeles)
Barkr	Arthur Barker (L)
BartH	Bart House (pb)
Baumg	Baumgardt Publishing Co. (Los Angeles)
Beagl	Beagle (pb) (NY)
Beauf	Beaufort
Bee-L	Bee-Line Books (pb)
Behrm	Behrman's Jewish Book House (NY)
Belmt	Belmont (pb) (NY)
Benn	Ernest Benn (L)
Benty	Bentley
Berk	Berkley Books (pb) (NY)
Bjay	Bluejay Books (NY)
BkKnt	Black Knight (Leicester, UK)
BkLtd	Books Ltd. (L)
Bkslr	Bookseller

Bles	Geoffrey Bles (L)
Blk&S	Blackie & Son (L)
Blkwd	William Blackwood & Sons (L)
Bob-M	The Bobbs-Merrill Co. (Indianapolis)
BodH	The Bodley Head, John Lane (L)
Bohn	H.G. Bohn (L)
Boni	A. & C. Boni; or Boni & Liveright (NY)
Brand	Brandon House (N. Hollywood, CA)
Braz	George Braziller (NY)
Brent	Brentano's (NY)
Brock	Brockhampton Press (Leicester, UK)
BuffB	Buffalo Book Co. (Providence, RI)
Burke	Burke (L)
Burt	A. L. Burt (NY)
Bush	C. Bush (Toronto)
C&W	Chatto & Windus (L)
CambU	Cambridge University Press
Camer	Cameron & Co.
Canav	Canaveral Press (NY)
Cape	Jonathan Cape (L)
Carco	Carcosa Press
Carlt	Carlton Press (NY)
Cass	Cassell & Co. (L)
CCTP	Collins Clear-Type Press (L)
CdRdr	Candid Reader (pb) (San Diego)
CECaz	Camille E. Cazedessus, Jr. (Baton Rouge, LA)
Centr	Cantaur (NY)
Centy	Century (NY)
ChapH	Chapman & Hall (L)
Chart	Charter (pb) (NY)
Chav	Chavannes & Co. (Knoxville, TN)
Chilt	Chilton (Philadelphia)
Clode	Edward J. Clode (NY)
Colwd	Collingwood Bros. (L)
Comp	Compact (pb) (L)
Const	Constable & Co. (L)
Conti	Continuum (NY)
Corgi	Corgi Books (pb) (L)
Corin	Corinth (pb) (San Diego)
Coron	Coronet (NY)
Cosmo	Cosmopolitan Book Corporation (NY)
CosSF	Cosmos Science Fiction Series (Wallsend, UK)
Covi	Covici, Friede (NY)
CowMc	Coward-McCann (NY)
CriCl	Crime Club, Doubleday (NY)
Crite	Criterion (L)
Crowl	Crowell
Crown	Crown Publishers (NY)
Cunni	J. Cunningham (L)

Cup&L	Cupples & Leon
Curt	Curtis Publishing
Curwg	Currawong Publishing Co. (Sydney, Australia)
Curwn	Curwen Press (Plainstow, UK)
Daker	Andrew Dakers (L)
Dark	Darkroom
DAW	DAW Books, New American Library (pb) (NY)
Dbdy	Doubleday & Co.; Doubleday, Page; Doubleday, Doran (NY)
Delac	Delacorte (NY)
Dell	Dell Publishing Co. (pb) (NY)
DelR	Del Rey, Ballantine Books (NY)
Dent	J.M. Dent & Sons (L)
Dial	Dial Press (NY)
Digit	Digit (pb) (L)
Dik&T	L. Dickson & Thompson (L)
Dillg	Dillingham
DimeP	Dimeda Pulp
Dobs	Dennis Dobson (L)
Dodd	Dodd, Mead & Co. (NY)
Donng	Donning (NY)
Doran	George H. Doran Co. (NY)
Dover	Dover Books (L)
EdArn	Edward Arnold (L)
Elsev	Elsevier
EMath	Elkin Mathews (L)
Ember	Ember Library (pb) (San Francisco)
EPDut	E.P. Dutton & Co. (NY)
Epic	Epic (pb) (Los Angeles)
Epwth	Epworth Press (L)
ERB	Edgar Rice Burroughs, Inc. (Tarzana, CA)
Eros	Eros Goldstripe (Wilmington, Delaware)
Essex	Essex House (N. Hollywood)
Evans	Evans Bros. (L)
Expo	Exposition Press (pb) (NY)
Eyre	Eyre & Spottiswoode (L)
Faber	Faber & Faber (L)
FantP	Fantasy Press (Reading, PA)
Farr	Farrar & Rinehart; Farrar, Strauss & Cudahy; Farrar, Strauss & Giroux; Farrar, Strauss & Rinehart (NY)
Fawc	Fawcett World Library (pb) (NY)
Fed	Federal
Fell	Frederick Fell (NY)
FictB	Fictioneer Books (Lakemont, CA)
Fires	Fireside
Font	Fontana (pb) (L)

Forum	Forum Publishing Co. (Boston)
FourS	Four Square (pb) (L)
FoWri	Fowler Wright (L)
FPCI	Fantasy Publishing Co., Inc. (NY)
Freew	Freeway Press (NY)
FunkW	Funk & Wagnalls Co. (NY)
Futur	Futura
FyFic	Fantasy Fiction (Sydney, Australia)
G&D	Grosset & Dunlap (NY)
Gawth	P.R. Gawthorn (L)
GHill	George M. Hill
Gnome	Gnome Press (NY)
Goldn	Golden Press (NY)
GoldM	Gold Medal Books (pb) (NY)
GoldS	Gold Star (pb) (Derby, Connecticut)
Gollz	Victor Gollancz (L)
Gould	Mark Goulden (L)
GPier	G. Pierce
Grana	Granada
Grand	Grandon Company (Providence, RI)
Grant	Donald M. Grant (W. Kingston, RI)
Green	Greening & Co. (L)
Gregg	Gregg Press (NY)
Greys	House of Greystoke
GRich	Grant Richards (L)
Griff	Charles Griffen (L)
Grnbg	Greenberg (NY)
Grnlf	Greenleaf Classic (pb) (San Diego)
Grnw	Greenwillow
Grove	Grove Press (NY)
GSmit	Goldsmith
GSwan	Gerald G. Swan (L)
Gylen	Gylendal (L)
H&B	Hurst & Blackett (L)
H&S	Hodder & Stoughton (L)
Hadly	Hadley Publishing Co. (Providence, RI)
Hale	Robert Hale & Co. (L)
Ham&C	Hamilton & Co. (L)
HamiH	Hamish Hamilton (L)
Harb	Harborough Publishing Co. (pb) (UK)
Harc	Harcourt, Brace & Co.; Harcourt, Brace & World; Harcourt-Brace-Jovanovich (NY)
Harmy	Harmony Books (NY)
Harpr	Harper & Brothers; Harper & Row (NY)
Harri	Harrison
Harrp	George G. Harrap (L)
HartD	Rupert Hart-Davis (L)
Hawth	Hawthorn Books (Englewood Cliffs, NJ)

Heine	Heinemann Publishers (L)
Herit	Heritage Press
HILib	Hearst's International Library (NY)
Hillm	Hillman Periodicals (pb) (NY)
HMiff	Houghton Mifflin Co. (Boston)
Hmlyn	The Hamlyn Publishing Group (Feltham, UK)
Holt	Henry Holt & Co.; Holt, Rinehart & Winston (NY)
Howe	Gerald Howe (L)
Howtz	Horowitz
Hurst	Hurst & Co. (NY)
Hutch	Hutchinson & Co., Publishers (L)
Hyper	Hyperion Press (NY)
IvesW	Ives, Washburn
Jarrd	Jarrolds Publishers (L)
Jay	Jay Books (L)
JCald	J. Calder
JDay	The John Day Co. (NY)
Jenk	Herbert Jenkins (L)
JJohn	J. Johnson (L)
JLane	John Lane (L)
JLong	John Long (L)
JMurr	John Murray Publishers (L)
Josph	Michael Joseph (L)
Jove	Jove (pb), Berkley Publishing
JThom	J. Thomas (L)
JTons	Jacob Tonson (L)
Kears	G. Kearsley (L)
Kimbl	H. Ingalls Kimball (NY)
Knopf	Alfred A. Knopf (NY)
Krueg	Krueger, Hamburg (NY)
Lance	Lancer Books (pb) (NY)
Lantn	Lantern Press (NY)
Laser	Laser Books (pb) (NY)
LateH	Late-Hour (pb)
Lee&S	Lee & Shepard (Boston)
Lehmn	John Lehmann (L)
Leisr	Leisure Books (pb) (N. Hollywood)
Lemur	Lemurian Press (Milwaukee)
Lipp	J.B. Lippincott & Co. (Philadelphia)
Liver	Liveright Publishers (NY)
LogoP	Logographic Press (L)
LongG	Longmans, Green & Co. (L)
Lothr	Lothrop Publishing Co. (Boston)
Lovel	John W. Lovell (NY)
Low,M	Low, Marsten & Co.; Sampson, Low (L)
LtBrn	Little, Brown & Co. (Boston)
Luttr	Lutterworth Press (L)

M&M	Mycroft & Moran (Sauk City, Wisconsin)
Macau	Macauley Co. (NY)
Macd	Macdonald & Co. (L)
Macf	Macfadden-Bartell (NY)
MacGi	MacGibbon & Kee (L)
Macm	The Macmillan Co. (NY)
MacmL	Macmillan (L)
Macq	John Macqueen (L)
Manus	Manuscript Press
Mastr	Master Publications (California)
MaxP	Maxfield Parrish
Mayfl	Mayflower (pb) (L)
McbrH	Macabre House
McBri	Robert M. McBride & Co. (NY)
McCal	McCall Books (NY)
McClg	A.C. McClurg (Chicago)
McClr	McClure Co.; McClure & Phillips (NY)
McGrH	McGraw-Hill Book Co. (NY)
Melro	Andrew Melrose (L)
Mermk	Merrimack
Mertn	Merton Press (L)
Mesnr	Julian Messner (NY)
Meth	Methuen & Co. (L)
Metro	Metropolitan (NY)
MiJos	Michael Joseph (L)
Mills	Mills & Boon (L)
Milne	Milne & Co. (L)
Mitre	Mitre Press (L)
Mnyld	Manyland
Moody	Moody Press
Morph	Joseph Morphew & James Woodward (L)
MStar	Morningstar
Mullr	Frederick Muller (L)
Munro	George Munro's Sons (NY)
Murry	John Murray Publishers (L)
MusPr	Museum Press (L)
MystP	Mysterious Press
NAL	New American Library (pb) (NY)
NEL	New English Library (pb) (L)
NewC	New Century Press (Sydney, Australia)
Newne	George Newnes (L)
Night	Nightstand Book (pb) (San Diego)
NonPP	Non-Profit Press (Tacoma, Washington)
NWrit	Northern Writers
Ogilv	J.S. Ogilvie (NY)
Olymp	Olympia Press (Paris)
Osbor	J. Osborn (L)
OxfUn	Oxford University Press (L)

P&C	Pellegrini & Cudahy (NY)
Page	L.C. Page (Boston)
Paget	Paget Literary Agency (NY)
PAlan	Philip Allan (L)
Pan	Pan Books (pb) (L)
Pantn	Pantheon Books (NY)
Pantr	Panther Books (pb) (L)
Parlo	Parlour Library
ParnP	Parnassus Press (Berkley, CA)
PB	Pocket Books (pb) (NY)
PbLib	Paperback Library (pb) (NY)
PDavi	Peter Davies (L)
PFCol	P.F. Collier (NY)
Pears	C. Arthur Pearson (L)
Peirc	George Peirce (L)
Peng	Penguin Books (pb) (L)
Peter	T.B. Peterson & Bros. (Philadelphia)
Phant	Phantasia Press (Huntington Woods, Michigan)
Philo	Philosophical Library (NY)
Phnix	Phoenix
Picco	Piccolo/TV Times (L)
Pinn	Pinnacle (pb) (NY)
Play	Playboy Press
Pleas	Pleasure Reader (pb) (San Diego)
PLunn	Peter Lunn (L)
Pop	Popular Library (pb) (NY)
Powel	Powell Publications (Reseda, CA)
POwen	Peter Owen (L)
Pr-H	Prentice-Hall
Priet	Benedict Prieth (Newark, NJ)
Prime	Prime Press (Philadelphia)
PulpP	Pulp Press
Putn	G.P. Putnam's Sons (NY)
Pyr	Pyramid Books (pb) (NY)
Pytho	Python Books
QualP	Quality Press (L)
Quart	Quartet (pb) (L)
Rain	Raintree
RandH	Random House (NY)
RdMcN	Rand McNally & Co. (Chicago)
Regcy	Regency (pb) (Evanston, Illinois)
Rei&B	Reilly & Britton (Chicago)
Rei&L	Reilly & Lee (Chicago)
Rey&H	Reynal & Hitchcock (NY)
RHale	Robert Hale & Co. (L)
RichP	Richards Press (L)
Rine	Rinehart & Co. (NY)
River	Riverside Press (Cambridge, MA)

Routl	George Routledge & Sons (L)
S&J	Sidgwick & Jackson (L)
S&S	Simon & Schuster (NY)
Saalf	Saalfield Publishing Co. (Akron, OH)
Schol	Scholastic Book Services (pb) (NY)
SchPl	Schoolboys Pocket Library (pb) (L)
Scion	Scion (L)
Scott	W.R. Scott (NY)
Scrib	Charles Scribner's Sons (NY)
ScrPr	Scream Press
Seaby	Seabury
Sears	Sears Publishing Co.; J.H. Sears (NY)
Seck	Secker & Warburg; Martin Secker (L)
Seely	Seely & Co. (L)
Sel&B	Selwyn & Blount (L)
Seltz	Thomas Seltzer (L)
SevHs	Severn House
SFBC	Science Fiction Book Club (NY)
Shast	Shasta Publishers (Chicago)
Sign	Signet (pb) (NY) New American Library
Simpk	Simpkin
SimPr	Simons Press (NY)
Skeff	Skeffington & Son (L)
Sloan	William Sloane Associates (NY)
S,Low	Sampson, Low (NY)
SmMay	Small, Maynard (Boston)
Souv	Souvenir Press (L)
SpBkt	Spencer Blackett (L)
Spear	Spearman
Spher	Sphere (pb) (L)
St&Sm	Street & Smith (NY)
Stacy	Tom Stacey (L)
Stalk	Charles Stalker (L)
Stein	Stein & Day (NY)
StM	St. Martin's Press (NY)
Stock	R. Stockwell (L)
Stoke	Frederick A. Stokes Co. (Philadelphia)
Strah	Strahan (NY)
StroB	Strothers Bookshops (L)
Swift	S. Swift (L)
Symnd	Symonds
Tand	Tandem (pb) (L)
Tapl	Taplinger (NY)
Targ	Target (pb) (L)
TBPet	T.B. Peterson
Tempo	Tempo (pb) (NY)
Tick	Ticknor & Co. (Boston)
TitB	Tit-Bits Science Fiction Library (pb) (L)

T-K	T-K Graphics (Baltimore)
TNels	Thomas Nelson & Sons (L)
Tor	Tor/Pinnacle (pb) (NY)
Tower	Tower Books (World Publishing) (Chicago)
TowrL	Tower Publishing Co. (L)
Trans	Transport (Australia)
Trueb	Truebner & Co. (L)
TrueN	True Nationalist Publishing Co. (NY)
Tuckr	C. Tuckr (L)
Tudor	Tudor Books (NY)
U-M	Underwood-Miller
Unicn	Unicorn Books
UnTex	University of Texas Press
Unwin	Allen & Unwin; T. Fisher Unwin (L)
Vang	Vanguard Press (NY)
Vant	Vantage
VCori	Vernon Coriell
Vik	Viking Press (NY)
Vint	Vintage Books/Knopf (pb) (NY)
Voll	P.F. Volland (Joliet, Illinois)
Walck	Henry Z. Walck (NY)
Walkr	Walker & Co. (NY)
WardL	Ward, Lock (L)
Warne	Frederick Warne & Co. (L)
Warnr	Warner Books (pb) (NY)
Warrn	C. Warren (L)
WDist	World Distributors (Manchester)
Weide	Weidenfield
Weinb	Weinberg
Westb	Westbrook
Westm	Westminster Press (Philadelphia)
WHAll	W.H. Allen & Co. (L)
WHDav	W.H. Davis (NY)
WhitH	Whittlesey House (NY)
Whitm	Whitman Publishing Co. (Racine, Wisconsin)
WilCl	Willett, Clark (Chicago)
Winst	John C. Winston Co. (Philadelphia)
Wintb	Joseph Winterburn (San Francisco)
WKent	W. Kent (L)
WmCol	William Collins & Sons (L)
WmMor	William Morrow & Co. (NY)
World	World Publishing Co. (Cleveland)
Wr&Br	Wright & Brown (L)
WWork	World's Work/Heinemann (L)
Zebra	Zebra (pb) (NY)
ZiffD	Ziff-Davis Publishing Co. (NY)

SPECIAL ACKNOWLEDGMENTS

We would like to thank the following for their aid in compiling this index:

DALE SHERMAN — for assistance in compiling the "Doctor Who" sequence.

JEFF ALLRED — for providing complete details to the "Perry Rhodan" series.

HARRY JOHNSON — for permitting us use of "The Book Store".

ROBERT E. MANNERS — for access to his considerable collection of SF paperbacks.

BOOKERY FANTASY and its customers — for providing the impetus for this project.

A

ABBEY, LYNN

    also see: collaboration with ROBERT LYNN ASPRIN

  <u>Rifkind</u>
1. Daughter of the Bright Moon
2. The Black Flame

ABBOTT, EDWIN A. (1838-1926)

    <u>Flatland</u> (pseud.-- A. Square)
1. Flatland; A Romance of Many Dimensions
                                  1884   Seely
    (sequel)
2. Sphereland; A Fantasy About Curved
   Spaces and an Expanding Universe   '65   Crowl
   (by Dionys Burger)

ABRASHKIN, RAYMOND (1911-1960)
    (see collaboration with JAY WILLIAMS)

ADAMS, DOUGLAS (b.1952)

    The Hitchhiker Series *
1. Hitchhiker's Guide to the Galaxy   '79   Harmy
2. Restaurant at the End of the Universe '80   Harmy
3. Life, the Universe, and Everything   '82   Harmy
4. So Long, and Thanks For All the Fish '84   Harmy
   * The first 3 volumes collected as:
     Hitchhiker's Trilogy; The Omnibus Edition
                                          ('84/Harmy)

ADAMS, EUSTACE L. (b.1891)

    <u>Andy Lane</u>
    (Note-- it is possible some of the titles below
    may not be part of the Andy Lane series; the pre-
    cise order of publication is only approximate).
1. Racing Around the World   '28   G&D
2. Over the Polar Ice   '28   G&D
3. On the Wings of Flame   '29   G&D

                      (cont.)

(Eustace L. Adams, cont.)

4. The Runaway Airship	'29	G&D
5. Pirates of the Air	'29	G&D
6. The Flying Windmill	'30	G&D
7. The Mysterious Monoplane	'30	G&D
8. The Plane Without A Pilot	'30	G&D
9. Across the Top of the World	'31	G&D
10. Wings of Adventure	'31	G&D
11. Prisoners of the Clouds	'32	G&D
12. Doomed Demons	'35	G&D
13. Wings of the Navy	'36	G&D
14. War Wings	'37	G&D

ADAMS, RICHARD

The Beklan Empire
1. Shardik	'74	S&S
2. Maia	'84	Vik

ADAMS, ROBERT (b.1932)

Horseclans Series
1. The Coming of the Horseclans	'75	Pinn
2. The Sword of the Horseclans	'77	Pinn
3. Revenge of the Horseclans	'78	Pinn
4. A Cat of Silvery Hue	'79	Sign
5. The Savage Mountains	'80	Sign
6. The Patrimony	'80	Sign
7. Horseclans Odyssey	'81	Sign
8. The Death of a Legend	'81	Sign
9. The Witch Goddess	'82	Sign
10. Bili the Axe	'82	Sign
11. Champion of the Last Battle	'83	Sign
12. A Woman of the Horseclans	'83	Sign
13. Horses of the North	'85	Sign

Note: First 3 titles collected as:
"Tales of the Horseclans" ('85/NAL)

Castaways in Time
1. Castaways in Time	'84	Sign
2. The Seven Magical Jewels of Ireland	'85	Sign

ADAMS, SAMUEL HOPKINS
(see collaboration with STEWART EDWARD WHITE)

"THE ADDAMS FAMILY"

   1. The Addams Family (Jack Sharkey)   '65   Pyr
   2. The Addams Family Strikes Back
      (William Miksch)   '65   Pyr

ADLARD, MARK (b.1932)

   TCity
   1. Interface   '71   S&J
   2. Volteface   '72   S&J
   3. Multiface   '73   S&J

AHERN, JERRY

   The Survivalist
   1. Total War   '81   Zebra
   2. The Nightmare Begins   '81   Zebra
   3. The Quest   '81   Zebra
   4. The Doomsayer   '81   Zebra
   5. The Web   '83   Zebra
   6. The Savage Horde   '83   Zebra
   7. The Prophet   '84   Zebra
   8. The End is Coming   '84   Zebra
   9. Earth Fire   '84   Zebra
  10. The Awakening   '84   Zebra

AIKEN, JOAN (b.1924)

   Willoughby Chase
   1. The Wolves of Willoughby Chase   '62   Cape
   2. Black Hearts in Battersea   '64   Dbdy
   3. Nightbirds on Nantucket   '66   Cape
   4. The Stolen Lake
   5. The Cuckoo Tree   '71   Cape
   6. The Whispering Mountain   '68   Cape

   Go Saddle the Sea
   1. Go Saddle the Sea   '77   Dbdy
   2. Bridle the Wind   '83   Delac

AKERS, ALAN BURT
     (pseud.— see KENNETH BULMER)

ALDISS, BRIAN W. (b.1925)

    Helliconia
1. Helliconia Spring   '82 Athen
2. Helliconia Summer   '83 Athen
3. Helliconia Winter   '85 Athen

ALEXANDER, LLOYD (b.1924)

    Chronicles of Prydain
1. The Book of Three   '64 Holt
2. The Black Cauldron   '65 Holt
3. The Castle of Llyr   '66 Holt
4. Taran Wanderer   '67 Holt
5. The High King   '68 Holt
    related titles
6. Coll and His White Pig   '65 Holt
7. The Truthful Harp   '67 Holt
8. The Foundling, and Other Tales of Prydain   '73 Holt

ALLAN, ANGUS P. (see JOHN THEYDON)

ALLISON, CLYDE (pseud. of William Knowles)

    Agent 008
1. Our Man From SADISTO   '65 Ember
2. Our Girl From MEPHISTO   '65 Ember
3. Nautipuss   '65 Ember
4. Go-Go SADISTO   '66 Ember
5. The Desdemona Affair   '66 Ember
6. Gamefinger   '66 Ember
7. SADISTO Royale   '66 Ember
8. 008 Meets Modesta Blaze   '66 Leisr
9. For Your Sighs Only   '66 Ember
10. The Lost Bomb   '66 Ember
11. The Merciless Mermaids   '66 Leisr
12. Mondo SADISTO   '66 Leisr
13. 008 Meets Gnatman   '66 Leisr
14. The Sex-Ray   '66 Leisr
15. Roburta the Conqueress   '66 Corin
16. From Rapture with Love   '66 Leisr
17. The Ice Maiden   '67 Ember
18. The Sin Funnel   '67 CdRdr
19. Platypussy   '68 Night
20. The Desert Damsels   '68 CdRdr

ALLONBY, EDITH

    <u>Lucifram</u> (published anonymously)
1. Jewel Sowers   '03 Green
2. Marigold   '05 Green

"AMITYVILLE"

1. The Amityville Horror (Jay Anson)   '77 Pr-H
2. The Amityville Horror II (John G. Jones)   '82 Warnr
3. Amityville: The Final Chapter
   (John G. Jones)   '85 Jove

ANDERSON, CHESTER, MICHAEL KURLAND & T.A. WATERS

    <u>Greenwich Village Trilogy</u>
1. The Butterfly Kid
   (Chester Anderson)   '67 Pyr
2. The Unicorn Girl
   (Michael Kurland)   '69 Pyr
3. The Probability Pad
   (T.A. Waters)   '70 Pyr

ANDERSON, MARGARET J. (b.1931)

    <u>The Time Trilogy</u>
1. In the Keep of Time   '77 Knopf
2. In the Circle of Time   '79 Knopf
3. The Mists of Time   '84 Knopf

ANDERSON, POUL (b.1926)

    also see: ROBERT E. HOWARD, "Conan" series
    also see: FRED SABERHAGEN, for collaboration

    Anderson's future-history series is extremely complex. The first sequence concerns Nicholas van Rijn and the Polesotechnic League of merchants. The second sequence takes place in the same universe about 500 years later, revolving around agent Dominic Flandry of the Terran Empire. Novels listed in parenthesis are related to the historical sequence but do not involve Flandry or van Rijn. The following list is based on rough internal chronology, but the books need not be read in a precise order.

(Poul Anderson, cont.)

THE TECHNIC HISTORY SERIES
The Polesotechnic League

1. War of the Wing Men   '58 Ace
     aka: The Man Who Counts ('78)
2. Trader to the Stars   '64 Dbdy
3. The Trouble Twisters   '66 Dbdy
4. Satan's World   '69 Dbdy
5. Mirkheim   '77 Berk
6. The Earth Book of Stormgate   '78 Berk
7. (The People of the Wind)   '73 Sign

Dominic Flandry

8. Ensign Flandry   '66 Chilt
9. A Circus of Hells   '70 Sign
10. The Rebel Worlds   '69 Sign
11. (The Day of Their Return)   '73 Dbdy
12. Flandry of Terra   '65 Chilt
     contains: Mayday Orbit ('61/Ace)
               Earthman, Go Home ('61/Ace)
13. Agent of the Terran Empire   '65 Chilt
     contains: We Claim These Stars! ('59/Ace)
14. A Knight of Ghosts and Shadows   '75 Dbdy
15. A Stone in Heaven   '79 Ace
16. The Game of Empire   '85 Baen
     (This title features Dominic's daughter Diana)

Post-Flandry

17. Let the Spacemen Beware   '63 Ace
     aka: The Night Face ('78/Ace)
18. The Long Night   '83

The Hoka Series (with Gordon R. Dickson)
1. Earthman's Burden   '57 Gnome
2. Star Prince Charlie   '75 Putn
3. Hoka!   '84 Tor

Alternate World Sequence
1. Three Hearts and Three Lions   '61 Dbdy
2. Midsummer Tempest   '74 Dbdy

The Last Viking
1. The Golden Horn
2. The Road of the Sea Horse
3. The Sign of the Raven   '80

The Psychotechnic League
(not related to first series)
1. The Psychotechnic League   '81 Tor
2. Cold Victory   '82 Tor
3. Starship   '82 Tor

       Annals of the Time Patrol (coll.'84/SFBC)
1. Guardians of Time   '60 Ball
2. Time Patrolman   '83 Tor

ANDERSON, WILLIAM C. (b.1920)

       Penelope
1. Penelope   '63 Crown
2. Penelope, the Damp Detective '74 Crown

ANDREWS, ALLEN (b.1913)

       Plantagenet
1. The Pig Plantagenet   '80 Vik
2. Castle Crespin   '82 Hutch

ANSON, JAY (see "AMITYVILLE")

ANTHONY, PIERS (b.1934)

       Chthon
1. Chthon   '67 Ball
2. Phthor   '75 Berk

       Battle Circle (coll.)
1. Sos the Rope   '68 Pyr
2. Var the Stick   '72 Faber
3. Neq the Sword   '75 Corgi

       Omnivore
1. Omnivore   '68 Ball
2. Orn   '71 Dbdy
3. Ox   '76 Dbdy

       Jason Striker
       (written with Roberto Fuentes)
1. Kiai!   '74 Berk
2. Mistress of Death   '74 Berk
3. The Bamboo Bloodbath   '74 Berk

       Cluster
1. Cluster   '77 Avon
2. Chaining the Lady   '78 Avon
3. Kirlian Quest   '78 Avon
4. Thousandstar   '80 Avon
5. Viscous Circle   '82 Avon

(Piers Anthony, cont.)

The Magic of Xanth
1. A Spell for Chameleon   '77   DelR
2. The Source of Magic   '79   DelR
3. Castle Roogna   '79   DelR
4. Centaur Aisle   '81   DelR
5. Ogre, Ogre   '82   DelR
6. Night Mare   '82   DelR
7. Dragon on a Pedestal   '83   DelR
8. Crewel Lye   '84   DelR

Tarot
1. God of Tarot   '79   Jove
2. Vision of Tarot   '80   Berk
3. Faith of Tarot   '80   Berk

The Apprentice Adept
1. Split Infinity   '81   DelR
2. Blue Adept   '82   DelR
3. Juxtaposition   '83   DelR

Bio of a Space Pirate
1. Refugee   '83   Avon
2. Mercenary   '84   Avon
3. Politician   '85   Avon

Incarnations of Immortality
1. On a Pale Horse   '83   DelR
2. Bearing an Hourglass   '84   DelR

APPLETON, VICTOR & VICTOR APPLETON II. (House Pseudonyms)

Tom Swift (by Victor Appleton)
(Note-- titles 1-35 written by Howard Garis)
1. Tom Swift and His Motor-Cycle   '10   G&D
2. Tom Swift and His Motor-Boat   '10   G&D
3. Tom Swift and His Airship   '10   G&D
4. Tom Swift and His Submarine-Boat   '10   G&D
5. Tom Swift and His Electric Runabout '10   G&D
6. Tom Swift and His Wireless Message   '11   G&D
7. Tom Swift Among the Diamond Makers   '11   G&D
8. Tom Swift in the Caves of Ice   '11   G&D
9. Tom Swift in His Sky Racer   '11   G&D
10. Tom Swift and His Electric Rifle   '11   G&D
11. Tom Swift in the City of Gold   '12   G&D
12. Tom Swift and His Air Glider   '12   G&D
13. Tom Swift in Captivity   '12   G&D
14. Tom Swift and His Wizard Camera   '12   G&D

15. Tom Swift and His Great Searchlight	'12	G&D
16. Tom Swift and His Giant Cannon	'13	G&D
17. Tom Swift and His Photo Telephone	'14	G&D
18. Tom Swift and His Aerial Warship	'15	G&D
19. Tom Swift and His Big Tunnel	'16	G&D
20. Tom Swift in the Land of Wonders	'17	G&D
21. Tom Swift and His War Tank	'18	G&D
22. Tom Swift and His Air Scout	'19	G&D
23. Tom Swift and His Undersea Search	'20	G&D
24. Tom Swift Among the Fire Fighters	'21	G&D
25. Tom Swift and His Electric Locomotive	'22	G&D
26. Tom Swift and His Flying Boat	'23	G&D
27. Tom Swift and His Giant Oil Gusher	'24	G&D
28. Tom Swift and His Chest of Secrets	'25	G&D
29. Tom Swift and His Airline Express	'26	G&D
30. Tom Swift Circling the Globe	'27	G&D
31. Tom Swift and His Talking Pictures	'28	G&D
32. Tom Swift and His House on Wheels	'29	G&D
33. Tom Swift and His Big Dirigible	'30	G&D
34. Tom Swift and His Sky Train	'31	G&D
35. Tom Swift and His Giant Magnet	'32	G&D
36. Tom Swift and His Television Detector	'33	G&D
37. Tom Swift and His Ocean Airport	'34	G&D
38. Tom Swift and His Planet Stone	'35	G&D

Tom Swift Jr. (by Victor Appleton II)

39. Tom Swift and His Flying Lab	'54	G&D
40. Tom Swift and His Jetmarine	'54	G&D
41. Tom Swift and His Rocket Ship	'54	G&D
42. Tom Swift and His Giant Robot	'54	G&D
43. Tom Swift and His Atomic Earth Blaster	'54	G&D
44. Tom Swift and His Outpost in Space	'55	G&D
45. Tom Swift and His Diving Seacopter	'56	G&D
46. Tom Swift in the Caves of Nuclear Fire	'56	G&D
47. Tom Swift on the Phantom Satellite	'57	G&D
48. Tom Swift and His Ultrasonic Cycloplane	'57	G&D
49. Tom Swift and His Deep-Sea Hydrodome	'58	G&D
50. Tom Swift in the Race to the Moon	'58	G&D
51. Tom Swift in His Space Solartron	'58	G&D
52. Tom Swift and His Electronic Retroscope	'59	G&D
53. Tom Swift and His Spectromarine Selector	'60	G&D
54. Tom Swift and the Cosmic Astronauts	'60	G&D
55. Tom Swift and the Visitor From Planet X	'61	G&D
56. Tom Swift and the Electronic Hydrolung	'61	G&D
57. Tom Swift and His Triphibian Atomicar	'62	G&D
58. Tom Swift and His Megascope Space Prober	'62	G&D
59. Tom Swift and the Asteroid Pirates	'63	G&D
60. Tom Swift and His Repelatron Skyway	'63	G&D
61. Tom Swift and His Aquatomic Tracker	'64	G&D

(cont.)

(Appleton, cont.)

 62. Tom Swift and His 3-D Telejector   '64   G&D
 63. Tom Swift and His Polar-Ray Dynasphere   '65   G&D
 64. Tom Swift and His Sonic Boom Trap   '65   G&D
 65. Tom Swift and His Subocean Geotron   '66   G&D
 66. Tom Swift and the Mystery Comet   '66   G&D
 67. Tom Swift and the Captive Planetoid   '67   G&D
 68. Tom Swift and His G-Force Inverter   '68   G&D
 69. Tom Swift and His Dyna-4 Capsule   '69   G&D
 70. Tom Swift and His Cosmotron Express   '70   G&D
 71. Tom Swift and the Galaxy Ghosts   '71   G&D

   Don Sturdy (by Victor Appleton)
 1. Don Sturdy in the Land of Volcanoes   '25   G&D
 2. Don Sturdy in the Tombs of Gold   '25   G&D
 3. Don Sturdy on the Desert of Mystery   '25   G&D
 4. Don Sturdy With the Big Snake Hunters   '25   G&D
 5. Don Sturdy Across the North Pole   '25   G&D
 6. Don Sturdy Captured by Headhunters   '28   G&D
 7. Don Sturdy in Lion Land   '29   G&D
 8. Don Sturdy in the Land of the Giants   '30   G&D
 9. Don Sturdy on the Ocean Bottom   '31   G&D
 10. Don Sturdy in the Temples of Fear   '32   G&D
 11. Don Sturdy Trapped in the Flaming Wilderness
                    '34   G&D
 12. Don Sturdy with the Harpoon Hunters   '35   G&D

ARLEN, MICHAEL (1895-1956)

   Lord Tarlyon et.al.
 1. These Charming People...   '23   WmCol
 2. May Fair   '25   WmCol

ARONIN, BEN (b.1904)

   Raphael Drale
 1. The Lost Tribe   '34   SimPr
 2. Cavern of Destiny   '43   Behrm

ARROW, WILLIAM (see "PLANET OF THE APES")

ASCHER, EUGENE

   Lucian Carolus
 1. The Grim Caretaker   '44   StroB

2. There Were No Asper Ladies   '44   Mitre
      aka: To Kill A Corpse ('59/World)

ASIMOV, ISAAC (b.1920)

     The Trantorian Empire *
1. Pebble in the Sky   '50   Dbdy
2. The Stars, Like Dust   '51   Dbdy
3. The Currents of Space   '52   Dbdy
      * all 3 collected as: Triangle ('61/Dbdy)
        aka: An Issac Asimov Second Omnibus ('69/S&J)

     The Robot Series
1. I, Robot   '50   Gnome
2. The Caves of Steel   '54   Dbdy
3. The Naked Sun   '57   Dbdy
4. The Rest of the Robots   '64   Dbdy
      (Note-- some editions contain "Caves of Steel"
      and "The Naked Sun").
      abridged as: Eight Stories From The
                    Rest of the Robots ('66/Pyr)
5. The Robots of Dawn   '83   Dbdy
6. Robots and Empire   '85   Phant

     The Foundation Series *
1. Foundation   '51   Gnome
      abridged as: The 1,000 Year Plan ('55/Ace)
2. Foundation and Empire   '52   Gnome
      aka: The Man Who Upset the Universe ('55/Ace)
3. Second Foundation   '53   Gnome
4. Foundation's Edge   '82   Dbdy
      * First 3 titles collected as:
        The Foundation Trilogy ('63/Dbdy)
        aka: An Isaac Asimov Omnibus ('66/S&J)

     Lucky Starr (pseud.— Paul French)
1. David Starr, Space Ranger   '52   Dbdy
2. Lucky Starr and the Pirates of the Asteroids
                                           '53   Dbdy
3. Lucky Starr and the Oceans of Venus   '54   Dbdy
4. Lucky Starr and the Big Sun of Mercury   '56   Dbdy
5. Lucky Starr and the Moons of Jupiter   '57   Dbdy
6. Lucky Starr and the Rings of Saturn   '58   Dbdy
      titles 1 & 2 combined as:
        An Isaac Asimov Double ('72/NEL)
      titles 3 & 4 combined as:
        A Second Isaac Asimov Double ('73/NEL)
      titles 5 & 6 combined as:
        The Third Isaac Asimov Double ('73/NEL)

ASPRIN, ROBERT LYNN   (b.1946)

    The Myth Series
1. Another Fine Myth   '78   Donng
2. Myth Conceptions   '80   Donng
3. Myth Directions   '82   Donng
4. Hit or Myth   '83   Donng
5. Myth-ing Persons   '84   Donng

    Sanctuary *
(Note-- Asprin created and edited this series of tightly-woven short stories wherein various authors continue a basic storyline and set of characters within a pre-set structure.

1. Thieves' World   '79   Ace
2. Tales From the Vulgar Unicorn   '80   Ace
3. Shadows of Sanctuary   '81   Ace
4. Storm Season   '82   Ace
5. The Face of Chaos   '83   Ace
6. Wings of Omen   (co-edited by Lynn Abbey) '84   Ace
7. The Dead of Winter (with Lynn Abbey) '85   Ace
    * The first 3 titles are collected as: Sanctuary
    * The second 3 titles are collected as:
      Cross-Currents ('84/SFBC)
  (sequel)
8. Beyond Sanctuary (by Janet Morris)   '85   Baen
   (note-- this is a novel)

AUBREY, FRANK   (1840-1927)

    Monella
1. The Devil-Tree of El Dorado   1897   Hutch
2. A Queen of Atlantis   1899   Hutch
3. King of the Dead   '03   Macq

AUEL, JEAN   (b.1936)

    Earth's Children
1. The Clan of the Cave Bear   '80   Crown
2. The Valley of Horses   '82   Crown

AUSTIN, RICHARD

    The Guardians
1. The Guardians   '85   Jove
2. Trial by Fire   '85   Jove

AVALLONE, MICHAEL (b.1924)

    also see: TROY CONWAY, pseud.
    also see: "U.N.C.L.E."
    also see: "PLANET OF THE APES"

    Craghold (pseud.— Edwina Noone)
1. The Craghold Legacy   '71   Beagl
2. The Craghold Curse   '72   Beagl
3. The Craghold Creatures   '72   Beagl
4. The Craghold Crypt   '73   Curt

"THE AVENGERS"

    The Avengers
1. Deadline (Peter Leslie writing as Patrick McNee)
                                                 '65   H&S
2. Dead Duck (Peter Leslie writing as Patrick McNee)
                                                 '66   H&S
3. The Floating Game (John Garforth)   '67   Pantr
4. The Laugh Was On Lazarus (John Garforth)   '67   Pantr
5. The Passing of Gloria Mundy (J. Garforth)   '67   Pantr
6. Heil Harris! (John Garforth)   '67   Pantr
7. The Afrit Affair (Keith Laumer)   '68   Berk
8. The Drowned Queen (Keith Laumer)   '68   Berk
9. The Gold Bomb (Keith Laumer)   '68   Berk
10. The Magnetic Man (Norman Daniels)   '68   Berk
11. Moon Express (Norman Daniels)   '68   Berk

    The New Avengers
    (order of publication may not be precise)
1. The Eagle's Nest (John Carter)   '76   Berk
2. House of Cards (Peter Cave)   '76   Futur
3. Hostage (Peter Cave)   '77   Futur
4. Last of the Cybernauts (Peter Cave)   '77   Futur
5. Fighting Men (Justin Cartwright)   '77   Futur
6. To Catch a Rat (Walter Harris)   '77   Barkr

AVERY, RICHARD (pseud.— see EDMUND COOPER)

AYME, MARCEL (1902-1967)

    The Wonderful Farm
1. The Wonderful Farm   '51   Harpr
2. Return to the Wonderful Farm   '54   BodH
       aka: The Magic Pictures; More About
              the Wonderful Farm ('54/Harpr)

B

BAEN, JIM (see collaboration with BARRY COHEN)

BAILEY, GERALD EARL (b.1929)

    The Nurlingas Series
1. Madame Trinh   '66 Phnix
2. Winnowing Winds   '67 Mnyld
3. House of a Stranger   '79 Mnyld
4. Sword of the Nurlingas   '79 Berk
5. Sword of Poyana   '79 Berk

BAKER, W. HOWARD (see PETER SAXON, pseud.)

BALL, BRIAN N. (b.1932) (also see: "SPACE: 1999")

    The Time Trilogy
1. Timepiece   '68 Dobs
2. Timepivot   '70 Ball
3. Timepit   '71 Dobs

    Frames Sequence
1. The Probability Man   '72 DAW
2. Planet Probability   '73 DAW

BALMER, EDWIN (see collaboration with PHILIP WYLIE)

BANGS, JOHN KENDRICK (1862-1922)

    also see: "BARON MUNCHAUSEN"

    The House-Boat
1. A House-Boat on the Styx   1896 Harpr
2. The Pursuit of the House-Boat   1897 Harpr
3. The Enchanted Type-Writer   1899 Harpr

BARBET, PIERRE (b.1925)

    Eridanus
1. The Napoleons of Eridanus   '76 DAW
2. Emperor of Eridanus   '83 DAW

BARBREE, JAY (see MARTIN CAIDIN)

BARCLAY, BILL (pseud.— see MICHAEL MOORCOCK)

BARKER, ALBERT W. (b.1900)

    Reefe King
1. Gift From Berlin '69 Award
2. The Apollo Legacy '70 Award

BARKER, G.P. (1879-1951)

    The Greenwood Sequence
1. The Magic Tale of Harvanger and Yolande '14 Mills
2. The Romance of Palombris and Pallogris '15 Mills

"BARON MUNCHAUSEN"

    Baron Munchausen
1. Baron Munchausen's Narrative of His Marvellous Travels and Campaigns in Russia... 1786 Smith
(1st ed., actually published 1785)
(49pp.) (by Rudolf Erich Raspe)

The following subsequent editions carry additional Munchausen stories by various anonymous authors:

2. Singular Travels, Campaigns, Voyages, and Sporting Adventures of Baron Munnikhouson, Commonly Pronounced Munchausen...
(2nd ed.) (87pp.) 1786 Smith
3. Gulliver Revived; or, The Singular Travels, Campaigns, Voyages, and Adventures of Baron Munikouson, Commonly Called Munchausen.
(3rd ed.) (156pp.) 1786 Kears
4. Gulliver Revived, Containing Singular Travels, Campaigns, Voyages, and Adventures in Russia, Iceland, Turkey, Egypt, Gibralter, and on the Atlantic Ocean; also, an Account of a Voyage into the Moon...
(4th ed.) (172pp.) 1786 Kears
5. Gulliver Revived... Russia, Caspian Sea, Ireland, Turkey, Egypt, Gibralter, up the Mediterranean... Atlantic Ocean... Through the Centre of Mount Etna... the South Sea... to the Moon and Dog Star... (5th ed.) (208pp.) 1787 Kears

("Baron Munchausen", cont.)

6. Gulliver Revived; or, The Vice of Lying
   Properly Exposed...
   (6th ed.) (252pp.)   1789   Kears

   Additional Anonymous Publications, or versions
   credited to Raspe:
   (the list is by no means complete)
7. A Sequel to the Adventures of Baron Munchausen, Humbly Dedicated to Mr. Bruce the Abys-
   sinian Traveller, as the Baron Conceives
   That It May Be of Some Service to Him Making
   Another Expedition into Abyssinia; But If
   This Does Not Delight Mr. Bruce, the Baron
   is Willing to Fight Him on Any Terms He
   Pleases.   1792   Symnd
8. The Surprising Travels and Adventures of
   Baron Munchausen...   1792   Bkslr
9. The Surprising Adventures of Baron
   Munchausen. (a novel)   1793   Kears
10. The Travels By Sea and Land of the Re-
    nowned Baron Munchausen, Including a Tour
    Through the United States in the Year 1803.
                                   c.1803   Nafis
11. The Surprising Adventures of the
    Renowned Baron Munchausen Abridged...   1804   Camer
12. Gulliver Redivious; or, the Celebrated
    & Entertaining Travels... of Baron
    Munchausen, Including a Tour to the Uni-
    ted States of America in the Year 1803. 1805   Dublin
13. Munchausen at Walcheron... Exploits at
    Walcheron, the Dardanelles, Talavera,
    Cintra, etc.   1811   JJohn
14. Gulliver Revived... Baron Munchausen,
    Including a Tour of the United States of
    America in 1803, and the First Two Chap-
    ters of a Second Tour in 1810.   1813   (NY)
15. "Complete Original Edition" of the Sur-
    prising Travels and Adventures of Baron
    Munchausen... to Which is Added, A Sequel,
    Containing His Expedition into Africa.   1819   Kirby
16. Munchausen at the Pole... Together with
    a Correct List of the Curiosities Brought
    Home and Deposited in the Museum and Tower
    of London. (by Capt. Munchausen)   1819   JJohn
17. The Surprising Adventures... Miracu-
    lous Escapes, and Wonderful Voyages...
    of the Renowned Baron Munchausen...
    (24pp)   1830   Rich.

18.	The Travels and Adventures by Sea and Land of Baron Munchausen.	1834	Nick.
19.	The Curious and Entertaining Adventures... of the Renowned Baron Munchausen, Including a Tour Through the United States in the Year MDCCCIII.	1845	Farmr
20.	The Travels and Surprising Adventures of Baron Munchausen.	1859	Trueb
21.	The Travels of Baron Munchausen.	1862	Vickr
22.	The Adventures of Baron Munchausen.	1865	Cass
23.	The Travels and Surprising Adventures of Baron Munchausen.	1867	Tegg
24.	Original Travels and Surprising Adventures of Baron Munchausen	1889	Trueb
25.	The Surprising Adventures of Baron Munchausen.	1895	Lawr.
26.	Original Travels of Baron Munchausen.	1900	RdMcN
27.	Tales From the Travels of Baron Munchausen.	1900	Heath
28.	The Surprising Adventures of Baron Munchausen	'28	Boni
29.	Baron Munchausen's Miraculous Adventures on Land.	'33	USLib
30.	12 Adventures of the Celebrated Baron Munchausen.	'47	PLunn
31.	Singular Travels, Campaigns, and Adventures of Baron Munchausen.	'48	Cress
32.	The Singular Adventures of Baron Munchausen.	'50	MaxP
33.	The Singular Adventures of Baron Munchausen.	'52	Herit
34.	The Real Munchausen	'60	Devin

author-designated sequels

35.	Mr. Munchausen, Being a True Account of Some of the Recent Adventures Beyond the Styx... (by John Kendrick Bangs)	'01	Noyes
36.	Munchausen XX, by the Baron, Being the Wondrous but Veracious Happenings Which Befell My Ancestors... (by W.G. Worfel)	'04	RdMcN
37.	The Extraordinary Exploits and Experiences of Munchausen, M.D. (by Julian Walter Brandeis)	'24	Quip

BARRETT, NEAL Jr.

Time Sequence
1.	The Gates of Time	'70	Ace
2.	The Leaves of Time	'71	Lance

(Barrett, cont.)
Aldair
1. Aldair in Albion   '76 DAW
2. Aldair, Master of Ships   '77 DAW
3. Aldair: Across the Misty Sea   '80 DAW
4. Aldair: The Legion of Beasts   '82 DAW

BARRIE, J.M. (1860-1937)

Peter Pan
1. The Little White Bird; or, Adventures
   in Kensington Gardens   '02 Scrib
        rev.: Peter Pan in Kensington Gardens   ('06/H&S)
2. Peter and Wendy   '11 H&S
        aka: Peter Pan and Wendy ('21/H&S)

(plays)
1. Peter Pan; or, The Boy Who Would Not
   Grow Up   '28 Scrib
2. When Wendy Grew Up: An Afterthought   '57 TNels

BARRINGER, LESLIE (1895-1968)

The Neustrian Cycle
1. Gerfalcon   '27 Heine
2. Joris of the Rock   '28 Heine
3. Shy Leopardess   '48 Meth

BARTHOLOMEW, BARBARA

The Timeways Trilogy
1. The Time Keeper   '85 Sign
2. Child of Tomorrow   '85 Sign
3. When Dreamers Cease to Dream   '85 Sign

BARTON, JAMES

Wasteworld
1. Aftermath   '83 Grana
2. Resurrection   '83 Grana

BASS, T.J. (b.1932)

The Hive
1. Half Past Human   '71 Ball
2. The Godwhale   '74 Ball

BATCHELOR, JOHN M.

    A Strange Conflict
1. A Strange Conflict   1888   Ogilv
2. A Strange People   1888   Ogilv

BAUM, FRANK JOSLYN (see L. FRANK BAUM)

BAUM, L. FRANK (1856-1919)

    Oz
1. The Wonderful Wizard of Oz   1900   GHill
    aka: The Wizard of Oz
    aka: The New Wizard of Oz ('03/Bob-M)
2. The Marvelous Land of Oz   '04   Rei&B
    aka: The Land of Oz ('14/Rei&B)
3. Ozma of Oz   '07   Rei&B
4. Dorothy and the Wizard in Oz   '08   Rei&B
5. The Road to Oz   '09   Rei&B
6. The Emerald City of Oz   '10   Rei&B
7. The Patchwork Girl of Oz   '13   Rei&B
8. Tik-Tok of Oz   '14   Rei&B
9. The Scarecrow of Oz   '15   Rei&B
10. Rinkitink in Oz   '16   Rei&B
11. The Lost Princess of Oz   '17   Rei&B
12. The Tin Woodman of Oz   '18   Rei&B
13. The Magic of Oz   '19   Rei&L
14. Glinda of Oz   '20   Rei&L

    (following titles by RUTH PLUMLY THOMPSON):
15. The Royal Book of Oz   '21   Rei&L
    (title credits Baum, but written by Thompson)
16. Kabumpo in Oz   '22   Rei&L
17. The Cowardly Lion of Oz   '23   Rei&L
18. Grampa in Oz   '24   Rei&L
19. The Lost King of Oz   '25   Rei&L
20. The Hungry Tiger of Oz   '26   Rei&L
21. The Gnome King of Oz   '27   Rei&L
22. The Giant Horse of Oz   '28   Rei&L
23. Jack Pumpkinhead of Oz   '29   Rei&L
24. The Yellow Knight of Oz   '30   Rei&L
25. Pirates in Oz   '31   Rei&L
26. The Purple Prince of Oz   '32   Rei&L
27. Ojo in Oz   '33   Rei&L
28. Speedy in Oz   '34   Rei&L
29. The Wishing Horse of Oz   '35   Rei&L
30. Captain Salt in Oz   '36   Rei&L
31. Handy Mandy in Oz   '37   Rei&L

(Baum, "Oz" cont.)

   32. The Silver Princess in Oz   '38 Rei&L
   33. Ozoplaning with the Wizard of Oz   '39 Rei&L

      <u>(the series continues with various authors as follows)</u>:
   34. The Wonder City of Oz
       (John R. Neill)   '40 Rei&L
   35. The Scalawagons of Oz (John R. Neill) '41 Rei&L
   36. Lucky Bucky in Oz (John R. Neill)   '42 Rei&L
   37. The Magical Mimics in Oz   (Jack Snow)   '46 Rei&L
   38. The Shaggy Man of Oz   (Jack Snow)   '49 Rei&L
   39. The Hidden Valley of Oz
       (Rachel Cosgrove)   '51 Rei&L
   40. Merry Go Round in Oz
       (Eloise Jarvis McGraw & Lauren McGraw Wagner)
                                              '63 Rei&L
   41. Yankee in Oz
       (Ruth Plumly Thompson)   '72 OzClb
   42. The Enchanted Island of Oz
       (Ruth Plumly Thompson)   '76 OzClb
   43. The Forbidden Fountain of Oz
       (Eloise Jarvis McGraw & Lauren McGraw Wagner)
                                              '80
   44. A Barnstormer in Oz (Philip Jose Farmer) '83
   45. Return to Oz (Joan D. Vinge)   '85 DelR

      additional Oz-related titles:
   46. The Woggle-Bug Book (L. Frank Baum)   '05 Rei&B
   47. Little Wizard Stories of Oz
       (L. Frank Baum)   '14 Rei&B
       (Note-- these were first published in
       1913 as 6 separate 29-page booklets)
   48. The Laughing Dragon of Oz
       (Frank Joslyn Baum)   '34 Whitm
   49. The Visitors From Oz   '60 Rei&L
      (Rewritten from a Baum comic strip of 1904-05)

BEAR, GREG (see "STAR TREK")

BEATTY, JEROME Jr. (b.1918)

      Matthew Looney
   1. Matthew Looney's Voyage to Earth   '61 Scott
   2. Matthew Looney's Invasion of the Earth '65 Scott
   3. Matthew Looney in the Outback   '69 Scott
   4. Matthew Looney and the Space Pirates   '72 Scott

BECK, L. ADAMS (?-1931)

    Ormond
1. The Ninth Vibration and Other Stories   '22 Dodd
    (title story)
2. The House of Fulfillment: The Romance
    of a Soul   '27 Unwin

BECKFORD, WILLIAM (1760-1844)

    Vathek
1. Vathek: An Arabian Tale   1786 JJohn
    aka: The History of the Caliph Vathek
                    (1868/S,Low)
2. The Episodes of Vathek   '12 Swift

BEDFORD-JONES, H. (1887-1949)

    John Solomon
1. Solomon's Quest   '24
2. The Seal of John Solomon   '24 H&B
3. Gentleman Solomon   '25
    aka: The Shawl of Solomon ('25/H&B)

BEERE, PETER

    Trauma 2020
1. Urban Prey   '84 Arrow
2. The Crucifiction Squad   '84 Arrow

BEGBIE, HAROLD (1871-1929) (see CAROLINE LEWIS, pseud.)

BELL, CLARE

    Clan Ground
1. Ratha's Creature   '83 Athen
2. Clan Ground   '84 Athen

BELLAIRS, JOHN (b.1938)

    Johnny Dixon
1. The Curse of the Blue Figurine   '83 Dial
2. The Mummy, The Will, and The Crypt   '83 Dial
                        (cont.)

(Bellairs, "Johnny Dixon", cont.)
3. The Spell of the Sorcerer's Skull '84 Dial
4. The Revenge of the Wizard's Ghost '85 Dial

BELLAMY, EDWARD (1850-1898)

    Julian West
1. Looking Backward, 2000-1887   1888 Tick
2. Equality   1897 Apple

BENCHLEY, PETER (see "JAWS")

BENFORD, GREGORY (b.1941)

    In the Ocean of Night
1. In the Ocean of Night '77 Dial
2. Across the Sea of Suns '83 PB
3. Deeper Than the Darkness '70 Ace
   revised as: The Stars in Shroud ('78/Berk)

BENNETT, MARCIA J.

    The Ni-Lach
1. Where the Ni-Lach
2. Shadow Singer '84 DelR

BENOIT, HENDRA (see "PSI PATROL")

BENSON, E.F. (1867-1940)

    David Blaize
1. David Blaize '16 H&S
2. David Blaize and the Blue Door '18 H&S

    Colin
1. Colin '23 Hutch
2. Colin II '25 Hutch

BERNA, PAUL (b.1913)

    Michael Jousse
1. Threshold of the Stars '58 BodH
2. Continent in the Sky '59 BodH

BERNARD, JOEL (see "U.N.C.L.E.")

BERNARD, RAFE (see "THE INVADERS")

BERRY, ADRIAN (b.1937)

    1. Koyama's Diamond
    2. Labyrinth of Lies   '84 Vant

BERRY, BRYAN (1930-1955)

    The Venus Trilogy (aka: Kennet Trilogy)
    1. Resurgent Dust   '53 Pantr
    2. The Immortals   '53 Pantr
    3. The Indestructible   '54 Pantr

"BEWITCHED"

    1. Bewitched (Al Hine)   '65 Dell
    2. Bewitched: The Opposite Uncle
       (William Johnston)   '70 Whitm

BIDMEAD, CHRISTOPHER H. (see "DOCTOR WHO")

BIEMILLER, CARL L. (b.1912-1979)

    Jonny
    1. The Magic Ball From Mars   '53 WmMor
    2. Starboy   '56 Holt

    The Hydronauts
    1. The Hydronauts   '70 Dbdy
    2. Follow the Whales; Hydronauts Meet the
       Otter-People   '73 Dbdy
    3. Escape From the Crater   '74 Dbdy

BIGGLE, LLOYD Jr. (b.1923)

    Jan Darzek
    1. All the Colors of Darkness   '63 Dbdy
    2. Watchers of the Dark   '66 Dbdy
    3. This Darkening Universe   '75 Dbdy
    4. Silence is Deadly   '77 Dbdy

BINDER, EANDO
   (pseud. of OTTO BINDER (1911-1975) & EARL BINDER (b.1904))

      Adam Link
  1. Adam Link in the Past   '50 FyFic
  2. Adam Link-- Robot   '65 PbLib

      The Saucers
  1. Menace of the Saucers   '69 Belmt
  2. Night of the Saucers   '71 Belmt

BINDER, OTTO (see "MARVEL SUPER HEROES")

BINGHAM, CARSON   see: collaboration with LEE FALK
                      also see: ALEX RAYMOND

"BIONIC MAN, THE"
   (aka The "Six-Million Dollar Man", see MARTIN CAIDIN)

"BIONIC WOMAN, THE" (see EILEEN LOTTMAN)

BISCHOFF, DAVID F.

      Dragonstar
      (in collaboration with Thomas F. Monteleone)
  1. Day of the Dragonstar
  2. Night of the Dragonstar   '85 Berk

      The Gaming Magi
  1. The Destiny Dice   '85 Sign
  2. Wraith Board   '85 Sign

      The Star Hounds
  1. The Infinite Battle   '85 Ace
  2. Galactic Warriors   '85 Ace

BLACK, CAMPBELL (see "INDIANA JONES")

BLACKWOOD, ALGERNON (1869-1951)

      Uncle Paul
  1. The Education of Uncle Paul   '09 Macm
  2. A Prisoner in Fairyland   '13 Macm

Jules LeVallon
1. Jules LeVallon   '16 Cass
2. The Bright Messenger   '21 Cass

BLAINE, JOHN
(pseud. of Harold Leland Goodwin, b.1914)

Rick Brant
1. The Rocket's Shadow   '47 G&D
2. The Lost City   '47 G&D
3. Sea Gold   '47 G&D
4. 100 Fathoms Under   '47 G&D
5. The Whispering Box Mystery   '48 G&D
6. The Phantom Shark   '49 G&D
7. Smuggler's Reef   '50 G&D
8. The Caves of Fear   '51 G&D
9. Stairway to Danger   '52 G&D
10. The Golden Skull   '54 G&D
11. The Wailing Octopus   '56 G&D
12. The Electronic Mind Reader   '57 G&D
13. The Scarlet Lake Mystery   '58 G&D
14. The Pirates of Shan   '58 G&D
15. The Blue Ghost Mystery   '60 G&D
16. The Egyptian Cat Mystery   '61 G&D
17. The Flaming Mountain   '63 G&D
18. The Flying Stingaree   '63 G&D
19. The Ruby Ray Mystery   '64 G&D
20. The Veiled Raiders   '65 G&D
21. The Rocket Jumper   '66 G&D
22. The Deadly Dutchman   '67 G&D

BLAIR, ERIC ARTHUR (see GEORGE ORWELL, pseud.)

BLAMIRES, HARRY (b.1916)

Heaven and Hell
1. The Devil's Hunting-Grounds; A Fantasy   '54 LongG
2. Cold War in Hell   '55 LongG
3. Blessing Unbounded   '55 LongG
    aka: Highway to Heaven ('84/TNels)

BLAYLOCK, JAMES P. (b.1950)

The Elfin Sequence
1. The Elfin Ship   '82 DelR
2. The Disappearing Dwarf   '83 DelR

BLAYRE, CHRISTOPHER
   (pseud. of Edward Heron-Allen, 1861-1943)

   The University of Cosmopoli
   1. The Purple Sapphire   '21 PAlan
      rev. as: The Strange Papers of Dr. Blayre
                                   ('32/PAlan)
   2. The Cheetah-Girl   '23
   3. Some Women of the University   '34 Stock

BLISH, JAMES (1921-1975)

   also see: "STAR TREK"

   Cities in Flight (coll.'70/Avon)
   1. They Shall Have Stars   '56 Faber
      rev. as: Year 2018! ('57/Avon)
   2. A Life for the Stars   '62 Putn
   3. Earthman, Come Home   '55 Putn
   4. The Triumph of Time   '58 Avon
      aka: A Clash of Cymbals ('59/Faber)

   After Such Knowledge *
   1. Doctor Mirabilis   '64 Faber
   2. Black Easter   '68 Dbdy
   3. The Day After Judgement   '71 Dbdy
   4. A Case of Conscience   '58 Ball
      * Listed by internal chronology, this is
        not strictly a series as such. Rather,
        the books form a thematic "trilogy"
        ("Black Easter" and "The Day After Judge-
        ment" are considered parts I and II of a
        single work). "Doctor Mirabilis" is an
        historical novel.

BLOCH, ROBERT (see H.P. LOVECRAFT, "Cthulhu Mythos)

BLOOM, WILLIAM (b.1948)

   Qhe (pseud.— W.W.)
   1. The Taming Power; The First Qhe
      Adventure   '74 Mayfl
   2. White Fire   '74 Mayfl

BOGART, WILLIAM (1907-1977) (see KENNETH ROBESON)

BONNER, RICHARD

    The Boy Inventors
1. The Boy Inventors' Wireless Triumph   '12 Hurst
2. The Boy Inventors and the Vanishing Gun   '12 Hurst
3. The Boy Inventors' Diving Torpedo Boat   '12 Hurst
4. The Boy Inventors' Flying Ship   '13 Hurst
5. The Boy Inventors' Electric Hydroaeroplane
    '14 Hurst
6. The Boy Inventors' Radio-Telephone   '15 Hurst

BOOTHBY, GUY (1867-1905)

    Dr. Nikola
1. A Bid for Fortune   1895 WardL
    aka: Dr. Nikola's Vendetta ('08/Westb)
2. Doctor Nikola   1896 WardL
3. The Lust of Hate   1898 WardL
4. Dr. Nikola's Experiment   1899 H&S
5. "Farewell, Nikola!"   '01 WardL

BOSTON, L.M. (Lucy Maria Boston, b.1892)

    Green Knowe
1. The Children of Green Knowe   '54 Faber
2. The Chimneys of Green Knowe   '58 Faber
    aka: The Treasure of Green Knowe
              ('58/Harc)
3. The River at Green Knowe   '59 Faber
4. A Stranger at Green Knowe   '61 Faber
5. An Enemy at Green Knowe   '64 Harc

BOULLE, PIERRE (b.1912)
    (see "PLANET OF THE APES")

BOVA, BEN (b.1932)

    The Exiles Trilogy (coll.'80/Berk)
1. Exiled From Earth   '71 EPDut
2. Flight of Exiles   '72 EPDut
3. End of Exile   '75 EPDut

    Orion
1. Orion   '85 Tor
2. As On A Darkling Plain

BOWEN, ROBERT SIDNEY (1900-1977)

    Dusty Ayres
1. Black Lightning   '66 Corin
2. Crimson Doom   '66 Corin
3. Purple Tornado   '66 Corin
4. The Telsa Raiders   '66 Corin
5. Black Invaders Vs. The Battle Birds   '66 Corin

BRACKETT, LEIGH (1915-1978)

    ERIC JOHN STARK
    Eric John Stark: Outlaw of Mars   (coll.'82)
1. The Secret of Sinharat   '64 Ace
2. People of the Talisman   '64 Ace
3. The Halfling, and Other Stories   '73 Ace
    (contains some Stark stories)
    The Book of Skaith   (coll.'76/Dbdy)
4. The Ginger Star   '74 Ball
5. The Hounds of Skaith   '74 Ball
6. The Reavers of Skaith   '76 Ball

BRADBURY, EDWARD P. (pseud.— see MICHAEL MOORCOCK)

BRADLEY, MARION ZIMMER (b.1930)

    Note— the Darkover novels require no specific reading sequence for the most part, and are listed here in order of publication.

    Darkover
1. The Sword of Aldones   '62 Ace
2. The Planet Savers   '62 Ace
3. The Bloody Sun   '64 Ace
4. Star of Danger   '65 Ace
5. Winds of Darkover   '70 Ace
6. The World Wreckers   '71 Ace
7. Darkover Landfall   '72 DAW
    (The above title is the first in terms of internal chronology)
8. The Spell Sword   '74 DAW
9. The Heritage of Hastur   '75 DAW
10. The Shattered Chain *   '76 DAW
11. The Forbidden Tower   '77 DAW
12. Stormqueen   '78 DAW

    (cont.)

(Bradley, cont.)

13. The Keeper's Price	'80	DAW
14. Two to Conquer	'80	DAW
15. Shaara's Exile	'81	DAW
16. Sword of Chaos	'82	DAW
17. Hawkmistress!	'82	DAW
18. Thendara House *	'83	DAW
19. City of Sorcery	'84	DAW

    * Note-- "The Shattered Chain" and "Thendara House" have been published in one volume as:
        Oath of the Renunciates ('83/Dbdy)

The Survivors
(in collaboration with Paul Edwin Zimmer)

1. Hunters of the Red Moon	'73	DAW
2. The Survivors	'79	DAW

Arwen

1. The Jewel of Arwen	'74	T-K
2. The Parting of Arwen	'74	T-K

Leslie Barnes

1. Dark Satanic	'72	Berk
2. The Inheritor	'84	Tor

Atlantis

1. Web of Light	'83	PB
2. Web of Darkness	'84	Donng

The Mists of Avalon (coll.'82/Knopf)

1. Mistress of Magic	'84
2. The High Queen	(NYP)
3. The King Stag	(NYP)
4. The Prisoner in the Oak	(NYP)

BRADSHAW, GILLIAN

King Arthur

1. Hawk of May	'80	S&S
2. Kingdom of Summer	'81	S&S
3. In Winter's Shadow	'82	S&S

BRADWELL, JAMES
    (pseud. of Arthur William Charles Kent, b.1925)
    (see "LAND OF THE GIANTS")

BRAMAH, ERNEST (1868-1942)

    Kai Lung *
1. The Wallet of Kai Lung   1900 GRich
    aka: The Celestial Omnibus ('63/RichP)
    abr. as: The Transmutation of Ling ('11/GRich)
2. Kai Lung's Golden Hours   '22 GRich
3. Kai Lung Unrolls His Mat   '28 RichP
4. The Moon of Much Gladness   '32 Cass
    aka: The Return of Kai Lung ('37/Sheridan)
5. Kai Lung Beneath the Mulberry Tree   '40 RichP
6. Kai Lung: Six   '74 NonPP
    * The first 3 titles collected as:
      The Kai Lung Omnibus ('36/PAlan)

BRAND, KURT (see "PERRY RHODAN")

BRANDEIS, JULIAN WALTER (1875-?) (see "BARON MUNCHAUSEN")

BRANDNER, GARY (b.1933)

    Big Brain
1. The Aardvark Affair   '75 Zebra
2. The Beelzebub Business   '75 Zebra
3. Energy Zero   '76 Zebra

    The Howling
1. The Howling   '77 Fawc
2. The Howling II   '78 Fawc

BRECKENRIDGE, GERALD (1889?-1964)

    The Radio Boys
    (Note— probably not a complete listing)
1. Radio Boys on Secret Service Duty   '22 Burt
2. Radio Boys on the Mexican Border   '22 Burt
3. Radio Boys Search for the Incas Treasure '22 Burt
4. Radio Boys with the Revenue Guards   '22 Burt
5. Radio Boys Seek the Lost Atlantis   '23 Burt
6. Radio Boys with the Border Patrol   '24 Burt

BRENNAN, JOSEPH PAYNE

    Lucius Leffing
                                (cont.)

1. The Casebook of Lucius Leffing	'73	McbrH
2. The Chronicles of Lucius Leffing	'77	Grant

BRONTE, CHARLOTTE (1816-1855)

    Angria
1. The Twelve Adventurers, and Other Stories   '25 H&S
2. Legends of Angria   '33 OxfUn

BROOKS, TERRY (b.1944)

    Shannara
1. The Sword of Shannara   '77 DelR
2. The Elfstones of Shannara   '83 DelR
3. The Wishsong of Shannara   '85 DelR

BROOKS, WALTER R. (1886-1958)

    Freddy
1. To and Again   '27 Knopf
    aka: Freddy's First Adventure ('49/BodH)
    aka: Freddy Goes to Florida ('49/Knopf)
2. More To and Again   '30 Knopf
    aka: Freddy Goes to the North Pole ('51/Knopf)
3. Freddy the Detective   '32 Knopf
4. Wiggins for President   '39 Knopf
    aka: Freddy the Politician ('48/Knopf)
5. Freddy's Cousin Weedly   '40 Knopf
6. Freddy and the Ignoramus   '41 Knopf
7. Freddy and the Perilous Adventure   '42 Knopf
8. Freddy and the Bean Home News   '43 Knopf
9. Freddy and Mr. Camphor   '44 Knopf
10. Freddy and the Popinjay   '45 Knopf
11. Freddy the Pied Piper   '46 Knopf
12. Freddy the Magician   '47 Knopf
13. Freddy Goes Camping   '48 Knopf
14. Freddy Plays Football   '49 Knopf
15. Freddy the Cowboy   '50 Knopf
16. Freddy Rides Again   '51 Knopf
17. Freddy the Pilot   '52 Knopf
18. Freddy and the Space Ship   '53 Knopf
19. Freddy and the Men From Mars   '54 Knopf
20. Freddy and the Baseball Team From Mars   '56 Knopf
21. Freddy and Simon the Dictator   '56 Knopf
22. Freddy and the Flying Saucer Plans   '57 Knopf
23. Freddy and the Dragon   '58 Knopf

BROWN, ROSEL GEORGE (1926-1967)

    Sibyl Sue Blue
1. Sibyl Sue Blue   '66 Dbdy
    aka: Galactic Sybil Sue Blue ('68/Berk)
2. The Waters of Centaurus   '70 Dbdy

BROWNE, HOWARD (b.1908)

    Tharn
1. Warrior of the Dawn   '43 Rei&L
2. The Return of Tharn   '56 Grand

BRUNNER, JOHN (b.1934)

    Zarathustra Refugee Planets
1. Castaway's World   '63 Ace
    rev. as: Polymath ('74/DAW)
2. Secret Agent of Terra   '62 Ace
    rev. as: The Avengers of Carrig ('69/Dell)
3. The Repairmen of Cyclops   '65 Ace

    Zanzibar
1. Stand on Zanzibar   '68 Dbdy
2. The Sheep Look Up   '72 Harpr

BRUST, STEVEN

    Vlad Taltos
1. Jhereg   '83 Ace
2. Yendi   '84 Ace

BRYANT, EDWARD (see collaboration with FRED SABERHAGEN)

"BUCK ROGERS"

1. Armageddon 2419, A.D.
    (by Philip Francis Nowlan)   '29/'62 Avalo
2. Mordred (by John Eric Holmes) *   '80
3. Warrior's World (Richard S. McEnroe) *   '81
4. Rogers' Rangers (John Silbersack)
    * (volumes 2 and 3 are based on outlines
      by Larry Niven and Jerry Pournelle)

TV adaptations
(by Richard A. Lupoff writing under pseud.
Addison E. Steele)
1. Buck Rogers in the 25th Century '78 Dell
2. That Man on Beta '79 Dell

BULMER, KENNETH (b.1921)

also see: NEIL LANGHOLM, pseud.

Keys to the Dimensions
1. Land Beyond the Map '65 Ace
2. The Key to Irunium '67 Ace
3. The Key to Venudine '68 Ace
4. The Wizards of Senuchria '69 Ace
5. The Ships of Durostorum '70 Ace
6. The Hunters of Jundagai '71 Ace
7. The Chariots of Ra '72 Ace

Dray Prescott (pseud.-- Alan Burt Akers) *
1. Transit to Scorpio '72 DAW
2. The Suns of Scorpio '73 DAW
3. Warrior of Scorpio '73 DAW
4. Swordships of Scorpio '73 DAW
5. Prince of Scorpio '74 DAW
6. Manhounds of Antares '74 DAW
7. Arena of Antares '74 DAW
8. Fliers of Antares '75 DAW
9. Bladesmen of Antares '75 DAW
10. Avenger of Antares '75 DAW
11. Armada of Antares '75 DAW
12. The Tides of Kregen '76 DAW
13. Renegades of Kregen '76 DAW
14. Krozair of Kregen '77 DAW
15. Secret Scorpio '77 DAW
16. Savage Scorpio '77 DAW
17. Captive Scorpio '77 DAW
18. Golden Scorpio '78 DAW
19. A Life for Kregen '79 DAW
20. A Sword for Kregen '79 DAW
21. A Fortune for Kregen '79 DAW
22. A Victory for Kregen '79 DAW
23. Beasts of Antares '80 DAW
24. Rebel of Antares '80 DAW
25. Legions of Antares '81 DAW
26. Allies of Antares '81 DAW

(cont.)

(Bulmer, "Dray Prescott", cont.)

27. Mazes of Scorpio	'81	DAW
28. Delia of Vallia	'82	DAW
29. Fires of Scorpio	'83	DAW
30. Talons of Scorpio	'83	DAW
31. Masks of Scorpio	'84	DAW
32. Seg the Bowman	'84	DAW
33. Werewolves of Kregen	'85	DAW
34. Witches of Kregen	'85	DAW
35. Storm Over Vallia	'85	DAW

* Titles 12, 13, & 14 collected as:
"The Krozair Cycle"

Wolfshead (writing as Arthur Frazier)
1. Oath of Blood '73
2. The King's Death '73
3. A Light in the West '73
4. Viking Slaughter '74
5. A Flame in the Fens '74
6. An Axe in Miklagard '75

The Hook Series (pseud.— Telly Zetford)
1. Whirlpool of Stars '74 NEL
2. The Boosted Man '74 NEL
3. Star City '74 NEL
4. The Virility Gene '75 NEL

Odan the Half-God (pseud.— Manning Norvil)
1. Dream Chariots '77 DAW
2. Whetted Bronze '78 DAW

BULWER-LYTTON, EDWARD GEORGE (1803-1873)

Glyndon
1. Falkland and Zicci   1841/1876   Routl
2. Zanoni   1842   Saund

BUNCH, CHRIS (see collaboration with ALAN COLE)

BURGER, DIONYS (see EDWIN A. ABBOTT)

BURKE, JOHN (b.1922)

(cont.)

34

(Burke, cont.)

    <u>UFO</u> (pseud.-- Robert Miall)
1. UFO   '70 Pan
    aka: UFO-1; Flesh Hunters ('73/Warnr)
2. UFO 2   '71 Pan
    aka: UFO-2; Sporting Blood ('73/Warnr)

BURMAN, BEN LUCIEN (b.1896)

    <u>Catfish Bend</u> *
1. High Water at Catfish Bend   '52 Mesnr
2. Seven Stars for Catfish Bend   '56 FunkW
3. The Owl Hoots Twice at Catfish Bend   '61 Tapl
    * all 3 collected as:
      "Three From Catfish Bend" ('67/Tapl)

BURROUGHS, EDGAR RICE (1875-1950)

    <u>Tarzan</u>
1. Tarzan of the Apes   '14 McClg
2. The Return of Tarzan   '15 McClg
3. The Eternal Lover   '25 McClg
    aka: Th Eternal Savage ('63/Ace)
    (Tarzan is a minor character in the above novel)
4. The Beasts of Tarzan   '16 McClg
5. The Son of Tarzan   '17 McClg
6. Tarzan and the Jewels of Opar   '18 McClg
7. Jungle Tales of Tarzan   '19 McClg
8. Tarzan the Untamed   '20 McClg
9. Tarzan the Terrible   '21 McClg
10. Tarzan and the Golden Lion   '23 McClg
11. Tarzan and the Ant Men   '24 McClg
12. The Tarzan Twins   '27 Voll
13. Tarzan, Lord of the Jungle   '28 McClg
14. Tarzan and the Lost Empire   '29 Metro
15. Tarzan at the Earth's Core   '30 Metro
    (note-- this book simultaneously continues
    both the Tarzan and Pellucidar series)
16. Tarzan the Invincible   '31 ERB
17. Tarzan Triumphant   '32 ERB
18. Tarzan and the City of Gold   '33 ERB
19. Tarzan and the Lion Man   '34 ERB
20. Tarzan and the Leopard Men   '35 ERB
21. Tarzan and the Tarzan Twins with
    Jad-Bal-Ja, the Golden Lion   '36 Whitm
                        (cont.)

(Burroughs, "Tarzan", cont.)

22. Tarzan's Quest	'36	ERB
23. Tarzan and the Forbidden City	'38	ERB
24. Tarzan the Magnificent	'39	ERB
25. Tarzan and the Foreign Legion	'47	ERB
26. Tarzan and the Madman	'64	Canav
27. Tarzan and the Castaways	'65	Canav
28. The Mark of the Red Hyena	'67	Whitm

authorized sequels

29. Tarzan and the Lightning Man (by William Gilmour)	'63	Greys
30. Tarzan and the Lost Safari (movie edition— anonymous author)	'66	Whitm
31. Tarzan and the Valley of Gold (by Fritz Leiber)	'66	Ball

In addition, 5 unauthorized Tarzan novels were written by Barton Werper (pseud. of Peter T. Scott and Peg O'Neill Scott) before the Burroughs estate halted distribution.

1. Tarzan and the Silver Globe	'64	GoldS
2. Tarzan and the Cave City	'64	GoldS
3. Tarzan and the Snake People	'64	GoldS
4. Tarzan and the Abominable Snowman	'65	GoldS
5. Tarzan and the Winged Invaders	'65	GoldS

Mars Series

1. A Princess of Mars	'17	McClg
2. The Gods of Mars	'18	McClg
3. The Warlord of Mars	'19	McClg
4. Thuvia, Maid of Mars	'20	McClg
5. The Chessmen of Mars	'22	McClg
6. The Master Mind of Mars	'28	McClg
7. A Fighting Man of Mars	'31	Metro
8. Swords of Mars	'36	ERB
9. Synthetic Men of Mars	'40	ERB
10. Llana of Gathol	'48	ERB
11. John Carter of Mars aka: John Carter and the Giant of Mars	'64	Canav

authorized sequels

12. Lost on Jupiter (William Gilmour)	'61	VCori
13. The Forgotten Sea of Mars (Michael D. Resnick)	'65	CECaz

Pellucidar Series

1. At the Earth's Core	'22	McClg
2. Pellucidar	'23	McClg
3. Tanar of Pellucidar	'30	Metro

4. Tarzan at the Earth's Core	'30	Metro
5. Back to the Stone Age	'37	ERB
6. Land of Terror	'44	ERB
7. Savage Pellucidar	'63	Canav
authorized sequel		
8. Mayhars of Pellucidar		
(John Eric Holmes)	'76	Ace

    <u>Barney Custer</u>

1. The Eternal Lover	'25	McClg
(Custer appears as minor character)		
2. The Mad King	'26	McClg

    <u>Caspak Series</u> *

1. The Land That Time Forgot	'63	Ace
2. The People That Time Forgot	'63	Ace
3. Out of Time's Abyss	'63	Ace

    * all 3 segments were originally
      published in a single volume:
      "The Land That Time Forgot" ('24/McClg)

    <u>Moon Sequence</u> *

1. The Moon Maid	'62	Ace
2. The Moon Men	'62	Ace

    * originally published in one volume as:
      "The Moon Maid" ('26/McClg)
      aka: The Moon Men ('62/Canav)

    <u>Venus Series</u>

1. Pirates of Venus	'34	ERB
2. Lost on Venus	'35	ERB
3. Carson of Venus	'39	ERB
4. Escape on Venus	'46	ERB
5. The Wizard of Venus	'70	Ace

    also included in: "Tales of Three Planets"
                         ('64/Canav)

BURROUGHS, WILLIAM S. (b.1914)

    <u>Nova Sequence</u>

1. The Ticket That Exploded	'62	Olymp
2. Nova Express	'64	Grove

BUSBY, F.M. (b.1921)

    <u>The Demu Trilogy</u> (coll.'80/PB)

1. Cage a Man	'73	Dbdy

                    (cont.)

(Busby, "Demu Trilogy", cont.)

    2. The Proud Enemy   '75 Berk
    3. End of the Line   '80 PB

    <u>The Saga of Rissa Kerguelen/Hulzein Chronicles</u>
    1. Rissa Kerguelen   '77 Berk
       (2-vol. version)
       A. Rissa Kerguelen ('76/Berk)
       B. The Long View ('76/Berk)
       (3-vol. version)
       A. Young Rissa ('84/Berk)
       B. Rissa and Tregare ('84/Berk)
       C. The Long View ('84/Berk)
    2. Star Rebel   '84 Bant
    3. Alien Debt   '84 Bant
    4. Rebel's Quest   '85 Bant

BUTLER, SAMUEL (1835-1902)

    <u>Erewhon</u>
    1. Erewhon; or, Over the Range   1872 Trueb
    2. Erewhon Revisited Twenty Years Later   '01 GRich

BUTTERWORTH, MICHAEL (see "SPACE: 1999")

BUTTERWORTH, OLIVER (b.1915)

    <u>Nate Twitchell</u>
    1. The Enormous Egg   '56 LtBrn
    2. The Narrow Passage   '73 LtBrn

BYRNE, S.J.

    STAR MAN (also see: "Perry Rhodan" series)
    (Note-- the series is in 2 volumes containing
    11 novelettes. The first 5 titles are in the
    same volume with Perry Rhodan title #137).

    <u>Volume 1</u>
    1. Supermen of Alpha   '79 Mastr
    2. Time Window   '79 Mastr
    3. Interstellar Mutineers   '79 Mastr
    4. The Cosmium Raiders   '79 Mastr
    5. The World Changer   '79 Mastr

                    (cont.)

(Byrne, "Star Man", cont.)

    Volume 2

6. The Slaves of Venus	'80 Mastr
7. Lost in the Milky Way	'80 Mastr
8. Time Trap	'80 Mastr
9. The Centaurians	'80 Mastr
10. The Emperor	'80 Mastr
11. The Return of Star Man	'80 Mastr

C

CABELL, JAMES BRANCH (1879-1958)

Biography of the Life of Manuel of Poictesme
1. Beyond Life   '19   McBri
2. Figures of Earth   '21   McBri
3. The Silver Stallion   '26   McBri
4. Music From Behind the Moon *   '26   JDay
5. The Way of Ecben *   '29   McBri
6. The White Robe *   '28   McBri
7. The Soul of Melicent   '13   Stoke
   aka: Domnei ('20/McBri)
* 8. Chivalry (rev.'21/McBri)   '09   Harpr
9. Jurgen   '19   McBri
10. The Line of Love (rev.'21/McBri)   '05   Harpr
11. The High Place   '23   McBri
12. Gallantry (rev.'28/McBri)   '07   JLane
13. Something About Eve   '27   McBri
14. The Certain Hour   '16   McBri
15. The Cords of Vanity (rev.'20/McBri)   '09   Dbdy
16. From the Hidden Way (rev.'24/McBri)   '16
17. The Jewel Merchants   '21
18. The Rivet in Grandfather's Neck   '15   McBri
19. The Eagle's Shadow (rev.'23/McBri)   '04   McBri
20. The Cream of the Jest   '17   McBri
21. The Lineage of Lichfield   '22   McBri
22. Straws and Prayer-Books   '24   McBri

   * Note— "Music From Behind the Moon",
     "The Way of Ecben", and "The White
     Robe" appeared in one volume as:
     "The Witch Woman" ('48/Farr)

The Nightmare Has Triplets (coll.'72)
1. Smirt   '34   McBri
2. Smith   '35   McBri
3. Smire   '37   Dbdy

Heirs and Assigns
1. Hamlet Had an Uncle   '40   Farr
2. The King Was in His Counting House   '38   Farr
3. The First Gentleman of America   '42   Farr

The Green Stone
1. There Were Two Pirates   '46   Farr
2. The Devil's Own Dear Son   '49   Farr

40

CAIDIN, MARTIN (b.1927)

    Steve Austin (aka: "The Six Million Dollar Man")
1. Cyborg '72 Arbor
2. Operation Nuke '73 Arbor
3. High Crystal '74 Arbor
4. Cyborg IV '75 Arbor
    sequels
5. Wine, Women and Wars (by Michael Jahn) '75 Warnr
6. The Solid Gold Kidnapping
   (by Evan Richards) '75 Warnr
7. Pilot Error (by Jay Barbree) '75 Warnr
8. The Rescue of Athena One '77 Warnr
9. The Secret of Bigfoot Pass (by Michael Jahn)
    '76 Berk
10. International Incidents (Michael Jahn) '77 Berk

CALVINO, ITALO (b.1923)

    The Qfwfq Sequence
1. Cosmicomics '68 Harc
2. T Zero '69 Harc
   aka: Time and the Hunter ('70/Cape)

CAMERON, BERL (pseud. of Arthur Roberts and John Glasby)

    Terran Empire Series
1. Cosmic Echelon '52 Warrn
2. Time and Space '52 Warrn

CAMERON, ELEANOR (b.1912)

    Tycho Bass
1. The Wonderful Flight to the Mushroom Planet
    '54 LtBrn
2. Stowaway to the Mushroom Planet '56 LtBrn
3. Mr. Bass's Planetoid '58 LtBrn
4. A Mystery For Mr. Bass '60 LtBrn
5. Time and Mr. Bass '67 LtBrn

CAMERON, LOU (b.1924)

    The Swinging Spy (pseud.-- Dagmar)
1. The Spy With the Blue Kazoo '67 Lance
2. The Spy Who Came in from the Copa '67 Lance

CAMPBELL, H.J. (b.1925)

    Magdah Sequence (pseud.— Roy Sheldon)
1. Mammoth Man   '52 Ham&C
2. Two Days of Terror   '52 Pantr

    Shiny Spear Sequence (pseud.— Roy Sheldon)
1. Atoms in Action   '53 Pantr
2. House of Entropy   '53 Pantr

CAMPBELL, JOHN W. (1910-1971)

    Aarn Munro
1. The Mightiest Machine   '47 Hadly
2. The Incredible Planet   '49 FantP

    Arcot, Wade & Morey *
1. The Black Star Passes   '53 FantP
2. Islands of Space   '56 FantP
3. Invaders From the Infinite   '61 Gnome
    * coll. as: John W. Campbell Anthology ('73/Dbdy)

CAMPBELL, RAMSEY (see H.P. LOVECRAFT, "Cthulhu Mythos")

CAPON, PAUL (b.1912)

    Antigeos Trilogy
1. The Other Side of the Sun   '50 Heine
2. The Other Half of the Planet   '52 Heine
3. Down to Earth   '54 Heine

CARLSEN, CHRIS (pseud., see ROBERT P. HOLDSTOCK)

CARNELLE, INGE

    Jane Blonde
1. The Girl From B.U.S.T.   '66 Bee-L
2. Joy Ride   '67 Bee-L

CARR, CHARLES

    Bel
1. Colonists of Space   '54 WardL
2. Salamander War   '55 WardL

CARR, JOHN F.
    ("Paratime Police sequence"-- see H. BEAM PIPER)

CARROLL, LEWIS
    (pseud. of CHARLES LUTWIDGE DODGSON, 1832-1898)

    Alice
1. Alice's Adventures in Wonderland   1865 MacmL
    aka: Alice in Wonderland ('44/Gawth)
2. Through the Looking-Glass, and What
   Alice Found There   1872 MacmL
    aka: Alice Through the Looking-Glass ('30/Whitm)

CARTER, JOHN (see "THE AVENGERS")

CARTER, LIN (b.1930)

    also see: ROBERT E. HOWARD, for "Conan" titles
    also see: collaboration with DONALD A. WOLLHEIM

    Thongor Series
1. The Wizard of Lemuria   '65 Ace
   rev. as:
   Thongor and the Wizard of Lemuria ('69/Berk)
2. Thongor of Lemuria   '66 Ace
   rev. as:
   Thongor and the Dragon City ('70/Berk)
3. Thongor Against the Gods   '67 PbLib
4. Thongor in the City of Magicians   '68 PbLib
5. Thongor at the End of Time   '68 PbLib
6. Thongor Fights the Pirates of Tarakus   '70 Berk

    The Great Imperium
1. The Man Without a Planet   '66 Ace
2. Star Rogue   '70 Lance
3. Outworlder   '71 Lance

    Hautley Quicksilver
1. The Thief of Thoth   '68 Belmt
2. The Purloined Planet   '69 Belmt

    The Green Star Rises
1. Under the Green Star   '72 DAW
2. When the Green Star Calls   '73 DAW
3. By the Light of the Green Star   '74 DAW
4. As the Green Star Rises   '75 DAW
5. In the Green Star's Glow   '76 DAW

(Lin Carter, cont.)

Callisto Series
1. Jandar of Callisto — '72 Dell
2. Black Legion of Callisto — '72 Dell
3. Sky Pirates of Callisto — '73 Dell
4. Mad Empress of Callisto — '75 Dell
5. Mind Wizards of Callisto — '75 Dell
6. Lankar of Callisto — '75 Dell
7. Ylana of Callisto — '77 Dell
8. Renegade of Callisto — '78 Dell

World's End Series/aka: The Gondwane Epic
1. The Warrior of World's End — '74 DAW
2. The Enchantress of World's End — '75 DAW
3. The Immortal of World's End — '76 DAW
4. The Barbarian of World's End — '77 DAW
5. The Pirate of World's End — '78 DAW
6. Giant of World's End — '69 Belmt

Zarkon, Lord of the Unknown
1. The Nemesis of Evil — '75 Dbdy
2. Invisible Death — '75 Dbdy
3. The Volcano Ogre — '76 Dbdy

Eric Carstairs of Zanthodon
1. Journey to the Underground World — '79 DAW
2. Zanthodon — '80 DAW
3. Hurok of the Stone Age — '81 DAW
4. Darya of the Bronze Age — '81 DAW
5. Eric of Zanthodon — '82 DAW

Kesrick
1. Kesrick — '82 DAW
2. Dragonrouge — '84 DAW

CARTWRIGHT, JUSTIN (see "THE AVENGERS")

CASSERLY, GORDON (?-1947)

Badshah
1. The Elephant God — '20 PAlan
2. The Jungle Girl — '21 PAlan

CAVE, HUGH B. (b.1910) (see H.P. LOVECRAFT)

CAVE, PETER (b.1940) (see "THE AVENGERS")

CEBULASH, MEL (b.1937)

    Herbie
1. The Love Bug   '69 Schol
2. Herbie Rides Again   '74 Schol

CHADWICK, PAUL (see "SECRET AGENT X")

CHALKER, JACK L. (b.1944)

    The Well of Souls
1. Midnight at the Well of Souls   '77 DelR
2. Exiles at the Well of Souls   '78 DelR
3. Quest for the Well of Souls   '78 DelR
4. The Return of Nathan Brazil   '80 DelR
5. Twilight at the Well of Souls: The Legacy of Nathan Brazil   '80 DelR

    The Four Lords of the Diamond (coll.'83/Dbdy)
1. Lilith: A Snake in the Grass   '81 DelR
2. Cerberus: A Wolf in the Fold   '81 DelR
3. Charon: A Dragon at the Gate   '82 DelR
4. Medusa: A Tiger by the Tail   '83 DelR

    The Dancing Gods
1. River of the Dancing Gods   '84 DelR
2. Demons of the Dancing Gods   '84 DelR
3. Vengeance of the Dancing Gods   '85 DelR

    Soul Rider
1. Spirits of Flux and Anchor   '84 Tor
2. Empires of Flux and Anchor   '84 Tor
3. Masters of Flux and Anchor   '85 Tor

CHAMBERS, ROBERT W. (1865-1933)

    Tales of a Naturalist
1. In Search of the Unknown   '04 Harpr
2. Police!!!   '15 Apple

    Athalie
1. Quick Action   '14 Apple
2. Athalie   '15 Apple

CHANDLER, A. BERTRAM (1912-1984)

(A) Derek Calver
1. The Rim of Space   '61 Avalo
2. The Ship From Outside   '63 Ace

(B) John Grimes: Federation Survey Service
3. The Road to the Rim   '67 Ace
4. To Prime the Pump   '71 Curt
5. The Hard Way Up   '72 Ace
6. The Broken Cycle   '75 Hale
7. False Fatherland   '68 Howtz
    aka: Spartan Planet ('69/Dell)
8. The Inheritors   '72 Ace
9. The Big Black Mark   '75 DAW
10. Star Courier   '77 DAW

(C) John Grimes: Rim Runners (no set sequence)
11. Rendezvous on a Lost World   '61 Ace
12. Beyond the Galactic Rim   '63 Ace
13. Into the Alternate Universe   '64 Ace
14. Contraband From Otherspace   '67 Ace
15. The Rim Gods   '69 Ace
16. The Dark Dimensions   '71 Ace
17. Alternate Orbits   '71 Ace
18. The Gateway to Never   '72 Ace
19. The Way Back   '76 Hale
20. To Keep the Ship   '78 DAW
21. The Far Traveller   '79 DAW
22. Matilda's Stepchildren   '79 DAW
23. The Anarch Lords   '81 DAW
24. The Last Amazon   '84 DAW
25. The Wild Ones   '85 DAW
26. Kelly Country   '85 DAW

The Empress Series
1. Empress of Outer Space   '65 Ace
2. Space Mercenaries   '65 Ace
3. Nebula Alert   '67 Ace

CHANNING, MARK

Colin Gray
1. King Cobra   '33 Hutch
2. White Python   '34 Hutch
3. The Poisoned Mountain   '35 Hutch
4. Nine Lives   '37 Harrp

CHANT, JOY (b.1945)

(cont.)

Red Moon and Black Mountain
1. Red Moon and Black Mountain '70 Unwin
2. The Grey Mane of Morning '77 Unwin
   (this is a "prequel" to the first book)
3. When Voiha Wakes '83 Unwin

CHARNAS, SUZY McKEE (b.1939)

Motherlines
1. Walk to the End of the World '74 Ball
2. Motherlines '78 Berk

CHASE, GLEN (pseud., see GARDNER F. FOX)

CHAVANNES, ALBERT (1836-1903)

Socioland
1. The Future Commonwealth; or, What Samuel Balcom Saw in Socioland 1892 TrueN
2. In Brighter Climes; or, Life in Socioland 1895 Chav

CHERRYH, C.J. (b.1942)

The Quest of Morgaine
1. Gate of Ivrel '76 DAW
2. Well of Shiuan '78 DAW
3. Fires of Azeroth '79 DAW

The Faded Sun
1. Kesrith '78 SFBC
2. Shon'Jir '79 SFBC
3. Kutath '80 SFBC

Downbelow Station
1. Downbelow Station '81 DAW
2. Merchanter's Luck '82 DAW

Captain Pyanfar
1. The Pride of Chanur '82 DAW
2. Chanur's Venture '84 Phant
3. The Kif Strike Back '85 Phant

Arafel's Saga ('83/SFBC)
1. The Dreamstone '83 DAW
2. The Tree of Swords and Jewels '83 DAW

CHESTER, WILLIAM L.   (b.1907)

    Kioga Series
1. Hawk of the Wilderness   '36 Harpr
2. Kioga of the Wilderness   '37/'76 DAW
3. One Against a Wilderness   '37/'77 DAW
4. Kioga of the Unknown Land   '38/'78 DAW

CHILTON, CHARLES   (b.1927)

    Jet Morgan
1. Journey into Space   '54 Jenk
2. The Red Planet   '56 Jenk
3. The World in Peril   '60 Jenk

CHRISTOPHER, JOHN   (b.1922)

    Tripods
1. The White Mountains   '67 Macm
2. The City of Gold and Lead   '67 Ham&C
3. The Pool of Fire   '68 Ham&C

    The Luke Trilogy
1. The Prince in Waiting   '70 Macm
2. Beyond the Burning Lands   '71 HamiH
3. The Sword of the Spirits   '72 HamiH

CLARKE, ARTHUR C.   (b.1917)

    Space Odyssey
1. 2001: A Space Odyssey   '68 NAL
2. 2010: Odyssey Two   '82 DelR

CLAUDY, CARL H.   (1879-1957)

    Adventures in the Unknown
1. The Mystery Men of Mars   '33 G&D
2. A Thousand Years a Minute   '33 G&D
3. The Land of No Shadow   '33 G&D
4. The Blue Grotto Terror   '34 G&D

CLAYTON, JO   (b.1939)

    Diadem Series
1. Diadem From the Stars   '77 DAW

(cont.)

   2. Lamarchos '78 DAW
   3. Irsud '78 DAW
   4. Maeve '79 DAW
   5. Star Hunters '80 DAW
   6. The Nowhere Hunt '81 DAW
   7. Ghosthunt '83 DAW
   8. The Snares of Ibex '84 DAW

   The Duel of Sorcery
   1. Moongather '82 DAW
   2. Moonscatter '83 DAW
   3. Changer's Moon '85 DAW

CLEGG, BARBARA (see "DOCTOR WHO")

CLEMENT, HAL (b.1922)

   Needle
   1. Needle '50 Dbdy
      aka: From Outer Space ('57/Avon)
   2. Through the Eye of the Needle '78 DelR

   Mesklin
   1. Mission of Gravity '54 Dbdy
   2. Close to Critical '64 Ball
   3. Star Light '71 Ball

CLEVE, JOHN
   (pseud., see ANDREW J. OFFUTT)

COBLENTZ, STANTON A. (1896-1982)

   Outlander Series
   1. The Moon People '64 Avalo
   2. The Crimson Capsule '67 Avalo
      aka: The Animal People ('70/Belmt)
   3. The Island People '71 Belmt

COE, ROSS ANTON

   Warrior of Vengeance
   1. Sorcerer's Blood '82 Pinn
   2. Trails of Peril '82 Pinn

COFFMAN, VIRGINIA (b.1914)

    Lucifer Cove
1. The Devil's Mistress   '70 Lance
2. Priestess of the Damned   '70 Lance
3. The Devil's Virgin   '71 Lance
4. Masque of Satan   '71 Lance
5. Chalet Diabolique   '71 Lance
6. From Satan, with Love   '71 Lance

COGSWELL, THEODORE (b.1918) (see "STAR TREK")

COHEN, BARRY

    Asher Bockhorn
1. The Taking of Satcon Station (with Jim Baen)   '82 Tor
2. Blood on the Moon   '84 Tor

COLE, ADRIAN

    The Dream Lords
1. A Plague of Nightmares   '75 Zebra
2. Lord of Nightmares   '75 Zebra
3. Bane of Nightmares   '76 Zebra

COLE, ALAN & CHRIS BUNCH

    Sten
1. Sten   '82 DelR
2. The Wolf Worlds   '84 DelR

COLES, CYRIL HENRY (1899-1965) & MANNING COLES (pseud. of Adelaide Manning)

    Latimer
1. Brief Candles   '54 Dbdy
    (also published as by Francis Gaite)
2. Happy Returns   '55 Dbdy
3. Come and Go   '58 Dbdy
    (also published as by Francis Gaite)

COLLINGWOOD, HARRY (pseud., 1851-1922)
    (cont.)

The "Flying Fish"
1. The Log of the "Flying Fish"; a Story of Aerial and Submarine Peril and Adventure — 1886 Blk&S
2. With Airship and Submarine; a Tale of Adventure — '07 Blk&S
3. The Cruise of the "Flying Fish", the Airship-Submarine — '24 Low,M

COMBE, WILLIAM (1741-1823) (see ALAIN RENE LE SAGE)

COMER, RALPH (pseud. of John Sanders)

Robert Lawson
1. The Witchfinders — '68 Tand
2. The Mirror of Dionysos — '69 Tand
   aka: To Dream of Evil ('73/Award)

COMSTOCK, JARROD

The Lawless Worlds
1. The Love Machine — '84 Pinn
2. Scales of Justice — '84 Pinn
3. Kingdom Come — '84 Pinn
4. Hammer Home — '85 Pinn

CONEY, MICHAEL (b.1932)

Song of Earth
1. The Celestial Steam Locomotive — '83 HMiff
2. Gods of the Greataway — '84 HMiff

CONNELL, ALAN

Serpent Land
1. Lords of Serpent Land — '45 Curwg
2. Prisoners in Serpent Land — '45 Curwg
3. Warriors of Serpent Land — '45 Curwg

CONWAY, GERALD F. (see WALLACE MOORE, pseud.)

CONWAY, TROY (House Pseudonym)

(cont.)

(Troy Conway, cont.)

Coxeman

1. Don't Bite Off More Than You Can Chew	'68	PbLib
2. A Hard Act to Follow	'68	PbLib
3. The Billion Dollar Snatch	'68	PbLib
4. The Wham! Bam! Thank You, Ma'am Affair	'68	PbLib
5. It's Getting Harder All the Time	'68	PbLib
6. Come One, Come All (Michael Avallone)	'68	PbLib
7. Last Licks	'68	PbLib
8. Keep It Up, Rod!	'68	PbLib
9. The Man-Eater (Michael Avallone)	'68	PbLib
10. The Best Laid Plans	'69	PbLib
11. It's What's Up Front That Counts	'69	PbLib
12. Had Any Lately? (Michael Avallone)	'69	PbLib
13. Whatever Goes Up	'69	PbLib
14. A Good Peace (Michael Avallone)	'69	PbLib
15. I'd Rather Fight Than Swish (Michael Avallone)	'69	PbLib
16. Just a Silly Millimeter Longer	'69	PbLib
17. The Big Broad Jump (Michael Avallone)	'69	PbLib
18. The Sex Machine	'70	PbLib
19. The Blow-Your-Mind Job (Michael Avallone)	'70	PbLib
20. The Cunning Linguist (Michael Avallone)	'70	PbLib
21. Will the Real Rod Please Stand Up?	'70	PbLib
22. All Screwed Up (Michael Avallone)	'70	PbLib
23. The Master Baiter	'70	PbLib
24. Turn the Other Sheik	'70	PbLib
25. It's Not How Long You Make It	'70	PbLib
26. Son of a Witch	'71	PbLib
27. The Penetrator (Michael Avallone)	'71	PbLib
28. A Stiff Proposition (Michael Avallone)	'71	PbLib
29. The Harder You Try, The Harder It Gets	'71	PbLib
30. Up and Coming	'71	PbLib
31. The Cockeyed Cuties	'72	PbLib
32. I Can't Believe I Ate the Whole Thing	'72	PbLib
33. Eager Beaver	'72	PbLib
34. A Hard Man is Good to Find	'73	PbLib

COOK, GLEN

The Dread Empire

1. A Shadow of All Night Falling	'79	Berk
2. October's Baby	'80	Berk
3. All Darkness Met	'80	Berk

(related titles)

4. The Fire in His Hands	'83	PB
5. With Mercy Toward None	'85	Baen

(Glen Cook, cont.)

The Starfishers Trilogy
1. Shadowline '82 Warnr
2. Starfishers '82 Warnr
3. Stars' End '82 Warnr

The Black Company Trilogy
1. The Black Company '84 Tor
2. Shadows Linger '84 Tor
3. The White Rose '85 Tor

COON, SUSAN

The Living Planet
1. Rahne '80 Avon
2. Cassilee '80 Avon
3. The Virgin '81 Avon
4. Chiy-Une '82 Avon

COOPER, EDMUND (1926-1982)

The Expendables
(pseud.— Richard Avery)
1. Deathworms of Kratos '75 Coron
2. The Rings of Tantalus '75 Coron
3. The War Games of Zelos '75 Coron
4. The Venom of Argus '76 Coron

COOPER, MORTON (see "THE MUNSTERS")

COOPER, SONNI (see "STAR TREK")

COOPER, SUSAN (b.1935)

The Dark is Rising
1. Over Sea, Under Stone '65 Cape
2. The Dark is Rising '73 Athen
3. Greenwitch '73 C&W
4. The Grey King '74 C&W
5. Silver on the Tree '77 Athen

COPPEL, ALFRED (b.1921)
(see ROBERT CHAN GILMAN, pseud.)

COPPER, BASIL (see collaboration with LEE FALK)

CORBY, ADAM

    The Doom-Quest of Ara-Karn
1. The Former King   '81 PB
2. The Divine Queen   '82 PB

CORELLI, MARIE (1855-1924)

    Heliobas
1. A Romance of Two Worlds   1886 Benty
2. Ardath, The Story of a Dead Self   1889 Benty

CORREY, LEE (pseud. of G. Harry Stine, b.1928)
    (see "STAR TREK")

CORY, DESMOND
    (pseud. of Shaun Lloyd McCarthy, b.1928)

    Johnny Fedora
1. High Requiem   '55 Mullr
2. Sunburst   '71 H&S

COSGROVE, RACHEL
    ("Oz" series-- see L. FRANK BAUM)

COULSON, JUANITA (b.1933)

    Children of the Stars
1. Tomorrow's Heritage   '81 Ball
2. Outward Bound   '82 DelR

COULSON, ROBERT (b.1924)
    (see "U.N.C.L.E.")

CRADOCK, PHYLLIS (b.1910)

    Amartus
1. Gateway to Remembrance   '49 Daker
2. The Eternal Echo   '50 Daker

CRAIG, DAVID (pseud. of Allan James Tucker, b.1929)

    Roy Rickman
1. The Alias Man   '68 Cape
2. Message Ends   '69 Cape
3. Contact Lost   '70 Cape

CRAINE, E.J. (1881-?)

    The Airplane Boys/(aka: The Sky Buddies) *
1. Airplane Boys on the Border Line   '30 World
2. Airplane Boys at Cap Rock   '30 World
3. Airplane Boys Discover the Secrets of Cuzco   '30 World
4. Airplane Boys Flying to Amy-Ran Fastness   '30 World
    aka: Flying to Amy-Ran Fastness ('30/World)
5. Airplane Boys at Platinum River   '31 World
    aka: At Platinum River ('31/World)
6. Airplane Boys with the Revolutionists in Bolivia   '31 World
    aka: With the Revolutionists in Bolivia ('31/World)
7. Airplane Boys in the Black Woods   '32 World
8. Airplane Boys at Belize   '32 World
    * Some editions change the name of the "Airplane Boys" to the "Sky Buddies".

CRAWLEY, RAYBURN

    Ned Shackleton
1. The Valley of Creeping Men   '30 Harpr
2. Chattering Gods   '31 Harpr

CREASEY, JOHN (1908-1973)

    Dr. Palfrey
    (Note-- some novels contain more SF elements than others, particularly after the first eight).

1. Traitors' Doom   '42 Walkr
2. The Valley of Fear   '43 JLong
    aka: The Perilous Country ('49/JLong)
3. The Legion of the Lost   '43 JLong
4. Dangerous Quest   '44 JLong
5. The Hounds of Vengeance   '45 JLong

(cont.)

(John Creasey, cont.)

6. Death in the Rising Sun	'45	Walkr
7. Shadow of Doom	'46	JLong
8. The House of the Bears	'47	JLong
9. Dark Harvest	'47	JLong
10. Sons of Satan	'48	JLong
11. The Wings of Peace	'48	JLong
12. The Dawn of Darkness	'49	JLong
13. The League of Light	'49	Evans
14. The Man Who Shook the World	'50	Evans
15. The Prophet of Fire	'51	Evans
16. The Children of Hate	'52	Evans
aka: The Children of Despair ('58/Jay)		
aka: The Killers of Innocence ('71/Walkr)		
17. The Touch of Death	'54	H&S
18. The Mists of Fear	'55	H&S
19. The Flood	'56	H&S
20. The Plague of Silence	'58	H&S
21. The Drought	'59	Walkr
aka: Dry Spell ('67/NEL)		
22. The Terror	'62	H&S
23. The Depths	'63	H&S
24. The Sleep	'64	H&S
25. The Inferno	'65	H&S
26. The Famine	'67	H&S
27. The Blight	'68	H&S
28. The Oasis	'69	H&S
29. The Smog	'70	H&S
30. The Unbegotten	'71	H&S
31. The Insulators	'72	H&S
32. The Voiceless Ones	'73	H&S

CRISPIN, A.C.   see: collaboration with ANDRE NORTON
                see: "STAR TREK"
                see: "V" series

CRISTABEL
   (pseud. of Christine Elizabeth Abrahamson, b.1916)

   Veltakin
1. Menalacor of Veltakin	'70	Curt
2. The Cruachen and the Killane	'70	Curt

CROFT, SIR HERBERT (1751-1816)
                               (cont.)

Kilkhampton and Westminster
1. The Abbey of Kilkhampton; or, Monumental
   Records for the Year 1980.   1780 Kears
2. The Second Part of the Abbey of Kilkhampton
                                             1780 Kears
3. The Wreck of Westminster Abbey, Alias the
   Year Two Thousand, Alias the Ordeal of Sepulchral Candour (actually printed 1788)   2001 Stalk

CROSS, JOHN KEIR (1914-1967)

      Stephen MacFarlane
1. The Angry Planet; An Authentic First-
   Hand Account of a Journey to Mars in
   the Spaceship "Albatross"   '45 PLunn
2. SOS From Mars   '54 Hutch
      aka: The Red Journey Back; A First-Hand
         Account of the Second and Third
         Martian Expeditions by the Space-
         Ships "Albatross" and "Comet" ('54/CowMc)

CRUMP, IRVING (1887-1979)

      Og
1. Og-- Son of Fire   '22 Dodd
2. Og-- Boy of Battle   '25 Dodd
3. Og of the Cave People   '35 Dodd
4. Og, Son of Og   '65 Dodd

"CTHULHU MYTHOS"   (see H.P. LOVECRAFT)

CULBREATH, MYRNA (see "STAR TREK")

CUMMINS, RAY (1887-1957)

      MATTER, SPACE & TIME SERIES
      Matter
1. The Girl in the Golden Atom   '22   Methn
      Space
2. The Princess of the Atom   '29/'50   Avon
      Time
3. The Man Who Mastered Time   '24/'29   McClg
4. The Shadow Girl   '29/'46   GSwan
5. The Exile of Time   '31/'64   Avalo

(Ray Cummings, cont.)

Tama
1. Tama of the Light Country   '30/'65   Ace
2. Tama, Princess of Mercury   '31/'66   Ace

Gregg Haljan
1. Brigands of the Moon   '31   McClg
2. Wandl the Invader   '32/'61   Ace

CURRY, JANE LOUISE (b.1932)

Prince Lincoas
1. The Daybreakers   '70   Harc
2. Over the Sea's Edge   '71   LongG

Professor Kurtz
1. Mindy's Mysterious Miniature   '70   Harc
     aka: The Housenapper ('71/LongG)
2. The Lost Farm   '74   Athen

D

DAGMAR (pseud., see LOU CAMERON)

DAHL, ROALD (b.1916)

    Charlie
1. Charlie and the Chocolate Factory   '64 Knopf
2. Charlie and the Great Glass Elevator   '72 Knopf

DAKE, CHARLES ROMYN (see EDGAR ALLAN POE)

DALEY, BRIAN

    also see: "STAR TREK"

    Coramonde
1. The Doomfarers of Coramonde   '77 DelR
2. The Starfollowers of Coramonde   '79 DelR

DALMAS, JOHN

    The Yngling
1. The Yngling   '83 Tor
2. The Homecoming   '84 Tor

DALOS, GYORGY ("1984" sequence— see GEORGE ORWELL)

DANIELS, DOROTHY (b.1915)

    Strange Paradise
1. Strange Paradise   '69 PbLib
2. Island of Evil   '70 PbLib
3. Raxl, Voodoo Priestess   '70 PbLib

DANIELS, LES (b.1943)

    Don Sebastian
1. The Silver Skull   '79 Scrib
2. Citizen Vampire   '81 Scrib
3. The Black Castle   '81 Scrib

DANIELS, NORMAN (see "THE AVENGERS")

DARLINGTON, W.A. (b.1890)

    Alf Higgins
1. Alf's Button   '19   Jenk
2. Alf's Carpet   '28   Jenk
3. Alf's New Button   '40   Jenk

DARLTON, CLARK (see "PERRY RHODAN")

DAVEY, NORMAN (1888-?)

    Matthew Sumner *
1. The Pilgrim of a Smile   '21   ChapH
2. The Penultimate Adventure   '24   EMath
    * coll. as: "The Pilgrim of a Smile" ('33/ChapH)

DAVIDSON, AVRAM (b.1923)

    Kar-Chee
1. Rogue Dragon   '65   Ace
2. The Kar-Chee Reign   '66   Ace

    Peregrine
1. Peregrine: Primus   '71   Walkr
2. Peregrine: Secundus   '81   Berk

DAVIES, FREDRIC (see "U.N.C.L.E.")

DAVIS, HAROLD A. (see "PERRY RHODAN")

DAVIS, GERRY (see "DOCTOR WHO")

DAWSON, CARLEY

    Mr. Wicker
1. Mr. Wicker's Window   '52   HMiff
2. The Sign of the Seven Seas   '54   HMiff

DE CAMP, CATHERINE CROOK (b.1907) (see L. SPRAGUE DE CAMP)

DE CAMP, L. SPRAGUE (b.1907)

    also see: ROBERT E. HOWARD for "Conan" series

Harold Shea
(written in collaboration with Fletcher Pratt)
1. The Incomplete Enchanter *   '41   Holt
2. The Castle of Iron *   '50   Gnome
3. The Wall of Serpents   '60   Avalo
   * Note-- the first two titles have been
     collected as: "The Compleat Enchanter"
                           ('75/Dbdy)

Krishna Series
1. Cosmic Manhunt   '54   Ace
   aka: A Planet Called Krishna ('66/Camp)
   aka: The Queen of Zamba ('77/Davis)
2. The Hand of Zei   '63   Avalo
   part I aka: The Search for Zei ('62/Avalon)
   part I aka: The Floating Continent ('66/Camp)
3. The Hostage of Zir   '77   Berk
4. The Virgin of Zesh   '76   Pop
5. The Tower of Zanid   '58   Avalo
6. The Prisoner of Zhamanak   '82   Phant
7. The Bones of Zora (with Catherine Crook De Camp)
                                  '83   Phant

Novaria Series *
1. The Goblin Tower   '68   Pyr
2. The Clocks of Iraz   '71   Pyr
3. The Fallible Fiend   '73   Sign
4. The Unbeheaded King   '83   DelR
   * Note-- Titles 1,2 and 4 have also been released
     as a trilogy entitled: "The Reluctant King"
                              ('84/SFBC)

DE CHANCIE, JOHN

Jake McGraw
1. Starrigger   '83   Ace
2. Red Limit Freeway   '84   Ace

DEEGAN, JON J. (House pseudonym)

Old Growler (by Robert Sharp)
1. Amateurs in Alchemy   '52   Pantr
2. Antro, the Life-Giver   '53   Pantr
3. The Great Ones   '53   Pantr

(Jon J. Deegan, cont.)

    Dysart (by Robert Sharp)
1. Corridors of Time   '53 Pantr
2. Beyond the Fourth Door   '54 Pantr
3. Exiles in Time   '54 Pantr

DELANY, SAMUEL R. (b.1942)

    The Fall of the Towers (coll.'70)
1. Captives of the Flame   '63 Ace
    rev. as: Out of the Dead City ('68/Spher)
2. The Towers of Toron   '64 Ace
3. City of a Thousand Suns   '65 Ace

    Neveryon
1. Tales of Neveryon   '79 Bant
2. Neveryona, or: The Tale of Signs and Cities
                                                   '83 Bant
3. Flight From Neveryon   '85 Bant

DE LARRABEITI, MICHAEL

    The Borribles
1. Borribles   '78 Macm
2. The Borribles Go for Broke   '81 BodH

DEL REY, LESTER (b.1915)

    Moon Series
1. Step to the Stars   '54 Winst
2. Mission to the Moon   '56 Winst
3. Moon of Mutiny   '61 Holt

DE LUBICZ, ISHA SCHWALLER (1885-?)

    Her-Bak
1. Her-Bak, "Chick-Pea"; the Living Face
   of Ancient Egypt   '54 H&S
2. Her-Bak, Egyptian Initiate   '67 H&S

DE MORGAN, JOHN (1848-?)

                                              (cont.)

Aristophano
1. He, a Companion to She, Being a History
   of the Adventures of J. Theodosius
   Aristaphano on the Island of Rapa Nui
   in Search of His Immortal Ancestor   1887 Munro
2. "It"; a Wild, Weird History of Marvelous,
   Miraculous, Phantasmagorical Adventures
   in Search of He, She, and Jess, and Leading to the Finding of "It"; a Haggard
   Conclusion.   1887 Munro

King Solomon's Mines Parodies
1. King Solomon's Wives   1887 Munro
2. King Solomon's Treasures   1887 Munro

DENNIS, ROBERT C. (1920-1983)

Paul Reeder
1. The Sweat of Fear   '73   Bob-M
2. Conversations with a Corpse   '74   Bob-M

DENT, LESTER (1905-1969) (see KENNETH ROBESON)

DERLETH, AUGUST (1909-1971) (see H.P. LOVECRAFT)

DeWEESE, THOMAS EUGENE (b.1934) (see "U.N.C.L.E.")

DEXTER, SUSAN (b.1955)

Tristan
1. The Ring of Allaire   '81   Ball
2. The Sword of Calandra   '85   DelR

DEXTER, WILLIAM (b.1909)

Denis Grafton
1. World in Eclipse   '54   POwen
2. Children of the Void   '55   POwen

DIAMOND, GRAHAM (b.1945)

(cont.)

(Graham Diamond, cont.)

    THE HAVEN SERIES
1. The Haven   '77 Play
    The Adventures of the Empire Princess
2. Lady of the Haven   '78 Play
3. Dungeons of Kuba   '79 Play
4. The Falcons of Eden   '80 Play
5. The Beasts of Hades   '81 Play

    Samarkind
1. Samarkind   '79 Play
2. Samarkind Dawn   '80 Play

DIBELL, ANSEN (pseud. of Nancy Ann Dibble, b.1942)

    The Kantmorie Saga
1. Pursuit of the Screamer   '78 DAW
2. Circle, Crescent, Star   '81 DAW
3. Summerfair   '82 DAW

DICKINSON, PETER (b.1927)

    The Changes Trilogy (coll.'75)
1. The Devil's Children   '70 Gollz
2. Heartsease   '69 Gollz
3. Weathermonger   '68 Gollz

DICKS, TERRANCE (see "DOCTOR WHO")

DICKSON, GORDON R. (b.1923)

    The Hoka Series (written with Poul Anderson)
1. Earthman's Burden   '57 Gnome
2. Star Prince Charlie   '75 Putn
3. Hoka!   '84 Tor

    Robby Hoenig
1. Secret Under the Sea   '60 Holt
2. Secret Under Antarctica   '63 Holt
3. Secret Under the Caribbean   '64 Holt

    The Dilbia Sequence
1. Spacial Delivery   '61 Ace
2. Spacepaw   '69 Putn

The Childe Cycle *
1. Necromancer   '62 Dbdy
     aka: No Room For Man ('63/Macf)
2. Tactics of Mistake   '71 Dbdy
3. Soldier, Ask Not   '67 Dell
4. The Genetic General   '60 Ace
     expanded as: Dorsai! ('76/DAW)
5. The Spirit of Dorsai   '79 Ace
6. Lost Dorsai   '80 Ace
7. The Final Encyclopedia   '84 Tor
   * Note-- titles 1,2 and 4 have been issued
     with some additional material as:
     Three to Dorsai! ('76)

DISCH, THOMAS M. (b.1940) (see "THE PRISONER")

DIXON, THOMAS (1864-1946)

The Fall of a Nation
1. The Clansman (this title is not SF)   '05 Heine
     aka: The Birth of a Nation ('15/Film Books)
2. The Fall of a Nation; a Sequel to
     the Birth of a Nation   '16 Apple

"DOCTOR WHO"

   The Doctor Who books published by the Target
divison of W.H. Allen are adaptations of the BBC television series. Each adaptation covers a series of
episodes which formed a particular storyline (the number of episodes comprising a story varied). The following list is in order of publication; however the
number in parenthesis preceding the title is the actual
order in which the story first aired (this order is as
of the end of 1984, since Target is still publishing
both early and later episodes in no specific pattern).
The author of each adaptation follows the title. Note--
many of the books actually begin with the words "Doctor
Who and..." which have been dropped for purposes of the
listing.

     Doctor Who
1. (2) Doctor Who in an Exciting Adventure
           with the Daleks (David Whittaker) '67 Avon
           aka: Doctor Who and the Daleks ('73/Targ)
                             (cont.)

("Doctor Who", cont.)

2. (6) Doctor Who and the Zarbi (Bill Strutton)
   reissued: ('73/Targ)
3. (7) The Crusaders (David Whittaker) '73 Targ
4. (20) The Cave Monsters (Malcolm Hulke) '74 Targ
5. (21) The Auton Invasion (Terrance Dicks) '74 Targ
6. (23) The Doomsday Weapon (Malcolm Hulke) '74 Targ
7. (25) The Day of the Daleks (T. Dicks) '74 Targ
8. (24) The Daemons (Barry Letts) '74 Targ
9. (27) The Sea Devils (Malcolm Hulke) '74 Targ
10. (12) The Abominable Snowmen (T. Dicks) '74 Targ
11. (26) The Curse of Peladon (Brian Hayles) '74 Targ
12. (10) The Cybermen (Gerry Davis) '75 Targ
13. (39) The Giant Robot (Terrance Dicks) '75 Targ
14. (19) The Terror of the Autons (T. Dicks) '75 Targ
15. (33) The Green Death (Malcolm Hulke) '75 Targ
16. (38) Planet of Spiders (Terrance Dicks) '75 Targ
17. (29) The Three Doctors (Terrance Dicks) '75 Targ
18. (44) The Loch Ness Monster (T. Dicks) '76 Targ
19. (8) The Tenth Planet (Gerry Davis) '76 Targ
20. (35) The Dinosaur Invasion (M. Hulke) '76 Targ
21. (13) The Ice Warriors (Brian Hayles) '76 Targ
22. (43) Revenge of the Cybermen (T. Dicks) '76 Targ
23. (42) Genesis of the Daleks (T. Dicks) '76 Targ
24. (15) The Web of Fear (Terrance Dicks) '76 Targ
25. (31) The Space War (Malcolm Hulke) '76 Targ
26. (32) Planet of the Daleks (T. Dicks) '76 Targ
27. (46) The Pyramids of Mars (T. Dicks) '76 Targ
28. (30) The Carnival Monsters (T. Dicks) '77 Targ
29. (49) The Seeds of Doom
   (Phillip Hinchcliffe) '77 Targ
30. (5) The Dalek Invasion of Earth
   (Terrance Dicks) '77 Targ
31. (22) The Claws of Axos (Terrance Dicks) '77 Targ
32. (48) The Brain of Morbius (T. Dicks) '77 Targ
33. (45) Planet of Evil (Terrance Dicks) '77 Targ
34. (28) The Mutants (Terrance Dicks) '77 Targ
35. (52) The Deadly Assassin (T. Dicks) '77 Targ
36. (55) The Talons of Weng-Chiang (T. Dicks) '77 Targ
37. (50) Masque of Mandragora (P. Hinchcliffe) '77 Targ
38. (53) The Face of Evil (Terrance Dicks) '78 Targ
39. (56) The Horror of Fang Rock (T. Dicks) '78 Targ
40. (11) The Tomb of the Cybermen (G. Davis) '78 Targ
41. (34) The Time Warrior
   (Terrance Dicks & Robert Holmes) '78 Targ
42. (36) Death to the Daleks (T. Dicks) '78 Targ
43. (47) The Android Invasion (T. Dicks) '78 Targ
44. (41) The Sontaran Experiment (Ian Marter) '78 Targ
45. (51) The Hand of Fear (Terrance Dicks) '79 Targ

46. (57) The Invisible Enemy   (T. Dicks)   '79 Targ
47. (54) The Robots of Death   (T. Dicks)   '79 Targ
48. (58) The Image of the Fendahl (T. Dicks)'79 Targ
49. (17) The War Games   (Malcolm Hulke)   '79 Targ
50. (67) The Destiny of the Daleks (T. Dicks)'79 Targ
51. (62) The Ribos Operation   (Ian Marter)   '79 Targ
52. (60) The Underworld (Terrance Dicks)   '80 Targ
53. (61) The Invasion of Time (T. Dicks)   '80 Targ
54. (63) The Stones of Blood   (T. Dicks)   '80 Targ
55. (64) The Androids of Tara (T. Dicks)   '80 Targ
56. (65) The Power of Kroll   (T. Dicks)   '80 Targ
57. (66) The Armageddon Factor (T. Dicks)   '80 Targ
58. (3) The Keys of Marinus   (P.Hinchcliffe)'80 Targ
59. (69) The Nightmare of Eden (T. Dicks)   '80 Targ
60. (70) The Horns of Nimon   (T. Dicks)   '80 Targ
61. (37) The Monster of Peladon (T. Dicks)   '80 Targ
62. (68) The Creature From the Pit
         (David Fisher)   '81 Targ
63. (14) The Enemy of the World (Ian Marter)'81 Targ
64. (1) An Unearthly Child (Terrance Dicks)'81 Targ
65. (74) The State of Decay (Terrance Dicks)'82 Targ
66. (75) Warriors' Gate (Steve Gallagher)   '82 Targ
67. (76) The Keeper of Traken (T. Dicks)   '82 Targ
68. (71) The Leisure Hive (David Fisher)   '82 Targ
69. (81) The Visitation (Eric Saward)   '82 Targ
70. (73) Full Circle (Andrew Smith)   '82 Targ
71. (59) The Sunmakers (Terrance Dicks)   '82 Targ
72. (77) Logopolis (Christopher H. Bidmead) '82 Targ
73. (83) Time Flight (Peter Grimwade)   '83 Targ
74. (72) Meglos (Terrance Dicks)   '83 Targ
75. (78) Castrovalva (Christopher H. Bidmead)
                                                 '83 Targ
76. (79) Four to Doomsday (Terrance Dicks)   '83 Targ
77. (82) Earthshock (Ian Marter)   '83 Targ
78. (87) Terminus (Steve Gallagher)   '83 Targ
79. (84) Arc of Infinity (Terrance Dicks)   '83 Targ
80. (89) The Five Doctors (Terrance Dicks)   '83 Targ
81. (86) Mawdryn Undead (Peter Grimwade)   '84 Targ
82. (80) Kinda (Terrance Dicks)   '84 Targ
83. (85) Snakedance (Terrance Dicks)   '84 Targ
84. (88) Enlightenment (Barbara Clegg)   '84 Targ
85. (16) The Dominators (Ian Marter)   '84 Targ
86. (90) Warriors of the Deep (T. Dicks)   '84 Targ
87. (4) The Aztecs (John Lucarotti)   '84 Targ
88. (18) Inferno (Terrance Dicks)   '84 Targ
89. (9) The Highlanders (Gerry Davis)   '84 Targ

Doctor Who— Pinnacle sequence
1. Doctor Who and the Day of the Daleks
   (Terrance Dicks)   Pinn

("Doctor Who", Pinnacle sequence cont.)

   2. Doctor Who and the Doomsday Weapon
      (Malcolm Hulke)   Pinn
   3. Doctor Who and the Dinosaur Invasion (Hulke)   Pinn
   4. Doctor Who and the Genesis of the Daleks
      (Terrance Dicks)   Pinn
   5. Doctor Who and the Revenge of the Cybermen
      (Terrance Dicks)   Pinn
   6. Doctor Who and the Loch Ness Monster (Dicks) Pinn
   7. Doctor Who and the Talons of Weng-Chiang
      (Terrance Dicks)   Pinn
   8. Doctor Who and the Masque of Mandragora
      (Hinchcliffe)   Pinn
   9. Doctor Who and the Android Invasion (Dicks)   Pinn
 10. Docto Who and the Seeds of Doom (Hinchcliffe)
                                                                             Pinn

DODGSON, CHARLES LUTWIDGE   (see LEWIS CARROLL, pseud.)

DOKE, JOSEPH J.

     Justin Retief
  1. The Secret City: A Romance of the Karroo   '13 H&S
  2. The Queen of the Secret City   '16 H&S

DOMBROWSKI, KATRINA (1881-?)

     Abdallah
  1. Abdallah and the Donkey   '28 Macm
  2. The Fat Camel of Bagdad   '29 Macm

DONALDSON, STEPHEN R. (b.1947)

     also see: collaboration with FRED SABERHAGEN

     THE CHRONICLES OF THOMAS COVENANT
     The First Chronicles
  1. Lord Foul's Bane   '77 Dbdy
  2. The Illearth War   '77 Holt
  3. The Power That Preserves   '77 Holt
     The Second Chronicles
  4. The Wounded Land   '80 DelR
  5. The One Tree   '82 DelR
  6. White Gold Wielder   '83 DelR

DONOVAN, LAURENCE (see KENNETH ROBESON)

DOUGLAS, CAROLE NELSON (b.1944)

    Kendric and Irissa
1. The Six of Swords   '82 DelR
2. Exiles of the Rynth   '84 DelR

DOYLE, SIR ARTHUR CONAN (1859-1930)

    The Professor Challenger Novels *
1. The Lost World   '12 H&S
2. The Poisoned Belt   '13 H&S
3. The Land of Mist   '26 Hutch
    * collected as:
      The Professor Challenger Stories ('52/JMurr)
    related anthology
4. The Maracot Deep, and Other Stories   '29 JMurr
   (contains 2 Challenger stories)

DRAKE, DAVID (b.1945)

    Don Slade
1. Hammer's Slammers   '79 Ace
2. Cross the Stars   '84 Tor
3. At Any Price   '85 Baen

"DRAY PRESCOTT" (see KENNETH BULMER)

DREW, WAYLAND

    The Erthring Cycle
1. The Memoirs of Alcheringia   '84 DelR
2. The Gaian Experiment   '85 DelR

DRUMM, D.B. (pseudonym)

    Traveler
1. First, You Fight   '84 Dell
2. Kingdom Come   '84 Dell
3. The Stalkers   '84 Dell
4. To Kill a Shadow   '84 Dell
5. Road War   '85 Dell
6. Border War   '85 Dell

DRURY, ALLEN (b.1918)

    Advise and Consent
1. Advise and Consent   '59 Dbdy
2. A Shade of Difference   '62 Dbdy
3. Capable of Honor   '66 Dbdy
4. Preserve and Protect   '68 Dbdy
5. Come Ninevah, Come Tyre; the Presidency of Edward M. Jason   '73 Dbdy

DRYASDUST (pseud. of M.Y. Halidom, also a pseudonym)

    Ye Headless Lady Inn
1. Tales of the Wonder Club   1899 Harri
2. Tales of the Wonder Club, Volume 2   1900 Harri

DUANE, DIANE

    also see: "STAR TREK"

    Epic Tale of the Five
1. The Door into Fire   '79
2. The Door into Shadow   '84 Bjay

    The Wizard Sequence
1. So You Want to Be a Wizard?
2. Deep Wizardry   '85 Delac

DUDLEY, OWEN FRANCIS (1882-1952)

    Problems of Human Happiness
1. Will Men Be Like Gods?   '24 LongG
2. The Shadow on the Earth   '26 LongG
3. The Masterful Monk   '29 LongG
4. Pageant of Life   '32 LongG
5. The Coming of the Monster; a Tale of the Masterful Monk   '36 LongG
6. The Tremaynes and the Masterful Monk   '40 LongG
7. Michael. A Tale of the Masterful Monk   '48 LongG

DUMAS, ALEXANDRE, pere (1802-1870)

    Memoirs of a Physician
1. Memoirs of a Physician   1846 G.Pier
    aka: Joseph Balsamo (1878/Peter)
    aka: Balsamo the Magician (1892/WHDav)

2. The Queen's Necklace　　　　　　　　1847　Parlo
    aka: Memoirs of a Physician (c.1850/Peter)
    aka: Joseph Balsamo, vol. II (1895/RdMcN)
    aka: The Elixir of Life ('28/CCTP)

DUNN, PHILIP

    The Cabal
1. The Cabal　　　　　　　　　　　　　　'78　Corgi
2. The Black Moon　　　　　　　　　　　'78　Corgi
3. The Evangelist　　　　　　　　　　　'79　Corgi

DUNSANY, LORD (1878-1957)

    The Gods of Pegana
1. The Gods of Pegana　　　　　　　　　'05　EMath
2. Time and the Gods　　　　　　　　　 '06　Heine

    The Jorkens Tales
1. The Travel Tales of Mr. Joseph Jorkens　'31　Putn
2. Jorkens Remembers Africa　　　　　　'34　LongG
3. Jorkens Has a Large Whiskey　　　　 '40　Putn
4. The Fourth Book of Jorkens　　　　　'47　Jarrd
5. Jorkens Borrows Another Whiskey　　 '54　MiJos

DURRELL, LAWRENCE (b.1912)

    Felix Charlock
1. Tunc　　　　　　　　　　　　　　　　'68　EPDut
2. Nunquam　　　　　　　　　　　　　　'70　EPDut

DVORKIN, DAVID (see "STAR TREK")

E

EAGER, EDWARD (1911-1964)

Magic
1. Half Magic	'54	Harc
2. Knight's Castle	'56	Harc
3. Magic By the Lake	'57	Harc
4. The Time Garden	'58	Harc

EARNSHAW, ANTHONY (b.1924) & ERIC THACKER (b.1923)

Wintersol
1. Musrum	'68	Cape
2. Wintersol	'71	Cape

EARNSHAW, BRIAN (b.1929)

Dragonfall 5
1. Dragonfall 5 and the Space Cowboys	'72	Meth
2. Dragonfall 5 and the Royal Beast	'72	Meth
3. Dragonfall 5 and the Empty Planet	'73	Meth
4. Dragonfall 5 and the Hijackers	'74	Meth
5. Dragonfall 5 and the Master Mind	'75	Meth
6. Dragonfall 5 and the Super Horse	'77	Meth
7. Dragonfall 5 and the Haunted World	'79	Meth

EDDINGS, DAVID (b.1931)

The Belgariad
1. Pawn of Prophecy	'82	DelR
2. Queen of Sorcery	'82	DelR
3. Magician's Gambit	'83	DelR
4. Castle of Wizardry	'84	DelR
5. Enchanter's End Game	'84	DelR

EDDISON, E.R. (1882-1945)

The Zimiamvian Trilogy
1. The Mezentian Gate	'58	Curwn
2. A Fish Dinner in Memison	'41	EPDut
3. Mistress of Mistresses	'35	Faber

related title (though only superficially)
4. The Worm Ouroboros	'22	

EDMONDSON, G.C. (b.1922)

    The "Alice"
1. The Ship That Sailed the Time Stream   '65 Ace
2. To Sail the Century Sea   '81 Ace

EFFINGER, GEORGE ALEC (b.1947) (see "PLANET OF THE APES")

EGLETON, CLIVE (b.1927)

    Garnett
1. A Piece of Resistance   '70 H&S
2. Last Post For a Partisan   '71 H&S
3. The Judas Mandate   '72 H&S

EGLINARDUS (pseud., see MARY DE LE RIVIERE MANLEY)

EKLUND, GORDON (b.1945)

    also see: "STAR TREK"

    Lord Tedric
1. Lord Tedric   '78 Ace
2. Space Pirates   '79 Ace
3. Black Knight of the Iron Sphere   '81 Ace

ELDER, MICHAEL (b.1931)

    Barclay Series
1. Nowhere on Earth   '72 Hale
2. The Perfumed Planet   '73 Hale
    aka: Flight to Terror ('73/Pinn)
3. Down to Earth   '73 Hale
4. The Seeds of Frenzy   '74 Hale

ELDRIDGE, PAUL
    (see collaboration with GEORGE SYLVESTER VIERECK)

ELGIN, SUZETTE HADEN (b.1936)

    Coyote Jones *
1. The Communipaths   '70 Ace

(cont.)

(Suzette Haden Elgin, cont.)

    2. Furthest   '71 Ace
    3. At the Seventh Level   '72 DAW
    4. Star Anchored, Star Angered   '79 Dbdy
       * The first 3 titles are collected in one volume as: Communipath Worlds ('80/PB)

Ozark Fantasy Trilogy
1. Twelve Fair Kingdoms   '81 Dbdy
2. The Grand Jubilee   '81 Dbdy
3. And Then There'll Be Fireworks   '81 Dbdy

ELIOTT, E.C. (pseud., b.1900)

Kemlo
1. Kemlo and the Crazy Planet   '54 TNels
2. Kemlo and the Zones of Silence   '54 TNels
3. Kemlo and the Sky Horse   '54 TNels
4. Kemlo and the Martian Ghosts   '54 TNels
5. Kemlo and the Craters of the Moon   '55 TNels
6. Kemlo and the Space Lanes   '55 TNels
7. Kemlo and the Star Men   '55 TNels
8. Kemlo and the Gravity Rays   '56 TNels
9. Kemlo and the Purple Dawn   '57 TNels
10. Kemlo and the End of Time   '57 TNels
11. Kemlo and the Zombie Men   '58 TNels
12. Kemlo and the Space Men   '59 TNels
13. Kemlo and the Satellite Builders   '60 TNels
14. Kemlo and the Space Invaders   '61 TNels
15. Kemlo and the Masters of Space   '63 TNels

Tas
1. Tas and the Space Machine   '55 TNels
2. Tas and the Postal Rocket   '55 TNels

ELLIOT, JOHN (see collaboration with FRED HOYLE)

ELLIOTT, GEORGE

Martin Speed
1. The Case of the Missing Airmen   '44 GSwan
2. The Mystery of the Missing Corpses   '45 GSwan

ELRICK, GEORGE S. (see "U.N.C.L.E.")

ENGDAHL, SYLVIA (b.1933)

    Elana
1. Enchantress From the Stars   '70 Athen
2. The Far Side of Evil   '71 Athen

    Noren
1. This Star Shall Abide   '72 Athen
    aka: Heritage of the Star ('73/Gollz)
2. Beyond the Tomorrow Mountains   '73 Athen

ENGEL, LYLE KENYON (b.1915)
    (see JEFFERY LORD, pseud.)

ENGLAND, GEORGE ALLAN (1877-1936)

    Darkness and Dawn (coll.'14/Sm,M) *
1. Darkness and Dawn   '65 Avalo
2. Beyond the Great Oblivion   '65 Avalo
3. The People of the Abyss   '66 Avalo
4. Out of the Abyss   '67 Avalo
5. The Afterglow   '67 Avalo
    * Note— a 3-volume version of the series
    has also been published.

ERNST, PAUL (b.1886)
    (see KENNETH ROBESON)

ERNSTING, WALTER
    (see "PERRY RHODAN")

ERSKINE, THOMAS (1788-1870)

    Armata
1. Armata: A Fragment   1816 JMurr
2. The Second Part of Armata   1817 JMurr

EULO, KEN (b.1939)

    Chandal Talon
1. The Brownstone   '80 PB
2. The Bloodstone   '81 PB
3. The Deathstone   '82 PB

EVANS, E. EVERETT (1893-1958)

    George Hanlon
1. Man of Many Minds   '53 FantP
2. Alien Minds   '55 FantP

EWERS, HANNS HEINZ (1871-1943)

    Frank Braun
1. The Sorcerer's Apprentice   '27 JDay
2. Alraune   '29 JDay

F

FAIRMAN, PAUL W. (1916-1977)

    also see: "VOYAGE TO THE BOTTOM OF THE SEA"

    The Man From S.T.U.D. (pseud.-- F.W. Paul) *
1. The Man From S.T.U.D. in The Solid
   Gold Screw   '68 Lance
2. The Orgy at Madame Dracula's   '68 Lance
3. Sock It To Me, Zombie!   '68 Lance
6. Rape is a No-No   '69 Lance
7. The Planned Parenthood Caper   '69 Lance
8. The Lay of the Land   '69 Lance
    * Titles 2,3, & 8 collected as:
    The Man From S.T.U.D. Vs. The Mafia ('72/Lance)

FALK, LEE (b.1915)
    Note: Frank S. Shawn is a pseudonym of Ron Goulart

    The Phantom
1. The Ghost Who Walks   '72 Avon
2. The Slave Market of Mucar
   (written with Basil Copper)   '72 Avon
3. The Scorpia Menace (with Basil Copper)   '72 Avon
4. The Veiled Lady (with Frank S. Shawn)   '73 Avon
5. The Golden Circle
   (with Frank S. Shawn)   '73 Avon
6. The Mysterious Ambassador   '73 Avon
7. The Mystery of the Sea Horse
   (with Frank S. Shawn)   '73 Avon
8. The Hydra Monster
   (with Frank S. Shawn)   '73 Avon
9. The Killer's Town   '73 Avon
10. The Goggle-Eyed Pirates
    (with Frank S. Shawn)   '74 Avon
11. The Swamp Rats (with Frank S. Shawn)   '74 Avon
12. The Vampires and the Witch   '74 Avon
13. The Island of Dogs
    (with Warren Shanahan)   '75 Avon
14. The Assassins
    (with Warren Shanahan)   '75 Avon
15. The Curse of the Two-Headed Bull   '75 Avon
    (with Carson Bingham)

FALLAW, L.M.

    The Ugglians
1. The Ugglians '57 Philo
2. The Ugglians at Large: Second Book of Ugg '59 Philo

FANE, BRON (pseud., see R. L. FANTHORPE)

FANTHORPE, R.L. (b.1935)

    The La Noire Series (pseud.-- Bron Fane)
1. The Intruders '63 Badgr
2. Somewhere Out There '63 Badgr
3. Softly By Moonlight '63 Badgr
4. Unknown Destiny '64 Badgr
5. Nemesis '64 Badgr
6. Suspension '64 Badgr
7. The Macabre Ones '64 Badgr
8. U.F.O. 517 '66 Badgr

FARADAY, ROBERT

    Adventures in the Time Machine
1. The Anytime Rings '63 Dell
2. Samax, the Gladiator '64 Dell

FARCA, MARIA (b.1935)

    Andrew Ames
1. Earth '72 Dbdy
2. Complex Man '73 Dbdy

FARLEY, RALPH MILNE (1887-1963)

    Miles Cabot
1. The Radio Man '24/'48 FPCI
    aka: An Earthman On Venus ('50/Avon)
2. The Radio Beasts '25/'64 Ace
3. The Radio Planet '26/'64 Ace

FARMER, PENELOPE (b.1939)

    Emma
1. The Summer Birds '62 Harc

   2. Emma in Winter   '66 Harc
   3. Charlotte Sometimes   '69 Harc

FARMER, PHILIP JOSE (b.1918)

also see: L. FRANK BAUM, "Oz" series

The World of Tiers
1. The Maker of Universes   '65 Ace
2. The Gates of Creation   '66 Ace
3. A Private Cosmos   '68 Ace
4. Behind the Walls of Terra   '70 Ace
5. The Lavalite World   '77 Ace

Herald Childe
1. The Image of the Beast   '68 Essex
2. Blown   '69 Essex
3. Traitor to the Living   '73 Ball

Doc Caliban
1. A Feast Unknown   '69 Essex
2. The Mad Goblin   '70 Ace

Lord Grandith
1. A Feast Unknown   '69 Essex
2. Lord of the Trees   '70 Ace

Riverworld *
1. To Your Scattered Bodies Go   '71 Putn
2. The Fabulous Riverboat   '71 Putn
3. The Dark Design   '77 Berk
4. The Magic Labyrinth   '80 Berk
5. Gods of Riverworld   '83 Phant
    * Note-- "River of Eternity" ('83) is the
      original, previously unpublished version of
      what later became the Riverworld series.

Ancient Africa
1. Time's Last Gift   '72 Ball
2. Hadon of Ancient Opar   '74 DAW
3. Flight to Opar   '76 DAW

FARREN, MICK

The Quest Trilogy
1. The Quest of the DNA Cowboys   '76
2. Synoptic Manhunt   '76
3. Neural Atrocity   '77 Mayfl

FAUCETTE, JOHN M. (b.1943)

    Peacemakers
1. The Warriors of Terra   '70 Belmt
2. Siege of Earth   '71 Belmt

FEARN, JOHN RUSSELL (1908-1960)

    The Golden Amazon
1. The Golden Amazon   '44 WWork
2. The Golden Amazon Returns   '48 WWork
    aka: The Deathless Amazon ('55/Harlequin)
3. The Golden Amazon's Triumph   '53 WWork
4. The Amazon's Diamond Quest   '53 WWork
5. The Amazon Strikes Again   '54 WWork
6. Twin of the Amazon   '54 WWork
7. Conquest of the Amazon   '73 CosSF

    Liners of Time (pseud.— Vargo Statten)
1. Liners of Time   '47 WWork
2. Zagribud   '52 Scion
    aka: Science Metropolis ('52/Scion)

    Clayton Drew
1. Emperor of Mars   '50 Ham&C
2. Warrior of Mars   '50 Ham&C
3. Red Men of Mars   '50 Ham&C
4. Goddess of Mars   '50 Ham&C

    Anjani (pseud.— Earl Titan)
1. The Gold of Akada   '51 Scion
2. Anjani the Mighty   '51 Scion

    Adam Quirke (pseud.— Volsted Gridban)
1. The Master Must Die   '53 Scion
2. The Lonely Astronomer   '54 Scion

    Herbert (pseud.— Volsted Gridban)
1. A Thing of the Past   '53 Scion
2. The Genial Dinosaur   '54 Scion

FEIST, RAYMOND

    The Riftwar Trilogy
1. Magician   '82 Dbdy
2. Silverthorn   '84 Dbdy
3. Darkness at Sethanon   (NYP)

FISHER, DAVID (see "DOCTOR WHO")

FISHER, PAUL R.

    The Ash Staff Series
1. The Ash Staff   '79 Athen
2. The Hawks of Fellheath   '80 Athen
3. The Princess and the Thorn '80 Athen
4. Mont Cant Gold   '84 Athen

FISHER, VARDIS (1895-1968)

    Testament of Man
1. Darkness and the Deep   '43 Vang
2. The Golden Rooms   '44 Vang
3. Intimations of Eve   '46 Vang
4. Adam and the Serpent   '47 Vang
5. The Divine Passion   '48 Vang

"FLASH GORDON" (see ALEX RAYMOND)

FLEMING-ROBERTS, G.T. (see "SECRET AGENT X")

FLETCHER, LAWRENCE

    Dick Grenville
1. Into the Unknown: A Romance of South Africa
                                                        1892 Cass
2. Zero the Slaver: A Romance of Equatorial Africa
                                                        1892 Cass

FLINT, HOMER EON (see collaboration with AUSTIN HALL)

FLINT, KENNETH C.

    The Sidhe
1. The Riders of the Sidhe   '84 Bant
2. Champion of the Sidhe   '84 Bant
3. Master of the Sidhe   '85 Bant

FORD, JOHN M. (see "STAR TREK")

FORSTCHEN, WILLIAM R.

    The New Ice Trilogy
1. Ice Prophet   '83 DelR
2. The Flame Upon the Ice   '84 DelR
3. A Darkness Upon the Ice   '85 DelR

FORTUNE, DION (pseud. of Violet M. Firth, 1890-1946)

    Lilith Le Fay Morgan
1. The Sea Priestess   '38 Firth
2. Moon Magic   '56 Aquar

FOSTER, ALAN DEAN (b.1946)

    also see: "STAR TREK"
    also see: "STAR WARS"

    HUMANX COMMONWEALTH SERIES
    (A) Flinx and Pip Titles
1. For Love of Mother-Not   '83 DelR
2. The Tar-Aiym Krang   '72 Ball
3. Orphan Star   '77 Ball
4. The End of the Matter   '77 Ball
5. Bloodhype   '73 Ball
    (B) Non-Flinx Titles
1. Nor Crystal Tears   '82 DelR
2. Midworld   '75 Dbdy
3. Icerigger   '74 Ball
4. Mission to Moulokin   '79 Dbdy
5. Voyage to the City of the Dead   '84 DelR

    Spellsinger
1. Spellsinger   '83 Warnr
2. The Hour of the Gate   '84 Warnr
3. The Day of the Dissonance   '84 Warnr
4. The Moment of the Magician   '85 Warnr

    Anthology Duet (short stories)
1. With Friends Like These...   '83 DelR
2. ... Who Needs Enemies   '84 DelR

FOSTER, M.A. (b.1939)

    The Ler Trilogy
1. The Gameplayers of Zan   '77 DAW

(cont.)

    2. The Warriors of Dawn   '75 DAW
    3. The Day of the Klesh   '78 DAW

The Morphodite
1. The Morphodite   '81 DAW
2. Transformer   '83 DAW

FOX, GARDNER F. (b.1911)

Alan Morgan
1. Warrior of Llarn   '64 Ace
2. Thief of Llarn   '66 Ace

Commander Craig (pseud.— Bart Somers)
1. Beyond the Black Enigma   '65 PbLib
2. Abandon Galaxy!   '67 PbLib

Lady From L.U.S.T. (pseud.— Rod Gray)
1. The Lady From L.U.S.T.   '67 Tower
2. Lay Me Odds   '67 Tower
3. The 69 Pleasures   '67 Tower
4. 5 Beds to Mecca   '68 Tower
5. The Hot Mahatma   '68 Tower
6. To Russia With L.U.S.T.   '68 Tower
7. Kiss My Assassin   '68 Tower
8. South of the Bordello   '68 Tower
9. The Poisoned Pussy   '69 Tower
10. The Big Snatch   '69 Tower
11. Lady in Heat   '69 Tower
12. Laid in the Future   '69 Tower
13. Blow My Mind   '70 Tower
14. The Copulation Explosion   '70 Belmt
15. Easy Ride   '70 Belmt
16. The Lady Takes It All Off   '71 Belmt
17. Turned on to L.U.S.T.   '71 Belmt
18. Skin Game Dame   '72 Belmt

Kothar
1. Kothar-- Barbarian Swordsman   '69 Belmt
2. Kothar of the Magic Sword   '69 Belmt
3. Kothar and the Demon Queen   '69 Tower
4. Kothar and the Conjurer's Curse   '70 Belmt
5. Kothar and the Wizard Slayer   '70 Belmt

Cherry Delight-- The Sexecutioner
(pseud.— Glen Chase)
1. The Italian Connection   '72 Leisr
2. Tong in Cheek   '72 Leisr

(cont.)

(Gardner F. Fox, "Cherry Delight", cont.)

3. Silverfinger	'72	Leisr
4. Up Your Ante	'73	Leisr
5. Crack Shot	'73	Leisr
6. I'm Cherry, Fly Me!	'73	Leisr
7. Chuck You, Farley!	'73	Leisr
8. Hot Rocks	'73	Leisr
9. The Jersey Bounce	'74	Leisr
10. Made in Japan	'74	Leisr
11. Broad Jump	'74	Leisr
12. Five in the Hole	'74	Leisr
13. Over the Hump	'74	Leisr
14. In a Pinch	'74	Leisr
15. What a Way to Go	'74	Leisr
16. Busted	'74	Leisr
17. Treasure Chest	'75	Leisr
18. Hang Loose	'75	Leisr
19. In a Bind	'75	Leisr
20. Always on Sunday	'75	Leisr
21. Mexican Standoff	'75	Leisr
22. The Big Bankroll	'75	Leisr
23. Lights! Action! Murder!	'75	Leisr
24. Roman Candle	'75	Leisr

Cherry Delight-- Agent of D.U.E.

25. Greek Fire	'77	Leisr
26. The Devil to Pay	'77	Leisr
27. The Moorland Monster	'77	Leisr
28. Where the Action Is	'77	Leisr
29. The Man Who Was God	'78	Leisr

Kyric

1. Kyric: Warlock Warrior	'75	Leisr
2. Kyric Fights the Demon World	'75	Leisr
3. Kyric and the Wizard's Sword	'76	Leisr
4. Kyric and the Lost Queen	'76	Leisr

FRANKAU, PAMELA (1908-1967)

Clothes of a King's Son

1. Sing For Your Supper	'63	Heine
2. Slaves of the Lamp	'65	Heine

FRASER, SIR RONALD (1888-1974)

Venus Series

1. A Visit From Venus	'58	Cape

(cont.)

2. Jupiter in the Chair	'58	Cape
3. Trout's Testament	'60	Cape
4. City of the Sun	'61	Cape

FRAZIER, ARTHUR (pseud., see KENNETH BULMER)

FRENCH, PAUL (pseud., see ISAAC ASIMOV)

FRETLAND, D. JOHN

The Oleandre Sequence
1. The Persimmon Sequence	'71	Apoll
2. Winds of the Heliopolis	'72	Apoll

FRIEDELL, EGON (1878-1938) see H.G. WELLS

FRIEL, ARTHUR O. (1885-1959)

McKay, Knowlton & Ryan
1. The Pathless Trail	'22	Harpr
2. Tiger River	'23	Harpr
3. The King of No Man's Land	'24	Harpr
4. Mountains of Mystery	'25	Harpr

FRIEND, ED (pseud., see "GREEN HORNET")

FROST, JASON

The Warlord
1. The Warlord	'83	Zebra
2. The Cutthroat	'83	Zebra
3. Badland	'84	Zebra
4. Prisonland	'85	Zebra

FUENTES, ROBERTO (see collaboration with PIERS ANTHONY)

G

GAITE, FRANCIS
    (pseud., see CYRIL HENRY COLES & MANNING COLES)

GALLAGHER, STEVE (see "DOCTOR WHO")

GALLAZIER, NATHAN (1866-1927)

1. Castel del Monte; A Romance of the Fall of the Hohenstaufen Dynasty in Italy   '05   Page
   (Note-- this title is not sf/fantasy)
2. The Sorceress of Rome   '07   Page
3. The Court of Lucifer; A Tale of the Renaissance   '10   Page

GAMOW, GEORGE (1904-1968)

    Mr. Tompkins
1. Mr. Tompkins in Wonderland; or, Stories of C, G, & H   '39   CambU
2. Mr. Tompkins Explores the Atom   '44   CambU
3. Mr. Tompkins Learns the Facts of Life   '54   CambU
4. Mr. Tompkins Inside Himself; Adventures in the New Biology (with Martynas Ycas)   '67   Vik

GANPAT (pseud. of Martin Louis Alan Gompertz, 1886-1951)

    Sakaeland
1. Harilek   '23   Blkwd
2. Wrexham's Romance   '35   H&S

GARBY, MRS. LEE HAWKINS
    (see collaboration with E.E. "DOC" SMITH)

GARDNER, MAURICE B. (b.1905)

    Bantan
    (Note--Some sources indicate there may be several titles in the series which precede those listed)
                                (cont.)

1. Bantan Incredible   '60 Forum
2. Bantan Primeval   '61 Forum
3. Bantan Fearless   '63 Forum
4. Bantan and the Mermaids   '70 Gaus

GARFORTH, JOHN (see "THE AVENGERS")

GARIS, HOWARD R. (1873-1962)

    also see: Victor Appleton, "Tom Swift" series

    Rocket Riders
1. Rocket Riders Across the Ice   '33 Burt
2. Rocket Riders Over the Desert   '33 Burt
3. Rocket Riders in Stormy Seas   '33 Burt
4. Rocket Riders in the Air   '34 Burt

GARNER, ALAN (b.1934)

    Colin and Susan
1. The Weirdstone of Brisingamen   '60 WmCol
    aka: The Weirdstone ('61/Watts)
2. The Moon of Gomrath   '63 WmCol

GARNER, ROLFE (pseud., see BRYAN BERRY)

GARRETT, RANDALL (b,1927)

    The Nidorian Sequence
    (pseud.-- Robert Randall; written in
    collaboration with Robert Silverberg)
1. The Shrouded Planet   '57 Gnome
2. The Dawning Light   '59 Gnome

    Ken Malone
    (pseud.-- Mark Phillips; written in collaboration
    with Laurence M. Janifer)
1. Brain Twister   '62 Pyr
2. The Impossibles   '63 Pyr
3. Supermind   '63 Pyr

    Lord Darcy
1. Murder and Magic   '79
2. Too Many Magicians   '67 Dbdy
3. Lord Darcy Investigates   '81 Ace

(Randall Garrett, cont.)

    The Gandalara Cycle (with Vicki Ann Heydron)
1. The Steel of Rathskar   '81 Bant
2. The Glass of Dyskornis   '82 Bant
3. The Bronze of Eddarta   '83 Bant
4. The Well of Darkness   '83 Bant
5. The Search for Ka   '84 Bant
6. Return to Eddarta   '85 Bant

GARRON, MARCO (pseud.)

    Azan
1. The Missing Safari   '50 Warrn
2. The Lost City   '50 Warrn
3. Jungle Fever   '50 Warrn
4. White Fangs   '51 Warrn
5. Tribal War   '51 Warrn
6. King Hunters   '51 Warrn

GARY, ROMAIN (b.1914)

    Genghis Cohn
1. The Dance of Genghis Cohn   '68 World
2. The Guilty Head   '69 World

GASKELL, JANE (b.1941)

    The Atlan Saga
1. The Serpent   '63 H&S
    (A) The Serpent ('77/StM)
    (B) The Dragon ('77/StM)
2. Atlan   '65 H&S
3. The City   '66 H&S
4. Some Summer Lands   '77 H&S

GEIS, RICHARD E. (b.1927)

    Roi Kunzer
1. The Sex Machine   '67 Brand
2. The Endless Orgy   '68 Brand

GENTLEMAN, FRANCIS (1728-1784)
    (see SIR HUMPHREY LUNATIC, pseud.)

GERROLD, DAVID (b.1944)

    also see: "PLANET OF THE APES"
    also see: "STAR TREK"

    The War Against the Chtorr *
1. A Matter for Men   '83 S&S
2. A Day for Damnation   '84 PB
   * both collected as:
     "The War Against the Chtorr: Invasion"
                                  ('84/SFBC)

GESTON, MARK S. (b.1916)

    Havengore
1. Lords of the Starship   '67 Ace
2. Out of the Mouth of the Dragon   '69 Ace

GIBSON, WALTER B. (b.1897) (see MAXWELL GRANT, pseud.)

GIBSON, WILLIAM

    Neuromancer
1. Neuromancer   '84 Ace
2. Count Zero   (NYP)

GIESY, J.U. (1877-1948)

    Jason Croft
1. Palos of the Dog Pack   '18/'65 Avalo
2. The Mouthpiece of Zitu   '19/'65 Avalo
3. Jason, Son of Jason   '21/'66 Avalo

GILBERT, STEPHEN (b.1912)

    Ben
1. Ratman's Notebooks   '68 Josph
   aka: Willard ('71/Lance)
   (sequel)
2. Ben (by Gilbert A. Ralston)   '72 Bant

GILLIAND, ALEXIS A. (b.1931)
                           (cont.)

(Alexis A. Gilliand, cont.)

    Rosinante
1. The Revolution From Rosinante   '81   DelR
2. Long Shot for Rosinante   '81   DelR
3. The Pirates of Rosinante   '82   DelR

GILMAN, ROBERT CHAM (pseud. of ALFRED COPPEL, b.1921)

    Rhada
1. The Rebel of Rhada   '68   Harc
2. The Navigator of Rhada   '69   Harc
3. The Starkhan of Rhada   '70   Harc
4. The Warlock of Rhada   '85   Ace

GILMOUR, WILLIAM (see EDGAR RICE BURROUGHS)

"THE GIRL FROM U.N.C.L.E." (see "U.N.C.L.E.")

GLASBY, JOHN (see BERL CAMERON, pseud.)

GLUT, DONALD F. (see "STAR WARS")

GODWIN, PARKE

    Masters of Solitude Sequence (with Marvin Kaye)
1. Masters of Solitude   '78   Dbdy
2. Wintermind   '84   Dbdy

    Camelot
1. Firelord   '80   Dbdy
2. Beloved Exile   '84   Dbdy

GODWIN, TOM (b.1915)

    Ragnarok
1. The Survivors   '58   Gnome
   aka: Space Prison ('60/Pyr)
2. The Space Barbarians   '64   Pyr

GOLDIN, STEPHEN (b.1947) see: E.E. "DOC" SMITH
                                  also see: "STAR TREK"

GOLDSTEIN, WILLIAM (b.1932)

    Dr. Phibes
1. Dr. Phibes   '71 Award
2. Dr. Phibes Rises Again   '73 Award

GOLL, REINHOLD W. (b.1897)

    Veta
1. The Visitors From Planet Veta   '61 Westm
2. Spaceship to Planet Veta   '62 Westm

GORDON, STUART (b.1947)

    The Eyes Trilogy
1. One-Eye   '73 DAW
2. Two-Eyes   '74 DAW
3. Three-Eyes   '75 NEL

GOTLEIB, PHYLLIS (b.1926)

    The Starcats Trilogy
1. A Judgement of Dragons   '80 Berk
2. Emperor, Swords, Pentacles   '82 Ace
3. Kingdom of the Cats   '85 Ace

GOULART, RON (b.1933)

    also see: GLEN A. LARSON, "Battlestar Galactica"
    also see: collaboration with LEE FALK
    also see: ALEX RAYMOND
    also see: KENNETH ROBESON

    The Chameleon Corps
1. The Sword Swallower   '68 Dbdy
2. The Chameleon Corps and Other Shape Changers   '72 Macm
3. Flux   '74 DAW
4. Spacehawk, Inc.   '74 DAW
5. A Whiff of Madness   '76 DAW

    Barnum System
1. The Fire-Eater   '70 Ace
2. Shaggy Planet   '73 Lance

(cont.)

(Ron Goulart, cont.)

Odd Jobs, Inc.
1. Odd Job No. 101   '75
2. Brainz, Inc.   '85   DAW

Vampirella
1. Bloodstalk   '75   Warnr
2. On Alien Wings   '75   Warnr
3. Deadwalk   '76   Warnr
4. Blood Wedding   '76   Warnr
5. Deathgame   '76   Warnr
6. Snakegod   '76   Warnr

The Gypsy Sequence
1. Quest of the Gypsy   '76   Pyr
2. Eye of the Vulture   '77   Jove

GRAAT, HEINRICH (pseud.)

Ben Camden
1. The Revenge of Increase Sewell   '69   Belmt
2. The Devil and Ben Camden   '70   Belmt
3. A Place of Demons   '72   Belmt

GRANT, CHARLES L.

Oxrun
1. The Hour of the Oxrun Dead   '77   Dbdy
2. The Sound of Midnight   '78   Dbdy
3. The Last Call of Mourning   '79   Dbdy

GRANT, JOAN (b.1907)

Ra-Ab Hotep
1. Eyes of Horus   '42   Meth
2. Lord of the Horizon   '43   Meth

GRANT, MAXWELL (House Pseudonym)
    Walter B. Gibson (b.1897)
    Dennis Lynds (b.1924)

The Shadow
(Note: Titles are listed in order of the original pulp publication)

(The following titles are by Walter B. Gibson)
1. The Living Shadow '31/'69 Bant
2. The Eyes of the Shadow '31/'69 Bant
3. The Shadow Laughs! '31/'69 Bant
4. Red Menace '31/'75 Pyr
5. Gangdom's Doom '31/'70 Bant
6. Death Tower '32/'69 Bant
7. Silent Seven '32/'75 Pyr
8. The Black Master '32/'74 Pyr
9. The Mobsmen on the Spot '32/'74 Pyr
10. Hands in the Dark '32/'75 Pyr
11. Double "Z" '32/'75 Pyr
12. The Crime Cult '32/'75 Pyr
13. Hidden Death '32/'70 Bant
14. Green Eyes '32/'77 Pyr
15. The Ghost Makers '32/'70 Bant
16. The Romanoff Jewels '32/'75 Pyr
17. Kings of Crime '32/'76 Pyr
18. Shadowed Millions '33/'76 Pyr
19. The Creeping Death '33/'77 Pyr
20. The Shadow's Shadow '33/'77 Pyr
21. Fingers of Death '33/'77 Jove
22. Murder Trail '33/'77 Jove
23. The Silent Death '33/'78 Jove
24. The Death Giver '33/'78 Jove
25. The Weird Adventures of the Shadow:
     Grove of Doom '33/'69 Tempo
26. Mox '33/'75 Pyr
27. The Wealth Seeker '34/'78 Jove
28. Grey Fist '34/'77 Pyr
29. Charge, Monster '34/'77 Jove
30. Zemba '35/'77 Jove
31. The Crime Oracle '36/'75 Dover
32. Teeth of the Dragon '37/'75 Dover
33. The Shadow and the Golden Master '39/'84 MystP
34. The Shadow and the Voice of Murder '40/'40 BantL
35. The Weird Adventures of the Shadow
     37-'44/'66 G&D
     (this title includes "The Grove of Doom")
36. The Freak Show Murders & A Quarter
     of Eight '44-'45/'78 Dbdy
37. The Mask of Mephisto & Murder By Magic
     '45/'75 Dbdy
38. Mother Goose Murders & Crime Over Casco
     '46/'79 Dbdy
39. Return of the Shadow '63 Belmt
     (The following are originals by Dennis Lynds):
40. The Shadow Strikes '64 Belmt

(cont.)

(Maxwell Grant, cont.)

41.	Shadow Beware	'65	Belmt
42.	Cry Shadow!	'65	Belmt
43.	The Shadow's Revenge	'65	Belmt
44.	Mark of the Shadow	'66	Belmt
45.	Shadow Go Mad	'66	Belmt
46.	The Night of the Shadow	'66	Belmt
47.	Destination Moon	'67	Belmt

Norgil (by Walter B. Gibson)
(Note-- originally appeared in pulps)

1.	Norgil the Magician	'77	MystP
2.	Norgil: More Tales of Prestidigitation	'79	MystP

GRAY, ROD (pseud., see Gardner F. Fox)

GREEN, ROLAND (b.1944)

also see: JEFFERY LORD, "Richard Blade Series"
also see: H. BEAM PIPER, "Paratime Police"

Wandor

1.	Wandor's Ride	'73	Avon
2.	Wandor's Journey	'75	Avon
3.	Wandor's Voyage	'79	Avon
4.	Wandor's Flight	'79	Avon
5.	Wandor's Battle		

GREEN, SHARON

Jalav: Amazon Warrior

1.	The Crystals of Mida	'82	DAW
2.	An Oath to Mida	'83	DAW
3.	Chosen of Mida	'84	DAW
4.	The Will of the Gods	'85	DAW

Terrilian Sequence

1.	The Warrior Within	'82	DAW
2.	The Warrior Enchained	'83	DAW
3.	The Warrior Rearmed	'84	DAW

"GREEN HORNET"

1. The Green Hornet in the Infernal Light   '66 Dell
   (by Richard Wormser, under pseud. of Ed Friend)

(cont.)
    2. The Case of the Disappearing Doctor   '66 Whitm
       (by Brandon Keith)

GREENE, JOSEPH (1897-1953)

    Dig Allen
1. The Forgotten Star   '59 Goldn
2. Captives in Space   '60 Goldn
3. Journey to Jupiter   '61 Goldn
4. Trappers of Venus   '61 Goldn
5. Robots of Saturn   '62 Goldn
6. Lost City of Uranus   '62 Goldn

GREENLEAF, WILLIAM

    UNSA
1. The Tartarus Incident   '83 Ace
2. The Pandora Stone   '84 Ace

GREGORIAN, JOYCE BALLOU

    Sybil Barron
1. The Broken Citadel   '75 Athen
2. Castledown   '77 Athen

GREGORY, JULIAN R. (see collaboration with ROGER PRICE)

GRIBBON, WILLIAM LANCASTER (see TALBOT MUNDY, pseud.)

GRIDBAN, VOLSTED (pseud.— see JOHN RUSSELL FEARN)

GRIFFITH, GEORGE (1857-1906)

    Romanoff Sequence
1. The Angel of the Revolution   1893 TowrL
2. Olga Romanoff   1894 TowrL

GRIMWADE, PETER (see "DOCTOR WHO")

GRINNELL, DAVID (pseud.— see DONALD A. WOLLHEIM)

GUARESCHI, GIOVANNI (1908-1968)

    Don Camillo
1. The Little World of Don Camillo   '57 Farr
2. Don Camillo and His Flock   '52 P&C
   aka: Don Camillo and the Prodigal Son
                  ('52/Gollz)
3. Don Camillo's Dilemma   '54 Farr
4. Don Camillo Takes the Devil By the Tail   '57 Farr
   aka: Don Camillo and the Devil ('57/Gollz)
5. Comrade Don Camillo   '64 Farr
6. Don Camillo Meets the Flower Children   '69 Farr
   aka: Don Camillo Meets Hell's Angels
                  ('70/Gollz)

GUTTERIDGE, LINDSAY (b.1923)

    Matthew Dilke
1. Cold War in a Country Garden   '71 Cape
2. Killer Pine   '73 Cape
3. Fratricide is a Gas   '75 Cape

HAGGARD, H. RIDER (1856-1925)

    Allan Quartermain
1. Marie   '12   Cass
2. Allan's Wife   1887   Munro
3. Child of Storm   '13   Cass
4. A Tale of Three Lions   1887   Lovel
5. Maiwa's Revenge   1888   LongG
6. Allan the Hunter   1898   Lothr
    aka: Hunter Quartermain's Story
7. "Long Odds" in: Allan's Wife and Other Tales
                              1889   SpBkt
8. The Holy Flower   '15   WardL
9. Heu-Heu; or, The Monster   '24   Hutch
10. She and Allan   '20   LongG
11. The Treasure of the Lake   '26   Dody
12. The Ivory Child   '16   Cass
13. Finished   '16   Paget
14. King Solomon's Mines   1885   Cass
15. The Ancient Allan   '20   Cass
16. Allan and the Ice Gods   '27   Hutch
17. Allan Quartermain   1887   LongG

    She
1. Wisdom's Daughter   '23   Hutch
2. She and Allan   '20   LongG
3. She   1886   Harpr
4. Ayesha: The Return of She '05   WardL

    Eric Brighteyes
1. Eric Brighteyes   1891
    (sequel)
2. Eric Brighteyes #2: A Witch's Welcome   '79   Zebra
    (by Sigfriour Skaldaspillir)

    Zulu Nation
1. Nada the Lily   1892   LongG
2. Marie   '12   Cass
3. Child of Storm   '13   Cass
4. Finished   '16   Paget

HALDEMAN II, JACK (see "STAR TREK")

HALDEMAN, JOE (b.1943)

    also see: "STAR TREK"

    Attar the Merman
1. Attar's Revenge   '75 PB
2. War of Nerves   '75 PB

    Marianne O'Hara
1. Worlds   '81 Vik
2. Worlds Apart   '83 Vik

HALIDOM, M.Y. (pseud., see DRYASDUST)

HALL, ANGUS (b.1932)

    Devilday
1. Devilday   '69 Spher
2. To Play the Devil   '71 Spher

HALL, AUSTIN (1886-1933)

    The Blind Spot
1. The Blind Spot
    (written with Homer Eon Flint)   '21/'51 Prime
2. The Spot of Life   '32/'65 Ace

"HALLOWEEN"

1. Halloween
    (Curtis Richards)
2. Halloween II
    (Jack Martin)   '81 Zebra
3. Halloween III: Season of the Witch
    (Jack Martin)   '82 Jove

HAMBLY, BARBARA

    also see: "STAR TREK"

    The Darwath Trilogy
1. The Time of the Dark   '82 DelR
2. Walls of Air   '83 DelR
3. The Armies of Daylight   '83 DelR

HAMILTON, EDMOND (1904-1977)

    Interstellar Patrol
    (originally serialized in pulps 1928-30)
1. Outside the Universe   '64 Ace
2. Crashing Suns   '65 Ace

    Captain Future (all by Hamilton unless noted)
    (the following are in order of original pulp publication):
1. Captain Future and the Space Emperor   '40/'69 PbLib
2. Calling Captain Future   '40/'69 PbLib
3. Captain Future's Challenge   '40/'69 PbLib
4. Galaxy Mission   '40/'69 PbLib
5. The Magician of Mars   '41/'69 PbLib
6. Quest Beyond the Stars   '42/'69 PbLib
7. Outlaws of the Moon   '42/'69 PbLib
8. The Comet Kings   '42/'69 PbLib
9. Planets in Peril   '42/'69 PbLib
10. The Tenth Planet
    (by Joseph Samachson writing as Brett Sterling)   '44/'69 PbLib
11. Danger Planet (by Hamilton as Brett Sterling)   '45/'68 PbLib
12. The Solar Invasion (By Manly Wade Wellman)   '46/'69 PbLib
13. Outlaw World   '46/'69 PbLib

    Star Kings
1. The Star Kings   '49 Fell
    aka: Beyond the Moon ('50/Sign)
2. Return to the Stars   '70 Lance

    Starwolf (coll.'82/Ace)
1. The Weapons From Beyond   '67 Ace
2. The Closed Worlds   '68 Ace
3. World of the Starwolves   '68 Ace

HAMILTON, VIRGINIA (b.1936)

    The Justice Cycle Trilogy
1. Justice and Her Brothers   '78 Grnw
2. Dustland   '80 Grnw
3. The Gathering   '81 Grnw

HANCOCK, H. IRVING

                    (cont.)

(H. Irving Hancock, cont.)

  Conquest of the United States
1. The Invasion of the United States   '16   Altem
2. In the Battle for New York   '16   Altem
3. At the Defense of Pittsburgh   '16   Altem
4. Making the Stand for Old Glory   '16   Altem

HANCOCK, NIEL (b.1941)

  ATALANTAN EARTH
  Circle of Light
1. Greyfax Grimwald   '77   Pop
2. Faragon Fairingay   '77   Pop
3. Calix Stay   '77   Pop
4. Squaring the Circle   '77   Pop
  The Wilderness of Four
1. Across the Far Mountain   '82   Pop
2. The Plains of the Sea   '82   Pop
3. On the Boundaries of Bleakness   '82   Pop
4. The Road to the Middle Islands   '82   Pop
  (related titles)
1. Dragon Winter   '78   Pop
2. The Fires of Windameir   '85   Warnr

HANDS, DIVERS
  (pseud. of August Derleth, see H.P. LOVECRAFT)

HARDING, RICHARD

  The Outrider
1. The Outrider   '84   Pinn
2. Fire and Ice   '84   Pinn
3. Blood Highway   '84   Pinn
4. Bay City Burnout   '85   Pinn
5. Built to Kill   '85   Pinn

HARDY, LYNDON

  The Principles of Magic
1. Master of the Five Magics   '80   DelR
2. Secret of the Sixth Magic   '84   DelR

HARDY, PHILIP

          (cont.)

       Smith Minor
1. The Buried Country   '45   SchPL
2. Smith Minor on the Moon   '45   SchPL

HARRIS, GERALDINE

       Seven Citadels
1. Prince of the Godborn   '82   Grnw
2. The Children of the Wind   '82   Grnw
3. The Dead Kingdom   '83   Grnw
4. The Seventh Gate   '83   MacmL

HARRIS, JOEL CHANDLER (1848-1908)

       Uncle Remus
1. Uncle Remus, His Songs and His Sayings:
    Folklore of the Old Plantation   1880 Apple
2. Nights with Uncle Remus: Myths and
    Legends of the Old Plantation   1883 HMiff
3. Daddy Jake the Runaway, and Short Stories
    Told After Dark by "Uncle Remus"   1889 Centy
4. Uncle Remus and His Friends: Old Planta-
    tion Stories, Songs, and Ballads   1892 HMiff
5. The Tar-Baby, and Other Rhymes of
    Uncle Remus   '04   Apple
6. Told By Uncle Remus: New Stories of the
    Old Plantation   '05   McClr
7. Uncle Remus and Brer Rabbit   '07   Stoke
8. Uncle Remus and the Little Boy   '10   SmMay
9. Uncle Remus Returns   '18   HMiff
10. The Witch Wolf: An Uncle Remus Story   '21   Bacon

HARRIS, ROSEMARY

       Reuben
1. The Moon in the Cloud   '68   Faber
2. The Shadow on the Sun   '70   Faber
3. The Bright and Morning Star   '72   Faber

HARRIS, WALTER (b.1925) (see "THE AVENGERS")

HARRISON, HARRY (b.1925)

       The Deathworld Trilogy (coll.'74/Dbdy)
                                        (cont.)

(Harry Harrison, "Deathworld Trilogy", cont.)

    1. Deathworld   '60   Bant
    2. Deathworld 2   '64   Bant
       aka: The Ethical Engineer ('64/Gollz)
    3. Deathworld 3   '68   Dell

       The Stainless Steel Rat *
    1. The Stainless Steel Rat   '61   Pyr
    2. The Stainless Steel Rat's Revenge   '70   Walkr
    3. The Stainless Steel Rat Saves the World '72   Putn
    4. The Stainless Steel Rat Wants You!   '79   Bant
    5. The Stainless Steel Rat for President   '82   Bant
    6. A Stainless Steel Rat is Born   '85   Bant
       * Note-- the first 3 titles have been collected
         as: "The Adventures of the Stainless Steel Rat"
                                                   ('77/Dbdy)

       Brion Brandd
    1. Planet of the Damned   '62   Bant
    2. Planet of No Return   '82   Tor

       To the Stars
    1. Homeworld   '80   Bant
    2. Wheelworld   '81   Bant
    3. Starworld   '81   Bant

HARRISON, M. JOHN (b.1945)

       Viriconium
    1. The Pastel City   '71   NEL
    2. A Storm of Wings   '79   Dbdy
    3. In Viriconium   '82   Gollz
       aka: The Floating Gods ('83/PB)
    4. Viriconium Nights (short stories)   '84   Ace

HATCH, RICHARD W. (b.1898)

       The Lobster Books (coll.'51/HMiff)
    1. The Curious Lobster   '37   Harc
    2. The Curious Lobster's Island   '39   Dodd

HATHAWAY, ALAN (see KENNETH ROBESON)

HAWKE, SIMON
       (pseud. of NICHOLAS YERMAKOV)

HAWKWOOD, ALLEN (pseud., see H. BEDFORD-JONES)

HAWTON, HECTOR (b.1901)

    Col. Max Masterson
1. Tower of Darkness   '50   H&S
2. Blue-Eyed Buddha   '51   H&S
3. Black Emperor   '52   H&S
4. The Lost Valley   '53   H&S

HAYLES, BRIAN (see "DOCTOR WHO")

HAZEL, PAUL

    The Finnbranch
1. Yearwood   '80   LtBrn
2. Undersea   '82   LtBrn
3. Winterking   '84   LtBrn

HEARD, H.F. (GERALD) (1889-1971)

    Mr. Mycroft
1. A Taste for Honey   '41   Vang
    aka: A Taste for Murder ('55/Avon)
2. Reply Paid   '42   Vang
3. The Notched Hairpin   '49   Vang

HEATH, PETER (b.1938)

    Mind Brothers
1. The Mind Brothers   '67   Lance
2. Assassins From Tomorrow   '67   Lance
3. Men Who Die Twice   '68   Lance

HECHT, BEN (1894-1964)

    Fantazius Mallare
1. Fantazius Mallare   '22   Covi
2. The Kingdom of Evil   '24   Covi

HEINLEIN, ROBERT A. (b.1907)

(cont.)

(Robert A. Heinlein, cont.)

THE FUTURE HISTORY SERIES *
1. The Man Who Sold the Moon   '50   Shast
2. The Green Hills of Earth   '51   Shast
3. Revolt in 2100   '53   Shast
4. Orphans in the Sky   '63   Gollz
    includes: Universe ('51/Dell)

Lazarus Long
5. Methuselah's Children   '58   Gnome
6. Time Enough For Love   '73   Putn
7. The Cat Who Walks Through Walls '85   Putn
    * Note-- This is a loosely-knit series
    whose titles can be read independently.
    Titles 1,2,3, & 5 are collected as:
    "The Past Through Tomorrow" ('67/Putn)

HENDERSON, ZENNA (b.1917)

The People
1. Pilgrimage: The Book of the People   '61   Dbdy
2. The People: No Different Flash   '66   Gollz

HERBERT, FRANK (b.1920)

Dune *
1. Dune   '65   Chilt
2. Dune Messiah   '69   Putn
3. Children of Dune   '76   Berk
4. God Emperor of Dune   '81   Putn
5. Heretics of Dune   '84   Putn
6. Chapter House: Dune   '85   Gollz
    aka: Chapterhouse: Dune ('85/Putn)
    * First 3 titles collected as:
    The Great Dune Trilogy ('79/Gollz)

Mekie
1. Whipping Star   '70   Putn
2. The Dosadi Experiment   '77   Putn

The Jesus Incident (with Bill Ransom)
1. The Jesus Incident   '79   Berk
2. The Lazarus Effect   '83   Putn

HERON-ALLEN, EDWARD
    (see CHRISTOPHER BLAYRE, pseud.)

HEYDRON, VICKI ANN
    (see collaboration with RANDALL GARRETT)

HICKMAN, TRACY (see collaboration with MARGARET WEIS)

HILL, DOUGLAS

    The Huntsman Series
1. Exiles of Colsec   '83 Gollz
2. The Caves of Klydor   '84 Athen
3. Alien Citadel   '84 Athen
4. Colsec Rebellion   '85 Gollz

HINCHCLIFFE, PHILLIP (see "DOCTOR WHO")

HINE, AL (see "BEWITCHED")

HITCHCOCK, RAYMOND (b.1922)

    Percy
1. Percy   '69 WHAll
2. Percy's Progress   '72 Spher

HOCH, EDWARD D. (b.1930)

    Simon Ark
1. The Judges of Hades and Other Simon Ark
   Stories   '71 Leisr
2. City of Brass and Other Simon Ark Stories
        '71 Leisr

    Carl Crader and Earl Jazine/aka: Computer Gods
1. The Transvection Machine   '71 Walkr
2. The Fellowship of the HAND   '73 Walkr
3. The Frankenstein Factory   '75 Warnr

HOGAN, JAMES P. (b.1941)

    The Minervan Experiment (coll.'81/SFBC)
1. Inherit the Stars   '77 DelR
2. The Gentle Giants of Ganymede   '78 DelR
3. Giants' Star   '81 DelR

HOGAN, ROBERT J.

    G-8 and His Battle Aces
    (Note-- originally appeared in pulps of the '30s)
1. Bat Staffel   '69 Berk
2. Purple Aces   '70 Berk
3. Ace of the White Death   '70 Berk
4. Bombs From the Murder Wolves   '71 Berk
5. Vultures of the White Death   '71 Berk
6. Flight From the Grave   '71 Berk
7. Fangs of the Sky Leopard   '71 Berk
8. Mark of the Vulture   '71 Berk

HOLDSTOCK, ROBERT P. (b.1948)

    (pseud.-- Chris Carlsen)
1. Shadow of the Wolf   '77
2. The Bull Chief   '77

HOLLY, J. HUNTER (1932-1982) (see "U.N.C.L.E.")

HOLMES, JOHN ERIC

    see: "BUCK ROGERS"
    see: EDGAR RICE BURROUGHS, "Pellucidar" series

HOLMES, ROBERT (see "DOCTOR WHO")

HOLZER, HANS (b.1920)

    Randy Knowles
1. The Red Chindvit Conspiracy   '70 Award
2. The Alchemy Deception   '73 Award
3. Psychic Detective: The Unicorn   '76 Manor

HOME-GALL, EDWARD R. (b.1899)

    The Human Bat
1. Caught in the Spider's Web   '50 Gould
2. The Human Bat Vs. The Robot Gangster   '50 Gould

HORLER, SYDNEY (1888-1954)

                         (cont.)

Paul Vivanti
1. The Mystery of No. 1   '25   H&S
   aka: The Order of the Octopus ('26/Doran)
2. The Worst Man in the World   '29   H&S
3. Lord of Terror   '35   WmCol
4. Virus X   '45   QualP

HOROWITZ, ANTHONY

Martin
1. The Devil's Doorbell   '83   Putn
2. The Night of the Scorpion   '85   Putn

HORSEMAN, ELAINE (b.1925)

Hubbles
1. Hubble's Bubble   '64   C&W
2. The Hubbles' Treasure Hunt   '65   C&W
3. Hubbles and the Robot   '68   C&W

HOSKINS, ROBERT (b.1933)

The Stars Sequence
1. To Control the Stars   '77   DelR
2. To Escape the Stars   '78   DelR

HOWARD, JOSEPH (see "THE OMEN")

HOWARD, ROBERT E. (1906-1936)

also see: H.P. LOVECRAFT

CONAN
Originally appearing in the pulps of the '30s, the Conan stories have since been published in book form in four distinct versions. The first 5 titles, published by Gnome Press, were collections of the original stories. The 6th title contained Howard stories which were re-written by L. Sprague DeCamp, while a final volume contained all-new stories by DeCamp & Nyberg.

The second series was published in paperback format by Lancer Books and consisted of 11 titles of mixed parentage, some by Howard, some revised, and some
(cont.)

(Robert E. Howard, "Conan", cont.)

completely new additions by other authors.

In the '70s Donald M. Grant printed a hardbound set which returned to the original unedited Howard stories, while a 4th series of Berkley paperbacks also contained Howard's stories as arranged by Karl Edward Wagner.

The Conan saga continues to date with a host of new titles by various authors and publishers.

1st book series
1. The Coming of Conan '53 Gnome
2. Conan the Barbarian '54 Gnome
3. The Sword of Conan '52 Gnome
4. King Conan '53 Gnome
5. Conan the Conqueror '50 Gnome
6. Tales of Conan
    (rewritten by L. Sprague DeCamp) '55 Gnome
7. The Return of Conan
    (by L. Sprague DeCamp & Bjorn Nyberg) '57 Gnome
    revised as: Conan the Avenger ('68/Lance)

2nd book series
1. Conan
    (by Howard, DeCamp, & Lin Carter) '67 Lance
2. Conan of Cimmeria
    (Howard, DeCamp, & Carter) '69 Lance
3. Conan the Freebooter
    (Howard & DeCamp) '68 Lance
4. Conan the Wanderer
    (Howard, DeCamp & Carter) '68 Lance
5. Conan the Adventurer
    (Howard & DeCamp) '66 Lance
6. Conan the Buccaneer
    (DeCamp & Carter) '71 Lance
7. Conan the Warrior
    (by Robert E. Howard) '67 Lance
8. Conan the Usurper
    (Howard & DeCamp) '67 Lance
9. Conan the Conqueror
    (Howard & DeCamp) '67 Lance
10. Conan the Avenger
    (L. Sprague DeCamp & Bjorn Nyberg) '68 Lance
11. Conan of the Isles
    (DeCamp & Carter) '68 Lance

3rd book series
1. The People of the Black Circle '74 Grant
2. A Witch Shall Be Born '75 Grant

3. The Tower of the Elephant   '75 Grant
4. Red Nails   '75 Grant
5. Rogues in the House   '76 Grant
6. The Devil in Iron   '76 Grant
7. Queen of the Black Coast   '78 Grant
8. Black Colossus   '79 Grant
9. Jewels of Gwahlur   '79 Grant

4th book series
(original texts by Howard, edited by
Karl Edward Wagner)
1. The Hour of the Dragon   '77 Berk
   this is a revision of: "Conan the Conqueror"
                                ('50/Gnome)
2. The People of the Black Circle   '77 Berk
3. Red Nails   '77 Berk

Additional Conan Titles
1. Conan of Aquilonia
   (L. Sprague DeCamp & Lin Carter)   '77 Ace
2. Conan the Swordsman
   (L. Sprague DeCamp & Lin Carter)   '78 Bant
3. Conan the Liberator
   (L. Sprague DeCamp & Lin Carter)   '78 Bant
4. Conan and the Sorcerer
   (Andrew J. Offutt)   '78 Ace
5. The Sword of Skelos (Andrew J. Offutt) '79 Bant
6. The Road of Kings
   (Karl Edward Wagner)   '79 Bant
7. Conan and the Spider God
   (L. Sprague DeCamp)   '80 Bant
8. Conan the Rebel (Poul Anderson)   '80 Bant
9. The Treasure of Tranicos
   (by Howard, revised by DeCamp)   '80 Ace
   appeared previously in: "King Conan"
   ('53) & "Conan the Usurper" ('67)
10. Conan the Mercenary (Andrew J. Offutt) '81 Ace
11. Conan! The Flame Knife
    (Robert E. Howard)   '81 Ace
12. Conan the Barbarian (DeCamp & Carter) '82 Bant
    (based on a screenplay by John Milius
    & Oliver Stone)
13. Conan the Invincible (Robert Jordan) '82 Pinn
14. Conan the Defender   (Jordan)   '82 Tor
15. Conan the Unconquered (Jordan)   '83 Tor
16. Conan the Triumphant (Jordan)   '83 Tor
17. Conan the Magnificent (Jordan)   '84 Tor
18. Conan the Destroyer (Jordan)   '84 Tor
19. Conan the Victorious (Jordan)   '84 Tor
20. Conan the Valorous (John Maddox Roberts) '85 Tor

(Robert E. Howard, cont.)

Tales of the Picts
1. King Kull (completed by Lin Carter)   '67 Lance
    slightly revised as: Kull ('78/Bant)
2. Bran Mak Morn   '69 Dell
    abridged as: Worms of the Earth ('74/Grant)
3. The Dark Man and Others   '63 ArkH
    (title story only)

Solomon Kane Series (series A) *
1. The Moon of Skulls   '69 Centr
2. The Hand of Kane   '70 Centr
3. Solomon Kane   '71 Centr
    * all 3 originally in one vol. as:
      Red Shadows ('68/Grant)
    (series B) *
1. Skulls in the Stars   '78 Bant
2. The Hills of the Dead   '79 Bant
    * Portions of the material in these two books
      were previously published in "Red Shadows"
      (see above); additional material is by Ramsey
      Campbell.

El Borak
1. The Lost Valley of Iskander   '74 FAX
2. Son of the White Wolf   '77 FAX
3. Three-Bladed Doom   '77 Zebra

HOWELLS, WILLIAM DEAN (1837-1920)

Altruria
1. A Traveler From Altruria   1894 Harpr
2. Through the Eye of the Needle   '07   Harpr

HOYLE, FRED (b.1915) & JOHN ELLIOT (b.1918)

Andromeda Sequence
1. A For Andromeda   '62 Souv
2. Andromeda Breakthrough   '64 Souv

HOYLE, TREVOR

The Q Series
1. Seeking the Mythical Future   '77 NWrit
2. Through the Eyes of Time   '77
3. The Gods Look Down   '77

110

HUGHES, ROBERT DON

    Pelman the Powershaper
1. The Prophet of Lamath   '79 DelR
2. The Wizard in Waiting   '82 DelR
3. The Power and the Prophet   '85 DelR

HULKE, MALCOLM (see "DOCTOR WHO")

HUNTINGTON, CHARLES

    Space Probe 6
1. The Soul Stealers   '72 Award
2. Nightmare on Vega 3   '72 Award

HURT, FREDA (b.1911)

    Crab Island
1. Benny and the Dolphin   '68 Epwth
2. Benny and the Space Boy   '70 Epwth

HURWOOD, BERNHARDT J. (b.1926)

    The Man From T.O.M.C.A.T.
    (pseud.— Mallory T. Knight)
1. The Dozen Deadly Dragons of Joy   '67 Award
2. The Million Missing Maidens   '67 Award
3. The Terrible Ten   '67 Award
4. The Dirty Rotten Depriving Ray   '67 Award
5. Tsimmis in Tangier   '68 Award
6. The Malignant Metaphysical Menace   '68 Award
7. The Ominous Orgy   '69 Award
8. The Peking Pornographer   '69 Award
9. The Bra-Burner's Brigade   '71 Award

    The Invisibles
1. The Invisibles   '71 Fawc
2. The Mind Master   '73 Fawc

HYNE, C.J. CUTCLIFFE (1866-1944)

    Capt. Kettle
1. Honour of Thieves   1895 C&W
    aka: The Little Red Captain: An Early
         Adventure of Captain Kettle ('02/Pears)

(C.J. Cutcliffe Hyne, "Captain Kettle", cont.)

2. The "Paradise" Coal-Boat, and Other
   Stories   1897   Bowdn
     (contains 1 Capt. Kettle story)
3. Adventures of Captain Kettle   1898   Pears
4. Further Adventures of Captain Kettle   1899   Pears
     aka: A Master of Fortune ('01/Dillg)
5. Captain Kettle, K.C.B.   '03   Pear
     aka: More Adventures of Captain
       Kettle, K.C.B. ('03/Fed)
6. The Escape Agents   '11   Lauri
     (contains several Kettle stories)
7. The Marriage of Kettle   '12   Heine
     aka: The Marriage of Captain Kettle ('12/Bob-M)
8. Captain Kettle on the War-Path   '16   Meth
9. Captain Kettle's Bit   '18   H&S
10. The Rev. Captain Kettle   '25   Harrp
11. President Kettle   '29   Nash
12. Mr. Kettle-- Third Mate   '31   WardL
13. Captain Kettle, Ambassador   '32   WardL
14. Ivory Valley; An Adventure of Captain Kettle
                                                   '38   WardL

I-J

"INDIANA JONES" (Based on stories by George Lucas)

1. Indiana Jones and the Temple of Doom
   (by James Kahn)   '84   Ball
   (precedes "Raiders" in internal chronology)
2. Raiders of the Lost Ark
   (by Campbell Black)   '81   Ball

"THE INVADERS"

1. The Invaders   (Keith Laumer)   '67   Pyr
2. Enemies From Beyond   (Keith Laumer)   '67   Pyr
3. Army of the Undead   (Rafe Bernard)   '67   Pyr
4. Alien Missle Threat   (Paul S. Newman)   '67   Pyr
5. The Halo Highway   (Rafe Bernard)   '67   Corgi
6. The Meteor Men   (Anthony LeBaron)   '68   Corgi
7. The Night of the Trilobites (Peter Leslie)
                                                '68   Corgi
8. The Autumn Accelerator   (Peter Leslie)   '69   Corgi

IRWIN, WALTER   (see "STAR TREK")

IVERSON, ERIC

    Gerin the Fox
1. Wereblood   '79   Belmt
2. Werenight   '79   Belmt

JACKS, L.P.   (1860-1955)

    Smokeover Series
1. The Heroes of Smokeover   '26   H&S
2. The Last Legend of Smokeover   '39   H&S

JACKSON, STEVE

    Sorcery
1. Sorcery 1: The Shamutanti Hills   '84   Peng
2. Sorcery 2: Khare-- Cityport of Traps   '84   Peng
                      (cont.)

(Steve Jackson, cont.)

    3. Sorcery 3: The Seven Serpents   '84 Peng
    4. Sorcery 4: The Crown of Kings   '85 Peng

JADE, SYMON

    Starship Orpheus
    1. Return From the Dead   '82
    2. Cosmic Carnage   '82
    3. Alter Evil   '83

JAHN, MICHAEL (see MARTIN CAIDIN)

JAKES, JOHN (b.1932)

    also see: "PLANET OF THE APES"

    II Galaxy
    1. When the Star Kings Die   '67 Ace
    2. The Planet Wizard   '69 Ace
    3. Tonight We Steal the Stars   '69 Ace

    Brak the Barbarian
    1. Brak the Barbarian   '68 Avon
    2. Brak the Barbarian Versus the Sorceress   '69 PbLib
    3. Brak the Barbarian Versus the Mark of
       the Demon   '69 PbLib
    4. Brak: When the Idols Walked   '78 PB
    5. The Fortunes of Brak   '80 Dell

    Gavin Black
    1. Master of the Dark Gate   '70 Lance
    2. Witch of the Dark Gate   '72 Lance

JAMES, LAURENCE

    also see: NEIL LANGHOLM, pseud.

    Simon Rack
    1. Earth Lies Sleeping   '74 Zebra
    2. War on Aleph   '74 Zebra
       aka: Starcross ('74/Spher)
    3. Backflash   '75 Pinn
    4. Planet of the Blind   '75 Pinn
    5. New Life For Old   '75 Pinn

JANIFER, LAURENCE M. (b.1933)

    Ken Malone
    (written with Randall Garrett under
    joint pseud. of Mark Phillips)
1. Brain Twister '62 Pyr
2. The Impossibles '63 Pyr
3. Supermind '63 Pyr

    Angelo Di Stefano
    (in collaboration with S.J. Treibich)
1. Target: Terra '68 Ace
2. The High Hex '69 Ace
3. The Wagered World '69 Ace

    Gerald Knave
1. Survivor '77 Ace
2. Knave in Hand '79 Ace

"JAWS"

1. Jaws (Peter Benchley) '74 Dbdy
2. Jaws 2 (Hank Searls) '78 Bant

JENSEN, JOHANNES V. (1873-1950)

    The Long Journey (coll.'33/Knopf)
1. Fire and Ice '22 Gylen
2. The Cimbrians '23 Gylen
3. Christopher Columbus '24 Gylen

JOHNS, W.E. (1893-1968)

    Rex Clinton
1. Kings of Space; a Story of Interplanetary Adventure '54 H&S
2. Return to Mars '55 H&S
3. Now To the Stars '56 H&S
4. To Outer Space '57 H&S
5. The Edge of Beyond '58 H&S
6. The Death Rays of Ardilla '59 H&S
7. To Worlds Unknown '60 H&S
8. The Quest For the Perfect Planet '61 H&S
9. Worlds of Wonder '62 H&S
10. The Man Who Vanished Into Space; Another Adventure of the Spacecraft 'Tavona' in the Great Unknown '63 H&S

JOHNSON, CROCKETT (pseud. of David J. Leisk)

> Barnaby
> 1. Barnaby   '43 Holt
> 2. Barnaby and Mrs. O'Malley   '44 Holt

JOHNSON, GEORGE CLAYTON   (see WILLIAM F. NOLAN)

JOHNSON, RYERSON (b.1901) (see KENNETH ROBESON)

JOHNSTON, JOE (see "STAR WARS")

JOHNSTON, WILLIAM (b.1924)

> also see: "BEWITCHED" & "THE MUNSTERS"
>
> Maxwell Smart
> 1. Get Smart!   '65 Tempo
> 2. Sorry, Chief...   '66 Tempo
> 3. Get Smart Once Again!   '66 Tempo
> 4. Max Smart and the Perilous Pellets   '66 Tempo
> 5. Missed It By That Much!   '67 Tempo
> 6. And Loving It!   '67 Tempo
> 7. Max Smart-- The Spy Who Went Out to the Cold
>   '68 Tempo
> 8. Max Smart Loses Control   '68 Tempo
> 9. Max Smart and the Ghastly Ghost Affair   '69 Tempo
>
> The Flying Nun
> 1. The Flying Nun: Miracle at San Tanco   '68 Ace
> 2. The Littlest Rebels   '68 Ace
> 3. Mother of Invention   '69 Ace
> 4. The Little Green Men   '69 Ace
> 5. The Underground Picnic   '70 Ace

JOHNSTONE, WILLIAM H.

> The Devil Series
> 1. The Devil's Kiss
> 2. The Devil's Heart
> 3. The Devil's Touch   '84 Zebra
>
> The Ashes Sequence
> 1. Out of the Ashes   '83 Zebra
> 2. Fire in the Ashes   '84 Zebra

JONES, D.F. (1916-1982)

Colossus
1. Colossus '66 HartD
2. The Fall of Colossus '74 Putn
3. Colossus and the Crab '77 Berk

JONES, DIANA WYNNE (b.1934)

The Dalemark Sequence
1. Drowned Ammet '77 Macm
2. Cart and Cwidder '76 Athen
3. The Spellcoats '79 Athen

Charmed Life
1. Charmed Life '77 Macm
2. The Magicians of Caprona '80 Grnw

JONES, JOHN G. (see "AMITYVILLE")

JONES, NEIL R. (b.1909)

The Professor Jameson Series
1. The Planet of the Double Sun '67 Ace
2. The Sunless World '67 Ace
3. Space War '67 Ace
4. Twin Worlds '67 Ace
5. Doomsday on Ajait '68 Ace

JONES, RAYMOND F. (b.1915)

also see: "VOYAGE TO THE BOTTOM OF THE SEA"

Ron Barron
1. Son of the Stars '52 Winst
2. Planet of Light '53 Winst

JORDAN, ROBERT see: ROBERT E. HOWARD, "Conan" series

K

KAGAN, JANET   (see "STAR TREK")

KAHN, JAMES   (b.1947)

    also see: "INDIANA JONES"
    also see: "STAR WARS"

    The New World Sequence
    1. World Enough, and Time   '80 DelR
    2. Time's Dark Laughter   '82 DelR

KANGLIASKI, JAAN

    The Seeking Sword
    1. The Seeking Sword   '77 Ball
    2. Hands of Glory   '80 DelR

KAPP, COLIN   (b.1929)

    Chaos Sequence
    1. Patterns of Chaos   '72 Gollz
    2. The Chaos Weapon   '77 DelR

    Cageworld
    1. Search For the Sun   '82 NEL
    2. The Lost Worlds of Cronus   '82 NEL
    3. The Tyrant of Hades   '83 NEL
    4. Star Search   '83 NEL

KARL, JEAN E.

    Turning Page Sequence
    1. The Turning Page
    2. Strange Tomorrow   '85 EPDut

KARR, PHYLLIS ANN   (b.1944)

    Frostflower
    1. Frostflower and Thorn   '80 Berk
    2. Frostflower and Windbourne   '85 Berk

KAYE, MARVIN
    (see collaboration with PARKE GODWIN)

KEITH, BRANDON
    see: "GREEN HORNET"
    see: "U.N.C.L.E."

KEITH, DONALD
    (pseud., see DONALD & KEITH MONROE)

KELLEAM, JOSEPH E. (1913-1975)

    Jack Odin
1. The Little Men   '60 Avalo
2. Hunters of Space   '60 Avalo

KELSEY, FRANKLYN

    James Armitage
1. The Island in the Mist   '37 Harrp
2. The Children of the Sun   '39 Harrp
3. The Prowlers of the Deep   '42 Harrp

KENDALL, CAROL (b.1917)

    The Minnipens
1. The Gammage Cup   '59 Harc
    aka: The Minnipens ('60/Dent)
2. The Whisper of Glocken   '65 Harc

KENYON, PAUL (pseud.)

    The Baroness
1. The Ecstasy Connection   '74 PB
2. Diamonds Are For Dying   '74 PB
3. Death Is a Ruby Light   '74 PB
4. Hard-Core Murder   '74 PB
5. Operation Doomsday   '74 PB
6. Sonic Slave   '74 PB
7. Flicker of Doom   '74 PB
8. Black Gold   '75 PB

KERN, GREGORY (pseud., see E.C. TUBB)

KEY, ALEXANDER (1904-1979)

    Sprockets
1. Sprockets, a Little Robot   '63   Westm
2. Rivets and Sprockets   '64   Westm
3. Bolts, a Robot Dog   '66   Westm

    Witch Mountain
1. Escape to Witch Mountain   '68   Westm
2. Return From Witch Mountain   '78   Westm

KEY, UEL (pseud. of Samuel Whittell Key, 1874-?)

    Professor Rhymer
1. The Broken Fang, and Other Experiences of a Specialist in Spooks   '20   H&S
2. Yellow Death; a Tale of Occult Mysteries   '21   BkLtd

KING, JOHN (pseud. of Ernest Lionel McKeag, b.1896)

    Shuna
1. Shuna, White Queen of the Jungle   '51   Harb
2. Shuna and the Lost Tribe   '51   Harb

KIPLING, RUDYARD (1865-1936)

    The Jungle Books
1. The Jungle Book   1894   MacmL
2. The Second Jungle Book   1895   MacmL

    Puck
1. Puck of Pook's Hill   '06   MacmL
2. Rewards and Fairies   '10   MacmL

KIPPAX, JOHN (1915-1974)

    Venturer Twelve Series
1. A Thunder of Stars (with Dan Morgan)   '68   Macd
2. Seed of Stars (with Dan Morgan)   '72   Ball
3. The Neutral Stars (with Dan Morgan)   '73   Ball
4. Where No Stars Guide   '75

KIRK, RICHARD

                   (cont.)

Raven Series
1. Swordsmistress of Chaos
2. A Time of Ghosts
3. The Frozen God
4. Lords of the Shadows
5. A Time For Dying

KLINE, OTIS ADELBERT (1891-1946)

Robert Grandon
1. The Planet of Peril   '29   McClg
2. The Prince of Peril   '30   McClg
3. The Port of Peril   '32/'49 Grand

Jan
1. The Call of the Savage   '31/'37 Clode
    aka: Jan of the Jungle ('66/Ace)
2. Jan in India   '35/'74 FictB

Mars Sequence
1. The Swordsman of Mars   '33/'60 Avalo
2. The Outlaws of Mars   '33/'61 Avalo

KNEALE, NIGEL (b.1922)

Professor Quatermass
1. The Quatermass Experiment   '59   Peng
    aka: The Creeping Unknown
2. Quatermass II   '60   Peng
    aka: Enemy From Space
3. Quatermass and the Pit   '60   Peng
    aka: Five Million Years to Earth

KNEIFEL, HANS (see "PERRY RHODAN")

KNIGHT, ERIC (1897-1943)

Sam Small
1. The Flying Yorkshireman   '40   Bush
2. Sam Small Flies Again; The Amazing
    Adventures of the Flying Yorkshireman   '42   Harpr
       aka: The Flying Yorkshireman ('46/World)

KNIGHT, MALLORY T. (pseud., see BERNHARDT J. HURWOOD)

KNOWLES, WILLIAM   (see CLYDE ALLISON, pseud.)

KORNBLUTH, C.M.   (1923-1958)
    (see collaboration with FREDERIK POHL)

KOTZWINKLE, WILLIAM   (b.1938)

    E.T.   (based on ideas by Steven Spielberg)
1. E.T. the Extra-Terrestrial in His
   Adventure On Earth   '82 Putn
2. E.T.— The Book of the Green Planet   '85 Berk

KRING, MICHAEL

    The Space Mavericks
1. The Space Mavericks   '80 Leisr
2. Children of the Night   '81 Leisr

KUMMER, FREDERIC ARNOLD   (1873-1943)

    Hades
1. Ladies in Hades; A Story of Hell's
   Smart Set   '28 Sears
2. Gentlemen in Hades; The Story of a
   Damned Debutante   '30 Sears

KURLAND, MICHAEL   (b.1938)   (see CHESTER ANDERSON)

KURTZ, KATHERINE   (b.1944)

    The Chronicles of Deryni
1. Deryni Rising   '70 Ball
2. Deryni Checkmate   '72 Ball
3. High Deryni   '73 Ball
    Legends of Camber of Culdi
4. Camber of Culdi   '76 Ball
5. Saint Camber   '78 Ball
6. Camber the Heretic   '80 Ball
    The Histories of King Kelson
7. The Bishop's Heir   '84 DelR
8. The King's Justice   '85 DelR

KYLE, DAVID A.   (see E.E. SMITH, "Lensmen" series)

L

LACH-SZYRMA, W.S. (1814-1915)

    Visitor From Venus Series
1. A Voice From Another World   1874   Parkr
    aka: Alerial; or, A Voyage to Other Worlds
                           (1883/Wyman)
2. Worlds Apart   1893/'72
3. Under Other Conditions   1892   A&CBk

LAFFERTY, R.A. (b.1914)

    The Devil is Dead Trilogy
1. Archipelago   '79   Manus
2. The Devil Is Dead   '71   Avon
3. More Than Melchisedech   '83   Donng

LAING, ALEXANDER (1903-1976)

    Dr. Scarlett
1. Dr. Scarlett: A Narrative of His
   Mysterious Behavior in the East   '36   Farr
2. The Methods of Dr. Scarlett   '38   Cass

LAKE, DAVID J. (b.1929)

    Dextra
1. The Right Hand of Dextra   '77   DAW
2. The Wildings of Westron   '77   DAW

    Xuma
1. The Gods of Xuma, or Barsoom Revisited   '78   DAW
2. Warlords of Xuma   '83   DAW

LAMBERT, WILLIAM J. III

    Adonis
1. Adonis   '69   Pleas
2. Adonis at Actum   '70   Pleas
3. Adonis at Bomasa   '70   Pleas

(cont.)

(William J. Lambert III, cont.)

Demon
1. Demon's Stalk   '70 Pleas
2. Demon's Coronation   '71 Pleas

Tlen
1. Five Roads to Tlen   '70 Grnlf
2. The Gods of Tlen   '70 Grnlf

LAMBOURNE, JOHN
(pseud. of John Battersby Crampton Lamburn, b.1893)

Professor Ellis
1. The Kingdom That Was   '31 Murry
2. The Second Leopard   '32 Murry

LANCOUR, GENE (pseud. of Gene L. Fisher, b.1947)

Dirshan the God-Killer
1. The Lerios Mecca   '73 Dbdy
2. The War Machines of Kalinth   '77 Dbdy
3. Sword For the Empire   '78 Dbdy

"LAND OF THE GIANTS"

1. Land of the Giants (Murray Leinster)   '68 Pyr
2. The Hot Spot (Murray Leinster)   '69 Pyr
3. Unknown Danger (Murray Leinster)   '69 Pyr
4. The Mean City (James Bradwell)   '69 WDist
5. Flight of Fear (Carl Henry Rathjen)   '69 Whitm

LANDIS, ARTHUR H.

Camelot in Space
1. A World Called Camelot   '76 DAW
2. Camelot in Orbit   '78 DAW
3. The Magick of Camelot   '81 DAW
4. Home-- To Avalon   '82 DAW

LANG, ANDREW (1844-1912)

Pantouflia *
1. Prince Prigio   1889 Arrow

(cont.)

    2. Prince Ricardo of Pantouflia   1893 Arrow
       * both collected in: "My Own Fairy Book"
                                        (1895/Arrow)

LANG, SIMON (pseud. of Darlene Hartman, b.1934)

      The Book of Han
  1. All the Gods of Eisernon   '73 Avon
  2. The Elluvon Gift   '75 Avon

LANGFORD, GEORGE (1876-1964)

      Pic
  1. Pic, the Weapon-Maker   '20 Boni
  2. Kutnar, Son of Pic   '21 Boni

LANGHOLM, NEIL (House Pseudonym)

      The Vikings
  1. Blood Sacrifice (Laurence James)   '75 Spher
  2. The Dark Return (Kenneth Bulmer)   '75 Spher
  3. Blood on the Sun (Laurence James)   '75 Spher
  4. Trail of Blood (Kenneth Bulmer)   '76 Spher

LANIER, STERLING E. (b.1927)

      Hiero Desteen (coll.'84/SFBC)
  1. Hiero's Journey   '73 Chilt
  2. The Unforsaken Hiero   '83 DelR

LARGE, E.C. (?-1976)

      Charles Pry
  1. Asleep in the Afternoon   '38 Cape
  2. Sugar in the Air   '37 Cape

LARSON, GLEN A.

      Battlestar Galactica
  1. Battlestar Galactica
     (with Robert Thurston)   '78 Berk
  2. The Cylon Death Machine
     (with Robert Thurston)   '79 Berk
                         (cont.)

(Glen A. Larson, "Battlestar Galactica", cont.)

  3. The Tombs of Kobol (with Robert Thurston)   '79 Berk
  4. The Young Warriors (with Robert Thurston)   '80 Berk
  5. Galactica Discovers Earth
     (with Michael Resnick)   '80 Berk
  6. The Living Legend (with Nicholas Yermakov) '81 Berk
  7. War of the Gods (with Nicholas Yermakov)   '82 Berk
  8. Greetings From Earth (with Ron Goulart)   '83 Berk
  9. Experiment in Terra (with Ron Goulart)   '84 Berk
10. The Long Patrol (with Ron Goulart)   '84 Berk

LATTER, SIMON (see "U.N.C.L.E.")

LAUMER, KEITH (b.1925)

    also see: "THE AVENGERS"
    also see: "THE INVADERS"

    The Imperium
1. Worlds of the Imperium   '62 Ace
2. The Other Side of Time   '65 Berk
3. Assignment in Nowhere   '68 Berk
4. Beyond the Imperium   '81 Pinn

    Retief Series
1. Envoy to New Worlds   '63 Ace
2. Galactic Diplomat   '65 Dbdy
3. Retief's War   '66 Dbdy
4. Reteif and the Warlords   '68 Dbdy
5. Retief: Ambassador to Space   '69 Dbdy
6. Retief of the CDT   '71 Dbdy
7. Retief's Ransom   '71 Putn
8. Retief: Emissary to the Stars   '75 Dell
9. Retief: Diplomat at Arms   '82 PB
    (collection of short stories published
    in the '60s)
10. Retief to the Rescue   '83 S&S
    reprint collections:
1. Retief at Large   '78 Ace
    (all reprints from previous collections)
2. Retief Unbound   '79 Ace
    (contains "Retief's Ransom" and 5 stories from
    "Envoy to New Worlds")

    Lafayette O'Leary
1. The Time Bender   '66 Berk

               (cont.)

2. The World Shuffler	'70	Putn
3. The Shape Changer	'72	Putn
4. The Galaxy Builder	'84	Ace

LAURIA, FRANK (b.1935)

Dr. Orient
1. Doctor Orient	'70	Bant
2. Raga Six	'72	Bant
3. Lady Sativa	'73	Curt
4. Baron Orgaz	'74	Bant
5. The Seth Papers	'79	Ball

LAW, WINIFRED

Ralph Hannon
1. Through Space to the Planets	'44	NewC
2. Rangers of the Universe	'45	NewC

LAWRENCE, J.A. (see "STAR TREK")

LAWRENCE, MARGERY (?-1969)

Club of the Round Table
1. Nights of the Round Table; A Book of Strange Tales	'26	Hutch
2. The Terraces of Night, Being Further Chronicles of the "Club of the Round Table"	'32	H&B

LeBARON, ANTHONY (see "THE INVADERS")

LECALE, ERROL
(pseud. of Wilfred Glassford McNeilly, b.1921)

The Specialist
1. The Tigerman of Terrahpur	'74	NEL
2. Castledoom	'74	NEL
3. The Severed Hand	'74	NEL
4. The Death Box	'74	NEL
5. Zombie	'75	NEL
6. Blood of My Blood	'76	NEL

LEE, ROBERT C. (b.1931)

(cont.)

(Robert C. Lee, cont.)

Mike Glenn
1. The Iron Arm of Michael Glenn '65 LtBrn
2. The Day It Rained Forever '68 LtBrn

LEE, TANITH (b.1947)

Birthgrave Series
1. The Birthgrave '75 DAW
2. Vazkor, Son of Vazkor '78 DAW
3. Quest For the White Witch '78 DAW

Don't Bite the Sun
1. Don't Bite the Sun '76 DAW
2. Drinking Sapphire Wine '77 DAW

Lords of Darkness
1. Night's Master '78 DAW
2. Death's Master '79 DAW
3. Delusion's Master '81 DAW

The Wars of Vis (coll.'84/SFBC)
1. The Storm Lord '78 DAW
2. Anackire '83 DAW

LEEMING, JOHN F. (b.1900)

Claudius
1. Claudius the Bee '36 Harrp
2. Thanks to Claudius '37 Harrp

LE GUIN, URSULA K. (b.1929)

The Earthsea Trilogy
1. A Wizard of Earthsea '68 ParnP
2. The Tombs of Atuan '71 Athen
3. The Farthest Shore '72 Athen

The League of All Worlds *
(Note-- The series comprises an expansive future history and is connected by certain terms, concepts, and populaces rather than by individual characters. Titles are listed by internal chronology, though they can be read independently).

1. The Dispossessed   '74 Harpr
2. The Word For World is Forest '76 Berk
3. Rocannon's World   '66 Ace
4. Planet of Exile   '66 Ace
5. City of Illusions   '67 Ace
6. The Left Hand of Darkness '69 Ace
   * Volumes 3, 4, & 5 have been published
   in one volume as: "Three Hainish Novels"

LEIBER, FRITZ (b.1910)

   also see: EDGAR RICE BURROUGHS, "Tarzan" series

   ### Changewar Sequence
1. The Big Time   '61 Ace
2. The Change War   '78 Gregg
   abridged as: Changewar ('83/Ace)

   ### Fafhrd and the Gray Mouser
1. Swords and Deviltry   '70 Ace
2. Swords Against Death   '70 Ace
   7 of 10 stories originally published as:
   Two Sought Adventure ('57/Gnome)
3. Swords in the Mist   '68 Ace
4. Swords Against Wizardry   '68 Ace
5. The Swords of Lankhmar   '68 Ace
6. Swords and Ice Magic   '77 Ace

LEIGH, STEPHEN

   ### The Hoorka Trilogy
1. Slow Fall to Dawn
2. Dance of the Hag   '83 Bant
3. A Quiet of Stone   '84 Bant

LEINSTER, MURRAY (1896-1975)

   ### Joe Kenmore Series
1. Space Platform   '53 Shast
2. Space Tug   '53 Shast
3. City on the Moon   '57 Avalo

   ### The Med Service Series *
1. S.O.S. From Three Worlds   '66 Ace

              (cont.)

(Murray Leinster, "Med Service", cont.)

   2. The Mutant Weapon   '59 Ace
   3. Doctor to the Stars   '64 Pyr
   4. This World is Taboo   '61 Ace
     * Titles 1, 2, & 4 have been collected as:
      The Med Series ('83/Ace)

Time Tunnel
1. The Time Tunnel   '67 Pyr
2. Time Slip   '67 Pyr

Land of the Giants (first 3 by Leinster)
1. Land of the Giants   '68 Pyr
2. The Hot Spot   '69 Pyr
3. Unknown Danger   '69 Pyr
4. The Mean City (by James Bradwell)   '69 WDist
5. Flight of Fear (by Carl H. Rathjen)   '69 Whitm

LEM, STANISLAW (b.1921)

The Ijon Tichy Stories
1. The Futurological Congress   '74 Conti
2. The Star Diaries   '76 Seaby

L'ENGLE, MADELEINE (b.1918)

Meg Murray
1. A Wrinkle in Time   '62 Ariel
2. A Wind in the Door   '73 Farr
3. A Swiftly Tilting Planet   '78 Farr

Canon Tellis
1. The Arm of the Starfish   '65 Ariel
2. The Young Unicorns   '68 Ariel

LE SAGE, ALAIN RENE (1668-1747)

The Devil Upon Two Sticks
1. Le Diable Boiteaux; or, The Devil Upon Two Sticks   1708 JTons
     aka: The Devil Upon Crutches (1750/Osbor)
     aka: The Devil Upon Two Sticks (1757/JTons)
     aka: The Devil On Two Sticks (1815/Walkr)
     aka: Asmodeus; or, The Devil On Two Sticks (1841/JThom)
     aka: The Lame Devil (1870/Tuckr)

(sequel)
2. The Devil Upon Two Sticks in England,
   Being a Continuation of Le Diable Boiteaux
   of Le Sage (by William Combe)   1790   LogoP

LESLIE, PETER
    see: "THE AVENGERS"
    also see: "THE INVADERS"
    also see: "U.N.C.L.E."

LESSING, DORIS (b.1919)

    Canopus in Argus: Archives
1. Re: Colonised Planet 5: Shikasta   '79   Knopf
2. The Marriages Between Zones Three,
   Four, and Five   '80   Knopf
3. The Sirian Experiments: Report By
   Ambien II of the Five   '81   Knopf
4. The Making of the Representative for
   Planet 8   '82   Knopf
5. Documents Relating to the Sentimental
   Agents in the Volyen Empire   '83   Knopf

LETTS, BARRY (see "DOCTOR WHO")

LEWIS, C.S. (1898-1963)

    The Perelandra Trilogy
1. Out of the Silent Planet   '38   BodH
2. Perelandra   '43   BodH
3. That Hideous Strength   '45   BodH
     abridged as: "The Tortured Planet"   ('58/Avon)

    Screwtape
1. The Screwtape Letters   '42   Bles
2. Screwtape Proposes a Toast, and Other Pieces
                                            '65   Font

    The Chronicles of Narnia
1. The Lion, the Witch, and the Wardrobe   '50   Bles
2. Prince Caspian: The Return to Narnia   '51   Bles
3. The Voyage of the Dawn Treader   '52   Bles
4. The Silver Chair   '53   Bles
5. The Horse and His Boy   '54   Bles
6. The Magician's Nephew   '55   BodH
7. The Last Battle: A Story For Children   '56   BodH

LEWIS, CAROLINE (pseud. of Harold Begbie [1871-1929],
J. Stafford Ransome [1860-1931], and M.H. Temple).

Clara
1. Clara in Blunderland   '02 Heine
2. Lost in Blunderland   '03 Heine

LEWIS, IRWIN (b.1916)

Horace Clarke
1. The Day They Invaded New York   '64 Avon
2. The Day New York Trembled   '67 Avon

LEWIS, WYNDHAM (1884-1957)

The Human Age
1. The Childermass   '28 C&W
2. Monstre Gai   '55 Meth
3. Malign Fiesta   '55 Meth

LICHTENBERG, JACQUELINE (b.1942)

The Sime/Gen Novels
1. House of Zeor   '74 Dbdy
2. Unto Zeor, Forever   '78 Dbdy
3. First Channel (with Jean Lorrah)   '80 Dbdy
4. Mahogany Trimrose   '81 Dbdy
5. Channel's Destiny (with Jean Lorrah)   '82 Dbdy
6. Rensime   '84 DAW

Molt Brother
1. Molt Brother   '84 Berk
2. City of a Million Legends   '85 Berk

The Dushau Trilogy
1. Dushau   '85 Pop
2. Farfetch   '85 Pop
3. (NYP)

LIEBERMAN, ROSALIE

Brother Angeto
1. The Man Who Sold Christmas   '51 LongG
2. The Man Who Captivated New York   '60 Dbdy

LIGHTNER, A.M.   (pseud. of Alice Lightner Hopf, b.1904)

    Rock
1. The Rock of Three Planets   '63   Putn
2. The Planet Poachers   '65   Putn
3. The Space Ark   '68   Putn

LINDHOLM, MEGAN

    Ki
1. Harpy's Flight   '83   Ace
2. The Windsingers   '84   Ace
3. The Limbreth Gate   '84   Ace

LIVINGSTON, MARJORIE   (b.1893)

    Karmic Destiny
1. Island Sonata   '44   Daker
2. Muted Strings   '46   Daker
3. Delphic Echo   '48   Daker

LLOYD, J. WM.   (1857-?)

    Natural Man
1. The Natural Man; A Romance of the
   Golden Age   '02   Priet
2. The Dwellers in Vale Sunrise   '04   Ariel

LOCKE, ASHLEY   (see collaboration with ARTHUR B. REEVE)

LOCKWOOD, INGERSOLL   (1841-1918)

    Baron Trump
1. Travels and Adventures of Little Baron
   Trump and His Wonderful Dog Bulger   1890   Lee&S
2. Baron Trump's Marvelous Underground
   Journey   1893   Lee&S

LOFTING, HUGH   (1886-1947)

    Doctor Doolittle

                         (cont.)

(Hugh Lofting, "Doctor Doolittle", cont.)

1. The Story of Doctor Doolittle '20 Stoke
   aka: Doctor Doolittle ('22/Cape)
2. The Voyages of Doctor Doolittle '22 Stoke
   aka: Doctor Doolittle and the Pirates
3. Doctor Doolittle's Post Office '23 Stoke
4. Doctor Doolittle's Circus '24 Stoke
5. Doctor Doolittle's Zoo '25 Stoke
6. Doctor Doolittle's Caravan '26 Stoke
7. Doctor Doolittle's Garden '27 Stoke
8. Doctor Doolittle in the Moon '28 Stoke
9. Gub-Gub's Book: An Encyclopedia of Food '32 Stoke
10. Doctor Doolittle's Return '33 Stoke
11. Doctor Doolittle and the Secret Lake '48 Lipp
12. Doctor Doolittle and the Green Canary '50 Lipp
13. Doctor Doolittle's Puddleby Adventure '52 Lipp

LONGYEAR, BARRY B. (b.1942)

Circus World
1. City of Baraboo '80 Putn
2. Elephant Song '82 Berk
3. Circus World '81 SFBC

The Tomorrow Testament
1. "Enemy Mine" a novella in the collection:
   Manifest Destiny '80 Berk
2. The Tomorrow Testament '83 Berk

LORD, BEMAN (b.1924)

The Spaceship
1. The Day the Spaceship Landed '67 Walck
2. The Spaceship Returns '70 Walck

LORD, JEFFERY
(House Pseudonym— most written by Lyle Kenyon Engel)

Richard Blade
1. The Bronze Axe '69 Macf
2. The Jade Warrior '69 Macf
3. Jewel of Tharn '69 Macf
4. Slave of Sarma '70 Macf
5. Liberator of Jedd '71 Macf
6. Monster of the Maze (by Roland Green) '72 Macf

7. Pearl of Patmos	'73	Pinn
8. Undying World	'73	Pinn
9. Kingdom of Royth (by Roland Green)	'74	Pinn
10. Ice Dragon (by Roland Green)	'74	Pinn
11. Dimension of Dreams (by Roland Green)	'74	Pinn
12. King of Zunga	'75	Pinn
13. The Golden Steed	'75	Pinn
14. The Temples of Ayocan	'75	Pinn
15. The Towers of Melnon	'75	Pinn
16. The Crystal Seas	'75	Pinn
17. Mountain of Brega	'76	Pinn
18. Warlords of Gaikan	'76	Pinn
19. Looters of Tharn	'76	Pinn
20. Guardians of the Coral Throne	'76	Pinn
21. Champion of the Gods	'76	Pinn
22. The Forests of Gleor	'77	Pinn
23. Empire of Blood	'77	Pinn
24. The Dragons of Englor	'77	Pinn
25. The Torian Pearls	'77	Pinn
26. City of the Living Dead	'78	Pinn
27. Master of the Hashomi	'78	Pinn
28. Wizard of Rentoro	'78	Pinn
29. Treasure of the Stars	'78	Pinn
30. Dimension of Horror	'79	Pinn
31. Gladiators of Hapanu	'79	Pinn
32. Pirates of Gohar	'79	Pinn
33. Killer Plants of Binaark	'80	Pinn
34. The Ruins of Kaldac	'81	Pinn
35. The Lords of the Crimson River	'81	Pinn
36. Return to Kaldac	'83	Pinn
37. Warriors of Laittan	'84	Pinn

LORRAH, JEAN (b. c.1940)

    also see: JACQUELINE LICHTENBERG, "Sime/Gen"
    also see: "STAR TREK"

The Savage Empire Series
1. Savage Empire	'81	Play
2. Dragon Lord of the Savage Empire	'83	Play
3. Captives of the Savage Empire	'84	Play

LORY, ROBERT (b.1936)

Trovo
1. The Eyes of Bolsk	'69	Ace
2. Master of the Etrax	'70	Dell

(Robert Lory, cont.)

Shamryke Odell
1. Masters of the Lamp   '70   Ace
2. The Veiled World   '72   Ace

Dracula Horror Series
1. Dracula Returns   '73   Pinn
2. The Hand of Dracula   '73   Pinn
3. Dracula's Brother   '73   Pinn
4. Dracula's Gold   '73   Pinn
5. Drums of Dracula   '74   Pinn
6. The Witching of Dracula   '74   Pinn
7. Dracula's Lost World   '74   Pinn
8. Dracula's Disciple   '75   Pinn

Horrorscope
1. Horrorscope; The Green Flames of Aries   '74   Pinn
2. Horrorscope; The Revenge of Taurus   '74   Pinn
3. Horrorscope; The Curse of Leo   '74   Pinn
4. Horrorscope; Gemini Smile, Gemini Kill   '75   Pinn

LOTTMAN, EILEEN (b.1927)

The Bionic Woman
1. Welcome Home, Jaime   '76   Berk
2. Extracurricular Activities   '77   Berk

LOVE, G.B. (see "STAR TREK")

LOVECRAFT, H.P. (1890-1937)

The Cthulhu Mythos
(The "Cthulhu Mythos" is a loosely connected group of stories whose common thread is their relationship, in varying degrees, to a vague but decidedly evil array of ancient other-dimensional forces whose goal is to supercede our own civilization.

Lovecraft created the concept, and it permeates most of his best-known works, but he also openly invited numerous other writers to add to the Mythos, and many authors continue today to write stories employing one or more of the elements Lovecraft developed.

The Mythos stories, however, are not always clear-cut, and there is debate among bibliographers as to which stories actually belong to the Cthulhu cycle and which are unrelated stories merely written in Lovecraftian style. The following list is far from complete, but includes the better-known works generally accepted as belonging to the series. Many of the earlier stories originally appeared in pulps).

1. The Outsider and Others (H.P. Lovecraft) '39 ArkH
    includes: "The Shadow Over Innsmouth" ('36)
2. Something Near (August Derleth)   '41 ArkH
    (contains several Cthulhu stories)
3. Beyond the Wall of Sleep (Lovecraft) '43 ArkH
    includes: "The Case of Charles Dexter Ward" ('51/Gollz)
4. The Lurker at the Threshold
    (Lovecraft & Derleth)   '45 ArkH
5. The Opener of the Way (Robert Bloch) '45 ArkH
    (contains several Cthulhu stories)
6. Skull-Face and Others
    (Robert E. Howard) (2 Cthulhu stories) '46 ArkH
7. The Web of Easter Island (Donald Wandrei) '48 ArkH
8. The Survivor and Others
    (Lovecraft & Derleth)   '57 ArkH
9. The Mask of Cthulhu (August Derleth) '58 ArkH
10. The Shuttered Room and Other Pieces '59 ArkH
    (Lovecraft & Divers Hands [pseud. of Derleth])
11. The Trail of Cthulhu (August Derleth) '62 ArkH
12. The Inhabitant of the Lake and Less
    Welcome Tenants (Ramsey Campbell) '64 ArkH
13. Colonel Markesan and Less Pleasant People
    (August Derleth) (2 stories belong to series)
                                        '66 ArkH
14. Tales of the Cthulhu Mythos   '69 ArkH
    (edited by August Derleth)
15. The Horror in the Museum and Other
    Revisions (edited by Lovecraft) '70 ArkH
16. Worse Things Waiting (Manly Wade Wellman)'73 Carco
    (1 story in Cthulhu sequence)
17. Murgunstrumm and Others (Hugh B. Cave) '77 Carco
    (at least 2 stories)
18. New Tales of the Cthulhu Mythos
    (edited by Ramsey Campbell)   '80 ArkH
19. The Color Out of Time (Michael Shea) '84 DAW
    (this is a direct sequel to "The Colour
    Out of Space")
20. Cold Print (Ramsey Campbell)   '85 ScrPr

ALSO SEE: Brian Lumley's "Titus Crow" series.

NOTE: Lovecraft's Cthulhu stories can also be found reprinted in the following collections:
(cont.)

(H.P. Lovecraft, reprint collections, cont.)

   1. The Dunwich Horror   '45 BartH
      abridged as: The Haunter of the Dark ('51/Gollz)
      expanded as: The Dunwich Horror and Others
            ('63/ArkH)
   2. At the Mountains of Madness and Other Novels   '64 ArkH
      aka: At the Mountains of Madness and Other
      Tales of Terror ('71/Ball) (2 stories)
   3. The Colour Out of Space   '64 Lance
   4. Dagon and Other Macabre Tales   '65 ArkH
   5. The Shadow Out of Time and Other Tales
     of Horror   '68 Gollz
      expanded as:
      The Watchers Out of Time and Others ('74/ArkH)
   6. The Tomb and Other Tales (1 story)   '70 Ball
   7. The Doom That Came to Sarnath and
     Other Stories (2 stories)   '71 Ball
   8. The Lurking Fear and Other Stories   '71 Ball
     (1 story)
   9. Bloodcurdling Tales of Horror and the
     Macabre (9 stories)   '82 DelR

LOVEJOY, JACK

    A Vision of Beasts
   1. Creation Descending   '84 Tor
   2. The Second Kingdom   '84 Tor
   3. The Brotherhood of Diablo   '85 Tor

LUCAROTTI, JOHN (see "DOCTOR WHO")

LUCAS, GEORGE (b.1944)
      see: "INDIANA JONES"
      see: "STAR WARS"

LUIGI, BELLI (pseud.)

    Vernon Templeton
   1. The Mummy Walks   '50 Trans
   2. Curse of the Mummy   '50 Trans

LUKEMAN, TIM
                      (cont.)

       Tales of Khe'chin
1. Rajan   '79 Dbdy
2. Koren   '81 Dbdy

LUMLEY, BRIAN (b.1937)

       The Titus Crow Series
1. The Burrowers Beneath   '74 DAW
2. The Transition of Titus Crow   '75 DAW
3. The Clock of Dreams   '78 Jove
4. Spawn of the Winds   '78 Jove
5. In the Moons of Borea   '79 Jove

LUNATIC, SIR HUMPHREY
     (pseud. of Francis Gentleman [1728-1784])

       Noibla
1. A Trip To the Moon, Containing an Account of the Island of Noibla, Its Inhabitants, Religious and Political Customs, Etc.   1764 WYork
2. A Trip to the Moon... Etc., Volume II   1765 Crowd

LUPOFF, RICHARD A. (b.1935) (see "BUCK ROGERS")

LYNDS, DENNIS (b.1924) (see MAXWELL GRANT, pseud.)

LYNN, ELIZABETH A. (b.1946)

       The Chronicles of Tornor
1. Watchtower   '79 Berk
2. The Dancers of Arun   '79 Berk
3. The Northern Girl   '80 Berk

MACAO, MARSHALL (pseud. of Thaddeus F. Tuleja, b.1944)

    K'ing Kung Fu
1. Son of the Flying Tiger   '73 Freew
2. Return of the Opium Wars   '73 Freew
3. The Rape of Sun Lee Fong   '73 Freew
4. The Kak-Abdullah Conspiracy   '73 Freew
5. Red Plague in Bolivia   '74 Freew
6. New York Necromancy   '74 Freew
7. Mark of the Vulture   '74 Freew

MacAVOY, R.A.

    A Trio For Lute (coll.'85/SFBC)
1. Damiano   '83 Bant
2. Damiano's Lute   '84 Bant
3. Raphael   '84 Bant

McBAIN, GORDON

    The Dawnstar
1. The Path of Exoterra
2. Quest of the Dawnstar   '84 Avon

McCAFFREY, ANNE (b.1926)

    THE DRAGON BOOKS
    The Dragonriders of Pern (coll.'78/Dbdy)
1. Dragonflight   '68 Ball
2. Dragonquest   '71 Ball
3. The White Dragon   '78 DelR
    Menolly the Singer *
4. Dragonsong   '76 Athen
5. Dragonsinger   '77 Athen
6. Dragondrums   '79 Athen
    Moreta
7. Moreta, Dragonlady of Pern   '83 SevHs
    * Note: titles 4-6 have been collected as:
        The Harper Hall of Pern ('79/Dbdy)

    Dinosaur Planet
1. Dinosaur Planet   '78 DelR
2. Dinosaur Planet Survivors   '84 DelR

McCUTCHAN, PHILIP (b.1920)

Commander Shaw
1. Gibralter Road — '60 Harrp
2. Redcap — '61 Harrp
3. Bluebolt One — '62 Harrp
4. The Man From Moscow — '63 Harrp
5. Warmaster — '63 Harrp
6. Moscow Coach — '64 Harrp
7. The Dead Line — '66 Harrp
8. Skyprobe — '66 Harrp
9. The Screaming Dead Balloons — '68 Harrp
10. The Bright Red Businessmen — '69 Harrp
11. The All-Purpose Bodies — '69 Harrp
12. Hartinger's Mouse — '70 Harrp
13. This Drakotny — '71 Harrp
14. Sunstrike — '79 H&S
15. Corpse — '80 H&S

McDANIEL, DAVID (1939-1977)

see: "U.N.C.L.E."
also see: "THE PRISONER"

MacDONALD, GEORGE (1824-1905)

A Faery Trilogy
1. At the Back of the North Wind — 1870 Strah
2. The Princess and the Goblin — 1871 Strah
3. The Princess and Curdie — 1882 C&W

McENROE, RICHARD S.

also see: "BUCK ROGERS"

Far Stars and Future Times
1. The Shattered Stars — '84 Bant
2. Flight of Honor — '84 Bant
3. Skinner — '85 Bant

McGILL, GORDON (see "THE OMEN")

McGRAW, ELOISE JARVIS & LAUREN McGRAW WAGNER
(see L. FRANK BAUM, "Oz" series)

MacGREGOR, ELLEN (1906-1954)

    Miss Pickerell
1. Miss Pickerell Goes to Mars   '51 WhitH
2. Miss Pickerell and the Geiger Counter   '53 WhitH
3. Miss Pickerell Goes Undersea   '53 WhitH
4. Miss Pickerell Goes to the Arctic   '54 WhitH
    (series continued by Dora Pantell):
5. Miss Pickerell on the Moon   '65 McGrH
6. Miss Pickerell Goes on a Dig   '66 McGrH
7. Miss Pickerell Harvests the Sea   '68 McGrH
8. Miss Pickerell and the Weather Satellite '71 McGrH
9. Miss Pickerell Meets Mr. H.U.M.   '74 McGrH
10. Miss Pickerell Takes the Bull By the Horns
    '76 McGrH
11. Miss Pickerell to the Earthquake Rescue '77 McGrH
12. Miss Pickerell and the Supertanker   '78 McGrH
13. Miss Pickerell Tackles the Energy Crisis '80 McGrH

McINTYRE, VONDA N. (b.1948) (see "STAR TREK")

McKENNEY, KENNETH

    Simon Blackstone
1. The Moonchild
2. The Changeling   '85 Avon

McKIERNAN, DENNIS L.

    The Iron Tower Trilogy
1. The Dark Tide   '84 Dbdy
2. Shadows of Doom   '84 Dbdy
3. The Darkest Day   '84 Dbdy

McKILLIP, PATRICIA (b.1948)

    Riddle of Stars (coll.'79/SFBC)
1. The Riddle-Master of Hed   '76 Athen
2. Heir of Sea and Fire   '77 Athen
3. Harpist in the Wind   '79 Athen

McKINLEY, ROBIN (b.1952)

    Damar

                           (cont.)

1. The Blue Sword '82 Grnw
2. The Hero and the Crown (a prequel) '84 WmMor

McNEE, PATRICK (see "THE AVENGERS")

MACPHERSON, DONALD

Reggie Brooks
1. Go Home, Unicorn '35 Faber
2. Men Are Like Animals '37 Faber

McQUAY, MIKE

Matthew Swain
1. Hot Time in Old Town '81 Bant
2. When Trouble Beckons '81 Bant
3. The Deadliest Show in Town '82 Bant
4. The Odds Are Murder '83 Bant

Morgan of Alb'ny
1. Pure Blood '85 Bant
2. Mother Earth '85 Bant

MacVICAR, ANGUS (b.1908)

Jeremy Grant
1. The Lost Planet '53 Burke
2. Return to the Lost Planet '54 Burke
3. Secret of the Lost Planet '55 Burke
4. Red Fire on the Lost Planet '59 Burke
5. Peril on the Lost Planet '60 Burke
6. Space Agent From the Lost Planet '61 Burke
7. Space Agent and the Isles of Fire '62 Burke
8. Space Agent and the Ancient Peril '64 Burke

Super Nova
1. 'Super Nova' and the Rogue Satellite '69 BkKnt
2. 'Super Nova' and the Frozen Man '70 Brock

MADDOCK, LARRY (b.1931)

Agent of T.E.R.R.A.
1. The Flying Saucer Gambit '66 Ace
2. The Golden Goddess Gambit '67 Ace

(cont.)

(Larry Maddock, cont.)

   3. The Emerald Elephant Gambit   '67 Ace
   4. The Time Trap Gambit   '69 Ace

MADLEE, DOROTHY (see collaboration with ANDRE NORTON)

MAGGIN, ELLIOT S.

     Superman (character created by DC Comics)
   1. Last Son of Krypton   '78 Warnr
   2. Miracle Monday   '81 Warnr

MAHR, KURT (see "PERRY RHODAN")

MAINE, CHARLES ERIC (pseud. of David McIlwain, b.1921)

     Mike Delaney
   1. The Isotope Man   '57 H&S
   2. Subterfuge   '59 H&S
   3. Never Let Up   '64 H&S

     World Without Men
   1. World Without Men   '58 Ace
   2. Alph   '72 Dbdy

MAITLAND, REGINALD (see "THE SPIDER")

MAJOR, H.M.

     Cord
   1. The Alien Trace   '84 Sign
   2. The Time Twister   '84 Sign

"THE MAN FROM U.N.C.L.E." (see "U.N.C.L.E." series)

MANLEY, MARY DE LA RIVIERE (1663-1724)

     New Atalantis
   1. Secret Memoirs and Manners of Several Persons
      of Quality of Both Sexes From the New Atalantis,
      an Island in the Mediterranean   1709 Morph

    2. Memoirs of Europe, Towards the Close of
       the Eighteenth Century
          (pseud.-- Eginardus)　　　　　　1710　Morph
    3. Court Intrigues in a Collection of
       Original Letters from the Island of
       the New Atalantis　　　　　　　　1711　Morph
    4. The Modern Atalantis; or, The Devil in
       an Air Balloon　　　　　　　　　 1784　Kears

MANN, JACK (pseud., see E. CHARLES VIVIAN)

MANNING, ADELAIDE (see CYRIL HENRY COLES & MANNING COLES)

MARSHAK, SONDRA (see "STAR TREK")

MARSHALL, DEBORAH A. (see "V")

MARTER, IAN (see "DOCTOR WHO")

MARTIN, JACK (see "HALLOWEEN")

"MARVEL SUPER-HEROES"

       Bantam sequence
   1. The Avengers Battle the Earth-Wrecker
     (Otto Binder)　　　　　　　　　　'67　Bant
   2. Captain America: The Great Gold Steal
     (Ted White)　　　　　　　　　　　'68　Bant
     Marvel Novel Series
   1. The Amazing Spider-Man in "Mayhem in Man-
     hatten" (Len Wein & Marv Wolfman)　'78　PB
   2. The Incredible Hulk in "Stalker From the
     Stars" (Len Wein, Marv Wolfman, & Joseph
     Silva)　　　　　　　　　　　　　'78　PB
   3. The Incredible Hulk in "Cry of the Beast"
     (Richard S. Meyers)　　　　　　　'79　PB
   4. Captain America in "Holocaust For Hire"
     (Joseph Silva)　　　　　　　　　 '79　PB
   5. The Fantastic Four in "Doomsday"
     (Marv Wolfman)　　　　　　　　　 '79　PB
   6. Iron Man in "And Call My Killer... Modok!"
     (William Rotsler)　　　　　　　　'79　PB
                      (cont.)

("Marvel Super-Heroes", cont.)
  7. Doctor Strange in "Nightmare"
    (William Rotsler)   '79 PB
  8. The Amazing Spider-Man in "Crime Campaign"
    (Paul Kupperberg)   '79 PB
  9. (?)
  10. The Avengers in "The Man Who Stole Tomorrow"
    (David Michelinie)   '79 PB
  11. The Hulk and Spider-Man in "Murdermoon"
    (Paul Kupperberg)   '79 PB

MASEFIELD, JOHN (1878-1967)

  <u>Kay Harker</u>
  1. The Midnight Folk   '27 Heine
  2. The Box of Delights, or, When the
    Wolves Were Running   '35 Heine

MASON, DAVID (1924-1974)

  <u>Kavin</u>
  1. Kavin's World   '69 Lance
  2. The Return of Kavin   '72 Lance

MASON, DOUGLAS R. (b.1918) (see JOHN RANKINE)

MASTIN, JOHN (1865-1932)

  <u>Regina</u>
  1. The Stolen Planet   '05 Griff
  2. Through the Sun in an Airship   '09 Griff

MATSON, N. (see collaboration with THORNE SMITH)

MAXWELL, ANN (b.1944)

  <u>The Dancer Trilogy</u>
  1. Fire Dancer   '82 Sign
  2. Dancer's Luck   '83 Sign
  3. Dancer's Illusion   '83 Sign

MAY, JULIAN (b.1931)

        (cont.)

The Saga of Pliocene Exile
1. The Many-Colored Land   '81 HMiff
2. The Golden Torc   '82 HMiff
3. The Nonborn King   '83 HMiff
4. The Adversary   '84 HMiff

MAYHAR, ARDATH (b.1930)

also see: H. BEAM PIPER, "Fuzzy" series

Tyrnos
1. Soul-Singer of Tyrnos   '81 Athen
2. Runes of the Lyre   '82 Athen

MEADE, RICHARD (1926-1977)

The Gray Lands
1. The Sword of Morning Star   '69 Sign
2. Exile's Guest   '70 Sign

MEANEY, DEE MORRISON

Lady Branwen
1. An Unkindness of Ravens   '83 Ace
2. Death of the Raven   '83 Ace

MEEK, COLONEL S.P. (1894-1972)

Troyana
1. The Drums of Tapajos   '30/'61 Avalo
2. Troyana   '32/'61 Avalo

MEIK, VIVIAN (b.1895)

Geoffrey Aylett
1. The Devils' Drums   '33 PAlan
2. Veils of Fear   '34 PAlan

MELTZER, DAVID (b.1937)

The Agency
1. The Agency   '68 Essex
2. The Agent   '68 Essex
3. How Many Blocks in the Pile?   '68 Essex

(David Meltzer, cont.)

The Brain-Plant Series
1. Lovely   '69 Essex
2. Healer   '69 Essex
3. Out   '69 Essex
4. Glue Factory   '69 Essex

MEREDITH, RICHARD C. (b.1937)

The Timeliner Trilogy
1. At the Narrow Passage   '73 Putn
2. No Brother, No Friend   '76 Dbdy
3. Vestiges of Time   '78 Dbdy

MERRITT, A. (1884-1943)

Dr. Goodwin
1. The Moon Pool   '19 Putn
2. The Metal Monster   '20/'46 Avon

Dr. Lowell
1. Burn, Witch, Burn!   '33 Liver
2. Creep, Shadow!   '34 Dbdy
    aka: Creep, Shadow, Creep ('35/Meth)

MERWIN, SAM Jr. (b.1910)

Elspeth Marriner
1. The House of Many Worlds   '51 Dbdy
2. Three Faces of Time   '55 Ace

MEYERS, RICHARD S. (see "MARVEL SUPER-HEROES")

MEYERS, ROY (1910-1974)

The Dolphin Trilogy
1. Dolphin Boy   '67 Ball
    aka: Dolphin Rider ('68/Rapp)
2. Daughters of the Dolphin   '68 Ball
3. Destiny and the Dolphins   '69 Ball

MEZO, FRANCINE

(cont.)

Captain Areia Darenga
1. The Fall of Worlds   '80 Avon
2. Unless She Burn   '81 Avon
3. No Earthly Shore   '81 Avon

MIALL, ROBERT (pseud., see JOHN BURKE)

MICHELINIE, DAVID
    (see "MARVEL SUPER-HEROES")

MIKSCH, WILLIAM (see "THE ADDAMS FAMILY")

MILAN, VICTOR
    (see collaboration with ROBERT E. VARDEMAN)

MILLER, CALVIN (b.1936)

Singreale Chronicles
1. Guardians of the Singreale   '82 Harpr
2. Star Riders of Ren   '83 Harpr
3. War of the Moonrhymes   '84 Harpr

MILLER, LEO E. (1887-1952)

The Hidden People
1. The Hidden People; The Story of a
   Search for Incan Treasure   '20 Scrib
2. In the Tiger's Lair   '21 Scrib

MILLS, ROBERT E.

The Star Quest Trilogy
1. Star Quest   '78 Belmt
2. Star Fighters   '78 Belmt
3. Star Force   '78 Belmt

MITFORD, BERTRAM (1855-1914)

Untuswa
1. The King's Assegai   1894 C&W
2. The White Shield   1895 Cass
3. The Word of the Sorceress   '02 Hutch

MOGRIDGE, STEPHEN

    <u>Peter</u>
1. Peter and the Flying Saucers   '54   Hutch
2. Peter and the Atomic Valley   '55   Hutch
3. Peter and the Moon Bomb   '56   Hutch

MOHOAO   (pseud., see EUGENE SUE)

MONACO, RICHARD   (b.1940)

    <u>Parsival</u>
1. Parsival, or A Knight's Tale   '77   Macm
2. The Grail War   '79   S&S
3. The Final Quest   '81   Putn
4. Blood and Dreams   '85   Berk

    <u>Runes</u>
1. Runes   '84   Ace
2. Broken Stone   '85   Ace

MONROE, DONALD   (1888-?) & KEITH MONROE   (b.1917)

    <u>Time Machine</u>   (pseud.— Donald Keith)
1. Mutiny in the Time Machine   '63   RandH
2. Time Machine to the Rescue   '67   RandH

MONTELEONE, THOMAS F. (see collaboration w. DAVID BISCHOFF)

MONTGOMERY, FRANCIS TREGO   (1858?-1925)

    <u>The Electric Elephant</u>
1. The Wonderful Electric Elephant   '03   Saalf
2. On a Lark to the Planets   '04   Saalf

MOON, SHEILA   (b.1910)

    <u>Maris</u>
1. Knee-Deep in Thunder   '67   Athen
2. Hunt Down the Prize   '71   Athen

MOORCOCK, MICHAEL   (b.1939)

                        (cont.)

Michael Kane
(originally under pseud.— Edward P. Bradbury)
1. Warriors of Mars '65 Comp
   aka: City of the Beast ('70/Lance)
2. Blades of Mars '65 Comp
   aka: The Lord of the Spiders ('70/Lance)
3. Barbarians of Mars '65 Comp
   aka: The Masters of the Pit ('70/Lance)

(pseud.— Bill Barclay)
1. Somewhere in the Night '66 Comp
   rev. as: The Chinese Agent ('70/Macm)
2. Printer's Devil '66 Comp
   rev. as: The Russian Intelligence ('80/Savoy)

The Runestaff
1. The Jewel in the Skull '67 Lance
   revised: ('77/DAW)
2. Sorcerer's Amulet '68 Lance
   aka: The Mad God's Amulet ('69/Mayfl)
3. The Sword of the Dawn '68 Lance
   revised: ('77/DAW)
4. The Secret of the Runestaff '69 Lance
   aka: The Runestaff ('69/Mayfl)

The Cornelius Chronicles (coll.'77/Avon)
1. The Final Programme '68 Avon
   aka: The Last Days of Man on Earth
2. A Cure For Cancer '71 A&B
3. The English Assassin '72 A&B
4. The Condition of Muzak '77 A&B
   related stories
5. The Lives and Times of Jerry Cornelius '76 A&B
6. The Adventures of Una Persson and Catherine
   Cornelius in the Twentieth Century '76 Quart
7. The Nature of the Catastrophe '71 Hutch
   (collection by Moorcock (5 stories) and
   others; edited by Michael Moorcock and
   Langdon Jones)
8. The Opium General '84 Harrp
   (contains one Cornelius novelette)

Karl Glogauer
1. Behold the Man '69 A&B
2. Breakfast in the Ruins '72 NEL

John Daker
1. The Eternal Champion '70 Dell
2. Phoenix in Obsidian '70 Mayfl
   aka: The Silver Warriors ('73/Dell)

(Michael Moorcock, cont.)

      The Nomad of Time
1. The Warlord of the Air   '71   Ace
2. The Land Leviathan   '74   Quart
3. The Steel Tsar   '81

      THE CHRONICLES OF CORUM
      The Swords Trilogy (coll.'77/Berk)
1. The Knight of the Swords   '71   Mayfl
2. The Queen of the Swords   '71   Berk
3. The King of the Swords   '71   Berk
      The Chronicles of Corum
4. The Bull and the Spear   '73   A&B
5. The Oak and the Ram   '73   A&B
6. The Sword and the Stallion   '74   Berk

      DANCERS AT THE END OF TIME/JERRY CARNELIAN SERIES
      The Dancers at the End of Time (coll.'76/Harpr)
1. An Alien Heat   '72   MacGi
2. The Hollow Lands   '74   Harpr
3. The End of All Songs   '76   Harpr
      additional titles
4. Legends From the End of Time   '76   Harpr
5. The Transformation of Miss Mavis Ming   '77   WHAll
    aka: A Messiah at the End of Time ('77/DAW)

      The Elric Saga
1. Elric of Melnibone   '72   Hutch
    abridged as: The Dreaming Jewels ('72/Lance)
2. The Sailor on the Seas of Fate   '76   Quart
3. The Weird of the White Wolf   '77   DAW
4. The Sleeping Sorceress   '71   NEL
    aka: The Vanishing Tower ('77/DAW)
5. The Bane of the Black Sword   '77   DAW
6. Stormbringer   '65   Jenk
    revised and expanded: ('77/DAW)
7. Elric at the End of Time   '85   DAW
    (additional titles)
8. The Stealer of Souls, and Other Stories   '63   Spear
9. Elric, the Return to Melnibone   '73   Unicn

      Count Brass
1. Count Brass   '73   Mayfl
2. Champion of Garathorm   '73   Mayfl
3. Quest For Tanelorn   '75   Mayfl

      Pyat
1. Byzantium Endures (revised: '81/RandH)   '80   Seck
2. The Laughter of Carthage   '84   RandH

MOORE, PATRICK (b.1923)

Grenfell and Wright
1. The Master of the Moon   '52   MusPr
2. The Island of Fear   '54   MusPr

Gregory Quest
1. Quest of the Spaceways   '55   Mullr
2. World of Mists   '56   Mullr

Maurice Gray
1. Mission to Mars   '55   Burke
2. The Domes of Mars   '56   Burke
3. The Voices of Mars   '57   Burke
4. Peril on Mars   '58   Burke
5. Raiders of Mars   '59   Burke

Robin North
1. Wanderer in Space   '61   Burke
2. Crater of Fear   '62   Burke
3. Invader From Space   '63   Burke
4. Caverns of the Moon   '64   Burke

MOORE, WALLACE (pseud. of Gerald F. Conway)

Balzan of the Cat People
1. The Bloodstone   '74   Pyr
2. The Caves of Madness   '75   Pyr
3. The Lights of Zetar   '75   Pyr

MORGAN, DAN (b.1925)

also see: collaboration with JOHN KIPPAX

Sixth Perception
1. The New Minds   '67   Corgi
2. The Several Minds   '69   Corgi
3. Mind Trap   '70   Avon
4. The Country of the Mind   '75

MORRESSY, JOHN (b.1930)

Del Whitby
1. Starbrat   '72   Walkr
2. Nail Down the Stars   '73   Walkr
    aka: Stardrift ('75/Pop)
3. Under a Calculating Star   '75   Dbdy

(John Morressy, cont.)

Iron Angel Series
1. Ironbrand   '80   Play
2. Greymantle   '81   Play
3. Kingsbane   '82   Play
4. The Time of the Annihilator   '85   Ace

MORRIS, JANET   (b.1946)

    also see: ROBERT LYNN ASPRIN, "Sanctuary"

Silistra Series
1. High Couch of Silistra   '77   Bant
    aka: Returning Creation ('84/Baen)
2. The Golden Sword   '77   Bant
3. Wind From the Abyss   '78   Bant
4. The Carnellian Throne   '79   Bant

The Kerrion Empire
1. Dream Dancer   '81   Putn
2. Cruiser Dreams   '81   Berk
3. Earth Dreams   '82   Berk

MUMFORD, E.E. (b.1932)

The Five Flights of the Starfire (coll.'74/Expo)
1. Flight of the Starfire   '72   Expo
2. The Second Flight of the Starfire   '72   Expo
3. The Third Flight of the Starfire   '72   Expo
4. The Fourth Flight of the Starfire   '73   Expo
5. The Voyage of the Starfire to Atlantis '73   Expo

"MUNCHAUSEN"   (see "BARON MUNCHAUSEN")

MUNDY, TALBOT
    (pseud. of William Lancaster Gribbon, 1879-1940)

The Jimgrim/Ramsden Series
(Note-- these titles are all related to some extent, though major characters in one volume may be minor ones in another, and some books may be connected only through references to events in previous stories. The titles are roughly arranged in order of publication).

1. King-- of the Khybers   '16   Bob-M
     aka: King-- of the Khyber Rifles
2. The Winds of the World   '16   Cass
3. Hira Singh's Tale   '18   Cass
4. Guns of the Gods   '21   Hutch
5. The Caves of Terror   '24   Hutch
6. Om: The Secret of Ahbor Valley   '24   Hutch
7. The Nine Unknown   '24   Hutch
8. Ramsden   '26   Hutch
     aka: The Devil's Guard ('26/Bob-M)
9. The Woman Ayisha   '30   Hutch
10. The Hundred Days   '30   Hutch
11. Jimgrim   '31   Hutch
     aka: Jimgrim Sahib ('53/Universal)
12. The Lost Trooper   '31   Hutch
13. C.I.D.   '32   Hutch
14. Jungle Jest   '32   Hutch
15. The Lion of Petra   '32   Hutch
16. The King in Check   '33   Hutch
     aka: Affair in Araby ('53/Universal)
17. The Gunga Sahib   '33   Hutch
18. The Mystery of Khufu's Tomb   '33   Hutch
19. Jimgrim and Allah's Peace   '33   Hutch
20. The Red Flame of Erinpura   '34   Hutch
21. The Seventeen Thieves of El-Kalil   '35   Hutch
22. The Thunder Dragon Gate   '37   Hutch
23. Old Ugly Face   '39   Hutch

     Tros of Samothrace
1. Tros of Samothrace   '34   Apple
     (4-volume edition)
   (A) Tros   ('67/Avon)
   (B) Helma   ('67/Avon)
   (C) Liafail ('67/Avon)
   (D) Helene ('67/Avon)
     (3-volume edition)
   (A) Lud of Lunden   ('76)
   (B) Avenging Liafail ('76)
   (C) The Praetor's Dungeon   ('76)
2. Queen Cleopatra   '29   Bob-M
3. Purple Pirate   '35   Apple
     aka: The Purple Pirate

MUNN, H. WARNER (1903-1981)

     Tales of the Werewolf Clan
1. The Werewolf of Ponkert   '29/'58 Grand
                         (cont.)

(H. Warner Munn, cont.)

   2. Tales of the Werewolf Clan I: In the
      Tomb of the Bishop   '79 Grant
   3. Tales of the Werewolf Clan II: The
      Master Goes Home

      The Merlin Trilogy *
   1. King of the World's Edge   '66 Ace
   2. The Ship From Atlantis   '67 Ace
   3. Merlin's Ring   '74 Ball
      * volumes 1 & 2 combined as: "Merlin's Godson"
                               ('76/Ball)

"THE MUNSTERS"

   1. The Munsters (Morton Cooper)   '64 Avon
   2. The Munsters and the Great Camera Caper   '65 Whitm
      (William Johnston)
   3. The Last Resort (William Johnston)   '66 Whitm

MURDOCH, M.S. (see "STAR TREK")

MURPHY, SHIRLEY ROUSSEAU (b.1928)

      The Children of Ynell/aka: The Seers of Ere
   1. The Ring of Fire   '77 Athen
   2. The Wolf Bell   '79 Athen
   3. The Castle of Hape   '80 Athen
   4. Caves of Fire and Ice   '80 Athen
   5. The Joining of the Stone   '81 Athen

N

NATHAN, ROBERT (b.1894)

    Professor Wutheridge
1. The Bishop's Wife   '28 Bob-M
   (Note-- The Professor is only a minor character in this book)
2. There Is Another Heaven   '29 Bob-M

    The Adventures of Tapiola (coll.'50)
1. Journey of Tapiola   '38 Knopf
2. Tapiola's Brave Regiment   '41 Knopf

NEILL, JOHN R. (see L. FRANK BAUM, "Oz" series)

NEILSON, ERIC

    Haakon
1. The Golden Ax   '84 Bant
2. The Viking's Revenge   '84 Bant
3. Haakon's Iron Hand   '84 Bant
4. The War God   '84 Bant

NESBIT, EDITH (1858-1924)

    The Five Children (coll.'30/CowMc)
1. The Five Children and It   '02 Unwin
2. The Phoenix and the Carpet   '04 Newne
3. The Story of the Amulet   '06 Unwin

    Arden
1. The House of Arden   '08 Unwin
2. Harding's Luck   '09 H&S

NEWMAN, PAUL S. (see "THE INVADERS")

NEWMAN, ROBERT (b.1909)

    Tertius
1. Merlin's Mistake   '70 Athen
2. The Testing of Tertius   '73 Athen

NEWMAN, SHARAN

Guinevere
1. Guinevere '81 StM
2. The Chessboard Queen '83 StM
3. Guinevere Evermore '85 StM

NIVEN, LARRY (b.1938)

also see: "BUCK ROGERS"
also see: collaboration with JERRY POURNELLE

Tales of Known Space
1. Tales of Known Space '75 Ball
2. World of Ptavvs '66 Ball
3. The Long ARM of Gil Hamilton '76 Ball
4. Protector '73 Ball
5. A Gift From Earth '68 Ball
6. Neutron Star '68 Ball
7. Ringworld '70 Ball
8. Ringworld Engineers '79 Phant

NIZZI, GUIDO "SKIPPER" (b.1900)

The Paralyzing Ray
1. The Victor '46 Expo
2. The Paralyzing Ray Vs. The Nuclears '64 Vant
3. The Daring Trip to the Moon '68 Carlt

NOLAN, WILLIAM F. (b.1928)

Logan
1. Logan's Run
   (written with George Clayton Johnson) '67 Dial
2. Logan's World '77 Bant
3. Logan's Search '80 Bant

Space For Hire
1. Space For Hire '71 Lance
2. Look Out For Space '84 IPL

NOONE, EDWINA (pseud., see MICHAEL AVALLONE)

NORMAN, JOHN (b.1931)

(cont.)

Gor *

1. Tarnsman of Gor — '66 Ball
2. Outlaw of Gor — '67 Ball
3. Priest-Kings of Gor — '68 Ball
4. Nomads of Gor — '69 Ball
5. Assassin of Gor — '70 Ball
6. Raiders of Gor — '71 Ball
7. Captive of Gor — '72 Ball
8. Hunters of Gor — '74 DAW
9. Marauders of Gor — '75 DAW
10. Tribesmen of Gor — '76 DAW
11. Slave Girl of Gor — '77 DAW
12. Beasts of Gor — '78 DAW
13. Explorers of Gor — '79 DAW
14. Fighting Slave of Gor — '80 DAW
15. Rogue of Gor — '81 DAW
16. Guardsman of Gor — '81 DAW
17. Savages of Gor — '82 DAW
18. Blood Brothers of Gor — '83 DAW
19. Kajira of Gor — '83 DAW
20. Players of Gor — '84 DAW
21. Mercenaries of Gor — '85 DAW

* Titles 1-3 collected as: Gor Omnibus ('72/S&J)

NORTH, ANDREW (pseud., see ANDRE NORTON)

NORTON, ANDRE (b.1912)

Astra Sequence
1. The Stars Are Ours! — '54 World
2. Star Born — '57 World

Dane Thorson/aka: Solar Queen
1. Sargasso of Space (pseud.— Andrew North) — '55 Gnome
2. Plague Ship (pseud.— Andrew North) — '56 Gnome
3. Voodoo Planet (pseud.— Andrew North) — '59 Ace
4. Postmarked the Stars — '69 Harc

Blake Walker
1. The Crossroads of Time — '56 Ace
2. Quest Crosstime — '65 Vik

Ross Murdock/aka: Time Agents
1. The Time Traders — '58 World
2. Galactic Derelict — '59 World
3. The Defiant Agents — '62 World
4. Key Out of Time — '63 World

(Andre Norton, cont.)

Hosteen Storm
1. The Beast Master — '59 Harc
2. Lord of Thunder — '62 Harc

The Forerunner Series
1. Storm Over Warlock — '60 World
2. Ordeal in Otherwhere — '64 World
3. Forerunner Foray — '73 Vik
4. Forerunner — '81 Tor
5. Forerunner: The Second Venture — '85 Tor

Dipple
1. Catseye — '61 Harc
2. Judgement on Janus
   (also see "Janus" sequence) — '63 Harc

Janus Sequence/aka: Niall Renfro
1. Judgement on Janus — '63 Harc
2. Victory on Janus — '66 Harc

Witch World (in order of publication)
1. Witch World — '63 Ace
2. Web of the Witch World — '64 Ace
3. Year of the Unicorn — '65 Ace
4. Three Against the Witch World — '65 Ace
5. Warlock of the Witch World — '67 Ace
6. Sorceress of the Witch World — '68 Ace
7. Spell of the Witch World — '72 DAW
8. The Crystal Gryphon
   (Kerovan & Joison v.1) — '72 Athen
9. The Jargoon Pard — '74 Athen
10. The Trey of Swords — '77 G&D
11. Zarsthor's Bane — '78 Ace
12. Lore of the Witch World — '80 DAW
13. Gryphon in Glory
    (Kerovan & Joison v.2) — '81 Athen
14. Ware Hawk — '83 Athen
15. Gryphon's Eyrie
    (Kerovan & Joison v.3) — '85 StM
    (in collaboration with A.C. Crispin)

Moon Singer/aka: Lyndis
1. Moon of Three Rings — '66 Vik
2. Exiles of the Stars — '71 Vik

Murdoc Jern
1. The Zero Stone — '68 Vik
2. Uncharted Stars — '69 Vik

Star Ka'at Series
(in collaboration with Dorothy Madlee)
1. Star Ka'at   '76 Walkr
2. Star Ka'at World   '78 Walkr
3. Star Ka'ats and the Plant People   '79 Walkr
4. Star Ka'ats and the Winged Invaders   '81 Walkr

NORTON, MARY (b.1903)

Bed-Knob and Broomstick (coll.'57/Dent)
1. The Magic Bed-Knob   '43 Hyper
2. Bonfires and Broomsticks   '47 Dent

The Borrowers *
1. The Borrowers   '52 Dent
2. The Borrowers Afield   '55 Dent
3. The Borrowers Afloat   '59 Dent
4. The Borrowers Aloft   '61 Dent
5. The Borrowers Avenged   '84 Harc
   * Titles 1-4 collected as:
     The Borrowers Omnibus ('66/Dent)

NORVIL, MANNING (pseud., see KENNETH BULMER)

NORWOOD, VICTOR (b.1920)

Jacare
1. The Untamed   '51 Scion
2. Caves of Death   '51 Scion
3. The Temple of the Dead   '51 Scion
4. The Skull of Kanaima   '51 Scion
5. The Island of Creeping Death   '52 Scion
6. Cry of the Beast   '52 Scion

NORWOOD, WARREN G.

The Windhover Tapes
1. An Image of Voices   '82 Bant
2. Fize of the Gabriel Ratchets   '83 Bant
3. Flexing the Warp   '83 Bant
4. The Planet of Flowers   '84 Bant

The Double Spiral War
1. Midway Between   '84 Bant
2. Polar Fleet   '85 Bant
3. Final Command   (NYP)

NOWLAN, PHILIP FRANCIS (1888-1940)   (see "BUCK ROGERS")

NUETZEL, CHARLES (b.1934)

    Noomas
1. Warriors of Noomas   '69 Powel
2. Raiders of Noomas   '69 Powel

NYBERG, BJORN (see ROBERT E. HOWARD, "Conan" series)

O'DONNELL, KEVIN Jr. (b.1950)

   The Journeys of McGill Feighan
1. Caverns   '81 Berk
2. Reefs   '81 Berk
3. Lava   '82 Berk

O'DUFFY, EIMAR (1893-1935)

   King Goshawk/Aloysius O'Kennedy
1. King Goshawk and the Birds   '26 Macm
2. The Spacious Adventures of the Man in the Street   '28 Macm
3. Asses in Clover   '33 Putn

OFFUTT, ANDREW J. (b.1937)

   also see: ROBERT E. HOWARD, "Conan" series

   Cormac Mac Art
1. Sword of the Gael   '75 Zebra
2. The Undying Wizard   '76 Zebra
3. Sign of the Moonbow   '77 Zebra
4. The Mists of Doom   '77 Zebra
5. The Tower of Death   '80 Ace
6. When Death Birds Fly   '80 Ace

   War of the Wizards
1. Demon in the Mirror   '78 PB
2. Eyes of Sarsis   '80 PB
3. Web of the Spider   '81 PB

   War of the Gods on Earth
1. The Iron Lords   '79 Jove
2. Shadows Out of Hell   '80 Berk
3. The Lady of the Snowmist   '83 Ace

   Spaceways (pseud.— John Cleve)
1. Of Alien Bondage   '82 Play
2. Corundum's Woman   '82 Play
3. Escape From Macho   '82 Play
4. Satana Enslaved   '82 Play

(cont.)

(Andrew J. Offutt, "Spaceways", cont.)

5. Master of Misfit	'82	Play
6. Purrfect Plunder	'82	Play
7. The Manhuntress	'82	Play
8. Under Twin Suns	'82	Play
9. The Quest of Qalara	'83	
10. The Yoke of Shen	'83	
11. The Iceworld Connection	'83	
12. Star Slaver	'83	
13. Jonuta Rising!	'83	
14. Assignment: Hellhole	'83	
15. Starship Sapphire	'84	Berk
16. The Planet Murderer	'84	Berk
17. Carnadyne Hoard	'84	Berk
18. A Race Across the Stars	'84	Berk
19. King of the Slavers	'85	Berk

OHLSON, HEREWARD

Thunderbolt
1. Thunderbolt of the Spaceways	'54	Luttr
2. Thunderbolt and the Rebel Planet	'54	Luttr

OLIPHANT, MARGARET (1828-1897)

The Little Pilgrim
1. A Little Pilgrim	1882	MacmL
2. The Land of Darkness, with Some Further Chapters in the Experiences of The Little Pilgrim	1888	MacmL

OLIVER, FREDERICK S. (see PHYLOS THE TIBETAN, pseud.)

"THE OMEN"

1. The Omen (David Seltzer)	'76	Sign
2. Damien: Omen II (Joseph Howard)	'78	Sign
3. Omen III: The Final Conflict (Gordon McGill)	'80	Sign
4. Omen IV: Armageddon 2000 (Gordon McGill)	'82	Sign
5. Omen V: The Abomination (Gordon McGill)	'85	Sign

ORAM, JOHN (see "U.N.C.L.E.")

ORWELL, GEORGE (pseud. of Eric Arthur Blair) (1903-1950)

    1984
1. 1984   '49 Seck
   (sequel)
2. 1985 (by Gyorgy Dalos)   '83 Pluto

O'SHEA, SEAN (pseud., see ROBERT TRALINS)

OWEN, FRANK (1893-1968)

    Scobee Trent
1. Rare Earth   '31 Lantn
2. The House Mother   '29 Lantn

PAGE, NORVELL W. (1904-1961)

    also see: "THE SPIDER"

    Prester John
1. Flame Winds   '39/'69 Berk
2. Sons of the Bear-God   '39/'69 Berk

PAL, GEORGE (b.1908) (see H.G. WELLS)

PALMER, BERNARD (b.1914)

    Pat Collins
1. Pat Collins and the Peculiar Dr. Brockton '57 Moody
2. Pat Collins and the Secret Engine   '57 Moody
3. Pat Collins and the Hidden Treasure '57 Moody
4. Pat Collins and the Wingless Plane   '57 Moody
5. Pat Collins and the Mysterious Orbiting Rocket
                                           '58 Moody
6. Pat Collins and the Captive Scientist '58 Moody

    Jim Dunlap
1. Jim Dunlap and the Strange Dr. Brockton '67 Moody
   (revision of Pat Collins #1)
2. Jim Dunlap and the Secret Rocket Formula '67 Moody
   (revision of Pat Collins #2)
3. Jim Dunlap and the Wingless Plane   '68 Moody
   (revision of Pat Collins #4)
                        (cont.)

(Bernard Palmer, cont.)

    4. Jim Dunlap and the Mysterious Orbiting Rocket
       (revision of Pat Collins #5)   '68 Moody
    5. Jim Dunlap and the Long Lunar Walk   '74 Moody
    6. Jim Dunlap and the Mysterious Spy   '74 Moody

PANSHIN, ALEXEI (b.1940)

    Anthony Villiers
    1. Star Well   '68 Ace
    2. The Thurb Revolution   '68 Ace
    3. Masque World   '69 Ace

PANTELL, DORA (see ELLEN McGREGOR, "Miss Pickerell")

PATERNOSTER, SIDNEY (1866-?)

    The Motor Pirate
    1. The Motor Pirate   '03 C&W
    2. The Cruise of the Conqueror, Being the
       Further Adventures of the Motor Pirate   '06 Page

PAUL, F.W. (pseud., see PAUL W. FAIRMAN)

PAXSON, DIANA

    The Books of Westria
    1. Lady of Light   '82 PB
    2. Lady of Darkness   '83 PB

PEAKE, MERVYN (1911-1968)

    The Gormenghast Trilogy
    1. Titus Groan   '46 Eyre
    2. Gormenghast   '50 Eyre
    3. Titus Alone   '59 Eyre

PEARL, JACK (b.1923)

    Space Eagle
    1. Space Eagle; Operation Doomsday   '67 Whitm
    2. The Space Eagle; Operation Star Voyage   '70 Whitm

PEMBERTON, MAX (1863-1950)

    Captain Black
1. The Iron Pirate   1893 Cass
    aka: The Shadow on the Sea ('07/Westbrook)
2. Captain Black   '11 Cass

"PERRY RHODAN"

    NOTE: Series created by Walter Ernsting and
          Karl-Herbert Scheer
    Other authors are: Kurt Mahr
                         William Voltz
                         Clark Darlton
                            (pseud. of Walter Ernsting)
                         Kurt Brand
                         W.W. Shols
                         Ernst Vlcek
                         Hans Kneifel

    Perry Rhodan
1. Enterprise Stardust (Scheer & Ernsting) '69 Ace
2. The Radiant Dome (Scheer & Ernsting)   '69 Ace
3. Galactic Alarm (Mahr & Shols)   '69 Ace
4. Invasion From Space (Ernsting & Mahr)   '70 Ace
5. The Vega Sector (Scheer & Mahr)   '70 Ace
6. Secret of the Time Vault (Darlton)   '71 Ace
7. Fortress of the Six Moons (Scheer)   '71 Ace
8. The Galactic Riddle (Darlton)   '71 Ace
9. Quest Through Space and Time (Darlton) '71 Ace
10. The Ghosts of Gol (Mahr)   '71 Ace
11. Planet of the Dying Sun (Mahr)   '72 Ace
12. Rebels of Tuglan (Darlton)   '72 Ace
13. The Immortal Unknown (Darlton)   '72 Ace
14. Venus in Danger (Mahr)   '72 Ace
15. Escape to Venus (Mahr)   '72 Ace
16. Secret Barrier X (Shols)   '72 Ace
17. The Venus Trap (Mahr)   '72 Ace
18. Menace of the Mutant Monster (Darlton) '72 Ace
19. Mutants Vs. Mutants (Darlton)   '72 Ace
20. The Thrall of Hypno (Darlton)   '72 Ace
21. The Cosmic Decoy (Scheer)   '73 Ace
22. Fleet of the Springers (Mahr)   '73 Ace
23. Peril of the Ice Planet (Mahr)   '73 Ace
24. Infinity Flight (Darlton)   '73 Ace
25. Snowman in Flames (Darlton)   '73 Ace
26. Cosmic Traitor (Darlton)   '73 Ace
27. Planet of the Gods (Mahr)   '73 Ace
                         (cont.)

("Perry Rhodan", cont.)

#	Title	Author	Year	Publisher
28.	The Plague of Oblivion	(Darlton)	'73	Ace
29.	A World Gone Mad	(Darlton)	'73	Ace
30.	To Arkon!	(Darlton)	'73	Ace
31.	Realm of the Tri-Planets	(Scheer)	'73	Ace
32.	Challenge of the Unknown	(Darlton)	'73	Ace
33.	The Giant's Partner	(Darlton)	'73	Ace
34.	SOS: Spaceship Titan	(Brand)	'73	Ace
35.	Beware the Microbots	(Mahr)	'73	Ace
36.	Man and Monster	(Scheer)	'73	Ace
37.	Epidemic Center: Aralon	(Darlton)	'74	Ace
38.	Project: Earthsave	(Brand)	'74	Ace
39.	The Silence of Gom	(Mahr)	'74	Ace
40.	The Red Eye of Betelgeuse	(Darlton)	'74	Ace
41.	The Earth Dies	(Darlton)	'74	Ace
42.	Time's Lonely One	(Scheer)	'74	Ace
43.	Life Hunt	(Brand)	'74	Ace
44.	The Pseudo One	(Darlton)	'74	Ace
45.	Unknown Sector: Milky Way	(Mahr)	'74	Ace
46.	Again: Atlan!	(Scheer)	'74	Ace
47.	Shadow of the Mutant Master	(Brand)	'74	Ace
48.	The Dead Live	(Darlton)	'74	Ace
49.	Solar Assassins	(Mahr)	'74	Ace
50.	Attack From the Unseen	(Darlton)	'74	Ace
51.	Return From the Void	(Mahr)	'74	Ace
52.	Fortress Atlantis	(Scheer)	'74	Ace
53.	Spybot!	(Darlton)	'74	Ace
54.	The Blue Dwarfs	(Mahr)	'74	Ace
55.	The Micro-Techs	(Darlton)	'74	Ace
56.	Prisoner of Time	(Darlton)	'74	Ace
57.	A Touch of Eternity	(Darlton)	'74	Ace
58.	The Guardians	(Mahr)	'74	Ace
59.	Interlude on Siliko 5	(Brand)	'74	Ace
60.	Dimension Search	(Mahr)	'74	Ace
61.	Death Waits in Semispace	(Mahr)	'75	Ace
62.	The Last Days of Atlantis	(Scheer)	'75	Ace
63.	The Tigris Leaps	(Brand)	'75	Ace
64.	Ambassadors From Auriegel	(Mahr)	'75	Ace
65.	Renegades of the Future	(Mahr)	'75	Ace
66.	The Horror	(Voltz)	'75	Ace
67.	Crimson Universe	(Scheer)	'75	Ace
68.	Under the Stars of Druufon	(Darlton)	'75	Ace
69.	The Bonds of Eternity	(Darlton)	'75	Ace
70.	Thora's Sacrifice	(Brand)	'75	Ace
71.	The Atom Hell of Grautier	(Mahr)	'75	Ace
72.	Caves of the Druufs	(Mahr)	'75	Ace
73.	Spaceship of Ancestors	(Darlton)	'75	Ace
74.	Checkmate: Universe	(Mahr)	'75	Ace
75.	Planet Topside, Please Reply	(Brand)	'75	Ace

#	Title	Author	Year	Publisher
76.	Recruits For Arkon	(Darlton)	'75	Ace
77.	Conflict Center: Naator	(Darlton)	'75	Ace
78.	Power Key	(Scheer)	'75	Ace
79.	The Sleepers	(Voltz)	'75	Ace
80.	The Columbus Affair	(Scheer)	'75	Ace
81.	Pucky's Greatest Hour	(Brand)	'75	Ace
82.	Atlan in Danger	(Brand)	'75	Ace
83.	Ernst Ellert Returns	(Darlton)	'75	Ace
84.	Secret Mission: Moluk	(Mahr)	'75	Ace
85.	Enemy in the Dark	(Mahr)	'76	Ace
86.	Blazing Sun	(Darlton)	'76	Ace
87.	The Starless Realm	(Darlton)	'76	Ace
88.	Mystery of the Anti	(Scheer)	'76	Ace
89.	Power's Price	(Brand)	'76	Ace
90.	Unleashed Powers	(Brand)	'76	Ace
91.	Friend to Mankind	(Voltz)	'76	Ace
92.	Target Star	(Scheer)	'76	Ace
93.	Vagabond of Space	(Darlton)	'76	Ace
94.	Action: Division Three	(Mahr)	'76	Ace
95.	Plasma Monster	(Mahr)	'76	Ace
96.	Horn: Green	(Voltz)	'76	Ace
97.	Phantom Fleet	(Darlton)	'76	Ace
98.	Idol From Passa	(Mahr)	'76	Ace
99.	Blue System	(Scheer)	'76	Ace
100.	Desert of Death	(Mahr)	'76	Ace
101.	Blockade: Lepso	(Brand)	'76	Ace
102.	Spoor of the Antis	(Voltz)	'76	Ace
103.	False Front	(Darlton)	'76	Ace
104.	The Man With Two Faces	(Brand)	'76	Ace
105.	Wonderflower of Utik	(Mahr)	'76	Ace
106.	Caller From Eternity	(Brand)	'76	Ace
107.	The Emperor and the Monster	(Voltz)	'76	Ace
108.	Duel Under the Double Sun	(Scheer)	'76	Ace

(Note: the following were published 2 titles per volume)

#	Title	Author	Year	Publisher
109.	The Stolen Spacefleet	(Darlton)	'77	Ace
110.	Sgt. Robot	(Mahr)	'77	Ace
111.	Seeds of Ruin	(Voltz)	'77	Ace
112.	Planet Mechanica	(Scheer)	'77	Ace
113.	Heritage of the Lizard People	(Darlton)	'77	Ace
114.	Death's Demand	(Mahr)	'77	Ace
115.	Saboteurs in A-1	(Brand)	'77	Ace
116.	The Psycho Duel	(Voltz)	'77	Ace
117.	Savior of the Empire	(Scheer)	'77	Ace
118.	The Shadows Attack	(Darlton)	'77	Ace

(The following were released as booklets from Master Publications)

#	Title	Author	Year	Publisher
119.	Between the Galaxies	(Mahr)	'78	Mastr
120.	Killers From Hyperspace	(Voltz)	'78	Mastr

(cont.)

("Perry Rhodan", cont.)

121.	Atom Fire on Mechanica (Darlton)	'78	Mastr
122.	Volunteers For Frago (Brand)	'78	Mastr
123.	Fortress in Time (Mahr)	'78	Mastr
124.	The Sinister Power (Brand)	'78	Mastr
125.	Robots, Bombs and Mutants (Voltz)	'79	Mastr
126.	The Guns of Everblack (Scheer)	'79	Mastr
127.	Sentinels of Solitude (Darlton)	'79	Mastr
128.	The Beasts Below (Mahr)	'79	Mastr
129.	Blitzkrieg Galactica (Brand)	'79	Mastr
130.	Peril Unlimited (Brand)	'79	Mastr
131.	World Without Mercy (Voltz)	'79	Mastr
132.	Deadmen Shouldn't Die (Darlton)	'79	Mastr
133.	Station of the Invisibles (Mahr)	'79	Mastr
134.	Agents of Destruction (Brand)	'79	Mastr
135.	Humans Keep Out! (Voltz)	'79	Mastr
136.	The Robot Invitation (Scheer)	'79	Mastr
137.	Phantom Horde (Darlton)	'79	Mastr

(# 137 bound with 5 episodes of "Star Man" by S.J. Byrne)
(see S.J. Byrne for titles listings)

Perry Rhodan Specials
(NOTE: The first four Specials contains 2 stories, some in the "Perry Rhodan" series, others in the "Atlan" series, which is also tied-in with Perry Rhodan's adventures.

1. Perry Rhodan #1: The Wasp Men Attack (Shols)
    Atlan #1: Spider Desert (Vlcek)   '77 Ace
2. Perry Rhodan #2: Menace of Atomigeddon (Mahr)
    Atlan #2: Flight From Tarkihl (Darlton) '77 Ace
3. Perry Rhodan #3: Robot Threat: New York (Shols)
    Atlan #3: Pale Country Pursuit (Kneifel) '77 Ace
4. Atlan #4: The Crystal Prince (Scheer)
    Atlan #5: War of the Ghosts (Darlton)   '77 Ace
5. Perry Rhodan #4: In the Center of the Galaxy
    (Darlton) (this is a full-length novel) '78 Ace

PETAJA, EMIL (b.1915)

The Kalevala Sequence
1. Saga of Lost Earths   '66 Ace
2. The Star Mill   '66 Ace
3. The Stolen Sun   '67 Ace
4. Tramontane   '67 Ace

Diarmid O'Dowd/aka: Green Planet
1. Lord of the Green Planet '67 Ace
2. Doom of the Green Planet '68 Ace

PFEIL, DON (see "PERRY RHODAN")

PHILLIFENT, JOHN T. (1916-1976)

    also see: "U.N.C.L.E."

    Space Puppet
1. Space Puppet   '54 TitB
2. The Master Weed   '54 TitB
3. Jupiter Equilateral   '54 TitB
4. Alien Virus   '54 TitB

PHILLIPS, MARK
    (pseud., see RANDALL GARRETT or LAURENCE M. JANIFER)

PHYLOS THE TIBETAN
    (pseud. of FREDERICK S. OLIVER, 1866-1899)

    Zalim
1. A Dweller on Two Planets   '05 Baumg
2. An Earth Dweller's Return   '40 Lemur

PIERCE, MEREDITH ANN (b.1958)

    Aeriel
1. The Darkangel   '82 LtBrn
2. A Gathering of Gargoyles   '84 LtBrn

PIERCE, TAMORA

    Song of the Lioness
1. Alanna   '83 Athen
2. In the Hand of The Goddess   '84 Athen

PINKWATER, DANIEL

    The Snarkout Boys
1. The Snarkout Boys and the Avocado of Death
2. The Snarkout Boys and the Baconburg Horror
    '84 WmMorw

PIPER, H. BEAM (1904-1964)
                          (cont.)

(H. Beam Piper, cont.)

The Fuzzy Series *
1. Little Fuzzy   '62 Avon
2. The Other Human Race   '64 Avon
   aka: Fuzzy Sapiens ('76/Ace)
3. Fuzzies and Other People   '84 Ace
   (sequels)
4. Fuzzy Bones (by William Tuning)   '81 Ace
5. Golden Dream: A Fuzzy Odyssey
   (by Ardath Mayhar)   '82 Ace

The Paratime Police/Lord Kalvan
1. Lord Kalvan of Otherwhen   '65 Ace
   aka: Gunpowder God ('78/Spher)
2. Paratime   '81 Ace
   (sequel)
3. Great Kings' War
   (by Roland King & John F. Carr)   '85 Ace

"PLANET OF THE APES"

PLANET OF THE APES
1. Planet of the Apes (Pierre Boulle)   '63 Vang
   movie adaptations
2. Beneath the Planet of the Apes
   (Michael Avallone)   '70 Bant
3. Escape From the Planet of the Apes
   (Jerry Pournelle)   '73 Award
4. Conquest of the Planet of the Apes
   (John Jakes)   '74 Award
5. Battle For the Planet of the Apes
   (David Gerrold)   '73 Award
   TV-series adaptations
6. Man the Fugitive (George Alec Effinger)   '74 Award
7. Escape to Tomorrow (George Alec Effinger)   '75 Award
8. Journey Into Terror (George Alec Effinger)   '75 Award
9. Lord of the Apes (George Alec Effinger)   '76 Award
   Return to the Planet of the Apes
   (written under House Pseud.-- William Arrow)
10. Visions of Nowhere (William Rotsler)   '76 Ball
11. Escape From Terror Lagoon (Don Pfeil)   '76 Ball
12. Man the Hunted Animal (William Rotsler)   '76 Ball

POE, EDGAR ALLAN (1809-1849)

Arthur Gordon Pym *

(cont.)

1. The Narrative of Arthur Gordon Pym
   of Nantucket...   1838   Harrp
   aka: Arthur Gordon Pym; or, Shipwreck...
                                   (1841/Cunni)
   aka: The Wonderful Adventures of
        Arthur Gordon Pym (1861/WKent)
   (sequels)
2. An Antarctic Mystery (by Jules Verne)
                                             1898   Low,M
3. A Strange Discovery (by Charles Romyn Dake)
                                             1899   Kimbl
   * NOTE-- Titles 1 & 2 are collected as:
     The Mystery of Arthur Gordon Pym ('60/Arco)

POHL, FREDERIK (b.1919)

    The Space Merchants
1. The Space Merchants
   (with C.M. Kornbluth)   '53   Ball
2. The Merchants' War   '85   StM

    Eden Series (with Jack Williamson)
1. Undersea Quest   '54   Gnome
2. Undersea Fleet   '56   Gnome
3. Undersea City   '58   Gnome

    The Starchild Trilogy (with Jack Williamson)
                             (coll.'77/PbLib)
1. The Reefs of Space   '64   Ball
2. Starchild   '65   Ball
3. Rogue Star   '69   Ball

    The Saga of Cuckoo (coll.'83)
   (with Jack Williamson)
1. Farthest Star   '75   Ball
2. Wall Around a Star   '83   DelR

    The Heechee Trilogy (with Jack Williamson)
1. Gateway   '77   StM
2. Beyond the Blue Event Horizon   '80   Ball
3. Heechee Rendezvous   '84   DelR

POTOCKI, JAN (1761-1815)

    The Saragossa Manuscript
1. The Saragossa Manuscript; A Collection
   of Weird Tales   '60   Orion
                          (cont.)

(Jan Potocki, cont.)

2. The New Decameron; Further Tales From
   the Saragossa Manuscript   '67   Orion

POURNELLE, JERRY (b.1933)

    also see: "BUCK ROGERS"
    also see: "PLANET OF THE APES"

THE CODOMINIUM SERIES
  Falkenberg
1. West of Honor   '76   Laser
2. The Mercenary   '77   PB
  Post-Falkenberg titles
3. A Spaceship For the King   '73   DAW
4. The Mote in God's Eye
   (written with Larry Niven)   '74   S&S
5. King David's Spaceship   '81   S&S

  Janissaries
1. Janissaries   '79   Ace
2. Janissaries: Clan and Crown   '83   Ace

  There Will Be War (editor and series creator)
1. There Will Be War   '83   Tor
2. Men of War   '84   Tor
3. Blood and Iron   '84   Tor
4. Day of the Tyrant   '85   Tor

PRATT, FLETCHER
    (see collaboration with L. SPRAGUE DE CAMP)

PRESCOTT, DRAY (see KENNETH BULMER)

PRICE, ROGER

  The Tomorrow People
1. The Tomorrow People in "The Visitor"   '73   Picco
   (written with Julian R. Gregory)
2. The Tomorrow People in "Three in Three"   '74   Picco

"THE PRISONER"
                     (cont.)

1. The Prisoner (Thomas Disch)   '69 Ace
2. Number Two (David McDaniel)   '70 Ace
3. A Day in the Life (Hank Stine)   '70 Ace

PROCTOR, GEO. W.
        see: collaboration with ROBERT E. VARDEMAN
        also see: "U.N.C.L.E."
        also see: "V"

"PSI PATROL"

1. Sal's Book   '85 Schol
2. Hendra's Book (Hendra Benoit)   '85 Schol

QUINN, SEABURY (1889-1969)

    Jules deGrandin
1. The Phantom Fighter   '66 M&M
2. The Adventures of Jules deGrandin   '76 Pop
3. The Casebook of Jules deGrandin   '76 Pop
4. The Skeleton Closet of Jules deGrandin   '76 Pop
5. The Devil's Bride   '76 Pop
6. The Hellfire Files of Jules deGrandin   '76 Pop
7. The Horror Chamber of Jules deGrandin   '77 Pop

RACKHAM, JOHN (pseud., see JOHN T. PHILLIFENT)

RALSTON, GILBERT A. (b.1912)
    (see STEPHEN GILBERT, "Ben" sequence)

RAMSAY, MARK

    The Falcon
1. The Falcon Strikes   '82 Sign
2. The Black Pope   '82 Sign
3. The Bloody Cross   '82 Sign

RANDALL, MARTA

    Journey
1. Journey   '78 PB
2. Dangerous Games   '80 PB

RANDALL, ROBERT
    (pseud., see ROBERT SILVERBERG & RANDALL GARRETT)

RANKINE, JOHN (pseud. of Douglas R. Mason, b.1918)

    also see: "SPACE: 1999"

    Dag Fletcher
1. Interstellar Two-Five   '66 Dobs
2. One is One   '68 Dobs

```
    3. The Plantos Affair                    '71  Dobs
    4. The Ring of Garamas                   '71  Dobs
    5. The Bromius Phenomenon                '73  Ace
```

RANSOM, BILL (b.1945)
        (see collaboration with FRANK HERBERT)

RANSOME, J. STAFFORD (1860-1931)
        (see CAROLINE LEWIS, pseud.)

RASPE, RUDOLF ERICH (1734-1794) (see "BARON MUNCHAUSEN")

RATHJEN, CARL H. (b.1909) (see "LAND OF THE GIANTS")

RAYMOND, ALEX (1909-1956)

        Flash Gordon
    1. Flash Gordon in the Caverns of Mongo   '37 G&D
        (as adapted by Con Steffanson [House Pseud.])
    2. The Lion Men of Mongo   (Ron Goulart)   '74 Avon
    3. The Plague of Sound   (Ron Goulart)   '74 Avon
    4. The Space Circus   (Ron Goulart)   '74 Avon
    5. The Time Trap of Ming XIII (Carson Bingham)
                                                 '74 Avon
    6. The Witch Queen of Mongo (Carson Bingham)'74 Avon
    7. The War of the Cybernauts (Carson Bingham)
                                                 '75 Avon

REEVE, ARTHUR B. (1880-1936)

        Craig Kennedy
    1. The Silent Bullet   '12 Dodd
        aka: The Black Hand ('12/Nash)
    2. The Poisoned Pen   '13 Dodd
    3. The Dream Doctor   '14 HILib
    4. The War Terror   '15 HILib
        aka: Craig Kennedy, Detective ('16/Simpk)
    5. The Gold of the Gods   '15 HILib
    6. The Exploits of Elaine   '15 HILib
    7. The Social Gangster   '16 HILib
        aka: The Diamond Queen ('17/H&S)
    8. The Ear in the Wall   '16 HILib
    9. The Romance of Elaine   '16 HILib
                        (cont.)

(Arthur B. Reeve, cont.)

10. The Triumph of Elaine	'16	H&S
11. The Treasure-Train	'17	Harpr
12. The Adventuress	'17	Harpr
13. The Panama Plot	'18	Harpr
14. The Soul Scar	'19	Harpr
15. The Film Mystery	'21	Harpr
16. Craig Kennedy Listens In	'23	Harpr
17. Atavar	'24	Harpr
18. The Fourteen Points	'25	Harpr
19. The Boy Scouts' Craig Kennedy	'25	Harpr
20. Craig Kennedy on the Farm	'25	Harpr
21. The Radio Detective	'26	G&D
22. Pandora	'26	Harpr
23. The Kidnap Club	'32	Macau
24. The Clutching Hand	'34	Rei&L
25. Enter Craig Kennedy (written with Ashley Locke)	'35	Macau
26. The Stars Scream Murder	'36	Apple

RESNICK, MIKE (b.1942)

also see: GLEN A. LARSON, "Battlestar Galactica"
also see: EDGAR RICE BURROUGHS, "Mars" series

Ganymede

1. The Goddess of Ganymede	'67	Grant
2. Pursuit on Ganymede	'68	PbLib

Tales of the Galactic Midway

1. Sideshow	'82	Sign
2. The Three-Legged Hootch Dancer	'83	Sign
3. The Wild Alien Tamer	'83	Sign
4. The Best Rootin' Tootin' Shootin' Gunslinger in the Whole Damned Galaxy	'83	Sign

Tales of the Velvet Comet

1. Eros Ascending	'84	Phant
2. Eros at Zenith	'84	Phant

"RETURN TO THE PLANET OF THE APES"
(see "PLANET OF THE APES")

REYNOLDS, MACK (1917-1983)

(cont.)

also see: "STAR TREK"

Joe Mauser
1. The Earth War   '63   Pyr
2. Time Gladiator   '66   FourS
3. Mercenary From Tomorrow   '68   Ace

Section G
1. Planetary Agent X   '65   Ace
2. Amazon Planet   '75   Ace
3. Dawnman Planet   '66   Ace
4. The Rival Rigelians   '67   Ace
5. Code Duello   '68   Ace
6. Section G: United Planets   '76   Ace

Homer Crawford
1. Blackman's Burden   '72   Ace
2. Border, Breed Nor Birth   '72   Ace
3. The Best Ye Breed   '78   Ace

Looking Back
1. Looking Backward From the Year 2000   '73   Ace
2. Equality: in the Year 2000   '77   Ace

2000 A.D. (a series in loose terms only)
1. Commune 2000 A.D.   '74   Bant
2. The Towers of Utopia   '75   Bant
3. Police Patrol: 2000 A.D.   '77   Ace

Rex Bader
1. The Five Way Secret Agent   '75   Ace
2. Satellite City   '75   Ace
3. Lagrange Five   '79   Bant
4. The Lagrangists   '83   Tor
5. Chaos in Lagrangia   '84   Tor

RHEINGOLD, HOWARD

Sisterhood Trilogy
1. Mama Liz Drinks Deep   '73   Freew
2. Mama Liz Tastes Flesh   '73   Freew
3. Secret Sisterhood   '73   Freew

Savage Report
1. Jack Anderson Against Dr. Tek!   '74   Freew
2. War of the Gurus   '74   Freew

"RHODAN, PERRY" (see "PERRY RHODAN")

RICE, JEFF (b.1944)

    Kolchak
1. The Night Stalker   '73 PB
2. The Night Strangler   '74 PB

RICHARDS, CURTIS (see "HALLOWEEN")

RICHARDS, EVAN (see MARTIN CAIDIN)

RICHARDS, HARVEY D.

    Sorak
1. Sorak of the Malay Jungle   '34 Cup&L
2. Sorak and the Clouded Tiger   '34 Cup&L
3. Sorak and the Sultan's Ankus   '34 Cup&L
4. Sorak and the Tree-Men   '36 Cup&L

RICHER, CLEMENT

    Ti-Coyo
1. Ti-Coyo and His Shark; An Immoral Fable   '51 HartD
2. Son of Ti-Coyo   '54 HartD

RIENOW, LEONA TRAIN (1903-1983)

    The Dark Pool Sequence
1. The Bewitched Caverns   '48 Scrib
2. The Dark Pool   '49 Scrib

ROBERSON, JENNIFER

    Chronicles of the Cheysuli
1. Shapechangers   '84 DAW
2. The Song of Homana   '85 DAW

ROBERTS, ARTHUR (see BERL CAMERON, pseud.)

ROBERTS, JOHN MADDOX

    also see: ROBERT E. HOWARD, "Conan" series
                        (cont.)

The Cingulum
1. The Cingulum   '85 Tor
2. Cloak of Illusion   '85 Tor

ROBESON, KENNETH (House Pseudonym)

Series Authors: Lester Dent (1905-1969)
William Bogart (1907-1977)
Laurence Donovan
Harold A. Davis
Alan Hathaway
Ryerson Johnson (b.1901)
Richard Sale (b.1911)

Doc Savage (original series)
1. The Man of Bronze   '33 St&Sm
2. The Land of Terror   '33 St&Sm
3. The Quest of the Spider   '33 St&Sm

Doc Savage (modern reprint series)
(stories originally appeared in pulps 1933-1949)
1. The Man of Bronze   '64 Bant
2. The Thousand-Headed Man   '64 Bant
3. Meteor Menace   '64 Bant
4. The Polar Treasure   '65 Bant
5. Brand of the Werewolf   '65 Bant
6. The Lost Oasis   '65 Bant
7. The Monsters   '65 Bant
8. The Land of Terror   '65 Bant
9. The Mystic Mullah   '65 Bant
10. The Phantom City   '66 Bant
11. Fear Cay   '66 Bant
12. Quest of Qui   '66 Bant
13. Land of Always-Night   '66 Bant
14. The Fantastic Island   '66 Bant
15. Murder Melody   '67 Bant
16. The Spook Legion   '67 Bant
17. The Red Skull   '67 Bant
18. The Sargasso Ogre   '67 Bant
19. Pirate of the Pacific   '67 Bant
20. The Secret of the Sky   '67 Bant
21. Cold Death   '68 Bant
22. The Czar of Fear   '68 Bant
23. Fortress of Solitude   '68 Bant
24. The Green Eagle   '68 Bant
25. The Devil's Playground   '68 Bant
26. Death in Silver   '68 Bant
27. The Mystery Under the Sea   '68 Bant

(cont.)

(Kenneth Robeson, cont.)

28. The Deadly Dwarf	'68	Bant
29. The Other World	'68	Bant
30. The Flaming Falcons	'68	Bant
31. The Annihilist	'68	Bant
32. The Squeaking Goblin	'69	Bant
33. Mad Eyes	'69	Bant
34. The Terror in the Navy	'69	Bant
35. Dust of Death	'69	Bant
36. Resurrection Day	'69	Bant
37. Hex	'69	Bant
38. Red Snow	'69	Bant
39. World's Fair Goblin	'69	Bant
40. The Dagger in the Sky	'69	Bant
41. Merchants of Disaster	'69	Bant
42. The Gold Ogre	'69	Bant
43. The Man Who Shook the Earth	'69	Bant
44. The Sea Magician	'70	Bant
45. The Man Who Smiled No More	'70	Bant
46. The Midas Man	'70	Bant
47. Land of Long Juju	'70	Bant
48. The Feathered Octopus	'70	Bant
49. The Sea Angel	'70	Bant
50. Devil on the Moon	'70	Bant
51. Haunted Ocean	'70	Bant
52. The Vanisher	'70	Bant
53. The Mental Wizard	'70	Bant
54. He Could Stop the World	'70	Bant
55. The Golden Peril	'70	Bant
56. The Giggling Ghosts	'71	Bant
57. Poison Island	'71	Bant
58. The Munitions Master	'71	Bant
59. The Yellow Cloud	'71	Bant
60. The Majii	'71	Bant
61. The Living Fire Menace	'71	Bant
62. The Pirate's Ghost	'71	Bant
63. The Submarine Mystery	'71	Bant
64. The Motion Menace	'71	Bant
65. The Green Death	'71	Bant
66. Mad Mesa	'72	Bant
67. The Freckled Shark	'72	Bant
68. Quest of the Spider	'72	Bant
69. The Mystery of the Snow	'72	Bant
70. Spook Hole	'72	Bant
71. Murder Mirage	'72	Bant
72. The Metal Monster	'73	Bant
73. The Seven Agate Devils	'73	Bant
74. The Derrick Devil	'73	Bant
75. Land of Fear	'73	Bant

76. The Black Spot	'74	Bant
77. The South Pole Terror	'74	Bant
78. The Crimson Serpent	'74	Bant
79. The Devil Genghis	'74	Bant
80. The King Maker	'75	Bant
81. The Stone Man	'76	Bant
82. The Evil Gnome	'76	Bant
83. The Red Terrors	'76	Bant
84. The Mountain Monster	'76	Bant
85. The Boss of Terror	'76	Bant
86. The Angry Ghost	'77	Bant
87. The Spotted Men	'77	Bant
88. The Roar Devil	'77	Bant
89. The Magic Island	'77	Bant
90. The Flying Goblin	'77	Bant
91. The Purple Dragon	'78	Bant
92. The Awful Egg	'78	Bant
93. Tunnel Terror	'79	Bant
94. The Hate Genius	'79	Bant
95. The Red Spider	'79	Bant
96. Mystery on Happy Bones	'79	Bant
97. Satan Black	'80	Bant
98. Cargo Unknown	'80	Bant
99. Hell Below	'80	Bant
100. The Lost Giant	'80	Bant
101. The Pharaoh's Ghost	'81	Bant
102. The Time Terror	'81	Bant
103. The Whisker of Hercules	'81	Bant
104. The Man Who Was Scared	'81	Bant
105. They Died Twice	'81	Bant
106. The Screaming Man	'81	Bant
107. Jiu San	'82	Bant
108. The Black, Black Witch	'82	Bant
109. The Shape of Terror	'82	Bant
110. Death Had Yellow Eyes	'82	Bant
111. One-Eyes Mystic	'82	Bant
112. The Man Who Fell Up	'82	Bant
113. The Talking Devil	'83	Bant
114. The Ten Ton Snakes	'83	Bant
115. Private Isle	'83	Bant
116. The Speaking Stone	'83	Bant
117. The Golden Man	'83	Bant
118. Peril in the North	'83	Bant
119. The Laugh of Death	'84	Bant
120. The King of Terror	'84	Bant
121. The Three Wild Men	'84	Bant
122. The Fiery Menace	'84	Bant
123. Devils of the Deep	'84	Bant
124. The Headless Men	'84	Bant

(cont.)

(Kenneth Robeson, cont.)

125. The Goblins '85 Bant
126. The Secret of the Su '85 Bant

The Avenger
<u>(original pulp stories from 30s & 40s)</u>
<u>titles 1-24 by Paul Ernst (b.1886)</u>
1. Justice, Inc. '72 PbLib
2. The Yellow Hoard '72 PbLib
3. The Sky Walker '72 PbLib
4. The Devil's Horns '72 PbLib
5. The Frosted Death '72 PbLib
6. The Blood Ring '72 PbLib
7. Stockholders in Death '72 PbLib
8. The Glass Mountain '73 PbLib
9. Tuned For Murder '73 PbLib
10. The Smiling Dogs '73 PbLib
11. River of Ice '73 PbLib
12. The Flame Breathers '73 PbLib
13. Murder on Wheels '73 PbLib
14. Three Gold Crowns '73 PbLib
15. House of Death '73 PbLib
16. The Hate Master '73 PbLib
17. Nevlo '73 PbLib
18. Death in Slow Motion '73 PbLib
19. Pictures of Death '73 PbLib
20. The Green Killer '74 PbLib
21. The Happy Killers '74 PbLib
22. The Black Death '74 PbLib
23. The Wilder Curse '74 PbLib
24. Midnight Murder '74 PbLib
    <u>(new additions)</u> (all by Ron Goulart)
25. The Man From Atlantis '74 Warnr
26. Red Moon '74 Warnr
27. The Purple Zombie '74 Warnr
28. Dr. Time '74 Warnr
29. The Nightwitch Devil '74 Warnr
30. Black Chariots '74 Warnr
31. The Cartoon Crimes '74 Warnr
32. The Death Machine '74 Warnr
33. The Blood Countess '75 Warnr
34. The Glass Man '75 Warnr
35. The Iron Skull '75 Warnr
36. Demon Island '75 Warnr

ROBINSON, SPIDER (b.1948)

(cont.)

Callahan's Crosstime Saloon
1. Callahan's Crosstime Saloon — '77 Ace
2. Time Travelers Strictly Cash — '81 Ace

ROCKWELL, CAREY (pseud.)

Tom Corbett, Space Cadet
1. Stand By For Mars! — '52 G&D
2. Danger in Deep Space — '53 G&D
3. On the Trail of Space Pirates — '53 G&D
4. The Space Pioneers — '53 G&D
5. The Revolt on Venus — '54 G&D
6. Treachery in Outer Space — '54 G&D
7. Sabotage in Space — '55 G&D
8. The Robot Rocket — '56 G&D

ROCKWOOD, ROY (House Pseudonym)

Great Marvel Series
1. Through the Air to the North Pole — '06 Cup&L
2. Under the Ocean to the South Pole — '07 Cup&L
3. Five Thousand Miles Underground — '08 Cup&L
4. Through Space to Mars — '10 Cup&L
5. Lost on the Moon — '11 Cup&L
6. On a Torn-Away World — '13 Cup&L
7. The City Beyond the Clouds — '25 Cup&L
8. By Air Express to Venus — '29 Cup&L
9. By Space Ship to Saturn — '35 Cup&L

Bomba the Jungle Boy
1. Bomba the Jungle Boy; or, The Old Naturalist's Secret — '26 Cup&L
2. Bomba the Jungle Boy at the Moving Mountain — '26 Cup&L
3. Bomba the Jungle Boy at the Great Cataract — '26 Cup&L
4. Bomba the Jungle Boy on Jaguar Island — '27 Cup&L
5. Bomba the Jungle Boy in the Abandoned City — '27 Cup&L
6. Bomba the Jungle Boy on Terror Trail — '28 Cup&L
7. Bomba the Jungle Boy in the Swamp of Death — '29 Cup&L
8. Bomba the Jungle Boy Among the Slaves — '29 Cup&L
9. Bomba the Jungle Boy on the Underground River — '30 Cup&L
10. Bomba the Jungle Boy and the Lost Explorers — '30 Cup&L

(cont.)

(Roy Rockwood, cont.)

11. Bomba the Jungle Boy in a Strange Land	'31	Cup&L
12. Bomba the Jungle Boy Among the Pygmies	'31	Cup&L
13. Bomba the Jungle Boy and the Cannibals	'32	Cup&L
14. Bomba the Jungle Boy and the Painted Hunters	'32	Cup&L
15. Bomba the Jungle Boy and the River Demons	'33	Cup&L
16. Bomba the Jungle Boy and the Hostile Chieftain	'34	Cup&L
17. Bomba the Jungle Boy Trapped by the Cyclone	'35	Cup&L
18. Bomba the Jungle Boy in the Land of Burning Lava	'36	Cup&L
19. Bomba the Jungle Boy in the Perilous Kingdom	'37	Cup&L
20. Bomba the Jungle Boy in the Steaming Grotto	'38	Cup&L

RODDENBERRY, GENE (b.1921) (see "STAR TREK")

RODGERS, MARY (b.1931)

Annabel Andrews
1. Freaky Friday	'72	Harpr
2. A Billion For Boris	'74	Harpr

ROHMER, SAX (pseud. of Arthur Sarsfield Ward, 1883-1959)

Fu Manchu
1. The Mystery of Dr. Fu Manchu	'13	Meth
aka: The Insidious Dr. Fu-Manchu ('13/McBri)		
2. The Devil Doctor	'16	Meth
aka: Return of Dr. Fu-Manchu ('16/McBri)		
3. The Si-Fan Mysteries	'17	Meth
aka: The Hand of Fu-Manchu ('17/McBri)		
4. The Golden Scorpion	'31	Cass
5. Daughter of Fu Manchu	'31	Cass
6. The Mask of Fu Manchu	'32	Dbdy
7. Fu Manchu's Bride	'33	Dbdy
aka: The Bride of Fu Manchu ('33/Cass)		
8. The Trail of Fu Manchu	'34	Cass
9. President Fu Manchu	'36	Cass
10. The Drums of Fu Manchu	'38	Cass
11. The Island of Fu Manchu	'41	Cass
12. The Shadow of Fu Manchu	'48	Dbdy

13.	Re-Enter Fu Manchu	'57	Jenk
	aka: Re-Enter Dr. Fu Manchu ('57/Jenk)		
14.	Emperor Fu Manchu	'59	Jenk
15.	The Wrath of Fu Manchu and Other Stories	'73	Stacy
	(includes 4 Fu Manchu Stories)		

Gaston Max
1. The Yellow Claw — '15 Meth
2. The Golden Scorpion — '19 Meth
3. The Day the World Ended — '30 Dody
4. Seven Sins — '43 McBri

Paul Harley
1. Bat-Wing — '21 Cass
2. Fire-Tongue — '21 Cass
3. Tales of Chinatown — '22 Cass
   (contains Harley stories)
4. Tales of East and West — '32 Cass
   (contains one Harley story)
5. Salute to Bazarada and Other Stories — '39 Cass
   (contains 3 Harley stories)

The Sumuru Series
1. Nude in Mink — '50 GoldM
   aka: Sins of Sumuru ('50/Jenk)
2. Sumuru — '51 GoldM
   aka: Slaves of Sumuru ('52/Jenk)
3. The Fire Goddess — '52 GoldM
   aka: Virgin in Flames ('53/Jenk)
4. Return of Sumuru — '54 GoldM
   aka: Sand and Satin ('55/Jenk)
5. Sinister Madonna — '56 GoldM

ROMERO, GEORGE A. (b.1939)

The Living Dead (The following titles by JOHN RUSSO based on ideas by George A. Romero):
1. The Night of the Living Dead — '74 Warnr
2. Return of the Living Dead — '78 Dale
   (following by George A. Romero & Susanna Sparrow)
3. Dawn of the Dead — '78 StM

ROSENBERG, JOEL

The Guardians of the Flame
1. The Sleeping Dragon — '83 Sign
2. The Sword and the Chain — '84 Sign
3. The Silver Crown — '85 Sign

ROSS, MARILYN
    (pseud. of William Edward Daniel Ross, b.1912)

    Dark Shadows
1. Dark Shadows   '66 PbLib
2. Victoria Winters   '67 PbLib
3. Strangers at Collins House   '67 PbLib
4. The Mystery at Collinwood   '67 PbLib
5. The Curse of Collinwood   '68 PbLib
6. Barnabas Collins   '69 PbLib
7. The Secret of Barnabas Collins   '69 PbLib
8. The Demon of Barnabas Collins   '69 PbLib
9. The Foe of Barnabas Collins   '69 PbLib
10. The Phantom and Barnabas Collins   '69 PbLib
11. Barnabas Collins Versus the Warlock   '69 PbLib
12. The Peril of Barnabas Collins   '69 PbLib
13. Barnabas Collins and the Mysterious Ghost   '70 PbLib
14. Barnabas Collins and Quentin's Dream   '70 PbLib
15. Barnabas Collins and the Gypsy Witch   '70 PbLib
16. House of Dark Shadows   '70 PbLib
17. Barnabas, Quentin, and the Mummy's Curse   '70 PbLib
18. Barnabas, Quentin, and the Avenging Ghost   '70 PbLib
19. Barnabas, Quentin, and the Nightmare Assassin   '70 PbLib
20. Barnabas, Quentin, and the Crystal Coffin   '70 PbLib
21. Barnabas, Quentin, and the Witch's Curse   '70 PbLib
22. Barnabas, Quentin, and the Haunted Cave   '70 PbLib
23. Barnabas, Quentin, and the Frightened Bride   '70 PbLib
24. Barnabas, Quentin, and the Scorpio Curse   '70 PbLib
25. Barnabas, Quentin, and the Serpent   '70 PbLib
26. Barnabas, Quentin, and the Magic Potion   '71 PbLib
27. Barnabas, Quentin, and the Body Snatchers   '71 PbLib
28. Barnabas, Quentin, and Dr. Jekyll's Son   '71 PbLib
29. Barnabas, Quentin, and the Grave Robbers   '71 PbLib
30. Barnabas, Quentin, and the Sea Ghost   '71 PbLib
31. Barnabas, Quentin, and the Mad Magician   '71 PbLib
32. Barnabas, Quentin, and the Hidden Tomb   '71 PbLib
33. Barnabas, Quentin, and the Vampire Beauty   '72 PbLib

ROTSLER, WILLIAM (b.1926)
    see: "PERRY RHODAN"
    also see: "MARVEL SUPER-HEROES"

ROWLAND, DONALD S. (b.1928)

    Omina (pseud.-- Roland Starr)
1. Operation Omina   '70 Lenox
2. Omina Uncharted   '74 Hale
3. Time Factor   '75 Hale
4. Return From Omina   '76 Hale

ROWLEY, CHRISTOPHER

    The War For Eternity
1. The War For Eternity   '83 DelR
2. The Blackship   '85 DelR

RUSS, JOANNA (b.1937)

    The Adventures oif Alyx (coll.'83/PB)
1. Picnic on Paradise   '68 Ace
2. Alyx   '76 Gregg
    contains: Picnic on Paradise ('68/Ace)

RYPEL, T.C.

    Gonji
1. Deathwind of Vedun
2. Samurai Steel
3. Samurai Combat   '83

S

SABERHAGEN, FRED (b.1930)

    Berserker Series
1. Berserker   '67   Ball
2. Brother Assassin   '69   Ball
3. Berserker's Planet   '75   DAW
4. Berserker Man   '79   Ace
5. The Ultimate Enemy   '79   Ace
6. Berserker Wars   '81   Tor
7. Berserker Base   '85   Tor
    (this title edited by Fred Saberhagen, with episodes by Saberhagen, Poul Anderson, Edward Bryant, Stephen R. Donaldson, Larry Niven, Connie Willis, & Roger Zelazny).
8. The Berserker Throne   '85   Fires

    Empire of the East *
1. The Broken Lands   '68   Ace
2. The Black Mountains   '71   Ace
3. Changeling Earth   '73   DAW
    * all 3 titles greatly revised as: Empire of the East ('79/Ace)

    Dracula Series
1. The Dracula Tapes   '75   Warnr
2. The Holmes-Dracula File   '78   Ace
3. An Old Friend of the Family   '79   Ace
4. Thorn   '80   Ace

    The Book of Swords *
1. The First Book of Swords   '83   Tor
2. The Second Book of Swords   '83   Tor
3. The Third Book of Swords   '84   Tor
    * all 3 collected as: The Complete Book of Swords ('85/SFBC)

SADLER, BARRY

    Casca: The Eternal Mercenary
1. The Eternal Mercenary   '79   Chart
2. God of Death   '79   Chart
3. The Warlord   '80   Chart
4. Panzer Soldier   '80   Chart
5. The Barbarian   '81   Chart

(cont.)
   6. The Persian   '82 Chart
   7. The Damned   '82 Chart
   8. Soldier of Fortune   '83 Chart
   9. The Sentinel   '83 Chart
 10. The Conquistador   '84 Chart
 11. The Legionnaire   '84 Chart
 12. The African Mercenary   '84 Chart
 13. The Assassin   '85 Chart
 14. The Phoenix   '85 Ace

SALE, RICHARD (b.1911) (see KENNETH ROBESON)

SALMONSON, JESSICA AMANDA

       Tomoe Gozen
  1. Tomoe Gozen   '81 Ace
  2. The Golden Naginata   '82 Ace
  3. Thousand Shrine Warrior   '84 Ace

SALTEN, FELIX
    (pseud. of Sigmund Salzmann, 1869-1945)

       Bambi
  1. Bambi, A Life in the Woods   '28 Cape
  2. Bambi's Children   '39 Bob-M

SAMACHSON, JOSEPH (see EDMOND HAMILTON)

SAUNDERS, CHARLES R.

       Imaro
  1. Imaro   '81 DAW
  2. The Quest For Cush   '84 DAW

SAVARIN, JULIUS JAY

       The Lemmus Trilogy
  1. Waiters on the Dance   '72 Arlin
  2. Beyond the Outer Mirr   '76 Corgi
  3. Archives of Haven   '77 Corgi

SAWARD, ERIC (see "DOCTOR WHO")

SAXON, PETER   (House Pseudonym)

    The Guardians Series
1. The Guardians (by W. Howard Baker)   '67   Mayfl
2. The Curse of Rathlaw (by Martin Thomas) '68   Lance
3. Through the Dark Curtain   '68   Lance
   aka: Guardians 2: Dark Ways to Death ('69/Berk)
4. Guardians 1: The Killing Bone   '69   Berk
5. Guardians 3: The Haunting of Alan Mais   '69   Berk
6. Guardians 4: The Vampires of Finisterre '70   Berk

SAYLER, H.L. (1863-1913)

    The Airship Boys
1. The Airship Boys   '09   Rei&B
2. The Airship Boys Adrift   '09   Rei&B
3. The Airship Boys Due North   '10   Rei&B
4. The Airship Boys in the Barren Lands   '10   Rei&B
5. The Airship Boys in Finance   '11   Rei&B
6. The Airship Boys' Ocean Flyer   '11   Rei&B

SCARBOROUGH, ELIZABETH

    Argonia
1. Song of Sorcery   '82   Bant
2. The Unicorn Creed   '83   Bant
3. Bronwyn's Bane   '83   Bant
4. The Christening Quest   '85   Bant

SCHEALER, JOHN M. (b.1920)

    Zip-Zip
1. Zip-Zip and His Flying Saucer   '56   EPDut
2. Zip-Zip Goes to Venus   '58   EPDut
3. Zip-Zip and the Red Planet   '61   EPDut

SCHEER, KARL-HERBERT (see "PERRY RHODAN")

SCHMIDT, DENNIS

    Kensho
1. The Way-Farer   '78   Ace
2. Kensho   '79   Ace
3. Satori
4. Wanderer   '85   Ace

SCHMITZ, JAMES H. (b.1911)

    The Hub
1. The Demon Breed   '68   Ace
2. A Nice Day For Screaming   '65   Chilt
3. A Pride of Monsters   '70   Macm
4. A Tale of Two Clocks   '62   Dodd

    Telzey Amberdon
1. The Universe Against Her   '64   Ace
2. The Telzey Toy   '73   DAW
3. The Lion Game   '73   DAW

SCHWALLER DE LUBICZ, ISHA (see DE LUBICZ, ISHA SCHWALLER)

SCOGGINS, C.E. (1888-1955)

    Colin O'Leary
1. The House of Dawn   '35   Skeff
2. Lost Road   '41   Dody

SCOTT, R.T.M. (pseud., see "THE SPIDER")

SEARLS, HANK (see "JAWS")

"SECRET AGENT X"

1. Torture Trust (Paul Chadwick)   '34/'66   Corin
2. Death Torch Terror (Paul Chadwick) '34/'66   Corin
3. City of the Living Dead (Paul Chadwick)
                                                   '34/'66   Corin
4. Octopus of Crime (Paul Chadwick)   '34/'66   Corin
5. Servants of the Skull
    (Paul Chadwick)   '34/'66   Corin
6. Sinister Scourge (Paul Chadwick)   '35/'66   Corin
7. Brand of the Metal Maiden
    (G.T. Fleming-Roberts)   '36/'74   Weinb
8. Curse of the Mandarin's Fan
    (Leo Zagat)   '38/'66   Corin

SELTZER, DAVID (see "THE OMEN")

SHANAHAN, WARREN (see collaboration with LEE FALK)

SHARKEY, JACK (b.1931) (see "THE ADDAMS FAMILY")

SHARP, MARGERY (b.1905)

    Miss Bianca
1. The Rescuers '59 LtBrn
2. Miss Bianca '62 LtBrn
3. The Turret '63 LtBrn
4. Miss Bianca in the Salt Mines '66 LtBrn
5. Miss Bianca in the Orient '70 LtBrn
6. Miss Bianca in the Antarctic '71 LtBrn
7. Miss Bianca and the Bridesmaid '72 LtBrn
8. Bernard the Brave '76 Heine
9. Bernard into Battle '79 Hutch

SHARP, ROBERT (see JON J. DEEGAN, pseud.)

SHAW, BOB (b.1931)

    Orbitsville
1. Orbitsville '75 Ace
2. Orbitsville Departure '83 Gollz

SHAWN, FRANK S.
    (pseud. of RON GOULART, see collab. with LEE FALK)

SHEA, MICHAEL (b.1946)
    see: JACK VANCE, "Dying Earth" sequence
    also see: H.P. LOVECRAFT, "Cthulhu Mythos"

SHEA, ROBERT (b.1933)
    (see collaboration with ROBERT ANTON WILSON)

SHELDON, ROY (pseud., see H.J. CAMPBELL)

SHERMAN, HAROLD (b.1898)

    Tahara
1. Tahara, Boy King of the Desert '33 Gsmit
2. Tahara Among African Tribes '33 Gsmit
3. Tahara, Boy Mystic of India '33 Gsmit
4. Tahara in the Land of Yucatan '33 Gsmit

SHERMAN, JORY

    The Chill Series
1. Satan's Seed   '78 Pinn
2. Chill   '78 Pinn
3. The Bamboo Demons   '79 Pinn
4. Vegas Vampire   '80 Pinn
    aka: Vampire ('81/NEL)
5. The Phoenix Man   '80 Pinn
6. House of Scorpions   '80 Pinn
7. Shadows   '80 Pinn

SHIRLEY, JOHN (see D.B. DRUMM, pseud.)

SHOLS, W.W. (see "PERRY RHODAN")

SIBSON, FRANCIS H.

    The Survivors
1. The Survivors   '32 Heine
2. The Stolen Continent   '34 Melro

SILBERSACK, JOHN (b.1954) (see "BUCK ROGERS")

SILVA, JOSEPH (see "MARVEL SUPER-HEROES")

SILVERBERG, ROBERT (b.1935)

    The Nidorian Sequence (with Randall Garrett, joint pseud.—Robert Randall)
1. The Shrouded Planet   '57 Gnome
2. The Dawning Light   '59 Gnome

    Majipoor Trilogy
1. Lord Valentine's Castle   '80 Harpr
2. Majipoor Chronicles   '82 Arbor
3. Valentine Pontifex   '83 Arbor

SIODMAK, CURT (b.1902)

    Cory
1. Donovan's Brain   '43 Knopf
2. Hauser's Memory   '68 Putn

SIROTA, MIKE

    Dannus
1. The Prisoner of Reglathium '78 Manor
2. The Conqueror of Reglathium '78 Manor
3. The Caves of Reglathium '78 Manor
4. Dark Straits of Reglathium '78 Manor
5. The Slaves of Reglathium '78 Manor

    Berbora
1. Berbora '78 Manor
2. Berbora #2 '78 Manor

    Ro-Lan
1. Master of Borango '80 Zebra
2. The Shrouded Walls of Borango '80 Zebra
3. Journey to Mesharra '81 Zebra
4. The Demons of Zammar '81 Zebra

"SIX MILLION DOLLAR MAN, THE" (see MARTIN CAIDIN)

SKALDASPILLIR, SIGFRIOUR (see H. RIDER HAGGARD)

SKY, KATHLEEN (see "STAR TREK")

SLEIGH, BARBARA (1906-1982)

    Carbonel
1. Carbonel '55 MaxP
    aka: Carbonel, the King of the Cats ('57/Bob-M)
2. The Kingdom of Carbonel '59 MaxP

SLOBODKIN, LOUIS (1903-1975)

    The Space Ship
1. The Space Ship Under the Apple Tree '52 Macm
2. The Space Ship Returns to the Apple Tree '58 Macm
3. The Three-Seated Space Ship '62 Macm
4. Round Trip Space Ship '68 Macm
5. The Space Ship in the Park '72 Macm

SMILIE, ELTON R. (or R. Elton Smilie)

                           (cont.)

Explorations Sequence
1. The Manatitlans; or, A Record of Recent
   Scientific Explorations in the Andean
   La Plata, S.A.   1877   River
2. Investigations and Experience of M.
   Shawtinbach at Saar Soong, Sumatra   1879   Wintb
   (published anonymously)

SMITH, ANDREW (see "DOCTOR WHO")

SMITH, CORDWAINER
     (pseud. of Paul M. A. Linebarger, 1913-1966)

The Instrumentality of Man *
1. The Planet Buyer   '64   Pyr
2. Quest of the Three Worlds   '66   Ace
3. Space Lords   '65   Pyr
4. Stardreamer   '71   Beagl
5. Under Old Earth, and Other Explorations   '70   Pantr
6. The Underpeople   '68   Pyr
7. You Will Never Be the Same   '63   Regcy
8. The Instrumentality of Mankind   '79   DelR
    * Titles 1 & 6 revised as: "Norstrilia"
                    ('75/Ball)

SMITH, DAVID C.

Oron
(Note-- proper sequence is as follows, despite
the publisher's numbering on the covers):
1. Oron: Mosutha's Magic (cover #3)   '82   Zebra
2. The Valley of Ogrum (cover #4)   '82   Zebra
3. Oron: The Ghost Army (cover #5)   '83   Zebra
4. Oron (cover #1)   '78   Zebra
5. The Sorcerer's Shadow (cover #2)   '78   Zebra

Red Sonja
(in collaboration with Richard Tierney)
1. The Ring of Ikribu   '81   Ace
2. Demon Night   '82   Ace
3. When Hell Laughs   '82   Ace
4. Endithor's Daughter   '82   Ace
5. Against the Prince of Hell   '83   Ace
6. Star of Doom   '83   Ace

The Fall of the First World
                    (cont.)

(David C. Smith, "Fall of the First World", cont.)

    1. Master of Evil   '83   Pinn
    2. Sorrowing Vengeance   '83   Pinn
    3. The Passing of the Gods   '83   Pinn

SMITH, DODIE (b.1896)

    <u>101 Dalmations</u>
    1. The Hundred and One Dalmations   '56   Heine
    2. The Starlight Barking   '67   Heine

SMITH, E.E. "DOC" (1890-1965)

    <u>The Skylark Series</u>
    1. The Skylark of Space
       (with Mrs. Lee Hawkins Garby)   '46   BuffB
    2. Skylark Three   '48   FantP
    3. Skylark of Valeron   '49   FantP
    4. Skylark DuQuesne   '66   Pyr

    <u>The Lensmen Series</u>
    1. Triplanetary   '48   FantP
    2. First Lensman   '50   FantP
    3. Galactic Patrol   '50   FantP
    4. Gray Lensman   '51   FantP
    5. Second Stage Lensman   '53   FantP
    6. Children of the Lens   '54   FantP
    7. The Vortex Blaster   '60   Gnome
       aka: Masters of the Vortex ('68/Pyr)
       (sequels)
    8. The Dragon Lensman (by David A. Kyle)   '80   Bant
    9. Lensman From Rigel (by David A. Kyle)   '82   Bant
  10. Z-Lensman (by David A. Kyle)   '83   Bant

    <u>Subspace Sequence</u>
    1. Subspace Explorers   '65   Canav
    2. Subspace Encounter   '83   Berk

    <u>The Family D'Alembert</u>
    (The first title is based on Smith's drafts and
    completed by Stephen Goldin, all others in the
    series are by Goldin)
    1. Imperial Stars   '76   Pyr
    2. Strangler's Moon   '76   Pyr
    3. The Clockwork Traitor   '77   Pyr
    4. Getaway World   '77   Pyr

                          (cont.)

5. Appointment at Bloodstar	'78	Jove
6. The Purity Plot	'80	Berk
7. Planet of Treachery	'82	Berk
8. Eclipsing Binaries	'83	Berk
9. The Omicron Invasion	'84	Berk
10. Revolt of the Galaxy	'85	Berk

SMITH, GEORGE H. (b.1922)

Duffus January
1. Druids' World	'67	Avalo
2. Witch Queen of Lochlann	'69	Sign

Annwn Series
1. Kar Karballa, King of the Gogs	'69	Ace
2. The Second War of the Worlds	'76	DAW
3. The Island Snatchers	'78	DAW

SMITH, L. NEIL (see "STAR WARS")

SMITH, THORNE (1892-1934)

Topper
1. Topper: An Impossible Adventure aka: The Jovial Ghosts ('33/Barkr)	'26	McBri
2. Topper Takes A Trip	'32	Dbdy

Jennifer
1. The Passionate Witch (with N. Matson) aka: I Married A Witch	'41	Dbdy
2. Bats in the Belfry (by N. Matson only)	'43	Dbdy

SMYTHE, R. JOHN (pseud.)

Conception
1. The Conception	'69	LateH
2. The Coming of Morikand	'70	Dark

SNELL, ROY J. (1878-?)

The Radio-Phone Boys
(Note-- there are probably other titles with fewer SF elements preceding these in the series)
1. The Seagoing Tank	'24	Rei&L
2. The Flying Sub	'25	Rei&L

SNODGRASS, MELINDA (see "STAR TREK")

SNOW, JACK (see L. FRANK BAUM, "Oz" series)

SNYDER, ZILPHA KEATLEY (b.1927)

    Green-Sky Trilogy
1. Below the Root   '75 Athen
2. And All Between   '76 Athen
3. Until the Celebration   '77 Athen

SOMERS, BART (pseud.— see GARDNER F. FOX)

SOUTHALL, IVAN (b.1921)

    Simon Black
1. Meet Simon Black   '50 Ang&R
2. Simon Black in Peril   '51 Ang&R
3. Simon Black in Coastal Command   '52 Ang&R
4. Simon Black in Space   '52 Ang&R
5. Simon Black in China   '54 Ang&R
6. Simon Black and the Spacemen   '55 Ang&R
7. Simon Black in the Antarctic
8. Simon Black Takes Over
9. Simon Black at Sea   '62 Ang&R

"SPACE: 1999"

    series authors: E.C. Tubb
                  John Rankine
                  Michael Butterworth
                  Brian Ball

    Space: 1999
1. Breakaway (Tubb)   '75 Futur
2. Moon Odyssey (Rankine)   '75 Futur
3. The Space Guardians (Ball)   '75 Futur
4. Collision Course (Tubb)   '75 Futur
5. Lunar Attack (Rankine)   '75 Futur
6. Astral Quest (Rankine)   '75 Dobs
7. Alien Seed (Tubb)   '76 Futur
8. Android Planet (Rankine)   '76 Futur
9. Rogue Planet (Tubb)   '76 Futur
10. Phoenix of Megaron (Rankine)   '76 PB

11. Earthfall (Butterworth)	'77	
12. Planets of Peril (Butterworth)	'77	Warnr
13. Mind-Breaks of Space (Butterworth)	'77	Warnr
14. The Space-Jackers (Butterworth)	'77	Warnr
15. The Psychomorph (Butterworth)	'77	Warnr
16. The Time Fighters (Butterworth)	'77	Warnr
17. On the Edge of the Infinite (Butterworth)	'78	Warnr

SPANO, CHARLES A. (b.1948) (see "STAR TREK")

"THE SPIDER"

(The following by Reginald Maitland under pseud. R.T.M. Scott):

1. The Spider Strikes	'33/'69	Berk
2. Wheel of Death	'33/'69	Berk

(The following by Norvell Page under pseud. Grant Stockbridge):

3. Wings of the Black Death	'33/'69	Berk
4. City of Flaming Shadows	'34/'70	Berk
5. Builders of the Black Empire	'34/'80	DimeP
6. City Destroyer	'35/'75	PB
7. Hordes of the Red Butcher	'35/'75	PB
8. Master of the Death Madness	'35/'80	DimeP
9. Overlord of the Damned	'35/'80	DimeP
10. Death Reign of the Vampire King	'35/'75	PB
11. Death and the Spider	'42/'75	PB
12. Blue Steel	'43/'79	Pytho

SPIELBERG, STEVEN (b.1946)
    (see WILLIAM KOTZWINKLE)

SPRINGER, NANCY (b.1948)

The Chronicles of Isle *

1. The White Hart	'79	PB
2. The Silver Sun	'80	PB

revised from an earlier work:
The Book of Suns ('77/PB)

3. The Sable Moon	'81	PB
4. The Black Beast	'82	PB
5. The Golden Swan	'83	PB

    * volumes 4 & 5 collected as:
      The Book of Vale ('83/Dbdy)

SPRUILL, STEVEN (b.1946)

    Elias Kane
1. The Psychopath Plague   '78 Dbdy
2. The Imperator Plot   '85 Tor

STABLEFORD, BRIAN (b.1948)

    The Dies Irae Series
1. Days of Glory   '71 Ace
2. In the Kingdom of the Beasts   '71 Ace
3. Day of Wrath   '71 Ace

    The Grainger Series
1. Halcyon Drift   '72 DAW
2. Rhapsody in Black   '73 DAW
3. Promised Land   '74 DAW
4. The Paradise Game   '74 DAW
5. The Fenris Device   '74 DAW
6. Swan Song   '75 DAW

    The Daedalus Series
1. The Florians   '76 DAW
2. Critical Threshold   '77 DAW
3. Wildeblood's Empire   '77 DAW
4. The City of the Sun   '78 DAW
5. Balance of Power

STABLES, GORDON (1840-1910)

    The Snowbird
1. The Cruise of the Snowbird   1882 H&S
2. Wild Adventures Round the Pole   1883 H&S

STACY, RYDER

    Doomsday Warrior
1. Doomsday Warrior   '84 Zebra
2. Red America   '84 Zebra
3. The Last American   '84 Zebra
4. Bloody America   '85 Zebra
5. America's Last Declaration   '85 Zebra
6. American Rebellion   '85 Zebra

STAHL, BEN (b.1910)

(cont.)

Blackbeard's Ghost
1. Blackbeard's Ghost   '65   HMiff
2. The Secret of Red Skull   '71   HMiff

STALLMAN, ROBERT (1930-1980)

The Book of the Beast
1. The Orphan   '80   PB
2. The Captive   '81   PB
3. The Beast   '82   PB

STAPLEDON, OLAF (1886-1950)

Last and First Men
1. Last and First Men   '30   Meth
2. Last Men in London   '32   Meth
3. Star Maker   '37   Meth

STARR, BILL

Farstar & Son
1. The Way to Dawnworld   '75   Ball
2. The Treasure of Wonderwhat   '77   Ball

STARR, ROLAND (pseud., see DONALD S. ROWLAND)

"STAR TREK"

Star Trek Novels
1. Star Trek: Mission to Horatius
     (Mack Reynolds)   '68   Whitm
2. Spock Must Die! (James Blish)   '70   Bant
3. Spock, Messiah!
     (Theodore Cogswell & Charles A. Spano) '76   Bant
4. The Price of the Phoenix
     (Sondra Marshak & Myrna Culbreath)   '77   Bant
5. Planet of Judgement (Joe Haldeman)   '77   Bant
6. Mudd's Angels (J.A. Lawrence)   '78   Bant
7. Vulcan! (Kathleen Sky)   '78   Bant
8. The Starless World (Gordon Eklund)   '78   Bant
9. Trek to Madworld (Stephen Goldin)   '79   Bant
10. World Without End (Joe Haldeman)   '79   Bant
11. The Fate of the Phoenix
     (Sondra Marshak & Myrna Culbreath)   '79   Bant
                             (cont.)

("Star Trek" cont.)

12. Devil World (Gordon Eklund)	'79	Bant
13. Star Trek: The Motion Picture (Gene Roddenberry)	'79	PB
14. Perry's Planet (Jack Haldeman II)	'80	Bant
15. The Galactic Whirlpool (David Gerrold)	'80	Bant
16. Death's Angel (Kathleen Sky)	'81	Bant
17. The Entropy Effect (Vonda N. McIntyre)	'81	PB
18. The Klingon Gambit (Robert E. Vardeman)	'81	PB
19. The Covenant of the Crown (Howard Weinstein)	'81	PB
20. The Prometheus Design (Sondra Marshak & Myrna Culbreath)	'82	PB
21. The Abode of Life (Lee Correy, pseud.)	'82	PB
22. Star Trek II: The Wrath of Khan (Vonda N. McIntyre)	'82	PB
23. Black Fire (Sonni Cooper)	'83	PB
24. Triangle (Sondra Marshak & Myrna Culbreath)	'83	PB
25. Web of the Romulans (M.S. Murdock)	'83	PB
26. Yesterday's Son (A.C. Crispin)	'83	PB
27. Mutiny on the Enterprise (Robert E. Vardeman)	'83	PB
28. The Wounded Sky (Diane Duane)	'83	PB
29. The Trellisane Confrontation (David Dvorkin)	'84	PB
30. Corona (Greg Bear)	'84	PB
31. The Final Reflection (John M. Ford)	'84	PB
32. Star Trek III: The Search For Spock (Vonda N. McIntyre)	'84	PB
33. My Enemy, My Ally (Diane Duane)	'84	PB
34. The Tears of the Singers (Melinda Snodgrass)	'84	PB
35. The Vulcan Academy Murders (Jean Lorrah)	'84	PB
36. Uhura's Song (Janet Kagan)	'85	PB
37. Shadow Lord (Lawrence Yep)	'85	PB
38. Ishmael (Barbara Hambly)	'85	PB
39. Killing Time (Della Van Hise)	'85	PB
40. Dwellers in the Crucible (Margaret Wander Bonanno)	'85	PB

<u>Star Trek TV Episode Adaptations</u>
(#s 1-11 by James Blish)

1. Star Trek	'67	Bant
2. Star Trek 2	'68	Bant
3. Star Trek 3	'69	Bant
4. Star Trek 4	'71	Bant
5. Star Trek 5	'72	Bant
6. Star Trek 6	'72	Bant

STEELE, CURTIS
    (pseud. of Frederick C. Davis, 1902-1977)

Operator 5
1. Legions of the Death Master   '66 Corin
2. The Army of the Dead   '66 Corin
3. The Invisible Empire   '66 Corin
    aka: Operator 5 #2: The Invisible Empire
        ('74/Freew)
4. Master of Broken Men   '66 Corin
5. Hosts of the Flaming Death   '66 Corin
6. Blood Reign of the Dictator   '66 Corin
7. March of the Flame Marauders   '66 Corin
8. Invasion of the Yellow Warlords   '66 Corin
9. The Masked Invasion   '74 Freew
    (labeled title #1 on cover)
10. The Yellow Scourge   '74 Freew
    (labeled title #3 on cover)
11. Cavern of the Damned   '80 PulpP

STEFFANSON, CON
    (see ALEX RAYMOND, "Flash Gordon" series)

STERLING, BRETT   (pseud., see EDMOND HAMILTON)

STERLING, PETER   (pseud., see DAVID STERN)

STERN, DAVID   (b.1909)

Francis
1. Francis... the Army Mule   '45 Adver
    (37pp. booklet written under pseud. of
    Peter Sterling)
2. Francis   '46 Farr
3. Francis Goes to Washington   '48 Farr

STEVENSON, FLORENCE

Kitty Telfair
1. The Witching Hour   '71 Award
2. Where Satan Dwells   '71 Award
3. Altar of Evil   '73 Award
4. Mistress of Devil's Manor   '73 Award
5. The Sorcerer of the Castle   '74 Award
6. The Silent Watcher   '75 Award

STEWART, MARY (b.1916)

    The Life of Merlin
1. The Crystal Cave   '70   H&S
2. The Hollow Hills   '73   H&S
3. The Last Enchantment   '79
4. The Wicked Day   '83   WmMor

STEWART, WILL (pseud., see JACK WILLIAMSON)

STILSON, CHARLES B.

    Polaris
1. Polaris of the Snows   '15/'65   Avalo
2. Minos of the Sardanes   '16/'66   Avalo
3. Polaris and the Immortals   '17/'68   Avalo

STINE, HANK (b.1945) (see "THE PRISONER")

STIVENS, DAL (b.1911)

    Ironbark Bill
1. The Gambling Ghost, and Other Tales   '53   Ang&R
2. Ironbark Bill   '55   Ang&R

STOCKBRIDGE, GRANT (pseud., see "THE SPIDER")

STOKER, BRAM (1847-1912)

    Dracula
1. Dracula   1897   Const
2. Dracula's Guest, and Other Weird Stories   '14   Routl
    aka: Dracula's Curse ('68/Tower)

STONEHAM, C.T. (b.1895)

    Kaspa
1. The Lion's Way; a Story of Men and Lions   '31   Hutch
    aka: King of the Jungle ('32/G&D)
2. Kaspa, the Lion Man   '33   Meth

STOREY, ANTHONY (b.1928)

(cont.)

The Rector
1. The Rector   '70   JCald
2. The Centre Holds   '73   JCald

STRATTON, CHRIS   (pseud. of Richard Hubbard)

Bugaloos
1. The Bugaloos and the Vile Vibes   '71   Curt
2. Rock City Rebels   '71   Curt
3. Benita's Platter Pollution   '71   Curt

STRATTON, THOMAS
    (pseud. of Thomas Eugene DeWeese &
    Robert Coulson)
    (see "U.N.C.L.E.")

STRUTTON, BILL   (see "DOCTOR WHO")

STURGEON, THEODORE   (1918-1985)
    (see "VOYAGE TO THE BOTTOM OF THE SEA")

SUCHARITKUL, SOMTOW

    also see: "V"

The Inquestor Trilogy
1. Light on the Sound   '82   PB
2. The Throne of Madness   '83   PB
3. Utopia Hunters   '84   Bant

SUE, EUGENE
    (pseud. of Marie Joseph, 1804-1857)

The Wandering Jew
1. The Wandering Jew   1844-45 ChapH
   (in 3 volumes)
2. The Ships of Tarshish, Being a Sequel
   to the "Wandering Jew"   1867   Hall
   (written under pseud.-- Mohoao)

SULLIVAN, TIM   (see "V")

SWANN, THOMAS BURNETT (1928-1976)

    Eunostos
1. Cry Silver Bells   '77 DAW
2. The Forest of Forever   '71 Ace
3. The Day of the Minotaur   '66 Ace

    The Prehumans
1. Lady of the Bees   '76 Ace
2. Green Phoenix   '72 DAW

SWEVEN, GODFREY
    (pseud. of John Macmillan Brown, 1846-1935)

    An Antarctic Utopia
1. Riallaro: The Archipelago of Exiles   '01 Putn
2. Limanora: The Island of Progress   '03 Putn

TABORI, PAUL (1908-1974)

    The Hunters
1. The Doomsday Brain   '67 Pyr
2. The Invisible Eye   '67 Pyr
3. The Torture Machine   '69 Pyr

TATE, PETER

    The Simeon Trilogy
1. The Thinking Seat   '69 Dbdy
2. Moon on an Iron Meadow   '74 Dbdy
3. Faces in the Flames   '76 Dbdy

TAYLOR, KEITH

    Bard
1. Bard   '81 Ace
2. Bard II   '84 Ace

TEDFORD, WILLIAM

    Timequest
1. Rashanyn Dark   Leisr
2. Hydrabyss Red   Leisr
3. Nemydia Deep   '81 Leisr

TEMPLE, M.H. (see CAROLINE LEWIS, pseud.)

TEMPLE, WILLIAM F. (b.1914)

    Martin Magnus
1. Martin Magnus, Planet Rover   '54 Mullr
2. Martin Magnus on Venus   '55 Mullr
3. Martin Magnus on Mars   '56 Mullr

TEPPER, SHERI S.

                   (cont.)

(Sheri S. Tepper, cont.)

    THE TRUE GAME
      The Mavin Trilogy

1. The Song of Mavin Manyshaped   '85 Ace
2. The Flight of Mavin Manyshaped   '85 Ace
3. The Search of Mavin Manyshaped   '85 Ace
      The True Game Trilogy
4. King's Blood Four   '83 Ace
5. Necromancer Nine   '83 Ace
6. Wizard's Eleven   '84 Ace
      Jinian
7. Jinian Footseer   '85 Tor

THACKER, ERIC (b.1923) (see ANTHONY EARNSHAW)

THEYDON, JOHN

    Stingray
1. Stingray   '65 Armad
2. Stingray and the Monster   '66 Armad

    Thunderbirds
1. Thunderbirds   '66 Armad
2. Calling Thunderbirds   '66 Armad
3. Thunderbirds Ring of Fire   '66 Armad
4. Thunderbirds Are Go
    (this title by Angus P. Allan) '66 Armad
5. Lady Penelope: The Albanian Affair '67 Armad

    Captain Scarlet
1. Captain Scarlet and the Mysterons   '67 Armad
2. Captain Scarlet and the Silent Saboteur '67 Armad

THOMAS, MARTIN (see PETER SAXON, pseud.)

THOMPSON, RUTH PLUMLY (1892-1976)
    (see L. FRANK BAUM, "Oz" series)

THURSTON, ROBERT (b.1936)
    (see GLEN A. LARSON, "Battlestar Galactica")

TIERNEY, RICHARD (b.1936)
    (see collaboration with DAVID C. SMITH)

TIGGES, JOHN

    Unto the Altar
1. Unto the Altar
2. Kiss Not the Child   '85 Leisr

TIMLETT, PETER VALENTINE (b.1933)

    The Serpent Trilogy
1. The Seedbearers   '74 Quart
2. The Power of the Serpent   '76 Bant
3. Twilight of the Serpent   '77 Bant

TITAN, EARL (pseud., see JOHN RUSSELL FEARN)

TODD, RUTHVEN

    Space Cat
1. Space Cat   '52 Scrib
2. Space Cat Visits Venus   '55 Scrib
3. Space Cat Meets Mars   '57 Scrib
4. Space Cat and the Kittens   '58 Scrib

TOLKIEN, J.R.R. (1892-1973)

    THE CHRONICLES OF MIDDLE-EARTH
1. The Hobbit   '37 Unwin
    The Lord of the Rings Trilogy (coll.'68/Unwin)
2. The Fellowship of the Ring   '54 Unwin
3. The Two Towers   '54 Unwin
4. The Return of the King   '55 Unwin
    additional titles of Middle Earth
5. The Silmarillion   '77 Unwin
   (Note— this book actually takes place
   long before the events in the other four,
   however it is likely to have more signi-
   ficance for the reader if read after the
   trilogy).
6. Unfinished Tales of Numenor and Middle-Earth
                                      '82 HMiff
7. The Book of Lost Tales, Part I   '83 Unwin
8. The Book of Lost Tales, Part II   '84 Unwin

"TOM SWIFT"

    (see VICTOR APPLETON, House pseudonym)

TOWNSEND, LARRY

    2069
1. 2069   '69 Pleas
2. 2069+1   '70 Pleas
3. 2069+2   '70 Pleas

TRACY, LOUIS (1863-1928)

    Vansittart
1. An American Emperor   1897 Pears
2. The Lost Provinces   1898 Pears

TRAIN, ARTHUR (1875-1945) & R.W. WOOD (1868-1955)

    Benjamin Hooker
1. The Man Who Rocked the Earth   '15 Dody
2. The Moon Maker   '58 Krueg

TRALINS, ROBERT (b.1926)

    Valentine Flynn (pseud.-- Sean O'Shea)
1. What a Way to Go!   '66 Belmt
2. Operation Boudoir   '67 Belmt
3. Win with Sin   '67 Belmt
4. The Nymph Island Affair   '67 Belmt
5. Invasion of the Nymphomaniacs '67 Belmt

    The Miss From S.I.S.
1. The Miss From S.I.S.   '66 Belmt
2. The Chic Chick Spy   '66 Belmt
3. The Ring-A-Ding UFOs   '67 Belmt

TRAVERS, P.L. (b.1906)

    Mary Poppins
1. Mary Poppins   '34 Howe
2. Mary Poppins Comes Back   '35 Dik&T
3. Mary Poppins Opens the Door '43 Rey&H
4. Mary Poppins in the Park   '52 PDavi
5. Mary Poppins From A to Z   '62 Harc
6. Mary Poppins in the Kitchen: A Cookery Book with a Story
    (written with Maurice Moore-Betty) '75 Harc
7. Mary Poppins in Cherry Tree Lane '82 WmCol

TREIBICH, S.J.
   (see collaboration with LAURENCE M. JANIFER)

TRIMBLE, LOUIS (b.1917)

   The Anthropol Bureau
1. Anthropol   '68 Ace
2. The Noblest Experiment in the Galaxy   '70 Ace

TUBB, E.C. (b.1919)

   also see: "SPACE: 1999"

   Dumarest of Terra
1. The Winds of Gath   '67 Ace
2. Derai   '68 Ace
3. Toyman   '69 Ace
4. Kalin   '69 Ace
5. The Jester at Scar   '70 Ace
6. Lallia   '71 Ace
7. Technos   '72 Ace
8. Veruchia   '73 Ace
9. Mayenne   '73 DAW
10. Jondelle   '73 DAW
11. Zenya   '74 DAW
12. Eloise   '75 DAW
13. Eye of the Zodiac   '75 DAW
14. Jack of Swords   '76 DAW
15. Spectrum of a Forgotten Sun   '76 DAW
16. Haven of Darkness   '77 DAW
17. Prison of Night   '77 DAW
18. Incident on Ath   '78 DAW
19. The Quillian Sector   '78 DAW
20. Web of Sand   '79 DAW
21. Iduna's Universe   '79 DAW
22. The Terra Data   '80 DAW
23. World of Promise   '80 DAW
24. Nectar of Heaven   '81 DAW
25. The Terridae   '81 DAW
26. The Coming Event   '82 DAW
27. Earth is Heaven   '82 DAW
28. Melome   '83 DAW
29. Angado   '84 DAW
30. Symbol of Terra   '84 DAW
31. The Temple of Truth   '85 DAW

(cont.)

(E.C. Tubb, cont.)

Cap Kennedy (pseud.— Gregory Kern)
1. Galaxy of the Lost   '73   DAW
2. Slave Ship From Sergan   '73   DAW
3. Monster of Metelaze   '73   DAW
4. Enemy Within the Skull   '74   DAW
5. Jewel of Jarhen   '74   DAW
6. Seetee Alert!   '74   DAW
7. The Gholan Gate   '74   DAW
8. The Eater of Worlds   '74   DAW
9. Earth Enslaved   '74   DAW
10. Planet of Dread   '74   DAW
11. Spawn of Laban   '74   DAW
12. The Genetic Buccaneer   '74   DAW
13. A World Aflame   '74   DAW
14. The Ghosts of Epidoris   '75   DAW
15. Mimics of Dephene   '75   DAW
16. Beyond the Galactic Lens   '75   DAW

TUCKER, WILSON (b.1914)

Gilbert Nash
1. The Time Masters   '53   Rine
2. Time Bomb   '55   Rine
    aka: Tomorrow Plus X ('57/Avon)

TUNING, WILLIAM (see H. BEAM PIPER, "Fuzzy" series)

"U.N.C.L.E."

    The Man From U.N.C.L.E.
    (NOTE— the British Four Square paperbacks number the series differently; the listing below is in the order of the American sequence).
1. The Thousand Coffins Affair
   (Michael Avallone)   '65 Ace
   aka: The Man From U.N.C.L.E.
   (FourS title #1, '65)
2. The Doomsday Affair (Harry Whittington) '65 Ace
   (FourS title #2, '65)
3. The Copenhagen Affair (John Oram) '65 Ace
   (FourS title #3, '66)
4. The Dagger Affair (David McDaniel) '65 Ace
   (FourS title #6, '66)
5. The Mad Scientist Affair
   (John T. Phillifent)   '66 Ace
   (FourS title #8, '66)
6. The Vampire Affair (David McDaniel) '66 Ace
   (FourS title #9, '66)
7. The Radioactive Camel Affair
   (Peter Leslie)   '66 Ace
   (FourS title #7, '66)
8. The Monster Wheel Affair
   (David McDaniel)   '67 Ace
   (FourS title #12, '67)
9. The Diving Dames Affair (Peter Leslie) '67 Ace
   (FourS title #10, '67)
10. The Assassination Affair (J. Hunter Holly)
        '67 Ace
11. The Invisibility Affair
    (Thomas Stratton) *   '67 Ace
12. The Mind-Twisters Affair
    (Thomas Stratton) *   '67 Ace
13. The Rainbow Affair (David McDaniel) '67 Ace
14. The Cross of Gold Affair (Fredric Davies) '68 Ace
15. The Utopia Affair (David McDaniel) '68 Ace
16. The Splintered Sunglasses Affair
    (Peter Leslie)   '68 Ace
    (FourS title #14, '68)
17. The Hollow Crown Affair (David McDaniel) '69 Ace
18. The Unfair Fare Affair (Peter Leslie) '69 Ace
    (FourS title #16, '68)

    (cont.)

("U.N.C.L.E.", cont.)

19. The Power Cube Affair
    (John T. Phillifent)   '69 Ace
    (FourS title #15,'68)
20. The Corfu Affair (John T. Phillifent)   '69 Ace
    (FourS title #13,'67)
21. The Thinking Machine Affair
    (Joel Bernard)   '70 Ace
    (FourS title #11,'67)
22. The Stone-Cold Dead in the Market Affair
    (John Oram)   '70 Ace
    (FourS title #4,'66)
23. The Finger in the Sky Affair
    (Peter Leslie)   '71 Ace
    (FourS title #5,'66)
24. The Man From U.N.C.L.E. and the Affair
    of the Gentle Saboteur (Brandon Keith)   '66 Whitm
25. The Calcutta Affair (George S. Elrick)   '67 Whitm

   * (Thomas Stratton is a joint pseudonym for
     Thomas Eugene DeWeese & Robert Coulson).

   The Girl From U.N.C.L.E.
1. The Birds-of-a-Feather Affair
   (Michael Avallone)   '66 Sign
2. The Blazing Affair (Michael Avallone)   '66 Sign
3. The Global Globules Affair (Simon Latter)   '67 FourS
4. The Golden Boats of Taradata Affair
   (Simon Latter)   '67 FourS
5. The Cornish Pixie Affair (Peter Leslie)   '67 FourS

"V"

1. V (A.C. Crispin)   '83 Pinn
2. V: East Coast Crisis
   (A.C. Crispin & Howard Weinstein)   '84 Pinn
3. The Pursuit of Diana (Allen Wold)   '84 Pinn
4. The Chicago Conversion (Geo. W. Proctor)   '85 Pinn
5. The Florida Project (Tim Sullivan)   '85 Pinn
6. Prisoners and Pawns (Howard Weinstein)   '85 Pinn
7. The Alien Swordmaster
   (Somtow Sucharitkul)   '85 Pinn
8. The Crivit Experiment (Allen Wold)   '85 Pinn
9. The New England Resistance
   (Tim Sullivan)   '85 Pinn
10. Death Tide
    (A.C. Crispin & Deborah A. Marshall)   '85 Pinn
11. The Texas Run (Geo. W. Proctor)   '85 Pinn

VAN ARNAM, DAVE

    Konarr
1. The Players of Hell　　　　　　　'68　Belmt
2. Wizard of Storms　　　　　　　　'70　Belmt

    Jamnar
1. Star Barbarian　　　　　　　　　'69　Lance
2. Lord of Blood　　　　　　　　　 '70　Lance

VANCE, JACK (b.1920)

    The Dying Earth
1. The Dying Earth　　　　　　　　　'50　Hillm
2. The Eyes of the Overworld　　　 '66　Ace
3. A Quest For Simbilis
   (this title by Michael Shea)　 '74　DAW
4. Cujel's Saga　　　　　　　　　　 '83　S&S
5. Rhialto the Marvelous　　　　　 '84　U-M

    The Demon Princes
1. Star King　　　　　　　　　　　　'64　Berk
2. The Killing Machine　　　　　　 '64　Berk
3. The Palace of Love　　　　　　　'67　Berk
4. The Face　　　　　　　　　　　　 '79　DAW
   (Note-- this edition was preceded by
   a Dutch translation)
5. The Book of Dreams　　　　　　　'81　DAW

    Tschai: Planet of Adventure
1. City of the Chasch　　　　　　　'68　Ace
2. Servants of the Wankh　　　　　 '69　Ace
3. The Dirdir　　　　　　　　　　　'69　Ace
4. The Pnume　　　　　　　　　　　 '70　Ace

    The Durdane Trilogy
1. The Anome　　　　　　　　　　　 '73　Dell
   aka: The Faceless Man ('78/Ace)
2. The Brave Free Men　　　　　　　'73　Dell
3. The Asutra　　　　　　　　　　　'74　Dell

    The Alastor Books (no specific reading sequence)
1. Trullion: Alastor 2262　　　　　'73　Ball
2. Marune: Alastor 933　　　　　　 '75　Ball
3. Wyst: Alastor 1716　　　　　　　'78　DAW

    Lyonesse
1. Lyonesse
2. Lyonesse II: The Green Pearl　 '85　U-M

VAN DER NAILLEN, A. (1830-1928)

    <u>The Magi</u>
1. On the Heights of Himalay   1890 ABC
2. In the Sanctuary   1896 Doxey
3. Balthazar the Magus   '04 Fenno

VAN HISE, DELLA (see "STAR TREK")

VAN LUSTBADER, ERIC

    <u>The Sunset Warrior Trilogy</u>
1. The Sunset Warrior   '77 Dbdy
2. Shallows of Night   '78 Dbdy
3. Dai-San   '78 Dbdy
    <u>Moichi</u>
4. Beneath an Opal Moon   '80 Dbdy

VAN SCYOC, SYDNEY J. (b.1939)

    <u>The Darkchild Trilogy</u> *
1. Darkchild   '82 Berk
2. Bluesong   '83 Berk
3. Starsilk   '84 Berk
    * all 3 collected as:
      Daughters of the Sunstone ('85/SFBC)

VAN VOGT, A.E. (b.1912)

    <u>Isher</u>
1. The Weapon Shops of Isher   '51 Grnbg
2. The Weapon Makers   '47 Hadly
    aka: One Against Eternity ('55/Ace)

    <u>Null-A</u>
1. The World of Null-A   '48 S&S
    aka: The World of $\overline{A}$
2. The Pawns of Null-A   '56 Ace
    revised as: The Players of Null-A
              ('66/Berk)
3. Null-A Three   '85 DAW

    <u>Linn</u>
1. Empire of the Atom   '57 Shast
2. The Wizard of Linn   '62 Ace

VARDEMAN, ROBERT E.

    also see: "STAR TREK"

    The War of the Powers (with Victor Milan)
1. The Sundered Realm   '80 Play
2. The City in the Glacier   '80 Play
3. The Destiny Stone   '80 Play
4. The Fallen Ones   '81 Play
5. In the Shadow of Omizantrim   '81 Play
6. Demon of the Dark Ages   '82 Play

    Cenotaph Road
1. Cenotaph Road   '83 Ace
2. The Sorcerer's Skull   '83 Ace
3. World of Mazes   '83 Ace
4. Iron Tongue   '84 Ace
5. Fire and Fog   '84 Ace
6. Pillar of Night   '84 Ace

    The Jade Demons
1. The Quaking Lands   '84 Avon
2. The Frozen Waves   '85 Avon
3. The Crystal Clouds   '85 Avon

    The Swords of Raemllyn (with Geo. W. Proctor)
1. To Demons Bound   '85 Ace
2. A Yoke of Magic   '85 Ace
3. Blood Fountain   '85 Ace

VARLEY, JOHN (b.1947)

    Gaea
1. Titan   '79 Putn
2. Wizard   '80 Putn
3. Demon   '84 Putn

VERNE, JULES (1828-1905)

    also see: EDGAR ALLAN POE, "Arthur Gordon Pym"

    NOTE-- determing the true first editions of Verne's books is extremely difficult, due to the innumerable printings, authorized and unauthorized, on both sides of the Atlantic. When possible, the earliest date is that of the original French publication.

(Jules Verne, cont.)

The Gun Club *
1. From the Earth to the Moon   1865
     aka: The American Gun Club
               (1874/Scrib)
     aka: The Baltimore Gun Club
               (1874/K&B)
2. Around the Moon   1870
     aka: Round the Moon
     * Both titles published in one volume as:
     "From the Earth to the Moon and A Trip
       Around It" (1873/S,Low)
     aka: All Around the Moon
     aka: The Moon-Voyage
     aka: A Voyage to the Moon
     aka: From Earth to Moon
     aka: A Tour of the Moon

The Adventures of Captain Hatteras
1. The English at the North Pole   1866
     aka: A Journey to the North Pole
2. Field of Ice   1866
     aka: The Desert of Ice
     aka: The Ice Desert
     aka: The Wilderness of Ice

Captain Nemo
1. Twenty Thousand Leagues Under the Sea   1870
2. The Mysterious Island   1875

The Floating City
1. A Floating City   1871
     aka: Propeller Island
2. The Blockade Runners   1876

Hector Servadac (coll. 1878)
1. Hector Servadac   1877
     aka: Astounding Adventures Among the
            Comets
     aka: To the Sun? A Journey Through
            Planetary Space
2. Off On a Comet!   1878
     aka: Homeward Bound
     aka: Anamalous Phenomena

Steam House Sequence
1. The Demon of Cawnpore   1880
2. Tigers and Traitors   1880

222

Kerban the Inflexible
1. The Captain of the Guidara   1883
2. Scarpante the Spy   1883

Robur the Conqueror
1. The Clipper of the Clouds   1886
   aka: Robur the Conqueror
   aka: A Trip Around the World
   in a Flying Machine
2. Master of the World   '04

Swiss Family Robinson
1. Their Island Home   1900
2. Castaways of the Flag   1900

Barsac Mission
1. Into the Niger Bend   '20
2. City in the Sahara   '20

VERRILL, A. HYATT (1871-1954)

The Trail Sequence
1. The Trail of the Cloven Foot   '18   EPDut
2. The Trail of the White Indians   '20   EPDut

The Boy Adventurers
1. The Boy Adventurers in the Land of El Dorado   c.'20   Putn
2. The Boy Adventurers in the Unknown Land   c.'20   Putn
3. The Boy Adventurers in the Land of the
   Monkey Men   '21   Putn
4. The Boy Adventurers in the Forbidden Land   '22   Putn

The Radio Detectives
(Note-- the following order of publication is uncertain)
1. The Radio Detectives   '22   Apple
2. The Radio Detectives in the Jungle   '22   Apple
3. The Radio Detectives Southward Bound   '22   Apple
4. The Radio Dertectives Under the Sea   '22   Apple

VIERECK, GEORGE S. (1884-1962) & PAUL ELDRIDGE

The Three Immortals
1. My First Two Thousand Years   '28   Macau
2. Salome: The Wandering Jewess   '30   Liver
   aka: Salome: 2000 Years of Love
3. The Invincible Adam   '32   Liver

VINGE, JOAN D. (b.1948)

    also see: L. FRANK BAUM, "Oz" series

    <u>The Snow Queen Sequence</u>
1. Snow Queen   '80 Dial
2. World's End   '84 Bjay

VIVIAN, E. CHARLES (1882-1947)

    <u>Aia</u>
1. Fields of Sleep   '23 Hutch
2. People of the Darkness   '24 Hutch

    <u>Detective Gees</u> (pseud.— Jack Mann)
1. Gees' First Case   '36 Wr&Br
2. Nightmare Farm   '37 Wr&Br
3. Grey Shapes   '37 Wr&Br
4. The Kleinert Case   '38 Wr&Br
5. Maker of Shadows   '38 Wr&Br
6. The Ninth Life   '39 Wr&Br
7. Her Ways Are Death   '39 Wr&Br
8. The Glass Too Many   '40 Wr&Br

VLCEK, ERNST (see "PERRY RHODAN")

VOLTZ, WILLIAM (see "PERRY RHODAN")

"VOYAGE TO THE BOTTOM OF THE SEA"

1. Voyage to the Bottom of the Sea
    (Theodore Sturgeon) (movie adaptation) '61 Pyr
2. City Under the Sea (Paul W. Fairman)   '65 Pyr
3. Voyage to the Bottom of the Sea
    (Raymond F. Jones)   '65 Whitm
    (TV adaptation)

W

W.W. (pseud., see WILLIAM BLOOM)

WAGNER, KARL EDWARD (b.1945)

    also see: ROBERT E. HOWARD, "Conan" series

    Kane
1. Darkness Weaves with Many Shades   '70   Powel
   aka: Darkness Weaves ('78/Warnr)
2. Death Angel's Shadow   '73   Warnr
3. Bloodstone   '75   Warnr
4. Dark Crusade   '76   Warnr
5. Night Winds   '78   Warnr

WALKER, HUGH (pseud. of Hubert Strassl)

    The Magira Series
1. War Gamers' World   '78   DAW
2. Army of Darkness   '79   DAW
3. Messengers of Darkness   '80   DAW

WALL, MERVYN (b.1908)

    Fursey
1. The Unfortunate Fursey   '46   Pilot
2. The Return of Fursey   '48   Pilot

WALLACE, IAN (pseud. of John Wallace Pritchard, b.1912)

    The Minds-in-Bodies Series
1. The World Asunder   '76   DAW
2. Pan Sagittarius   '73   Putn

    The Croyd Series
1. Croyd   '67   Putn
2. Dr. Orpheus   '68   Putn
3. A Voyage to Dari   '74   DAW
4. Z-Sting   '78   DAW
5. Door to Enigma   '79   DAW
6. Heller's Leap   '79   DAW

(Ian Wallace, cont.)

    Claudine St. Cyr
1. The Purloined Prince   '71   McCal
2. Deathstar Voyage   '69   Putn
3. The Sign of the Mute Medusa   '77   Pop
4. Heller's Leap   '79   DAW

WALTERS, HUGH (pseud. of Walter Llewellyn Hughes, b.1910)

    Chris Godfrey of the U.N. Exploration Agency
1. Blast Off at Woomera   '57   Faber
    aka: Blast-Off at 0300 ('58/Crite)
2. The Domes of Pico   '58   Faber
3. Operation Columbus   '60   Faber
    aka: First on the Moon ('60/Crite)
4. Moon Base One   '61   Faber
    aka: Outpost on the Moon ('62/Crite)
5. Expedition Venus   '62   Faber
6. Destination Mars   '63   Faber
7. Terror By Satellite   '64   Faber
8. Journey to Jupiter   '65   Faber
9. Mission to Mercury   '65   Faber
10. Spaceship to Saturn   '67   Faber
11. The Mohole Mystery   '68   Faber
    aka: The Mohole Menace ('69/Crite)
12. Nearly Neptune   '69   Faber
    aka: Neptune One is Missing ('70/IvesW)
13. First Contact?   '71   Faber
14. Passage to Pluto   '73   Faber
15. Tom Hale, Space Detective   '73   Faber
16. Murder on Mars   '75   Faber
17. Boy Astronaut   '77   Abeld
18. The Caves of Drach   '77   Faber
19. The Last Disaster   '79   Mermk
20. The Blue Aura   '79   Mermk
21. The Dark Triangle   '81   Faber
22. School on the Moon   '81   Abeld

WALTHER, DANIEL

    Shai
1. The Book of Shai   '84   DAW
2. Shai's Destiny   '85   DAW

WALTON, EVANGELINE (b.1907)

                                     (cont.)

The Books of the Welsh Mabinogion
1. Prince of Annwn '74 Ball
2. The Children of Llyr '71 Ball
3. The Song of Rhiannon '72 Ball
4. The Virgin and the Swine '36 WilCl
   aka: The Island of the Mighty ('70/Ball)

WANDREI, DONALD (b.1908) (see H.P. LOVECRAFT)

WANGERIN, WALTER Jr.

The Coop
1. The Book of the Dun Cow '78 Harpr
2. The Book of Sorrows '85 Harpr

WARD, HAROLD (see ZORRO, pseud.)

WATERS, T.A. (see CHESTER ANDERSON)

WATSON, IAN (b.1943)

The Books Sequence
1. The Book of the River '84 Gollz
2. The Book of the Stars '84 Gollz
3. The Book of Being '85 Gollz

WATT-EVANS, LAWRENCE (b.1954)

The Garth Series
1. The Lure of the Basilisk '80 DelR
2. The Seven Alters of Dusarra '81 DelR
3. The Sword of the Bheleu '82 DelR
4. The Book of Silence '84 DelR

WAYMAN, TONY RUSSELL (b.1929)

Dreamhouse
1. World of the Sleeper '67 Ace
2. Ads Infinitum '71 Curt

WEBB, SHARON

(cont.)

(cont.)
        The Earthchild Trilogy
1. Earthchild   '82 Athen
2. Earthsong   '83 Athen
3. Ramsong   '84 Athen

WEIN, LEN (see "MARVEL SUPER-HEROES")

WEINSTEIN, HOWARD (b.1954)
    see: "V"
    see: "STAR TREK"

WEINSTEIN, SOL (b.1928)

    Israel Bond
1. Loxfinger; a Thrilling Adventure of Hebrew Secret Agent Oy-Oy-7, Israel Bond   '65 PB
2. Matzohball; A New Adventure of Hebrew Secret Agent Oy-Oy-7, Israel Bond   '66 PB

WEIS, MARGARET & TRACY HICKMAN

    Dragonlance Chronicles
1. Dragons of Autumn Twilight   '85 TSR
2. Dragons of Winter Night   '85 TSR

WELLMAN, MANLY WADE (b.1903)

    also see: EDMOND HAMILTON, "Captain Future" series
    also see: H.P. LOVECRAFT

    Silver John
1. Who Fears the Devil?   '63 ArkH
2. Worse Things Waiting   '73 Carco
   (contains 2 Silver John stories)
3. The Old Gods Waken   '79 Dbdy
4. After Dark   '80 Dbdy
5. The Lost and the Lurking   '81 Dbdy
6. The Hanging Stones   '82 Dbdy
7. The Voice of the Mountain   '84 Dbdy

WELLS, H.G. (1866-1946)
                  (cont.)

The Time Machine
1. The Time Machine   1895   Heine
    (sequels)
2. The Return of the Time Machine   '46/'72 DAW
    (Egon Friedell)
3. The Time Machine II
    (George Pal & Joe Morhaim)   '81   Dell

WERPER, BARTON   (see EDGAR RICE BURROUGHS, "Tarzan" series)

WEVERKA, ROBERT   (b.1926)

Search
1. Search   '73   Bant
2. Moonrock   '73   Bant

WHEATLEY, DENNIS   (1897-1977)

Duc de Richleau
(Note-- only titles 2,5, & 11 are particularly
occult-related)
1. The Forbidden Territory   '33   Hutch
2. The Devil Rides Out   '34   Hutch
3. The Golden Spaniard   '38   Hutch
4. Three Inquisitive People   '40   Hutch
5. Strange Conflict   '41   Hutch
6. Codeword-- Golden Fleece   '46   Hutch
7. The Second Seal   '50   Hutch
8. The Prisoner in the Mask   '57   Hutch
9. Vendetta in Spain   '61   Hutch
10. Dangerous Inheritance   '65   Hutch
11. Gateway to Hell   '70   Hutch

Colonel Verney
1. To the Devil-- A Daughter   '53   Hutch
2. The Satanist   '60   Heine

WHITE, JAMES   (b.1928)

Sector General
1. Hospital Station   '62   Ball
2. Star Surgeon   '63   Ball
3. The Aliens Among Us   '69   Ball
    (not all stories are Sector General)
4. Major Operation   '71   Ball

(cont.)

(James White, cont.)

    5. Ambulence Ship   '79 Ball
    6. Futures Past   '82 DelR
    7. Sector General   '83 DelR
    8. Star Healer   '85 DelR

WHITE, STEWART EDWARD (1873-1946)

    Percy Darrow
    1. The Mystery (with Samuel Hopkins Adams)   '07 McClr
    2. The Sign at Six   '12 Bob-M

WHITE, T.H. (1906-1964)

    CAMELOT
        The Once and Future King (rev. & coll. '58/WmCol)
    1. The Sword in the Stone   '38 WmCol
    2. The Witch in the Wood   '39 Putn
    3. The Ill-Made Knight   '40 Putn
       additional title
    4. The Book of Merlyn   '77 UnTex

WHITE, TED (b.1938)

    also see: "MARVEL SUPER-HEROES"

    Android Tanner Sequence
    1. Android Avenger   '65 Ace
    2. The Spawn of the Death Machine   '68 PbLib

    Qanar
    1. Phoenix Prime   '66 Lance
    2. The Sorceress of Qar   '66 Lance
    3. Star Wolf!   '71 Lance

WHITTAKER, DAVID (see "DOCTOR WHO")

WHITTINGTON, HARRY (see "U.N.C.L.E.")

WIBBERLEY, LEONARD (1915-1983)

    Grand Fenwick
                        (cont.)

1. Beware of the Mouse '58 Putn
2. The Mouse That Roared '55 LtBrn
   aka: The Wrath of Grapes ('55/Hale)
3. The Mouse on the Moon '62 WmMor
4. The Mouse on Wall St. '69 WmMor
5. The Mouse That Saved the West '81 WmMorw

WILDER, CHERRY (pseud. of Cherry Barbara Grimm, b.1930)

The Torin Series
1. The Luck of Brin's Five '77 Athen
2. The Nearest Fire '80 Athen
3. Second Nature '82 PB

Rulers of Hylor
1. A Princess of the Chamelin '84 Athen
2. Yorath the Wolf '84 Athen

WILLIAMS, CHARLES (1886-1945)

Sir Giles Tumulty
1. War in Heaven '30 Gollz
2. Many Dimensions '31 Gollz

WILLIAMS, GORDON

The Micronauts
1. Micronauts '77 Bant
2. The Microcolony '79 Bant
3. Revolt of the Micronauts '81 Bant

WILLIAMS, JAY (1914-1978) & RAYMOND ABRASHKIN (1911-1960)

Danny Dunn
1. Danny Dunn and the Anti-Gravity Paint '56 WhitH
2. Danny Dunn on a Desert Island '57 WhitH
3. Danny Dunn and the Homework Machine '58 WhitH
   aka: The Homework Machine ('60/Brock)
4. Danny Dunn and the Weather Machine '59 WhitH
5. Danny Dunn on the Ocean Floor '60 WhitH
6. Danny Dunn and the Fossil Cave '61 WhitH
7. Danny Dunn and the Heat Ray '62 WhitH
8. Danny Dunn, Time Traveller '63 WhitH
9. Danny Dunn and the Automatic House '65 WhitH

(cont.)

(Williams & Abrashkin, cont.)

10. Danny Dunn and the Voice From Space	'67	McGrH
11. Danny Dunn and the Smallifying Machine	'69	McGrH
12. Danny Dunn and the Swamp Monster	'71	McGrH
13. Danny Dunn, Invisible Boy	'74	McGrH
14. Danny Dunn, Scientific Detective	'77	McGrH
15. Danny Dunn and the Universal Glue	'77	McGrH

WILLIAMS, PAUL O. (b.1935)

The Pelbar Cycle

1. The Breaking of Northwall	'81	DelR
2. Ends of the Circle	'81	DelR
3. The Dome in the Forest	'81	DelR
4. The Fall of the Shell	'82	DelR
5. An Ambush of Shadows	'83	DelR
6. The Song of the Axe	'84	DelR

WILLIAMS, ROBERT MOORE (1907-1978)

Jongor

1. Jongor of the Lost Land	'40/'70	Pop
2. The Return of Jongor	'44/'70	Pop
3. Jongor Fights Back	'51/'70	Pop

Zanthar

1. Zanthar of the Many Worlds	'67	Lance
2. Zanthar at the Edge of Never	'68	Lance
3. Zanthar at Moon's Madness	'68	Lance
4. Zanthar at Trip's End	'69	Lance

WILLIAMSON, J.N.
(pseud. of Gerald Neal Williamson, b.1932)

Lamia Zacharius

1. Death-Coach	'81	Zebra
2. Death-Angel	'81	Zebra
3. Death-School	'82	Zebra
4. Death-Doctor	'82	Zebra

WILLIAMSON, JACK (b.1908)

The Legion of Space

1. Legion of Space	'47	FantP

(cont.)

2. The Cometeers   '50   FantP
   abridged version: ('67/Pyr)
3. One Against the Legion   '67   Pyr
   (title story originally in "The Cometeers",
   plus a new novelette added to it for this
   publication)
4. The Queen of the Legion   '83   PB

   The Humanoids
1. The Humanoids   '49   S&S
2. The Humanoid Touch   '80   Phant

   Seetee   (pseud.— Will Stewart)
1. Seetee Ship   '51   Gnome
2. Seetee Shock   '50   S&S

   The Legion of Time   (coll.'52/Fantasy Pr)
1. The Legion of Time   '61   Digit
2. After World's End   '61   Digit

   Eden Series   (written with Frederik Pohl)
1. Undersea Quest   '54   Gnome
2. Undersea Fleet   '56   Gnome
3. Undersea City   '58   Gnome

   The Starchild Trilogy   (coll.'77/PbLib)
   (written with Frederik Pohl)
1. The Reefs of Space   '64   Ball
2. Starchild   '65   Ball
3. Rogue Star   '69   Ball

   Heechee Trilogy   (written with Frederik Pohl)
1. Gateway   '77   StM
2. Beyond the Blue Event Horizon   '80   Ball
3. Heechee Rendezvous   '84   DelR

   The Saga of Cuckoo   (coll.'83)
   (written with Frederik Pohl)
1. Farthest Star   '75   Ball
2. Wall Around a Star   '83   DelR

WILSON, COLIN   (b.1931)

        Gerard Sorme
1. Ritual in the Dark   '60   Gollz
2. Man Without a Shadow   '63   Barkr
   aka: The Sex Diary of Gerard Sorme   ('63/Dial)
3. The God of the Labyrinth   '70   HartD
   aka: The Hedonists   ('71/Sign)

WILSON, HAZEL (b.1898)

    Herbert
1. Herbert   '50 Knopf
2. Herbert's Space Trip   '65 Knopf

WILSON, ROBERT ANTON (b.1932)

    ILLUMINATUS!
    The Illuminatus Trilogy
1. The Eye in the Pyramid (with Robert Shea) '75 Dell
2. The Golden Apple (with Robert Shea) '75 Dell
3. Leviathan (with Robert Shea) '75 Dell
    The Historical Illuminatus Chronicles
4. The Earth Will Shake '84

    Schrodinger's Cat
1. The Universe Next Door '79 PB
2. The Trick Top Hat '81 PB
3. The Homing Pigeons '81 PB

WOLD, ALLEN (see "V")

WOLFE, GENE (b.1931)

    The Book of the New Sun
1. The Shadow of the Torturer '80 S&S
2. The Claw of the Conciliator '81 S&S
3. The Sword of the Lictor '81 S&S
4. The Citadel of the Autarch '83 S&S
5. The Castle of the Otter (NYP)

WOLFMAN, MARV (see "MARVEL SUPER-HEROES")

WOLLHEIM, DONALD A. (b.1914)

    Mike Mars
1. Mike Mars, Astronaut '61 Dbdy
2. Mike Mars Flies the X-15 '61 Dbdy
3. Mike Mars at Cape Canaveral '61 Dbdy
4. Mike Mars in Orbit '61 Dbdy
5. Mike Mars Flies the Dyna-Soar '62 Dbdy
6. Mike Mars, South Pole Spaceman '62 Dbdy
7. Mike Mars and the Mystery Satellite '63 Dbdy
8. Mike Mars Around the Moon '64 Dbdy

(Donald A. Wollheim, cont.)

    Destiny (pseud.— David Grinnell)
1. Destiny's Orbit   '61 Avalo
2. Destination: Saturn (with Lin Carter)   '67 Avalo

WOOD, MRS. HENRY (1814-1887)

    Johnny Ludlow
1. Johnny Ludlow   1874 Benty
2. Johnny Ludlow, Second Series   1880 Benty
3. Johnny Ludlow, Third Series   1885 Benty
4. Johnny Ludlow, Fourth Series   1890 Benty
5. Johnny Ludlow, Fifth Series   1890 Benty
6. Johnny Ludlow, Sixth Series   1899 Benty

WOOD, R.W.
    (see collaboration with ARTHUR TRAIN)

WORFEL, W.G. (see "BARON MUNCHAUSEN")

WORMSER, RICHARD (see "GREEN HORNET")

WREDE, PATRICIA C.

    Lyra
1. Shadow Magic   '82 Ace
2. The Harp of Imach Thyssel   '85 Ace

WREN, M.K.
    (pseud. of Martha Kay Renfroe, b.1938)

    The Phoenix Legacy
1. Sword of the Lamb   '81 Berk
2. Shadow of the Swan   '81 Berk
3. House of the Wolf   '81 Berk

WRIGHT, S. FOWLER (1874-1965)

    The World Below (coll.'29/WmCol)
1. The Amphibians   '25 Mertn
2. The World Below   '29 WmCol
    aka: The Dwellers ('54/Pantr)

(S. Fowler Wright, cont.)

Martin Webster
1. Deluge   '27   FoWri
2. Dawn   '29   Cosmo

Marguerite Cranleigh
1. Dream; or, The Simian Maid   '31   Harrp
2. Spiders' War   '54   Abeld

The War of 1938
1. Prelude in Prague: A Story of the
 War of 1938   '35   Newne
2. Four Days War   '36   Hale
3. Megiddo's Ridge   '37   Hale

WRIGHTSON, PATRICIA (b.1921)

The Australian Trilogy
1. The Ice is Coming   '77   Hutch
2. The Dark Bright Water   '78   Hutch
3. Behind the Wind   '81   Hutch
 aka: Journey Behind the Wind ('81/Athen)

WYLIE, PHILIP (1902-1971) & EDWARD BALMER (1883-1959)

Bronson Beta
1. When Worlds Collide   '33   Stoke
2. After Worlds Collide   '34   Stoke

X-Y-Z

YARBRO, CHELSEA QUINN (b.1942)

The Saint-Germain Series
1. Hotel Transylvania   '78 StM
2. The Palace   '78 StM
3. Blood Games   '80 StM
4. Path of the Eclipse   '81 StM
5. Tempting Fate   '82 StM
6. The Saint-Germain Chronicles '83 PB

YCAS, MARTYNAS (see collaboration with GEORGE GAMOW)

YEP, LAWRENCE (b.1948)

also see: "STAR TREK"

Shimmer and Thorn
1. The Dragon of the Lost Sea
2. Dragon Steel   '85 Harpr

YERMAKOV, NICHOLAS

also see: GLEN A. LARSON, "Battlestar Galactica"

Last Communion Sequence
1. Last Communion   '81 Sign
2. Epiphany   '82 Sign
3. Jehad   '84 Sign

Time War Series (pseud.-- Simon Hawke)
1. The Ivanhoe Gambit   '84 Ace
2. The Timekeeper Conspiracy   '84 Ace
3. The Pimpernel Plot   '84 Ace
4. The Zenda Vendetta   '85 Ace

YOLEN, JANE

Dragon Sequence
1. Dragon's Blood   '82 Delac
2. Heart's Blood   '84 Delac

ZAGAT, LEO (1895-1949) (see "SECRET AGENT X")

ZEBROWSKI, GEORGE (b.1945)

    The Omega Point Trilogy (coll.'83/Ace)
1. Ashes and Stars   '77 Ace
2. The Omega Point   '72 Ace
3. Mirror of Minds

ZELAZNY, ROGER (b.1937)

    Isle of the Dead
1. Isle of the Dead   '69 Ace
2. To Die in Italbar   '73 Dbdy

    The Amber Series
1. Nine Princes in Amber   '70 Dbdy
2. The Guns of Avalon   '72 Dbdy
3. The Sign of the Unicorn   '75 Dbdy
4. The Hand of Oberon   '76 Dbdy
5. The Courts of Chaos   '78 Dbdy
6. Trumps of Doom   '85 Arbor

    The Changeling Saga
1. Changeling   '80 Ace
2. Madwand   '81 Phant

    Dilvish of Dilvar
1. The Changing Land   '81 DelR
2. Dilvish, the Damned   '82 DelR

ZETFORD, TELLY (pseud., see KENNETH BULMER)

ZIMMER, PAUL EDWIN

    The Survivors Sequence
    (in collaboration with Marion Zimmer Bradley)
1. Hunters of the Red Moon   '73 DAW
2. The Survivors   '79 DAW

    The Dark Border
1. The Lost Prince   '82 Berk
2. King Chondo's Ride   '82 Berk

ZORRO (pseud. of Harold Ward)

    Doctor Death
1. 12 Must Die   '66   Corin
2. The Gray Creatures   '66   Corin
3. The Shriveling Murders   '66   Corin
4. Stories From Doctor Death   '66   Corin

ANTHOLOGIES

ABBEY, LYNN
    (see collaboration with ROBERT LYNN ASPRIN)

ACKERMAN, FORREST J. (b.1916) (see FREDERIK POHL)

ALDISS, BRIAN W. (b.1925)

    also see: collaboration with HARRY HARRISON
    also see: "NEBULA AWARD SERIES"

The Penguin SF Series
1. Penguin Science Fiction   '61   Peng
2. More Penguin Science Fiction   '63   Peng
3. Yet More Penguin Science Fiction   '64   Peng

Decades
(with Harry Harrison)
1. Decade the 1940s   '75   MacmL
2. Decade the 1950s   '76   MacmL
3. Decade the 1960s   '77   MacmL

Galactic Empires
1. Galactic Empires, Volume One   '76   Weide
2. Galactic Empires, Volume Two   '76   Weide

ALLEN, DICK

Science Fiction: The Future
1. Science Fiction: The Future   '71   Harc
2. Science Fiction: The Future, Second Edition
     '83   Harc

AMIS, KINGSLEY (b.1922) & ROBERT CONQUEST (b.1917)

Spectrum
1. Spectrum   '62   Harc
2. Spectrum 2   '63   Harc
3. Spectrum 3   '64   Harc
4. Spectrum 4   '65   Harc
5. Spectrum 5   '67   Harc

"ANALOG YEARBOOK"

    1. Analog Yearbook (Ben Bova)   '77 Ace
    2. Analog Yearbook II (Stanley Schmidt)   '81 Ace

ANDERSON, POUL (b.1926) (see "NEBULA AWARDS SERIES")

"THE ARBOR HOUSE SERIES"

    1. The Arbor House Treasury of Modern Science Fiction
       (Robert Silverberg & Martin H. Greenberg)
                                                         '80 Arbor
    2. The Arbor House Treasury of Great Science
       Fiction Short Novels
       (Robert Silverberg & Martin H. Greenberg)
                                                         '80 Arbor
    3. The Arbor House Treasury of Horror and the
       Supernatural (Bill Pronzini, Barry N. Malz-
       berg, Martin H. Greenberg)   '81 Arbor
    4. The Arbor House Celebrity Book of Horror Stories
       (Charles G. Waugh & Martin H. Greenberg)
                                                       '83 Arbor
    5. The Arbor House Treasury of Science Fiction
       Masterpieces (Robert Silverberg & Martin H.
       Greenberg)   '83 Arbor

ARNOLD, MARK ALAN (see collaboration with TERRI WINDLING)

ASHLEY, MICHAEL (b.1948)

        The History of the Science Fiction Magazine
    1. Part 1, 1926-1935   '74 NEL
    2. Part 2, 1936-1945   '75 NEL
    3. Part 3, 1946-1955   '76 NEL
    4. Part 4, 1956-1965   '78 NEL

        The Best of British SF
    1. The Best of British SF 1   '77 Futur
    2. The Best of British SF 2   '77 Futur

ASIMOV, ISAAC (b.1920)

            also see: "NEBULA AWARD SERIES"
            also see: GEORGE H. SCITHERS

The Hugo Winners
1. The Hugo Winners (vol.1)   '62   Dbdy
2. The Hugo Winners (vol.2)   '71   Dbdy
3. The Hugo Winners (vol.3)   '77   Dbdy
4. The Hugo Winners (vol.4)   '85   Dbdy

100 Short Short Stories
1. 100 Great Science Fiction Short Short Stories (with Martin H. Greenberg & Joseph D. Olander)   '78   Dbdy
2. 100 Great Fantasy Short Short Stories (with Terry Carr & Martin H. Greenberg) '84   Dbdy

The Great SF Stories (with Martin H. Greenberg)
1. The Great SF Stories 1 (1939)   '79   DAW
2. The Great SF Stories 2 (1940)   '79   DAW
3. The Great SF Stories 3 (1941)   '80   DAW
4. The Great SF Stories 4 (1942)   '80   DAW
5. The Great SF Stories 5 (1943)   '81   DAW
6. The Great SF Stories 6 (1944)   '81   DAW
7. The Great SF Stories 7 (1945)   '82   DAW
8. The Great SF Stories 8 (1946)   '82   DAW
9. The Great SF Stories 9 (1947)   '83   DAW
10. The Great SF Stories 10 (1948)   '83   DAW
11. The Great SF Stories 11 (1949)   '84   DAW
12. The Great SF Stories 12 (1950)   '84   DAW

Space Mail
1. Space Mail (with Martin H. Greenberg & Joseph D. Olander)   '80   Fawc
2. Space Mail Vol.II (with Martin H. Greenberg & Charles G. Waugh)   '82   Fawc

The "7" Duet
(with Martin H. Greenberg & Charles G. Waugh)
1. The 7 Deadly Sins of Science Fiction   '80   Fawc
2. The 7 Cardinal Virtues of Science Fiction '81   Fawc

The Raintree Series
(with Martin Harry Greenberg & Charles Waugh)
1. After the End   '81   Rain
2. Thinking Machines   '81   Rain
3. Travels Through Time   '81   Rain
4. Wild Inventions   '81   Rain
5. Earth Invaded   '82   Rain
6. Mad Scientists   '82   Rain
7. Mutants   '82   Rain
8. Tomorrow's TV   '82   Rain

(cont.)

(Isaac Asimov, cont.)

   9. Bug Awful '84 Rain
10. Children of the Future '84 Rain
11. The Immortals '84 Rain
12. Time Warps '84 Rain

Isaac Asimov Presents:
(with Martin H. Greenberg & Charles G. Waugh)
1. The Best Science Fiction of the 19th Century '81 Beauf
2. The Best Fantasy of the 19th Century '82 Beauf
3. The Best Horror and the Supernatural of the 19th Century '83 Beauf

The Science in Science Fiction
(with Martin H. Greenberg & Charles G. Waugh)
1. Caught in the Organ Draft: Biology in Science Fiction '83 Farr
2. Hallucination Orbit: Psychology in Science Fiction '83 Farr

Isaac Asimov's Wonderful Worlds of Science Fiction
(with Martin H. Greenberg & Charles G. Waugh)
1. Intergalactic Empires '83 Sign
2. The Science Fictional Olympics '84 Sign
3. Supermen '84 Sign

Isaac Asimov's Magical Worlds of Fantasy
(with Martin H. Greenberg & Charles G. Waugh)
1. Wizards '83 Sign
2. Witches '84 Sign
3. Cosmic Knights '85 Sign
4. Spells '85 Sign

ASPRIN, ROBERT LYNN (b.1946)

Sanctuary *
1. Thieves' World '79 Ace
2. Tales From the Vulgar Unicorn '80 Ace
3. Shadows Over Sanctuary '81 Ace
4. Storm Season '82 Ace
5. The Face of Chaos '83 Ace
6. Wings of Omen (with Lynn Abbey) '84 Ace
7. The Dead of Winter (with Lynn Abbey) '85 Ace

    * The first 3 titles are collected as: Sanctuary
    * The last 3 titles are collected as: Cross-Currents ('84/SFBC)

"THE AVON DECADE SERIES"

    1. Science Fiction of the 30s (Damon Knight) '75 Avon
    2. Science Fiction of the 40s
        (Frederik Pohl, Martin H. Greenberg,
        & Joseph D. Olander) '78 Avon
    3. Science Fiction of the 50s
        (Martin H. Greenberg & Joseph D. Olander)
          '79 Avon

BAEN, JAMES (b.1943)

    also see: "EDITORS OF GALAXY"
    also see: "EDITORS OF IF"
    also see: collaboration with JERRY POURNELLE

  Destinies
1. Destinies, Vol.1, no.1   '78 Ace
2. Destinies, Vol.1, no.2   '79 Ace
3. Destinies, Vol.1, no.3   '79 Ace
4. Destinies, Vol.1, no.4   '79 Ace
5. Destinies, Vol.1, no.5   '79 Ace
6. Destinies, Vol.2, no.1   '80 Ace
7. Destinies, Vol.2, no.2   '80 Ace
8. Destinies, Vol.2, no.3   '80 Ace
9. Destinies, Vol.2, no.4   '80 Ace
10. The Best of Destinies   '80 Ace
11. Destinies, Vol.3, no.1   '81 Ace
12. Destinies, Vol.3, no.2   '81 Ace

"THE BALLANTINE 'BEST OF' SERIES"

1. The Best of Fritz Leiber   '74 Dbdy
2. The Best of Stanley G. Weinbaum   '74 Ball
3. The Best of Henry Kuttner   '75 Dbdy
4. The Best of C.L. Moore   '75 Dbdy
5. The Best of Frederik Pohl   '75 Dbdy
6. The Best of Cordwainer Smith   '75 Dbdy
7. The Best of Frederic Brown   '76 Dbdy
8. The Best of John W. Campbell, Jr.   '76 Dbdy
9. The Best of Damon Knight   '76 Dbdy
10. The Best of C.M. Kornbluth   '76 Dbdy
11. The Best of Robert Bloch   '77 Ball
12. The Best of Leigh Brackett   '77 Dbdy
13. The Best of Philip K. Dick   '77 Ball
14. The Best of Edmond Hamilton   '77 Dbdy
15. The Best of L. Sprague De Camp   '78 Ball

(cont.)

("Ballantine", cont.)

```
16. The Best of Lester Del Rey          '78  Ball
17. The Best of Raymond Z. Gallun       '78  Ball
18. The Best of Murray Leinster         '78  Ball
19. The Best of Eric Frank Russell      '78  Ball
20. The Best of Jack Williamson         '78  Ball
21. The Best of James Blish             '79  Ball
22. The Best of Hal Clement             '79  Ball
```

BAXTER, JOHN (b.1939)

<u>The Pacific Books</u>
```
1. Pacific Book of Australian Science Fiction
                                         '68  Ang&R
2. The Second Pacific Book of Science Fiction
                                         '71  Ang&R
```

BENSEN, DONALD R. (b.1927)

<u>The Unknown</u>
```
1. The Unknown                           '63  Pyr
2. The Unknown 5                         '64  Pyr
```

"BEST FROM FANTASY AND SCIENCE FICTION"

```
         (edited by Anthony Boucher & J. Francis McComas)
 1. Volume 1                             '52  LtBrn
 2. Volume 2                             '53  LtBrn
 3. Volume 3                             '54  Dbdy
         (edited by Anthony Boucher)
 4. Volume 4                             '55  Dbdy
 5. Volume 5                             '56  Dbdy
 6. Volume 6                             '57  Dbdy
 7. Volume 7                             '58  Dbdy
 8. Volume 8                             '59  Dbdy
         (edited by Robert P. Mills)
 9. Volume 9                             '60  Dbdy
10. Volume 10                            '61  Dbdy
11. Volume 11                            '62  Dbdy
         (edited by Avram Davidson)
12. Volume 12                            '63  Dbdy
13. Volume 13                            '64  Dbdy
14. Volume 14                            '65  Dbdy
         (edited by Edward L. Ferman)
15. Volume 15                            '66  Dbdy
```

(cont.)

("Best From Fantasy & Science Fiction", cont.)

```
16. Volume 16                                      '67  Dbdy
17. Volume 17                                      '68  Dbdy
18. Volume 18                                      '69  Dbdy
19. Volume 19                                      '71  Dbdy
20. Volume 20                                      '73  Dbdy
21. Best From Fantasy and Science Fiction:
    25th Anniversary                               '74  Dbdy
22. 22nd Series                                    '77  Dbdy
23. The Magazine of Fantasy and Science Fiction:
    A Thirty Year Retrospective                    '80  Dbdy
24. 23rd Series                                    '80  Dbdy
25. 24th Series                                    '82  Scrib
```

BIGGLE, LLOYD, JR. (b.1923) (see "NEBULA AWARD SERIES")

"BINARY STARS"

```
1. Destiny Times Three  (Fritz Leiber)
   Riding the Torch  (Norman Spinrad)              '78  Dell
2. The Twilight River  (Gordon Eklund)
   The Tery  (F. Paul Wilson)                      '79  Dell
3. Dr. Scofflaw  (Ron Goulart)
   Outerworld  (Isadore Haiblum)                   '79  Dell
4. Legacy  (Joan Vinge)
   The Janus Equation  (Steven G. Spruill)         '79  Dell
5. Nightflyers  (George R.R. Martin)
   True Names  (Vernor Vinge)                      '79  Dell
```

BISCHOFF, DAVID

The Raintree Books
```
1. Quest                                           '77  Rain
2. Strange Encounters                              '77  Rain
```

BLEILER, EVERETT (b.1910) & T.E. DIKTY (b.1920)

The Best Science-Fiction Stories
```
1. The Best Science-Fiction Stories: 1949          '49  Fell
2. The Best Science-Fiction Stories: 1950          '50  Fell
3. The Best Science-Fiction Stories: 1951          '51  Fell
4. The Best Science-Fiction Stories: 1952          '52  Fell
5. The Best Science-Fiction Stories: 1953          '53  Fell
6. The Best Science-Fiction Stories: 1954          '54  Fell
```
(cont.)

(Bleiler & Dikty, cont.)

<u>(The Following are by T.E. Dikty only)</u>:
7. The Best Science-Fiction Stories and Novels: 1955   '55 Fell
8. The Best Science-Fiction Stories and Novels: 1956   '56 Fell
9. The Best Science-Fiction Stories and Novels: 9th Series   '58 Fell

BLISH, JAMES (1921-1975) (see "NEBULA AWARD SERIES")

BOUCHER, ANTHONY (1911-1968)

    also see: "BEST FROM FANTASY AND SCIENCE FICTION"

<u>Science Fiction Treasuries</u>
1. A Treasury of Great Science Fiction Volume 1   '59 Dbdy
2. A Treasury of Great Science Fiction Volume 2   '59 Dbdy

BOVA, BEN (b.1932)

    also see: "ANALOG YEARBOOK"
    also see: "SCIENCE FICTION HALL OF FAME"

<u>The Best of Omni</u> (with Don Myrus)
1. The Best of Omni Science Fiction   '80 Omni
2. The Best of Omni Science Fiction No. 2   '81 Omni
3. The Best of Omni Science Fiction No. 3   '82 Omni
4. The Best of Omni Science Fiction No. 4   '83 Omni
    <u>(the following are by Don Myrus only)</u>:
5. The Best of Omni Science Fiction No. 5   '83 Omni
6. The Best of Omni Science Fiction No. 6   '83 Omni

BRADLEY, MARION ZIMMER (b.1930)

<u>Sword and Sorceress</u>
1. Sword and Sorceress I   '84 DAW
2. Sword and Sorceress II   '85 DAW

BRETNOR, REGINALD (b.1911)

(cont.)

The Future at War
1. The Future at War Vol. 1: Thor's Hammer   '79 Ace
2. The Future at War Vol. 2: The Spear of Mars
                                              '80 Ace
3. The Future at War Vol. 3: Orion's Sword   '80 Ace

BROWN, CHARLES N.

The Mews Duet
1. Alien Worlds   '76 Mews
2. Far Travellers   '76 Mews

BULMER, KENNETH (b.1921)   (see "NEW WRITINGS IN SF")

CAMPBELL, JOHN W., Jr. (1910-1971)

Analog
1. Prologue to Analog   '62 Dbdy
2. Analog 1   '63 Dbdy
3. Analog 2   '64 Dbdy
4. Analog 3   '65 Dbdy
5. Analog 4   '66 Dbdy
6. Analog 5   '67 Dbdy
7. Analog 6   '68 Dbdy
8. Analog 7   '70 Dbdy
9. Analog 8   '71 Dbdy
10. Analog 9   '73 Dbdy

CAMPBELL, RAMSEY

New Terrors
1. New Terrors 1   '80 Pan
2. New Terrors 2   '80 Pan

CARD, ORSON SCOTT

Dragons
1. Dragons of Light   '80 Ace
2. Dragons of Darkness   '81 Ace

CARNELL, JOHN (1912-1972)

    also see: "NEW WRITINGS IN SF"
                            (cont.)

(John Carnell, cont.)

Gateways
1. Gateway to Tomorrow   '54 MusPr
2. Gateway to the Stars   '55 MusPr

CARR, JOHN F. (see collaboration with JERRY POURNELLE)

CARR, TERRY (b.1937)

    also see: ISAAC ASIMOV
    also see: collaboration with DONALD A. WOLLHEIM

New Worlds of Fantasy
1. New Worlds of Fantasy   '67 Ace
2. New Worlds of Fantasy No. 2   '70 Ace
3. New Worlds of Fantasy No. 3   '71 Ace

Universe
1. Universe 1   '71 Ace
2. Universe 2   '72 Ace
3. Universe 3   '73 RandH
4. Universe 4   '74 RandH
5. Universe 5   '75 RandH
6. Universe 6   '76 Dbdy
7. Universe 7   '77 Dbdy
8. Universe 8   '78 Dbdy
9. Universe 9   '79 Dbdy
10. Universe 10   '80 Dbdy
11. Universe 11   '81 Dbdy
12. Universe 12   '82 Dbdy
13. Universe 13   '83 Dbdy
14. Universe 14   '84 Dbdy
15. Universe 15   '85 Dbdy

Best Science Fiction of the Year
1. The Best Science Fiction of the Year   '72 Ball
2. The Best Science Fiction of the Year No.2   '73 Ball
3. The Best Science Fiction of the Year No.3   '74 Ball
4. The Best Science Fiction of the Year No.4   '75 Ball
5. The Best Science Fiction of the Year No.5   '76 Ball
6. The Best Science Fiction of the Year No.6   '77 Holt
7. The Best Science Fiction of the Year No.7   '78 Ball
8. The Best Science Fiction of the Year No.8   '79 Ball
9. The Best Science Fiction of the Year No.9   '80 Ball
10. Best Science Fiction of the Year No.10   '81 PB
11. Best Science Fiction of the Year No.11   '82 PB
12. Best Science Fiction of the Year No.12   '83 PB

13. Best Science Fiction of the Year No.13   '84 Baen

Year's Finest Fantasy
1. Year's Finest Fantasy   '78 Berk
2. The Year's Finest Fantasy Volume 2   '79 Berk
3. Fantasy Annual III   '81 PB
4. Fantasy Annual IV   '81 PB
5. Fantasy Annual V   '82 PB

Best Science Fiction Novellas
1. The Best Science Fiction Novellas of the Year #1
                                              '79 Ball
2. The Best Science Fiction Novellas of the Year #2
                                              '80 Ball

CARTER, LIN (b.1930)

also see: "YEAR'S BEST FANTASY STORIES"

Flashing Swords!
1. Flashing Swords! #1   '73 Dell
2. Flashing Swords! #2   '74 Dell
3. Flashing Swords! #3   '76 Dell
4. Flashing Swords! #4   '77 Dell
5. Flashing Swords! #5: Demons and Daggers   '81 Dell

Weird Tales
1. Weird Tales #1   '81 Zebra
2. Weird Tales #2   '81 Zebra
3. Weird Tales #3   '81 Zebra
4. Weird Tales #4   '83 Zebra

CLARKE, ARTHUR C. (b.1917)
(see "SCIENCE FICTION HALL OF FAME")

CLEAR, VAL
(see "ST. MARTIN'S PRESS TEXTBOOK SERIES")

COLLINS, PAUL

Worlds
1. Envisaged Worlds   '78 Void
2. Other Worlds   '78 Void
3. Alien Worlds   '79 Void
4. Distant Worlds   '81 Corey

CONKLIN, GROFF (1904-1968)

    Vanguard Science Fiction Series
1. Science Fiction Thinking Machines   '54   Vang
2. Science Fiction Adventures in Dimension   '55   Vang
3. Science Fiction Adventures in Mutation   '55   Vang

    Collier's Great Science Fiction Series
1. Great Science Fiction By Scientists   '62   PFCol
2. Great Science Fiction By Doctors   '63   PFCol
   (edited with Noah Fabricant)

CONQUEST, ROBERT (see collaboration with KINGSLEY AMIS)

CRISPIN, EDMUND (1921-1978)

    Best SF
1. Best SF   '55   Faber
2. Best SF 2   '56   Faber
3. Best SF 3   '58   Faber
4. Best SF 4   '61   Faber
5. Best SF 5   '63   Faber
6. Best SF 6   '66   Faber
7. Best SF 7   '70   Faber

    Best Tales of Terror
1. Best Tales of Terror   '62   Faber
2. Best Tales of Terror 2   '65   Faber

CROSS, JOHN KEIR (1911-1967)

    Best Horror
1. Best Horror Stories   '56   Faber
2. Best Horror Stories 2   '65   Faber

DANN, JACK (b.1945)

    Wandering Stars
1. Wandering Stars   '74   Harpr
2. More Wandering Stars   '81   Dbdy

DATLOW, ELLEN

    Omni Science Fiction
1. The First Book of Omni Science Fiction   '83   Zebra

2. The Second Book of Omni Science Fiction   '83 Zebra
3. The Third Omni Book of Science Fiction   '85 Zebra

DAVIDSON, AVRAM (b.1923)
    (see "BEST FROM FANTASY AND SCIENCE FICTION")

DAVIS, RICHARD

    also see: "YEAR'S BEST HORROR STORIES"

    Space
1. Space 1   '73 Abeld
2. Space 2   '74 Abeld

    Armada
1. Armada Sci-Fi One   '75 Armad
2. Armada Sci-Fi Two   '75 Armad

"THE DAW 'BOOK OF' FAMOUS AUTHORS SERIES"

1. The Book of Brian Aldiss   '72 DAW
2. The Book of Van Vogt   '72 DAW
3. The Book of Philip K. Dick   '73 DAW
4. The Book of Gordon R. Dickson   '73 DAW
5. The Book of Philip Jose Farmer   '73 DAW
6. The Book of Frank Herbert   '73 DAW
7. The Book of Fritz Leiber   '74 DAW
8. The Second Book of Fritz Leiber   '75 DAW
9. The Book of Poul Anderson   '75 DAW
10. The Book of Andre Norton   '75 DAW
11. The Book of Saberhagen   '75 DAW
12. The Book of John Brunner   '76 DAW

DELANY, SAMUEL R. (b.1942) & MARILYN HACKER

    also see: "NEBULA AWARDS SERIES"

    Quark
1. Quark/1   '70 PbLib
2. Quark/2   '71 PbLib
3. Quark/3   '71 PbLib
4. Quark/4   '71 PbLib

DEL REY, JUDY-LYNN

                           (cont.)

(Judy-Lynn Del Rey, cont.)

Stellar
1. Stellar #1   '74 Ball
2. Stellar #2   '76 Ball
3. Stellar Short Novels   '76 Ball
4. Stellar #3   '77 Ball
5. Stellar #4   '78 Ball
6. Stellar #5   '80 Ball
7. Stellar #6   '81 Ball
8. Stellar #7   '81 Ball

DEL REY, LESTER (b.1915) & GARDNER DOZOIS (b.1947)

Best Science Fiction
(edited by Lester Del Rey):
1. Best Science Fiction Stories of the Year
   (1971)   '72 EPDut
2. Best Science Fiction Stories of the Year
   (1972)   '73 EPDut
3. Best Science Fiction Stories of the Year
   (1973)   '74 EPDut
4. Best Science Fiction Stories of the Year
   (1974)   '75 EPDut
5. Best Science Fiction Stories of the Year
   (1975)   '76 EPDut
   (edited by Gardner Dozois):
6. Best Science Fiction Stories of the Year
   (1976)   '77 EPDut
7. Best Science Fiction Stories of the Year
   (1977)   '78 EPDut
8. Best Science Fiction Stories of the Year
   (1978)   '79 EPDut
9. Best Science Fiction Stories of the Year
   (1979)   '80 EPDut
10. Best Science Fiction Stories of the Year
    (1980)   '81 EPDut

DICKSON, GORDON R. (b.1923) (see "NEBULA AWARDS SERIES")

DIKTY, T.E. (b.1920)

also see: collaboration with EVERETT BLEILER

Every Boy's Series
1. Every Boy's Book of Science Fiction   '55 Fell
2. Every Boy's Book of Space Stories   '60 Fell

Great Science Fiction Stories
1. Great Science Fiction Stories About Mars   '66   Fell
2. Great Science Fiction Stories About the Moon
                                                   '67   Fell

"THE DOUBLEDAY 'EARLY' SERIES"

1. The Early Asimov   '72   Dbdy
2. The Early Del Rey   '75   Dbdy
3. The Early Long   '75   Dbdy
4. The Early Williamson   '75   Dbdy
5. The Early Pohl   '76   Dbdy

DOZOIS, GARDNER (see collaboration with LESTER DEL REY)

DURWOOD, THOMAS

Ariel
1. Ariel, A Fantasy Magazine   '76   MStar
2. Ariel, the Book of Fantasy, Volume 2   '77   Ball
3. Ariel, the Book of Fantasy, Volume 3   '78   Ball
4. Ariel, the Book of Fantasy, Volume 4   '78   Ball

EDITORS OF "GALAXY"

1. The Best From Galaxy, Volume I   '72   Award
2. The Best From Galaxy, Volume II   '74   Award
3. The Best From Galaxy, Volume III
    (James Baen, ed.)   '75   Award
4. The Best From Galaxy, Volume IV
    (James Baen, ed.)   '76   Award

EDITORS OF "IF"

1. The Best From If, Volume I   '73   Award
2. The Best From If, Volume II   '74   Award
3. The Best From If, Volume III
    (James Baen, ed.)   '76   Award

ELLISON, HARLAN (b.1934)

Dangerous Visions
1. Dangerous Visions   '67   Dbdy
2. Again Dangerous Visions   '72   Dbdy

ELWOOD, ROGER (b.1933)

    Little Monsters (with Vic Ghidlia)
1. The Little Monsters   '69 Macf
2. More Little Monsters   '73 Manor

    Beasts (with Vic Ghidlia)
1. Beware the Beasts   '70 Macf
2. Beware More Beasts   '75 Manor

    Frontiers
1. Frontiers 1; Tomorrow's Alternatives   '73 Macm
2. Frontiers 2; The New Mind   '73 Macm

    Science Fiction Tales
1. Science Fiction Tales   '73 RandH
2. More Science Fiction Tales   '74 RandH

    Continuum
1. Continuum 1   '74 Putn
2. Continuum 2   '74 Berk
3. Continuum 3   '74 Berk
4. Continuum 4   '75 Berk

ERNSBERGER, GEORGE
    (see collaboration with DONALD A. WOLLHEIM)

EVANS, I.O. (1894-1977)

    Through the Ages
1. Science Fiction Through the Ages 1   '66 Panthr
2. Science Fiction Through the Ages 2   '66 Panthr

FADIMAN, CLIFTON

    The Mathematics Duet
1. Fantasia Mathematica   '58 S&S
2. The Mathematical Magpie   '62 S&S

FERMAN, EDWARD L. (b.1937)
    (see "BEST FROM FANTASY AND SCIENCE FICTION")

FRANKLIN, H. BRUCE (b.1934)

    Future Perfect

(cont.)
1. Future Perfect '66 OxfUn
2. Future Perfect, Revised Edition '78 OxfUn

FURMAN, A.L.

The Teen-Age Series
1. Teen-Age Science Fiction Stories '52 Lantn
2. Teen-Age Outer Space Stories '62 Lantn
3. Teen-Age Space Adventures '72 Lantn

GHIDLIA, VIC (see collaboration with ROGER ELWOOD)

GOLD, H.L. (b.1914)

The Galaxy Reader
1. Galaxy Reader of Science Fiction '52 Crown
2. Second Galaxy Reader of Science Fiction '54 Crown
3. The Third Galaxy Reader '58 Dbdy
4. The Fourth Galaxy Reader '59 Dbdy
5. The Fifth Galaxy Reader '61 Dbdy
6. The Sixth Galaxy Reader
(The following edited by Frederik Pohl):
7. The Seventh Galaxy Reader '64 Dbdy
8. The Eighth Galaxy Reader '65 Dbdy
9. The Ninth Galaxy Reader '66 Dbdy
10. The Tenth Galaxy Reader '67 Dbdy
11. The Eleventh Galaxy Reader '69 Dbdy

Galaxy Novella Series
1. 5 Galaxy Short Novellas '58 Dbdy
2. World That Couldn't and 8 Other SF Novelets
 '59 Dbdy
3. Bodyguard and 4 Other Short SF Novels
 From Galaxy '60 Dbdy
4. Mind Partner and 8 Other Novelets From Galaxy
 '61 Dbdy

GRANT, CHARLES L.

Shadows
1. Shadows '78 Dbdy
2. Shadows 2 '79 Dbdy
3. Shadows 3 '80 Dbdy
4. Shadows 4 '81 Dbdy

(cont.)

(Charles L. Grant, cont.)

    5. Shadows 5   '82   Dbdy
    6. Shadows 6   '83   Dbdy
    7. Shadows 7   '84   Dbdy

       The "Frights" Series
    1. Nightmares   '79   Play
    2. Horrors   '81   Play
    3. Terrors   '82   Play
    4. Fears   '83   Berk

GREENBERG, MARTIN H. (b.1941)

       also see: "ARBOR HOUSE SERIES"
       also see: collaborations with ISAAC ASIMOV
       also see: "AVON DECADES SERIES"
       also see: collaboration with JOSEPH D. OLANDER
       also see: "RAND McNALLY TEXTBOOK SERIES"
       also see: "ST. MARTIN'S PRESS TEXTBOOK SERIES"

       The "3000" Sequence (with Charles G. Waugh)
    1. Love 3000   '80   Elsev
    2. Baseball 3000 (with Frank D. McSherry Jr.)
                                                  '81   Elsev

GUNN, JAMES E. (b.1923)

       also see: "NEBULA AWARDS SERIES"
       The Road to Science Fiction:
    1. #1: From Gilgamesh to Wells   '77   Sign
    2. #2: From Wells to Heinlein   '79   Sign
    3. #3: From Heinlein to Here   '79   Sign
    4. #4: From Here to Forever   '82   Sign

HACKER, MARILYN (see collaboration with SAMUEL R. DELANY)

HALDEMAN, JOE W. (b.1943) (see "NEBULA AWARDS SERIES")

HARRISON, HARRY (b.1925)

       also see: "NEBULA AWARD SERIES"

       Author's Choice
    1. SF: Author's Choice   '68   Berk

2. SF: Author's Choice 2	'70	Berk
3. SF: Author's Choice 3	'71	Putn
4. SF: Author's Choice 4	'74	Putn

Best SF (with Brian W. Aldiss)
1. Best SF: 1967	'68	Berk
2. Best SF: 1968	'69	Putn
3. Best SF: 1969	'70	Putn
4. Best SF: 1970	'71	Putn
5. Best SF: 1971	'72	Putn
6. Best SF: 1972	'73	Putn
7. Best SF: 1973	'74	Putn
8. Best SF: 1974	'75	Bob-M
9. Best SF: 1975, The Ninth Annual	'76	Bob-M

Nova
1. Nova 1	'70	Delac
2. Nova 2	'72	Walkr
3. Nova 3	'73	Walkr
4. Nova 4	'74	Walkr

Astounding-Analog (with Brian W. Aldiss)
1. The Astounding-Analog Reader Volume One	'72	Dbdy
2. The Astounding-Analog Reader Volume Two	'73	Dbdy

Decades (with Brian W. Aldiss)
1. Decade the 1940s	'75	MacmL
2. Decade the 1950s	'76	MacmL
3. Decade the 1960s	'77	MacmL

HAY, GEORGE (b.1922)

Pulsar
1. Pulsar 1	'78	Peng
2. Pulsar 2	'79	Peng

HERBERT, FRANK (b.1920)
(see "NEBULA AWARDS SERIES")

HOSKINS, ROBERT (b.1933)

Infinity
1. Infinity 1	'70	Lance
2. Infinity 2	'71	Lance
3. Infinity 3	'72	Lance
4. Infinity 4	'72	Lance
5. Infinity 5	'73	Lance

(Robert Hoskins, cont.)

Wondermakers
1. Wondermakers   '72 Fawc
2. Wondermakers 2   '74 Fawc

JAKUBOWSKI, MAXIM (b.1944)

Lands of Never
1. Lands of Never   '83 Unwin
2. Beyond Lands of Never   '84 Unwin

KATZ, HARVEY (see "RAND McNALLY TEXTBOOK SERIES")

KELLEY, LEO P. (b.1928)

Themes
1. Themes in Science Fiction   '72 McGrH
2. Fantasy: The Literature of the Marvelous   '74 McGrH

KNIGHT, DAMON (b.1922)

also see: "AVON DECADE SERIES"
also see: "NEBULA AWARDS SERIES"

The Century Sequence
1. A Century of Science Fiction   '62 S&S
2. One Hundred Years of Science Fiction   '68 S&S

Orbit
1. Orbit   '66 Berk
2. Orbit 2   '67 Berk
3. Orbit 3   '68 Putn
4. Orbit 4   '68 Putn
5. Orbit 5   '69 Putn
6. Orbit 6   '70 Putn
7. Orbit 7   '70 Putn
8. Orbit 8   '70 Putn
9. Orbit 9   '71 Putn
10. Orbit 10   '72 Putn
11. Orbit 11   '73 Putn
12. Orbit 12   '73 Putn
13. Orbit 13   '74 Putn
14. Orbit 14   '74 Harpr
15. Orbit 15   '74 Harpr
16. Orbit 16   '75 Harpr

17. Orbit 17	'75	Harpr
18. The Best From Orbit	'75	Berk
19. Orbit 18	'76	Harpr
20. Orbit 19	'77	Harpr
21. Orbit 20	'78	Harpr
22. Orbit 21	'80	Harpr

LE GUIN, URSULA K. (b.1929) (see "NEBULA AWARDS SERIES")

LEIBER, FRITZ (b.1910) (see "WORLD FANTASY AWARDS")

LUPOFF, RICHARD A. (b.1935)

What If?

1. What If? Volume 1: Stories That Should Have Won The Hugo	'80	PB
2. What If? Volume 2: Stories That Should Have Won The Hugo	'81	PB
3. What If? Volume 3: Stories That Should Have Won The Hugo	('82)	*

* (Note-- This final volume was never actually published, and exists only as a few sets of publisher's galleys. However, at least one copy has been seen for sale, and so is noted here).

McCARTHY, SHAWNA (see GEORGE H. SCITHERS)

McCOMAS, J. FRANCIS (1911-1978)
(see "BEST FROM FANTASY AND SCIENCE FICTION")

McSHERRY, FRANK D. JR.
(see collaboration with MARTIN H. GREENBERG)

MAGIDORFF, ROBERT (b.1905)

Russian Science Fiction

1. Russian Science Fiction	'64	NYUnv
2. Russian Science Fiction, 1968	'68	NYUnv
3. Russian Science Fiction, 1969	'69	NYUnv

MALZBERG, BARRY N. (b.1939) (see "ARBOR HOUSE SERIES")

MARGULIES, LEO (1900-1975)

    Weird
1. Weird Tales   '64 Pyr
2. Worlds of Weird   '65 Pyr

MARTIN, GEORGE R.R. (b.1948)

    New Voices
1. New Voices in Science Fiction   '77 Macm
2. New Voices II   '79 Jove
3. New Voices III   '80 Berk
4. New Voices IV: The John W. Campbell Award
   Nominess   '81 Berk
5. The John W. Campbell Awards Volume 5   '84 Bjay

MASON, CAROL (see "ST. MARTIN'S PRESS TEXTBOOK SERIES")

MERRIL, JUDITH (b.1923)

    The Year's Best Series
1. SF: The Year's Greatest Science Fiction
   and Fantasy   '56 Gnome
2. SF 57: The Year's Greatest Science Fiction
   and Fantasy   '57 Gnome
3. SF 58: The Year's Greatest Science Fiction
   and Fantasy   '58 Gnome
4. SF 59: The Year's Greatest Science Fiction
   and Fantasy   '59 Gnome
5. 5th Annual of the Year's Best S-F   '60 S&S
6. 6th Annual of the Year's Best S-F   '61 S&S
7. 7th Annual of the Year's Best S-F   '62 S&S
8. 8th Annual of the Year's Best S-F   '63 S&S
9. 9th Annual of the Year's Best S-F   '64 S&S
10. 10th Annual of the Year's Best S-F   '65 Delac
11. 11th Annual of the Year's Best S-F   '66 Delac
12. SF: The Best of the Best   '67 Delac
13. SF 12   '68 Delac

MILLS, ROBERT P. (b.1920)
    (see "BEST FROM FANTASY AND SCIENCE FICTION")

MILSTEAD, JOHN W.
    (see "ST. MARTIN'S PRESS TEXTBOOK SERIES")

MOLONEY, KATHLEEN (see GEORGE H. SCITHERS)

MOORCOCK, MICHAEL (b.1939)

    New Worlds
1. The Best SF Stories From New Worlds No. 1 '67 Berk
2. The Best SF Stories From New Worlds No. 2 '68 Berk
3. The Best SF Stories From New Worlds No. 3 '68 Berk
4. Best SF From New Worlds 4 '69 Berk
5. Best SF From New Worlds 5 '69 Berk
6. Best SF From New Worlds 6 '70 Berk
7. Best SF From New Worlds 7 '71 Pantr
8. Best SF From New Worlds 8 '74 Pantr

    New Worlds Quarterly
1. New Worlds Quarterly No. 1 '71 Berk
2. New Worlds Quarterly No. 2 '71 Berk
3. New Worlds Quarterly No. 3 '72 Berk
4. New Worlds Quarterly No. 4 '72 Berk
5. New Worlds Quarterly No. 5 '73 Spher

MYRUS, DON (see collaboration with BEN BOVA)

"NEBULA AWARDS SERIES"

1. Nebula Award Stories (Damon Knight) '66 Dbdy
2. Nebula Award Stories No. 2
    (Brian W. Aldiss & Harry Harrison) '67 Dbdy
3. Nebula Award Stories No. 3 (Roger Zelazny)
    '68 Dbdy
4. Nebula Award Stories No. 4 (Poul Anderson)
    '69 Dbdy
5. Nebula Award Stories No. 5 (James Blish) '70 Dbdy
6. Nebula Award Stories No. 6
    (Clifford D. Simak) '71 Dbdy
7. Nebula Award Stories No. 7
    (Lloyd Biggle Jr.) '73 Harpr
8. Nebula Award Stories 8 (Isaac Asimov) '73 Harpr
9. Nebula Award Stories 9 (Kate Wilhelm) '74 Harpr
10. Nebula Award Stories 10 (James E. Gunn) '75 Harpr
11. Nebula Award Stories 11 (Ursula K. LeGuin)
    '77 Harpr
12. Nebula Winners 12 (Gordon R. Dickson) '78 Harpr
13. Nebula Winners 13 (Samuel R. Delany) '80 Harpr
14. Nebula Winners 14 (Frederik Pohl) '80 Harpr
15. Nebula Winners 15 (Frank Herbert) '81 Harpr
    (cont.)

("Nebula Award Series", cont.)

    16. Nebula Award Stories 16
        (Jerry E. Pournelle)   '82 Harpr
    17. Nebula Award Stories 17 (Joe W. Haldeman)
                                                   '83 Holt
    18. Nebula Award Stories 18 (Robert Silverberg)
                                                   '83 Arbor
    19. Nebula Award Stories 19 (Marta Randall) '84 Arbor

"NEW WRITINGS IN SF"

       (edited by John Carnell)
     1. New Writings in SF 1   '66 Bant
     2. New Writings in SF 2   '66 Bant
     3. New Writings in SF 3   '67 Bant
     4. New Writings in SF 4   '68 Bant
     5. New Writings in SF 5   '70 Bant
     6. New Writings in SF 6   '71 Bant
     7. New Writings in SF 7   '71 Bant
     8. New Writings in SF 8   '71 Bant
     9. New Writings in SF 9   '72 Bant
    10. New Writings in SF 10   '67 Dobs
    11. New Writings in SF 11   '68 Corgi
    12. New Writings in SF 12   '68 Corgi
    13. New Writings in SF 13   '68 Corgi
    14. New Writings in SF 14   '69 Dobs
    15. New Writings in SF 15   '69 Dobs
    16. New Writings in SF 16   '69 Dobs
    17. New Writings in SF 17   '70 Dobs
    18. New Writings in SF 18   '71 Dobs
    19. New Writings in SF 19   '71 Dobs
    20. New Writings in SF 20   '72 Dobs
    21. New Writings in SF 21   '73 S&J
       (edited by Kenneth Bulmer)
    22. New Writings in SF 22   '73 S&J
    23. New Writings in SF 23   '74 S&J
    24. New Writings in SF 24   '74 S&J
    25. New Writings in SF 25   '75 Dobs
    26. New Writings in SF 26   '75 S&J
    27. New Writings in SF 27   '75 S&J
    28. New Writings in SF 28   '76 Dobs
    29. New Writings in SF 29   '76 S&J
    30. New Writings in SF 30   '77 Corgi

NIVEN, LARRY (b.1938)

        Magic

(cont.)
1. The Magic Goes Away
2. The Magic May Return
3. More Magic '84 Berk

NOLANE, RICHARD D.

Terra SF
1. Terra SF '81 DAW
2. Terra SF II '83 DAW

NORTON, ANDRE (b.1912)

The Space Group
1. Space Service '53 World
2. Space Pioneers '54 World
3. Space Police '56 World

OFFUTT, ANDREW J. (b.1937)

The Swords Quintet
1. Swords Against Darkness '77 Zebra
2. Swords Against Darkness II '77 Zebra
3. Swords Against Darkness III '78 Zebra
4. Swords Against Darkness IV '79 Zebra
5. Swords Against Darkness V '79 Zebra

OLANDER, JOSEPH D.

also see: ISAAC ASIMOV
also see: "AVON DECADE SERIES"
also see: "RAND McNALLY TEXTBOOK SERIES"
also see: "ST. MARTIN'S PRESS TEXTBOOK SERIES"

Franklin Watts Textbook Series
(with Martin H. Greenberg)
1. Criminal Justice Through Science Fiction '77 Watts
2. International Relations Through Science Fiction '78 Watts

"OMNI" (see BEN BOVA or ELLEN DATLOW)

OWEN, MABLY
(see collaboration with AMABEL WILLIAMS-ELLIS)

PAGE, GERALD W. (see "YEAR'S BEST HORROR STORIES")

PIERCE, ROBERT

1. Science Fiction 1   '73 HMiff
2. Science Fiction 2   '73 HMiff
3. Science Fiction 3 (with Murray Suid)   '73 HMiff

"PLAYBOY SCIENCE FICTION SERIES"

1. The Playboy Book of Science Fiction and
   Fantasy   '66 Play
2. The Playboy Book of Horror and the Supernatural   '67 Play
3. The Playboy Book of the Sinister and Strange
                                                '69 Play
4. The Dead Astronaut: 10 Stories of Space
   Flight   '71 Play
5. The Fiend   '71 Play
6. From the "S" File   '71 Play
7. The Fully Automated Love Life of Henry
   Keanridge   '71 Play
8. Last Train to Limbo   '71 Play
9. Transit of Earth   '71 Play
10. Weird Show   '71 Play

POHL, FREDERIK (b.1919)

   also see: "AVON DECADE SERIES"
   also see: H.L. GOLD
   also see: "NEBULA AWARDS SERIES"

   Star Science Fiction
1. Star Science Fiction Stories   '53 Ball
2. Star Science Fiction Stories No. 2   '53 Ball
3. Star Science Fiction Stories No. 3   '54 Ball
4. Star Short Novels   '54 Ball
5. Star Science Fiction Stories No. 4   '58 Ball
6. Star Science Fiction Stories No. 5   '59 Ball
7. Star Science Fiction Stories No. 6   '59 Ball
8. Star of Stars   '60 Ball

   Best Science Fiction
1. Best Science Fiction For 1972   '72 Ace
     (Following edited by Forrest J. Ackerman)
2. Best Science Fiction For 1973   '73 Ace

The Great Years
1. Science Fiction: The Great Years   '73 Ace
2. Science Fiction: The Great Years Vol. II '76 Ace

POURNELLE, JERRY (b.1933)

also see: "NEBULA AWARDS SERIES"

The Endless Frontier
1. The Endless Frontier   '79 Ace
2. The Endless Frontier Vol. II
   (with John F. Carr)   '82 Ace

There Will Be War (with John F. Carr)
1. There Will Be War   '83 Tor
2. Men of War: There Will Be War Volume II   '84 Tor
3. Blood and Iron: There Will Be War Volume III
                                             '84 Tor
4. Day of the Tyrant: There Will Be War Volume IV
                                             '85 Tor

Far Frontiers (with Jim Baen)
1. Far Frontiers   '84 Baen
2. Far Frontiers 2   '85 Baen

PREISS, BYRON

Weird Heroes
1. Weird Heroes Volume 1   '75 Pyr
2. Weird Heroes Volume 2   '75 Pyr
3. Weird Heroes Volume 3   '77 Pyr
4. Weird Heroes Volume 4   '77 Jove

PROCTOR, GEORGE W. (see "SCIENCE FICTION HALL OF FAME")

PRONZINI, BILL

also see: "ARBOR HOUSE SERIES"

The Creature Series
1. Creature!   '77 Arbor
2. Voodoo!   '79 Arbor
3. Werewolf!   '79 Arbor
4. Mummy!   '80 Arbor

(cont.)

(Bill Pronzini, cont.)

    5. Specter!   '80 Arbor
    6. Ghoul!   '81 Arbor
       appears in: The Arbor House Necropolis ('81/Arbor)

QUINN, JAMES L. & EVE WULFF

    Worlds of If
    1. The First World of If   '57 Quinn
    2. The Second World of If   '58 Quinn

"RAND McNALLY TEXTBOOK SERIES"

    1. Introductory Psychology Through Science
       Fiction (Harvey Katz, Patricia S. Warrick,
       & Martin H. Greenberg)   '74 RdMcN
    2. American Government Through Science Fiction
       (Joseph D. Olander, Patricia S. Warrick,
       & Martin H. Greenberg)   '74 RdMcN
    3. School and Society Through Science Fiction
       (Joseph D. Olander, Patricia S. Warrick,
       & Martin H. Greenberg)   '74 RdMcN
    4. Introductory Psychology Through Science
       Fiction-- 2 (Harvey Katz, Patricia S. Warrick,
       & Martin H. Greenberg)   '77 RdMcN

RANDALL, MARTA
      see: "NEBULA AWARDS SERIES"
      also see: collaboration with ROBERT SILVERBERG

ROSELLE, DANIEL

    Transformations
    1. Transformations   '73 Fawc
    2. Transformations II   '74 Fawc

SAHA, ARTHUR W.
      see: collaboration with DONALD A. WOLLHEIM
      also see: "YEAR'S BEST FANTASY STORIES"

"ST. MARTIN'S PRESS TEXTBOOK SERIES"

    1. Anthropology Through Science Fiction
       (Carol Mason, Martin H. Greenberg,
       & Patricia Warrick)   '74 StM

    2. Sociology Through Science Fiction
       (John W. Milstead, Martin H. Greenberg,
       & Joseph D. Olander)   '74 StM
    3. Marriage and the Family Through Science
       Fiction (Val Clear, Warrick, Greenberg, & Olander)
                                         '75 StM
    4. Social Problems Through Science Fiction
       (Greenberg, Milstead, Olander, & Warrick)
                                         '76 StM

SALMONSON, JESSICA AMANDA

    Amazons
    1. Amazons!   '79 DAW
    2. Amazons II   '82 DAW

SANTESSON, HANS STEFAN

    Mighty Warriors
    1. The Mighty Barbarians   '69 Lance
    2. The Mighty Swordsmen   '70 Lance

SARGENT, PAMELA

    Women of Wonder
    1. Women of Wonder   '75 Vint
    2. More Women of Wonder   '76 Vint
    3. The New Women of Wonder   '78 Vint

SCHIFF, STUART DAVID

    also see: "WORLD FANTASY AWARDS"

    Whispers
    1. Whispers   '77 Dbdy
    2. Whispers II   '79 Dbdy
    3. Whispers III   '81 Dbdy
    4. Whispers IV   '83 Dbdy
    4. Whispers V   '85 Dbdy

SCHMIDT, STANLEY (b.1944)

    also see: "ANALOG YEARBOOK"

                                        (cont.)

(Stanley Schmidt, cont.)

The Analog Series
1. The Analog Anthology #1   '80 Davis
2. Analog: Reader's Choice   '82 Davis
3. Analog's Children of the Future   '82 Davis
4. Analog's Lighter Side   '82 Davis
5. Analog: Writer's Choice   '83 Davis
6. War and Peace   '83 Davis
7. Aliens From Analog   '83 Davis
8. Analog: Writer's Choice Volume II   '84 Davis
9. From Mind to Mind: Tales of Communication From Analog   '84 Davis

SCHOCHET, VICTORIA

Berkley Showcase
1. The Berkley Showcase Vol. 1 (with John W. Silbersack)   '80 Berk
2. The Berkley Showcase Vol. 2 (with Silbersack)   '80 Berk
3. The Berkley Showcase Vol. 3 (with Silbersack)   '81 Berk
4. The Berkley Showcase Vol. 4 (with Silbersack)   '81 Berk
5. The Berkley Showcase Vol. 5 (with Melissa Singer)   '82 Berk

"SCIENCE FICTION HALL OF FAME"

1. Science Fiction Hall of Fame Volume 1 (Robert Silverberg)   '70 Dbdy
2. Science Fiction Hall of Fame Volume 2A (Ben Bova)   '73 Dbdy
3. Science Fiction Hall of Fame Volume 2B (Ben Bova)   '73 Dbdy
4. Science Fiction Hall of Fame Volume III (Arthur C. Clarke & George W. Proctor)   '82 Avon

SCITHERS, GEORGE H. (b.1929)

Asimov's Choice
1. Astronauts & Androids   '77 Davis
2. Black Holes & Bug-Eyed Monsters   '77 Davis
3. Comets & Computers   '78 Davis
4. Dark Stars & Dragons   '78 Davis
5. Extraterrestrials & Eclipses   '78 Davis

Isaac Asimov's Series
1. Isaac Asimov's Masters of Science Fiction '78 Dial
2. Isaac Asimov's Marvels of Science Fiction '79 Dial
3. Isaac Asimov's Adventures of Science Fiction '80 Dial
4. Isaac Asimov's Worlds of Science Fiction '80 Dial
5. Isaac Asimov's Near Futures and Far '82 Dial
6. Isaac Asimov's Wonders of the World '82 Dial
   (ed. by Kathleen Moloney & Shawna McCarthy)
7. Isaac Asimov's Aliens & Outworlders '83 Dial
8. Isaac Asimov's Space of Her Own '83 Davis

SILBERSACK, JOHN W.
    (see collaboration with VICTORIA SCHOCHET)

SILVERBERG, ROBERT (b.1935)
    also see: "ARBOR HOUSE SERIES"
    also see: "NEBULA AWARDS SERIES"
    also see: "SCIENCE FICTION HALL OF FAME"

Alpha
1. Alpha 1 '70 Ball
2. Alpha 2 '71 Ball
3. Alpha 3 '72 Ball
4. Alpha 4 '73 Ball
5. Alpha 5 '74 Ball
6. Alpha 6 '76 Berk
7. Alpha 7 '77 Berk
8. Alpha 8 '77 Berk
9. Alpha 9 '78 Berk

New Dimensions
1. New Dimensions 1 '71 Dbdy
2. New Dimensions 2 '72 Dbdy
3. New Dimensions 3 '74 Sign
4. New Dimensions 4 '74 Sign
5. New Dimensions 5 '75 Harpr
6. New Dimensions 6 '76 Harpr
7. New Dimensions 7 '77 Harpr
8. New Dimensions 8 '78 Harpr
9. New Dimensions 9 '79 Harpr
10. The Best of New Dimensions '79 PB
11. New Dimensions 10 '80 Harpr
12. New Dimensions 11 (with Marta Randall) '80 PB
13. New Dimensions 12 (with Marta Randall) '81 PB

SIMAK, CLIFFORD D. (b.1904) (see "NEBULA AWARDS SERIES")

"SOVIET SCIENCE FICTION"

    1. Soviet Science Fiction   '62 PFCol
    2. More Soviet Science Fiction   '62 PFCol

SUID, MURRAY (see collaboration with ROBERT PIERCE)

SUTTON, DAVID A.

    1. New Writings in Horror and the
       Supernatural #1   '71 Spher
    2. New Writings in Horror and the
       Supernatural #2   '72 Spher

TORGESON, ROY

    Chrysalis
    1. Chrysalis   '77 Zebra
    2. Chrysalis 2   '78 Zebra
    3. Chrysalis 3   '78 Zebra
    4. Chrysalis 4   '79 Zebra
    5. Chrysalis 5   '79 Zebra
    6. Chrysalis 6   '80 Zebra
    7. Chrysalis 7   '80 Zebra
    8. Chrysalis 8   '80 Dbdy
    9. Chrysalis 9   '81 Dbdy
   10. Chrysalis 10   '83 Dbdy

    Other Worlds
    1. Other Worlds 1   '79 Zebra
    2. Other Worlds 2   '80 Zebra

WAGNER, KARL EDWARD (b.1945)
      (see "YEAR'S BEST HORROR STORIES")

WARRICK, PATRICIA S.
        see: "RAND McNALLY TEXTBOOK SERIES"
        also see: "ST. MARTIN'S PRESS TEXTBOOK SERIES"

WAUGH, CHARLES G.
        see: "ARBOR HOUSE SERIES"
        also see: ISAAC ASIMOV
        also see: MARTIN H. GREENBERG

WESTON, PETER (b.1944)

    Andromeda
1. Andromeda 1   '76 Futur
2. Andromeda 2   '77 Futur
3. Andromeda 3   '78 Futur

WILHELM, KATE (b.1928)
    (see "NEBULA AWARDS SERIES")

WILLIAMS-ELLIS, AMABEL & MABLY OWEN

    Out of This World
1. Out of This World 1   '60 Blk&S
2. Out of This World 2   '61 Blk&S
3. Out of This World 3   '61 Blk&S
4. Out of This World 4   '64 Blk&S
5. Out of This World 5   '65 Blk&S
6. Out of This World 6   '67 Blk&S
7. Out of This World 7   '68 Blk&S

WILSON, GAHAN
    (see "WORLD FANTASY AWARDS")

WILSON, ROBIN SCOTT (b.1928)

    Clarion
1. Clarion   '71 Sign
2. Clarion II   '72 Sign
3. Clarion III   '73 Sign

WINDLING, TERRI & MARK ALAN ARNOLD

    Elsewhere
1. Elsewhere   '81 Ace
2. Elsewhere Vol. II   '82 Ace
3. Elsewhere Vol. III   '84 Ace

WOLLHEIM, DONALD A. (b.1914)

    Adventures on Other Planets
1. Adventures on Other Planets   '55 Ace
2. More Adventures on Other Planets   '63 Ace

(Donald A. Wollheim, cont.)

World's Best (edited with Terry Carr)

1. World's Best Science Fiction: 1965   '65   Ace
2. World's Best Science Fiction: 1966   '66   Ace
3. World's Best Science Fiction: 1967   '67   Ace
4. World's Best Science Fiction: 1968   '68   Ace
5. World's Best Science Fiction: 1969   '69   Ace
6. World's Best Science Fiction: 1970   '70   Ace
7. World's Best Science Fiction: 1971   '71   Ace

Avon Fantasy Reader
(edited with George Ernsberger)

1. The Avon Fantasy Reader   '68   Avon
2. The Second Avon Fantasy Reader   '69   Avon

The Annual World's Best

1. The 1972 Annual World's Best SF   '72   DAW
2. The 1973 Annual World's Best SF   '73   DAW
3. The 1974 Annual World's Best SF   '74   DAW
4. The 1975 Annual World's Best SF   '75   DAW
5. The 1976 Annual World's Best SF   '76   DAW
6. The 1977 Annual World's Best SF   '77   DAW
7. The 1978 Annual World's Best SF   '78   DAW
8. The 1979 Annual World's Best SF   '79   DAW
9. The 1980 Annual World's Best SF   '80   DAW
10. The 1981 Annual World's Best SF   '81   DAW

(Following edited by Wollheim and Arthur W. Saha)

11. The 1982 Annual World's Best SF   '82   DAW
12. The 1983 Annual World's Best SF   '83   DAW
13. The 1984 Annual World's Best SF   '84   DAW
14. The 1985 Annual World's Best SF   '85   DAW

"WORLD FANTASY AWARDS"

1. First World Fantasy Awards (Gahan Wilson) '77   Dbdy
2. The World Fantasy Awards Volume Two
   (Fritz Leiber & Stuart David Schiff)   '80   Dbdy

"YEAR'S BEST FANTASY STORIES"

(edited by Lin Carter)

1. The Year's Best Fantasy Stories   '75   DAW
2. The Year's Best Fantasy Stories: 2   '76   DAW
3. The Year's Best Fantasy Stories: 3   '77   DAW
4. The Year's Best Fantasy Stories: 4   '78   DAW
5. The Year's Best Fantasy Stories: 5   '80   DAW
6. The Year's Best Fantasy Stories: 6   '80   DAW

    (edited by Arthur W. Saha)
7. The Year's Best Fantasy Stories: 7   '81 DAW
8. The Year's Best Fantasy Stories: 8   '82 DAW
9. The Year's Best Fantasy Stories: 9   '83 DAW
10. The Year's Best Fantasy Stories: 10   '84 DAW

"YEAR'S BEST HORROR STORIES"

    (edited by Richard Davis)
1. The Year's Best Horror Stories   '71 DAW
2. The Year's Best Horror Stories: Series II '74 DAW
3. The Year's Best Horror Stories: Series III
                                                         '75 DAW
    (edited by Gerald W. Page)
4. The Year's Best Horror Stories: Series IV '76 DAW
5. The Year's Best Horror Stories: Series V '77 DAW
6. The Year's Best Horror Stories: Series VI '78 DAW
7. The Year's Best Horror Stories: Series VII
                                                         '79 DAW
    (edited by Karl Edward Wagner)
8. The Year's Best Horror Stories: Series VIII
                                                         '80 DAW
9. The Year's Best Horror Stories: Series IX '81 DAW
10. The Year's Best Horror Stories: Series X '82 DAW
11. The Year's Best Horror Stories: Series XI
                                                         '83 DAW
12. The Year's Best Horror Stories: Series XII
                                                         '84 DAW

ZACHERLEY

1. Zacherley's Midnight Snacks   '60 Ball
2. Zacherley's Vulture Stew   '60 Ball

ZELAZNY, ROGER (b.1937) (see "NEBULA AWARDS SERIES")

ADDENDA

ANTHONY, PIERS

    The Magic of Xanth
9. Golem in the Gears   '85   DelR

    Bio of a Space Tyrant
4. Executive   '85   Avon

    Incarnations of Immortality
3. With a Tangled Skein   '85   DelR

ASIMOV, ISAAC

    The Great SF Stories (with Martin H. Greenberg)
13. The Great SF Stories 13 (1951)   '85   DAW

    Isaac Asimov's Magical Worlds of Fantasy
5. Giants   '85   Sign
    (with Martin H. Greenberg & Charles G. Waugh)

ASPRIN, ROBERT LYNN

    Myth Series
6. Little Myth Marker   '85   Donng

    Thieves' World
8. Soul of the City   '85   Ace

AUEL, JEAN

    Earth's Children
3. The Mammoth Hunters   '85   Crown

AUSTIN, RICHARD

    The Guardians
3. Thunder of Hell   '85   Jove

BRADLEY, MARION ZIMMER

    Darkover
20. Free Amazons of Darkover   '85   DAW

BRANDNER, GARY

    The Howling
  3. The Howling III   '85   Fawc

BULMER, KENNETH

    Dray Prescott
  36. Omens of Kregen   '85   DAW

CALDECOTT, MAYRA

    Tall Stories
  1. The Tall Stories   '80   Pop
  2. The Temple of the Sun   '80   Pop
  3. Shadow on the Stones   '80   Pop

CHALKER, JACK L.

    Soul Rider
  4. The Birth of Flux and Anchor   '85   Tor

CLOUGH, B.W.

    The Crystal Crown
  1. The Crystal Crown   '84   DAW
  2. The Dragon of Mishbil   '85   DAW

COOK, GLEN

    The Darkwar Trilogy
  1. Doomstalker   '85   Pop
  2. Warlock   '85   Pop

DALEY, BRIAN

    Alacrity Fitzhugh and Hobart Floyt
  1. Requiem for a Ruler of Worlds
  2. Jinx on a Terran Inheritance   '85   DelR

FORWARD, ROBERT L.

(cont.)

(Robert L. Forward, cont.)

Dragon's Egg Sequence
1. Dragon's Egg   '80 DelR
2. Starquake   '85 DelR

FOSTER, ALAN DEAN

Humanx Commonwealth (Non-Flinx)
6. Sentenced to Prism   '85 DelR

Spellsinger
5. The Paths of the Perambulator   '85 Phant

GOTLEIB, PHYLLIS

Note-- The series is also known as "The Ungruwarkh Trilogy"

GRANT, CHARLES L.

Oxrun
4. The Grave   '81 Pop
5. The Bloodwind   '82 Pop
6. The Soft Whisper of the Oxrun Dead '82 Grant

GREEN, SHARON

Diana Santee-- Spaceways Agent
1. Mind Guest   '84 DAW
2. Gateway to Xanadu   '85 DAW

HAGGARD, H. RIDER

She
(sequel)
5. Journey to the Flame (by Richard Monaco) '85 Bant

HAWKINS, WARD

Harry Borg and Guss
1. Red Flame Burning   '85 DelR
2. Sword of Fire   '85 DelR

JANSSON, TOVE

    The Moomin Books
1. Finn Family Moomintroll   '58 Walck
2. Moominland Midwinter   '58 Walck
3. Comet in Moominland   '59 Walck
4. Moominsummer Madness   '61 Walck
5. Tales From Moominvalley   '63 Walck
6. Exploits of Moominpappa   '66 Walck
7. Moominpappa at Sea   '66 Walck
8. Moominvalley in November   '71 Benn

LARSON, GLEN A.

    Battlestar Galactica
11. The Nightmare Machine
    (with Robert Thurston)   '85 Berk

LICHTENBERG, JACQUELINE

    The Dushau Trilogy
3. Outreach   '85 Pop

McCAFFREY, ANNE

    Crystal Singer
1. Crystal Singer   '82 DelR
2. Killashandra   '85 DelR

    Note-- "Dinosaur Planet" and "Dinosaur Planet Survivors" have been collected as: "The Ireta Adventure" ('85/SFBC)

McCOLLUM, MICHAEL

    Life Probe Sequence
1. Life Probe   '84 DelR
2. Procyon's Promise   '85 DelR

MASTERSON, GRAHAM

    The Manitou
1. The Manitou   '75 Spear
2. Revenge of the Manitou   '79 Pinn

MEYERS, RICHARD S.

    Doomstar
1. Doomstar   '78 Carly
2. Return to Doomstar   '85 Pop

MICHAELS, MELISA C.

    Skyrider
1. Skirmish   '85 Tor
2. First Battle   '85 Tor

MORRESSY, JOHN

    Ziak II
1. The Humans of Ziak II   '74 Walkr
2. The Drought of Ziak II   '78 Walkr

NORMAN, JOHN

    Gor
22. Dancer of Gor   '85 DAW

NORTON, ANDRE & ROBERT ADAMS (eds.)

    Ithkar Fair
1. Magic in Ithkar   '84 Tor
2. Magic in Ithkar 2   '85 Tor

POHL, FREDERIK & C.M. KORNBLUTH

    "Space Merchants" and "The Merchants' War" are collected in one volume as: "Venus, Inc." ('85/SFBC)

REINIUS, TRISH

    Planet of Tears
1. The Planet of Tears   '79 Dawne
2. Power of the White Wolf   '85 Iris

RESNICK, MIKE

    (cont.)

(Mike Resnick, cont.)

    <u>Tales of the Velvet Comet</u>
  3. Eros Descending   '85 Sign

RICE, ANNE

    <u>The Stories of the Vampire</u>
  1. Interview with the Vampire
  2. The Vampire Lestat   '85 Knopf

SADLER, BARRY

    <u>Casca</u>
  15. The Pirate   '85 Chart

SAUNDERS, CHARLES R.

    <u>Imaro</u>
  3. The Trail of Bohu   '85 DAW

SHERRED, T.L. (b.1915)

    <u>The Alien Sequence</u>
  1. Alien Island   '70
  2. Alien Main (with Lloyd Biggle Jr.)   '85 Dbdy

"STAR TREK"

    <u>Novels</u>
  41. Pawns and Symbols (Majliss Larson)   '85 PB
  42. Mindshadow (J.M. Dillard)   '85 PB

STASHEFF, CHRISTOPHER

    <u>Rod Gallowglass</u>
  5. The Warlock Enraged   '85 Ace

SUCHARITKUL, SOMTOW

    <u>The Inquestor Series</u>
  4. The Darkling Wind   '85 Bant

SWYCAFFER, JEFFERSON P.

    The Concordat
1. Not in Our Stars
2. Become the Hunted (prequel)   '85 Avon
3. The Universal Prey   '85 Avon

TARR, JUDITH

    The Hound and the Falcon
1. The Isle of Glass
2. The Golden Horn   '85 Bjay

TOLKIEN, J.R.R.

    additional titles of Middle Earth
9. The Lays of Beleriand
  (edited by Christopher Tolkien)   '85 HMiff

"V"

12. Path to Conquest (Howard Weinstein)   '85 Pinn

VAN VOGT, A.E.

    "Computerworld", aka: "Computer Eye" ('85/DAW)

VARDEMAN, ROBERT E.

    Jade Demons
4. The White Fire   '85 Avon

WEIS, MARGARET & TRACY HICKMAN

    Dragonlance Chronicles
3. Dragons of Spring Dawning   '85 TSR

WILLIAMS, PAUL O.

    Pelbar Cycle
7. The Sword of Forebearance   '85 DelR

YERMAKOV, NICHOLAS

    <u>Time War Series</u> (pseud.-- Simon Hawke)
5. The Nautilus Sanction   '85 Ace

PUBLISHING ADDENDA & ERRATA

1. ABBEY, LYNN. The "Rifkind" books were published by Ace in 1979 and 1980.
2. ANDERSON, POUL. The "Last Viking" series were all published by Zebra in 1980.
3. ANTHONY, PIERS. The series should read "Bio of a Space <u>Tyrant</u>."
4. BAUM, L. FRANK. Title #43 was published by Oz Club; Title #44 was published by Berkley.
5. BENNETT, MARCIA J. "Where the Ni-Lach" was published by Del Rey, 1983.
6. BERRY, ADRIAN. "Koyama's Diamond" was published by Vantage, 1982.
7. BISCHOFF, DAVID F. "Day of the Dragonstar" was published by Berkley, 1983.
8. BOVA, BEN. "Orion" should read '84/S&S; "As On a Darkling Plain" was published by Walker in 1972.
9. DREW, WAYLAND. The second title should read "The Gaian Expedient".
10. DUANE, DIANE. "The Door Into Fire" was published by Dell, 1979. "So You Want to be a Wizard" is Delacorte, 1983.
11. FARREN, MICK. All titles were published by Mayflower.
12. MOORCOCK, MICHAEL. The "Nomad of Time" titles have been collected as one volume, '82/SFBC. "The Steel Tsar" was published by Mayflower.
13. RYPEL, T.C. The "Gonji" books are published by Zebra.
14. VANCE, JACK. The title is "Cugel's Saga", not "Cujel's Saga".
15. YEP, LAWRENCE. "Dragon of the Lost Sea" was published by Harper in 1983.
16. ZEBROWSKI, GEORGE. "Mirror of Minds" was first published in the collected trilogy, '83/Ace.

Sequence Index

Aarn Munro (Campbell, J.), 42
Abdallah (Dombrowski), 68
Adam Link (Binder, E.), 24
Adam Quirke (Fearn), 80
Addams Family, 3
Adonis (Lambert), 123
Adventures in the Time Machine (Faraday), 78
Adventures in the Unknown (Claudy), 48
Adventures of Alyx (Russ), 189
Adventures of Captain Hatteras (Verne), 222
Adventures of Tapiola (Nathan), 157
Adventures of the Empire Princess (Diamond), 64
Adventures on Other Planets (Wollheim), 273
Advise and Consent (Drury), 70
Aeriel (Pierce, M.), 171
After Such Knowledge (Blish), 26
Agency (Meltzer), 147
Agent 008 (Allison), 4
Agent of T.E.R.R.A. (Maddock), 143, 144
Aia (Vivian), 224
Airplane Boys (Craine), 55
Airship Boys (Sayler), 192
Alacrity Fitzhugh and Hobart Floyt (Daley), 277
Alan Morgan (Fox), 83
Alastor Books (Vance), 219
Aldair (Barrett), 18
Alf Higgins (Darlington), 60
Alice (Caroll), 43
"Alice," The (Edmondson), 73
Alien Sequence (Sherred), 281
Allan Quartermain (Haggard), 97
Alpha (Silverberg), 271
Alternate World Sequence (Anderson, P.), 6
Altruria (Howells), 110
Amartus (Cradock), 54
Amazons (Salmonson), 269
Amber Series (Zelazny), 238
Amityville, 5
Analog (Campbell, J.), 249
Analog Series (Schmidt), 270
Analog Yearbook, 242
Ancient Africa (Farmer, P.J.), 79
Andrew Ames (Farca), 78
Android Tanner Sequence (White, T.), 230
Andromeda (Weston), 273
Andromeda Sequence (Hoyle, F.), 110
Andy Lane (Adams, E.), 1, 2
Angelo Di Stefano (Janifer), 115
Angria (Bronte), 31
Anjani (Fearn), 80
Annabel Andrews (Rodgers), 186
Annals of the Time Patrol (Anderson, P.), 7
Annual World's Best (Wollheim), 274
Annwn Series (Smith, G.), 199
Antarctic Utopia (Sweven), 210
Anthology Duet (Foster, A.), 82
Anthony Villiers

(Panshin), 166
Anthropol Bureau
  (Trimble), 215
Antigeos Trilogy (Capon), 42
Apprentice Adept
  (Anthony), 8
Arafel's Saga (Cherryh), 47
Arbor House Series, 242
Arcot, Wade & Morey
  (Campbell, J.), 42
Arden (Nesbit), 157
Argonia (Scarborough), 192
Ariel (Durwood), 255
Aristophano (De Morgan), 63
Armada (Davis), 253
Armata (Erskine), 75
Arthur Gordon Pym (Poe), 172, 173
Arwen (Bradley), 29
Ash Staff Series (Fisher, P.), 81
Asher Brockhorn (Cohen), 50
Ashes Sequence
  (Johnstone), 116
Asimov's Choice
  (Scithers), 270
Astounding-Analog
  (Harrison & Aldiss), 259
Astra Sequence (Norton, A.), 159
Atalantan Earth (Hancock, N.), 100
Athalie (Chambers), 45
Atlan Saga (Gaskell), 88
Atlantis (Bradley), 29
Attar the Merman
  (Haldeman), 98
Australian Trilogy
  (Wrightston), 236
Author's Choice
  (Harrison), 258
Avenger (Robeson), 184
Avengers, 13
Avon Decade Series, 245
Avon Fantasy Reader
  (Wollheim & Ernsberger), 274
Azan (Garron), 88

Badshah (Casserly), 44
Ballantine Best of
  Series, 245, 246
Balzan of the Cat People
  (Moore, W.), 153
Bambi (Salten), 191
Bantan (Gardner), 86, 87
Barclay Series (Elder), 73
Bard (Taylor), 211
Barnaby (Johnson, C.), 116
Barney Custer (E.R. Burroughs), 37
Barnum System (Goulart), 91
Baron Munchausen, 15-17
Baron Trump (Lockwood), 133
Baroness (Kenyon), 119
Barsac Mission (Verne), 223
Battle Circle (Anthony), 7
Battlestar Galactica
  (Larson), 125, 126, 279
Beasts (Elwood & Ghidlia), 256
Bed-Knob and Broomstick
  (Norton, M.), 161
Beklan Empire (Adams, Rd.), 2
Bel (Carr, C.), 42
Belgariad (Eddings), 72
Ben (Gilbert), 89
Ben Camden (Graat), 92
Benjamin Hooker (Train), 214
Berbora (Sirota), 196
Berkley Showcase
  (Schochet & Silbersack), 270
Berserker Series
  (Saberhagen), 190
Best From Fantasy and
  Science Fiction, 246, 247
Best Horror (Cross), 252

Best of British SF
  (Ashley), 242
Best of Omni (Bova &
  Myrus), 248
Best of Trek, 205
Best SF (Crispin), 252
Best SF (Harrison &
  Aldiss), 259
Best Science Fiction (Del
  Rey, L.), 254
Best Science Fiction
  (Pohl), 266
Best Science Fiction
  Novellas (Carr), 251
Best Science Fiction of
  the Year (Carr), 250,
  251
Best Science-Fiction
  Stories (Bleiler
  & Dikty), 247, 248
Best Tales of Terror
  (Crispin), 252
Bewitched, 23
Big Brain (Brandner), 30
Binary Stars, 247
Bio of a Space Tyrant
  (Anthony), 8, 276
Biography of the Life of
  Manuel of Poictesme
  (Cabell), 40
Bionic Woman (Lottman),
  136
Birthgrave Series (Lee,
  T.), 128
Black Company Trilogy
  (Cook), 53
Blackbeard's Ghost
  (Stahl), 203
Blake Walker (Norton,
  A.), 159
Blind Spot (Hall, Austin
  & Flint), 98
Bomba the Jungle Boy
  (Rockwood), 185, 186
Book of Han (Lang, S.),
  125
Book of Skaith
  (Brackett), 28
Book of Swords
  (Saberhagen), 190
Book of the Beast
  (Stallman), 203
Book of the New Sun
  (Wolfe), 234
Books of the Welsch
  Mabinogion (Walton), 227
Books of Westria
  (Paxson), 166
Books Sequence (Watson),
  227
Borribles (De Larra-
  beiti), 62
Borrowers (Norton, M.),
  161
Boy Adventurers
  (Verrill), 223
Boy Inventors (Bonner), 27
Brain-Plant Series
  (Meltzer), 148
Brak the Barbarian
  (Jakes), 114
Brion Brandd (Harrison,
  H.), 102
Bronson Beta (Wylie), 236
Brother Angeto (Lieber-
  man), 132
Buck Rogers, 32, 33
Bugaloos (Stratton, C.),
  209

Cabal, The (Dunn), 71
Cageworld (Kapp), 118
Callahan's Crosstime
  Saloon (Robinson), 185
Callisto Series (Carter,
  L.), 44
Camelot (Godwin, P.), 90
Camelot (White, T.H.), 230
Camelot in Space
  (Landis), 124
Canon Tellis (L'Engle),
  130
Canopus in Argus:
  Archives (Lessing), 131
Cap Kennedy (Tubb), 216
Captain Areia Darenga
  (Mezo), 149
Captain Black

(Pemberton), 167
Captain Future (Hamilton, E.), 99
Captain Kettle (Hyne), 111, 112
Captain Nemo (Verne), 222
Captain Pyanfar (Cherryh), 47
Captain Scarlet (Theydon), 212
Carbonel (Sleigh), 196
Carl Crader and Earl Jazine (Hoch), 105
Casca: The Eternal Mercenary (Sadler), 190, 281
Caspak Series (Burroughs, E.), 37
Castaways in Time (Adams, Rbt.), 2
Catfish Bend (Burman), 35
Cenotaph Road (Vardeman), 221
Century Sequence (Knight), 260
Chameleon Corps (Goulart), 91
Chandal Talon (Eulo), 75
Changeling Saga (Zelazny), 238
Changes Trilogy (Dickinson), 64
Changewar Sequence (Leiber), 129
Chaos Sequence (Kapp), 118
Charles Pry (Large), 125
Charlie (Dahl), 59
Charmed Life (Jones, D.W.), 117
Cherry Delight--Agent of D.U.E. (Fox), 84
Cherry Delight--The Sexecutioner (Fox), 83, 84
Childe Cycle (Dickson), 65
Children of the Stars (Coulson, J.), 54
Children of Ynell (Murphy), 156
Chill Series (Sherman, J.), 195
Chris Godfrey of the U.N. Exploratory Agency (Walters), 226
Chronicles of Corum (Moorcock), 152
Chronicles of Deryni (Kurtz), 122
Chronicles of Isle (Springer), 201
Chronicles of Middle-Earth (Tolkien), 213
Chronicles of Narnia (Lewis, C.S.), 131
Chronicles of Prydain (Alexander), 4
Chronicles of the Cheysuli (Roberson), 180
Chronicles of Thomas Covenant (Donaldson), 68
Chronicles of Tornor (Lynn), 139
Chrysalis (Torgeson), 272
Chthon (Anthony), 7
Cingulum (J.R. Roberts), 181
Circle of Light (Hancock, N.), 100
Circus World (Longyear), 134
Cities in Flight (Blish), 26
Clan Ground (Bell), 21
Clara (Lewis, C.), 132
Clarion (Wilson), 273
Claudine St. Cyr (Wallace), 226
Claudius (Leeming), 128
Clayton Drew (Fearn), 80
Clothes of a King's Son (Frankau), 84
Club of the Round Table (Lawrence, M.), 127
Cluster (Anthony), 7
Codominium Series (Pournelle), 174
Col. Max Masterson (Hawton), 103
Colin (Benson), 22

Colin and Susan (Garner, A.), 87
Colin Gray (Channing), 46
Colin O'Leary (Scoggins), 193
Collier's Great Science Fiction Series (Conklin), 252
Colonel Verney (Wheatley), 229
Colossus (Jones, D.F.), 117
Commander Craig (Fox), 83
Commander Shaw (McCutchan), 141
Computer Gods (Hoch), 105
Conan (Howard, R.), 107-109
Conception (Smythe), 199
Concordat (Swycaffer), 282
Conquest of the United States (Hancock, H.), 100
Continuum (Elwood), 256
Coop, The (Wangerin), 227
Coramonde (Daley), 59
Cord (Major), 144
Cormac Mac Art (Offutt), 163
Cornelius Chronicles (Moorcock), 151
Cory (Siodmak), 195
Count Brass (Moorcock), 152
Coxeman (Conway, T.), 52
Coyote Jones (Elgin), 73
Crab Island (Hurt), 111
Craghold (Avallone), 13
Craig Kennedy (Reeve), 177, 178
Creature Series (Pronzini), 267, 268
Croyd Series (Wallace), 225
Crystal Crown (Clough), 277
Crystal Singer (McCaffrey), 279
Cthulhu Mythos (Lovecraft), 136-138

Daedalus Series (Stableford), 202
Dag Fletcher (Rankine), 176, 177
Dalemark Sequence (Jones, D.W.), 117
Damar (McKinley), 142, 143
Dancer Trilogy (Maxwell), 146
Dancers at the End of Time (Moorcock), 152
Dancing Gods (Chalker), 45
Dane Thorson (Norton, A.), 159
Dangerous Visions (Ellison), 255
Dannus (Sirota), 196
Danny Dunn (Williams, J.), 231, 232
Dark Border (Zimmer), 238
Dark is Rising (Cooper, Susan), 53
Dark Pool Sequence (Rienow), 180
Dark Shadows (Ross), 188
Darkchild Trilogy (Van Scyoc), 220
Darkness and Dawn (England), 75
Darkover (Bradley), 28, 276
Darkwar Trilogy (Cook), 277
Darwath Trilogy (Hambly), 98
David Blaize (Benson), 22
Daw Book of Famous Authors Series, 253
Dawnstar (McBain), 140
Deathworld Trilogy (Harrison, H.), 101, 102
Decades (Aldiss & Harrison), 259
Del Whitby (Morressy), 153
Demon (Lambert), 124
Demon Princes (Vance), 219
Demu Trilogy (Busby), 37

Dennis Grafton (Dexter, W.), 63
Derek Calver (Chandler), 46
Destinies (Baen), 245
Destiny (Wolheim), 235
Detective Gees (Vivian), 224
Devil is Dead Trilogy (Lafferty), 123
Devil Series (Johnstone), 116
Devil Upon Two Sticks (Le Sage), 130
Devilday (Hall, Angus), 98
Dextra (Lake), 123
Diadem Series (Clayton), 48, 49
Diana Santee--Spaceways Agent (Green), 278
Diarmid O'Dowd (Petaja), 170
Dick Grenville (Fletcher), 81
Dies Irae Series (Stableford), 202
Dig Allen (Greene), 95
Dilbia Sequence (Dickson), 64
Dilvish of Dilvar (Zelazny), 238
Dinosaur Planet (McCaffrey), 140, 279
Dipple (Norton, A.), 160
Dirshan the God-Killer (Lancour), 124
Doc Caliban (Farmer, P.J.), 79
Doc Savage (Robeson), 181-184
Doctor Death (Zimmer), 239
Doctor Doolittle (Lofting), 133, 134
Dr. Goodwin (Merritt), 148
Dr. Lowell (Merritt), 148
Dr. Nikola (Boothby), 27
Dr. Orient (Lauria), 127
Dr. Palfrey (Creasey), 55, 56

Dr. Phibes (Goldstein), 91
Dr. Scarlet (Laing), 123
Doctor Who, 65-68
Dolphin Trilogy (Meyers), 148
Dominic Flandry (Anderson, P.), 6
Don Camillo (Guareschi), 96
Don Sebastian (Daniels, L.), 59
Don Slade (Drake), 69
Don Sturdy (Appleton), 10
Don't Bite the Sun (Lee, T.), 128
Doom-Quest of Ara-Karn (Corby), 54
Doomsday Warrior (Stacy), 202
Doomstar (Meyers), 280
Double Spiral War (Norwood, W.), 161
Doubleday Early Series, 255
Downbelow Station (Cherryh), 47
Dracula (Stoker), 208
Dracula Horror Series (Lory), 134
Dracula Series (Saberhagen), 190
Dragon Books (McCaffrey), 140
Dragon Sequence (Yolen), 237
Dragonfall 5 (Earnshaw, B.), 72
Dragonlance Chronicles (Weis & Hickman), 228, 282
Dragonriders of Pern (McCaffrey), 140
Dragons (Card), 249
Dragon's Egg Sequence (Forward), 278
Dragonstar (Bischoff), 24
Dray Prescott (Bulmer), 33, 34, 277
Dread Empire (Cook), 52

Dream Lords (Cole), 50
Dreamhouse (Wayman), 227
Duc de Richleau
  (Wheatley), 229
Duel of Sorcery
  (Clayton), 49
Duffus January (Smith,
  G.), 199
Dumarest of Terra (Tubb),
  215
Dune (Herbert), 104
Durdane Trilogy (Vance),
  219
Dushau Trilogy (Lichtenberg), 132, 279
Dusty Ayres (Bowen), 28
Dying Earth (Vance), 219
Dysart (Deegan), 62

E.T. (Kotzwinkle), 122
Earth's Children (Auel),
  12, 276
Earthchild Trilogy
  (Webb), 228
Earthsea Trilogy (Le
  Guin), 128
Eden Series (Pohl &
  Wiliamson), 173, 233
Editors of Galaxy, 255
Editors of IF, 255
El Borak (Howard, R.), 110
Elana (Engdahl), 75
Electric Elephant
  (Montgomery), 150
Elfin Sequence (Blaylock), 25
Elias Kane (Spruill), 202
Elric Saga (Moorcock), 152
Elsewhere (Windling &
  Arnold), 273
Elspeth Marriner
  (Merwin), 148
Emma (Farmer, P.), 78, 79
Empire of the East
  (Saberhagen), 190
Empress Series
  (Chandler), 46
Endless Frontier
  (Pournelle), 267

Epic Tale of the Five
  (Duane), 70
Erewhon (Butler), 38
Eric Brighteyes
  (Haggard), 97
Eric Carstairs of
  Zanthodon (Carter, L.),
  44
Eric John Stark: Outlaws
  of Mars (Brackett), 28
Eridanus (Barbet), 14
Erthring Cycle (Drew), 69
Eunostos (Swann), 210
Every Boy's Series
  (Dikty), 254
Ewoks (Star Wars), 206
Exiles Trilogy (Bova), 27
Expendables (Cooper, E.),
  53
Explorations Sequence
  Smilie), 197
Eyes Trilogy (Gordon), 91

Faded Sun (Cherryh), 47
Faery Trilogy
  (MacDonald), 141
Fafhrd and the Gray
  Mouser (Leiber), 129
Falcon (Ramsay), 176
Falkenberg (Pournelle),
  174
Fall of a Nation (Dixon),
  65
Fall of the First World
  (Smith, D.C.), 197, 198
Fall of the Towers
  (Delany), 62
Family D'Alembert (Smith,
  E.), 198, 199
Fantazius Mallare
  (Hecht), 103
Far Frontiers (Pournelle
  & Baen), 267
Far Stars and Future
  Times (McEnroe), 141
Farstar & Son (Starr,
  B.), 203
Felix Charlock (Durrell),
  71

Finnbranch (Hazel), 103
Five Children (Nesbit), 157
Five Flights of the Starfire (Mumford), 154
Flash Gordon (Raymond), 177
Flashing Swords (Carter), 251
Flatland (Abbott), 1
Flinx and Pip Titles (Foster, A.), 82,
Floating City (Verne), 222
Flying Fish (Collingwood), 51
Flying Nun (Johnston, W.), 116
Forerunner Series (Norton, A.), 160
Foundation Series (Asimov), 11
Four Lords of the Diamond (Chalker), 45
Frames Sequence (Ball), 14
Francis (Stern) 207
Frank Braun (Ewers), 76
Franklin Watts Textbook Series (Olander & Greenberg), 265
Freddy (Brooks, W.), 31
Frights Series (Grant), 258
Frontiers (Elwood), 256
Frostflower (Karr), 118
Fu Manchu (Rohmer), 186, 187
Fursey (Wall), 225
Future at War (Bretnor), 249
Future History Series (Heinlein), 104
Future Perfect (Franklin), 256, 257
Fuzzy Series (Piper), 172

G-8 and His Battle Aces (Hogan, R.), 106
Gaea (Varley), 221
Galactic Empires (Aldiss), 241
Galaxy Novella Series (Gold), 257
Galaxy Reader (Gold), 257
Gaming Magi (Bischoff), 24
Gandalara Cycle (Garrett & Heydron), 88
Ganymede (Resnick), 178
Garnett (Egleton), 73
Garth Series (Watt-Evans), 227
Gaston Max (Rohmer), 187
Gateways (Carnell), 250
Gavin Black (Jakes), 114
Genghis Cohn (Gary), 88
Geoffrey Aylett (Meik), 147
George Hanlon (Evans), 76
Gerald Knave (Janifer), 115
Gerard Sorme (Wilson, C.), 233
Gerin the Fox (Iverson), 113
Gilbert Nash (Tucker), 216
Girl from U.N.C.L.E., 218
Glyndon (Bulwer-Lytton), 34
Go Saddle the Sea (Aiken), 3
Gods of Pegana (Dunsany), 71
Golden Amazon (Fearn), 80
Gondwane Epic (Carter, L.), 44
Gonji (Rypel), 189
Gor (Norman), 159, 280
Gormenghast Trilogy (Peake), 166
Grainger Series (Stableford), 202
Grand Fenwick (Webberley), 230, 231
Gray Lands (Meade), 147
Great Imperium (Carter, L.), 43
Great Marvel Series

(Rockwood), 185
Great SF Stories (Asimov
 & Greenberg), 243, 276
Great Science Fiction
 Stories (Dikty), 255
Great Years (Pohl), 267
Green Hornet, 94
Green Knowe (Boston), 27
Green Planet (Petaja), 170
Green-Sky Trilogy
 (Snyder), 200
Green Star Rises (Carter,
 L.), 43
Green Stone (Cabell), 40
Greenwich Village Trilogy
 (Anderson, C., Kurland,
 Walters), 5
Greenwood Sequence
 (Barker, G.), 15
Gregg Haljan (Cummins), 58
Gregory Quest (Moore,
 P.), 153
Grenfell and Wright
 (Moore, P.), 153
Guardians (Austin), 12,
 276
Guardians of the Flame
 (Rosenberg), 187
Guardians Series (Saxon),
 192
Guinevere (Newman, S.),
 158
Gun Club (Verne), 222
Gypsy Sequence (Goulart),
 92

Haakon (Neilson), 157
Hades (Kummer), 122
Halloween, 98
Han Solo (Star Wars), 206
Harold Shea (De Camp &
 Pratt), 61
Harry Borg and Guss
 (Hawkins), 278
Hautley Quicksilver
 (Carter, L.), 43
Haven Series (Diamond), 64
Havengore (Geston), 89
Heaven and Hell
 (Blamires), 25
Hector Servadac (Verne),
 222
Heechee Trilogy (Pohl &
 Williamson), 173, 233
Heirs and Assigns
 (Cabell), 40
Heliobas (Corelli), 54
Helliconia (Aldiss), 4
Her-Bak (De Lubicz), 62
Herald Childe (Farmer,
 P.J.), 79
Herbert (Fearn), 80
Herbert (Wilson, H.), 234
Herbie (Cebulash), 45
Hidden People (Miller,
 L.), 149
Hiero Desteen (Lanier),
 125
Historical Illuminatus
 Chronicles (Wilson,
 R.), 234
Histories of King Kelson
 (Kurtz), 122
History of the Science
 Fiction Magazine
 (Ashley), 242
Hitchhiker Series (Adams,
 D.), 1
Hive (Bass), 18
Hoka Series (Anderson, P.
 & Dickson), 6, 64
Homer Crawford (Rey-
 nolds), 179
Hook Series (Bulmer), 34
Hoorka Trilogy (Leigh),
 129
Horace Clarke (Lewis,
 I.), 132
Horrorscope (Lory), 136
Horseclans Series (Adams,
 Rbt.), 2
Hosteen Storm (Norton,
 A.), 160
Hound and the Falcon
 (Tarr), 282
House-Boat (Bangs), 14
Howling (Brandner), 30,
 277

Hub (Schmitz), 193
Hubbles (Horseman), 107
Hugo Winners (Asimov), 243
Hulzein Chronicles
  (Busby), 38
Human Age (Lewis, W.), 132
Human Bat (Home-Gall), 106
Humanoids (Williamson,
  J.), 233
Humanx Commonwealth
  Series (Foster, A.),
  82, 278
Hunters (Tabori), 211
Huntsman Trilogy (Hill),
  105
Hydronauts (Biemiller), 23

Ijon Tichy Stories (Lem),
  130
Illuminatus (Wilson, R.),
  234
Illuminatus Trilogy
  (Wilson, R.), 234
Imaro (Saunders), 191, 281
Imperium (Laumer), 126
In the Ocean of the Night
  (Benford), 22
Incarnations of Immor-
  tality (Anthony), 8, 276
Indiana Jones, 113
Infinity (Hoskins), 259
Inquestor Trilogy
  (Sucharitkul), 209, 281
Instrumentality of Man
  (Smith, C.), 197
Interstellar Patrol
  (Hamilton, E.), 99
Invaders, 113
Invisibles (Hurwood), 111
Iron Angel Series
  (Morressy), 154
Iron Tower Trilogy
  (McKiernan), 142
Ironbark Bill (Stivens),
  208
Isaac Asimov Presents
  (Asimov, Greenberg, &
  Waugh), 244
Isaac Asimov's Magical

Worlds of Fantasy
  (Asimov, Greenberg, &
  Waugh), 244, 276
Isaac Asimov's Series
  (Scithers), 270
Isaac Asimov's Wonderful
  World of Science
  Fiction (Asimov,
  Greenberg, & Waugh), 244
Isher (Van Vogt), 220
Isle of the Dead
  (Zelazny), 238
Israel Bond (Weinstein),
  228
Ithkar Fair (Norton &
  Adams), 280

Jacare (Norwood, V.), 161
Jack Odin (Kelleam), 119
Jade Demons (Vardeman),
  221, 282
Jake McGraw (De Chancie),
  61
Jalav: Amazon Warrior
  (Green, S.), 94
James Armitage (Kelsey),
  119
Jamnar (Van Arnam), 219
Jan (Kline), 121
Jan Darzek (Biggle), 23
Jane Blonde (Carnelle), 42
Janissaries (Pournelle),
  174
Janus Sequence (Norton,
  A.), 160
Jason Croft (Giesy), 89
Jason Striker (Anthony), 7
Jaws, 115
Jennifer (Smith, T.), 199
Jeremy Grant (MacVicar),
  143
Jerry Carnelian Series
  (Moorcock), 152
Jesus Incident (Herbert &
  Ransom), 104
Jet Morgan (Chilton), 48
Jim Dunlap (Palmer), 165
Jimgrim/Ramsden Series
  (Mundy), 154, 155

Jinian (Tepper), 212
Joe Kenmore Series
  (Leinster), 129
Joe Mauser (Reynolds), 179
John Daker (Moorcock), 151
John Grimes: Federation
  Survey Service
  (Chandler), 46
John Grimes: Rim Runners
  (Chandler), 46
John Solomon (Bedford-
  Jones), 21
Johnny Dixon (Bellairs),
  21
Johnny Fedora (Cory), 54
Johnny Ludlow (Wood, Mrs.
  H.). 235
Jongor (Williams, R.), 232
Jonny (Biemiller), 23
Jorkens Tales (Dunsany),
  71
Journey (Randall, M.), 176
Journeys of McGill
  Feighan (O'Donnell), 163
Jules deGrandin (Quinn),
  176
Jules LeVallon (Black-
  wood), 25
Julian West (Bellamy), 22
Jungle Books (Kipling),
  120
Justice Cycle Trilogy
  (Hamilton, V.), 99
Justin Retief (Doke), 68

Kai Lung (Bramah), 30
Kalevala Sequence
  (Petaja), 170
Kane (Wagner), 225
Kantmorie Saga (Dibell),
  64
Kar-Chee (Davidson), 60
Karl Glogauer (Moorcock),
  151
Karmic Destiny (Living-
  ston), 133
Kaspa (Stoneham), 208
Kavin (Mason, D.), 146

Kay Harker (Masefield),
  146
Kemlo (Eliott, E.), 74
Ken Malone (Janifer &
  Garrett), 87, 115
Kendric and Irissa
  (Douglas), 69
Kennet Trilogy (Berry,
  B.), 23
Kensho (Schmidt), 192
Kerban the Inflexible
  (Verne), 223
Kerrion Empire (Morris),
  154
Kesrick (Carter, L.), 44
Keys to the Dimensions
  (Bulmer), 33
Ki (Lindholm), 133
Kilkhampton and West-
  minister (Croft), 57
King Arthur (Bradshaw), 29
King Goshawk/Aloysius
  O'Kennedy (O'Duffy), 163
K'ing Kung Fu (Macao), 140
King Solomon's Mines
  Parodies (De Morgan), 63
Kioga Series (Chester), 48
Kitty Telfair (Steven-
  son), 207
Kolchak (Rice), 180
Konarr (Van Arnam), 219
Kothar (Fox), 83
Krishna Series (De Camp),
  61
Kyric (Fox), 84

La Noire Series
  (Fanthorpe), 78
Lady Branwen (Meaney),
  147
Lady From L.U.S.T. (Fox),
  83
Lafayette O'Leary
  (Laumer), 126
Lamia Zacharius (William-
  son, J.N.), 232
Land of the Giants
  (Leinster, Bradwell,

& Rathjen), 124
Lando Calrissian (Star Wars), 206
Lands of Never (Jakubowski), 260
Last and First Men (Stapledon), 203
Last Communion Sequence (Yermakov), 237
Last Viking (Anderson, P.), 6
Latimer (Coles), 50
Lawless Worlds (Comstock), 51
Lazarus Long (Heinlein), 104
League of All Worlds (Le Guin), 128, 129
Legends of Camber of Culdi (Kurtz), 122
Legion of Space (Williamson, J.), 232, 233
Legion of Time (Williamson, J.), 233
Lemmus Trilogy (Savarin), 191
Lensmen Series (Smith, E.), 198
Ler Trilogy (Foster, M.), 82, 83
Leslie Barnes (Bradley), 29
Life of Merlin (Stewart, M.), 208
Life Probe Sequence (McCollum), 279
Lilith Le Fay Morgan (Fortune), 82
Liners of Time (Fearn), 80
Linn (Van Vogt), 220
Little Monsters (Elwood & Ghidlia), 256
Little Pilgrim (Oliphant), 164
Living Dead (Romero), 187
Living Planet (Coon), 53
Lobster Books (Hatch), 102
Logan (Nolan), 158
Long Journey (Jensen), 115
Looking Back (Reynolds), 179
Lord Darcy (Garrett), 87
Lord Grandith (Farmer, P.J.), 79
Lord Kalvan (Piper), 172
Lord of the Rings Trilogy (Tolkien), 213
Lord Tarlyon et al. (Arlen), 10
Lord Tedric (Eklund), 73
Lords of Darkness (Lee, T.), 128
Lucian Carolus (Ascher), 10, 11
Lucifer Cove (Coffman), 50
Lucifram (Allonby), 5
Lucius Leffing (Brennan), 30, 31
Lucky Starr (Asimov), 11
Luke Skywalker (Star Wars), 206
Luke Trilogy (Christopher), 48
Lyndis (Norton, A.), 160
Lyonesse (Vance), 219
Lyra (Wrede), 235

Magdah Sequence (Campbell, H.), 42
Magi (Van Der Naillen), 220
Magic (Eager), 72
Magic (Niven), 264, 265
Magic of Xanth (Anthony), 8, 276
Magira Series (Walker), 225
Majipoor Trilogy (Silverberg), 195
Man From S.T.U.D. (Fairman), 77
Man From T.O.M.C.A.T. (Hurwood), 111
Man From U.N.C.L.E., 217, 218
Manitou (Masterson), 279
Manuel of Pioctesme (Cabell), 40

Marguerite Cranleigh
  (Wright), 236
Marianne O'Hara
  (Haldeman), 98
Maris (Moon), 150
Mars Sequence (Kline), 121
Mars Series (Burroughs,
  E.), 36
Martin (Horowitz), 107
Martin Magnus (Temple),
  211
Martin Speed (Eliott,
  G.), 74
Martin Webster (Wright),
  236
Mary Poppins (Travers),
  214
Masters of Solitude Sequence (Godwin, P.), 90
Mathematics Duet
  (Faidman), 256
Matter (Cummins), 57
Matter, Space & Time
  Series (Cummins), 57
Matthew Dilke (Gutteridge), 96
Matthew Looney (Beatty),
  20
Matthew Sumner (Davey), 60
Matthew Swain (McQuay),
  143
Maurice Gray (Moore, P.),
  153
Mavin Trilogy (Tepper),
  212
Maxwell Smart (Johnston,
  W.), 116
McKay, Knowlton & Ryan
  (Friel), 85
Med Service Series
  (Leinster), 129, 130
Meg Murray (L'Engle), 130
Mekie (Herbert), 104
Memoirs of a Physician
  (Dumas), 70
Menolly the Singer
  (McCaffrey), 140
Merlin Trilogy (Munn), 156
Mesklin (Clement), 49

Mews Duet (Brown), 249
Michael Jousse (Berna), 22
Michael Kane (Moorcock),
  151
Micronauts (Williams,
  G.), 231
Middle Earth (Tolkien),
  213, 282
Mighty Warriors
  (Santesson), 269
Mike Delaney (Maine), 144
Mike Glenn (Lee, R.), 128
Mike Mars (Wollheim), 234
Miles Cabot (Farley), 78
Mind Brothers (Heath), 103
Minds-in-Bodies Series
  (Wallace), 225
Minervan Experiment
  (Hogan, J.), 105
Minnipens (Kendall), 119
Miss Bianca (Sharp, M.),
  194
Miss From S.I.S.
  (Tralins), 214
Miss Pickerell
  (MacGregor), 142
Mr. Mycroft (Heard), 103
Mr. Tompkins (Gamow), 86
Mr. Wicker (Dawson), 60
Mists of Avalon
  (Bradley), 29
Molt Brother
  (Lichtenberg), 132
Monella (Aubrey), 12
Moomin Books (Jansson),
  279
Moon Sequence (Burroughs,
  E.), 37
Moon Series (Del Rey), 62
Moon Singer (Norton, A.),
  160
Moreta (McCaffrey), 140
Morgan of Alb'ny
  (McQuay), 143
Morphodite (Foster, M.),
  83
Motherlines (Charnas), 47
Motor Pirate (Paternoster), 166

Munsters, 156
Murdoc Jern (Norton, A.), 160
Myth Series (Asprin), 12, 276

Nate Twitchell (Butterworth), 38
Natural Man (Lloyd), 133
Nebula Awards Series, 263, 264
Ned Shackleton (Crawley), 55
Needle (Clement), 49
Neuromancer (Gibson, Wm.), 89
Neustrian Cycle (Barringer), 18
Neveryon (Delany), 62
New Atalantis (Manley), 144
New Avengers, 13
New Dimensions (Silverberg), 271
New Ice Trilogy (Forestchen), 82
New Terrors (Campbell, R.), 249
New Voices (Martin), 262
New Voyages (Star Trek), 205
New World Sequence (Kahn), 118
New Worlds (Moorcock), 263
New Worlds of Fantasy (Carr), 250
New Worlds Quarterly (Moorcock), 263
New Writings in Horror and the Supernatural (Sutton), 272
New Writings in SF, 264
Ni-Lach (Bennett), 22
Niall Renfro (Norton, A.), 160
Nidorian Sequence (Garrett & Silverberg), 87, 195
Nightmare Has Triplets (Cabell), 40
1984 (Orwell), 165
Noibla (Lunatic), 139
Nomad of Time (Moorcock), 152
Noomas (Neutzel), 162
Noren (Engdahl), 75
Norgil (Grant, M.), 94
Nova (Harrison), 259
Nova Sequence (Burroughs, W.), 37
Novaria Series (De Camp), 61
Null-A (Van Vogt), 220
Nurlingas Series (Bailey), 14

Odan the Half-God (Bulmer), 34
Odd Jobs, Inc. (Goulart), 92
Og (Crump), 57
Old Growler (Deegan), 61
Oleandre Sequence (Fretland), 85
Omega Point Trilogy (Zebrowski), 238
Omen, 164
Omina (Rowland), 189
Omni Science Fiction (Datlow), 252, 253
Omnivore (Anthony), 7
Once and Future King (White, T.H.), 230
100 Short Short Stories (Asimov), 243
101 Dalmations (Smith, D.), 198
Operator 5 (Steele, C.), 207
Orbit (Knight), 260, 261
Orbitsville (Shaw), 194
Orion (Bova), 27
Ormond (Beck), 21
Oron (Smith, D.C.), 197
Other Worlds (Torgeson), 272
Out of This World (Williams-Ellis &

Owen), 273
Outlander Series
 (Coblentz), 49
Outrider (Harding), 100
Oxrun (Grant, C.), 92, 278
Oz (Baum), 19, 20
Ozark Fantasy Trilogy
 (Elgin), 74

Pacific Books (Baxter),
 246
Pantouflia (Lang, A.),
 124, 125
Paralyzing Ray (Nizzi),
 158
Paratime Police/Lord
 Kalvan (Piper), 172
Parsival (Monaco), 150
Pat Collins (Palmer), 165
Paul Harley (Rohmer), 187
Paul Reeder (Dennis), 63
Paul Vivanti (Horler), 107
Peacemakers (Faucette), 80
Pelbar Cycle (Williams,
 P.), 232, 282
Pellucidar Series
 (Burroughs, E.), 36, 37
Pelman the Powershaper
 (Hughes), 111
Penelope (Anderson, W.), 7
Penguin SF Series
 (Aldiss), 241
People (Henderson), 104
Percy (Hitchcock), 105
Percy Darrow (White, S.),
 230
Peregrine (Davidson), 60
Perelandra Trilogy
 (Lewis, C.S.), 131
Perry Rhodan, 167-170
Peter (Mogridge), 150
Peter Pan (Barrie), 18
Phantom (Falk), 77
Phoenix Legacy (Wren), 235
Pic (Langford), 125
Planet of Tears
 (Reinius), 280
Planet of the Apes, 172
Plantagenet (Andrews), 7

Playboy Science Fiction
 Series, 266
Polaris (Stilson), 208
Polesotechnic League
 (Anderson, P.), 6
Prehumans (Swann), 210
Prester John (Page), 165
Prince Lincoas (Curry), 58
Principles of Magic
 (Hardy, L.), 100
Prisoner, 174, 175
Problems of Human
 Happiness (Dudley), 70
Professor Challenger
 Novels (Doyle), 69
Professor Ellis
 Lambourne), 124
Professor Jameson Series
 (Jones, N.), 117
Professor Kurtz (Curry),
 58
Professor Quartermass
 (Kneale), 121
Professor Rhymer (Key,
 U.), 120
Professor Wutheridge
 (Nathan), 157
Psi Patrol, 175
Psychotechnic League
 (Anderson, P.), 6
Puck (Kipling), 120
Pulsar (Hay), 259
Pyat (Moorcock), 152

Q Series (Hoyle, T.), 110
Qanar (White, T.), 230
Qfwfq Sequence (Calvino),
 41
Qhe (Bloom), 26
Quark (Delany & Hacker),
 253
Quest of Morgaine
 (Cherryh), 47
Quest Trilogy (Farren), 79

Ra-Ab Hotep (Grant, J.),
 92
Radio Boys (Brecken-
 ridge), 30

Radio Detectives
  (Verrill), 223
Radio-Phone Boys (Snell),
  199
Ragnarok (Godwin, T.), 90
Raintree Books
  (Bischoff), 247
Raintree Series (Asimov,
  Greenberg, & Waugh), 243
Ralph Hannon (Law), 127
Rand McNally Textbook
  Series, 268
Randy Knowles (Holzer),
  106
Raphael Drale (Aronin), 10
Raven Series (Kirk), 121
Rector (Storey), 209
Red Moon and Black
  Mountain (Chant), 47
Red Sonja (Smith, D.C.),
  197
Reefe King (Barker, A.),
  15
Reggie Brooks
  (MacPherson), 143
Regina (Mastin), 146
Retief Series (Laumer),
  126
Return to the Planet of
  the Apes, 172
Reuben (Harris, R.), 101
Rex Bader (Reynolds), 179
Rex Clinton (Johns), 115
Rhada (Coppel), 90
Richard Blade (Lord, J.),
  134, 135
Rick Brant (Blaine), 25
Riddle of Stars
  (McKillip), 125
Rifkind (Abbey), 1
Riftwar Trilogy (Feist),
  80
Riverworld (Farmer,
  P.J.), 79
Ro-Lan (Sirota), 196
Road to Science Fiction
  (Gunn), 258
Robby Hoenig (Dickson), 64
Robert Grandon (Kline),
  121
Robert Lawson (Comer), 51
Robin North (Moore, P.),
  153
Robot Series (Asimov), 11
Robur the Conqueror
  (Verne), 223
Rock (Lightner), 133
Rocket Riders (Garis), 87
Rod Gallowglass (Stash-
  eff), 206, 281
Roi Kunzer (Geis), 88
Romanoff Sequence
  (Griffith), 95
Ron Barron (Jones, R.),
  117
Rosinante (Gilliand), 90
Ross Murdock (Norton,
  A.), 159
Roy Rickman (Craig), 55
Rulers of Hylor (Wilder),
  231
Runes (Manaco), 150
Runestaff (Moorcock), 151
Russian Science Fiction
  (Magidorff), 261

Saga of Cuckoo (Pohl &
  Williamson), 173, 233
Saga of Pliocene Exile
  (May), 147
Saga of Rissa Kerguelen
  (Busby), 38
Saint-Germain Series
  (Yarbro), 237
St. Martin's Press
  Textbook Series,
  268, 269
Sakaeland (Ganpat), 86
Sam Small (Knight, E.),
  121
Samarkind (Diamond), 64
Sanctuary (Asprin),
  12, 244, 276
Saragossa Manuscript
  (Potocki), 173, 174
Saucers (Binder, E.), 24
Savage Empire Series
  (Lorrah), 135

Savage Report
  (Rheingold), 179
Schrodinger's Cat
  (Wilson, R.), 234
Science Fiction: The
  Future (Allen), 241
Science Fiction Hall of
  Fame, 271
Science Fiction Tales
  (Elwood), 256
Science Fiction
  Treasuries (Boucher),
  248
Science in Science
  Fiction (Asimov,
  Greenberg, & Waugh), 244
Scobee Trent (Owen), 165
Screwtape (Lewis, C.S.),
  131
Search (Weverka), 229
Secret Agent X, 193
Section G (Reynolds), 179
Sector General (White,
  J.), 229, 230
Seeking Sword
  (Kangliaski), 118
Seers of Ere (Murphy),
  156
Seetee (Williamson, J.),
  233
Serpent Land (Connell), 51
Serpent Trilogy
  (Timlett), 213
Seven Citadels (Harris,
  G.), 101
7 Duet (Asimov, Greenberg, & Waugh), 243
Shadow (Grant, M.), 92-94
Shadows (Grant), 257, 258
Shai (Walther), 226
Shamryke Odell (Lory), 136
Shannara (Brooks, T.), 31
She (Haggard), 97, 278
Shimmer and Thorn (Yep),
  237
Shiny Spear Sequence
  (Campbell, H.), 42
Shuna (King), 120
Sibyl Sue Blue (Brown), 32

Sidhe (Flint, K.), 81
Silistra Series (Morris),
  154
Silver John (Wellman), 228
Sime/Gen Novels
  (Lichtenberg), 132
Simeon Trilogy (Tate), 211
Simon Ark (Hoch), 105
Simon Black (Southall),
  175
Simon Blackstone
  (McKenney), 142
Simon Rack (James), 114
Singreale Chronicles
  (Miller, C.), 149
Sir Giles Tumulty
  (Williams, C.), 231
Sisterhood Trilogy
  (Rheingold), 179
Six Million Dollar Man
  (Caidin), 41
Sixth Perception
  (Morgan), 153
Sky Buddies (Craine), 55
Skylark Series (Smith,
  E.), 198
Skyrider (Michaels), 280
Smith Minor (Hardy, P.),
  101
Smokeover Series (Jacks),
  113
Snarkout Boys
  (Pinkwater), 171
Snow Queen Sequence
  (Vinge), 224
Snowbird (Stables), 202
Socioland (Chavannes), 47
Solar Queen (Norton, A.),
  159
Solomon Kane Series
  (Howard, R.), 110
Song of Earth (Coney), 51
Song of the Lioness
  (Pierce, T.), 171
Sorak (Richards, H.), 180
Sorcery (Jackson), 113,
  114
Soul Rider (Chalker), 45,
  277

Soviet Science Fiction, 272
Space (Cummins), 57
Space (Davis), 253
Space Cat (Todd), 213
Space Eagle (Pearl), 166
Space For Hire (Nolan), 158
Space Group (Norton), 265
Space Mail (Asimov, Greenberg & Olander), 243
Space Mavericks (Kring), 122
Space Merchants (Pohl), 173
Space: 1999, 200, 201
Space Odyssey (Clarke), 48
Space Probe 6 (Huntington), 111
Space Puppet (Phillifent), 171
Space Ship (Slobodkin), 196
Spaceship (Lord, B.), 134
Spaceways (Offutt), 163, 164
Specialist (LeCale), 127
Spectrum (Amis), 241
Spellsinger (Foster, A.), 82, 278
Spider, The, 201
Sprockets (Key, A.), 120
Stainless Steel Rat (Harrison, H.), 102
Star Hounds (Bischoff), 24
Star Ka'at Series (Norton, A. & Madlee), 161
Star Kings (Hamilton, E.), 99
Star Man (Byrne), 38, 39
Star Quest Trilogy (Mills), 149
Star Science Fiction (Pohl), 266
Star Trek Animated TV Series Adaptations, 205
Star Trek Foto-Novels, 205
Star Trek Novels, 203, 204, 281

Star Trek TV Episode Adaptations, 204, 205
Star Wars Trilogy, 206
Starcats Trilogy (Gotleib), 91
Starchild Trilogy (Pohl & Williamson), 173, 233
Starfishers Trilogy (Cook), 53
Stars Sequence (Hoskins), 107
Starship Orpheus (Jade), 114
Starwolf (Hamilton, E.), 99
Steam House Sequence (Verne), 222
Stellar (Del Rey, J.), 254
Sten (Cole & Bunch), 50
Stephen MacFarlane (Cross), 57
Steve Austin (Caidin), 41
Stingray (Theydon), 212
Stories of the Vampire (Rice), 281
Strange Conflict (Batchelor), 19
Strange Paradise (Daniels, D.), 59
Subspace Sequence (Smith, E.), 198
Sumuru Series (Rohmer), 187
Sunset Warrior Trilogy (Van Lustbader), 220
Super Nova (MacVicar), 143
Superman (Maggin), 144
Survivalist (Ahern), 3
Survivors (Bradley & Zimmer), 29
Survivors (Sibson), 195
Survivors Sequence (Zimmer), 238
Swinging Spy (Cameron, L.), 41
Swiss Family Robinson (Verne), 223
Sword and Sorceress (Bradley), 248

Swords of Raemllyn (Vardeman & Proctor), 221
Swords Quintet (Offutt), 265
Swords Trilogy (Moorcock), 152
Sybil Barron (Gregorian), 95

Tahara (Sherman, H.), 194
Tales of a Naturalist (Chambers), 45
Tales of Khe'chin (Lukeman), 139
Tales of Known Space (Niven), 158
Tales of the Galactic Midway (Resnick), 178
Tales of the Picts (Howard, R.), 110
Tales of the Velvet Comet (Resnick), 178, 281
Tales of the Werewolf Clan (Munn), 155, 156
Tall Stories (Caldecott), 277
Tama (Cummins), 58
Tarot (Anthony), 8
Tarzan (Burroughs, E.), 35, 36
Tas (Eliott, E.), 74
TCity (Adlard), 3
Teen-Age Series (Furman), 257
Telzey Amberdon (Schmitz), 193
Terra SF (Nolane), 265
Terran Empire Series (Cameron, B.), 41
Terrilian Sequence (Green, S.), 94
Tertius (Newman, R.), 157
Testament of Man (Fisher, V.), 81
Tharn (Browne), 32
Themes (Kelley), 260
There Will Be War (Pournelle), 174

There Will Be War (Pournelle & Carr), 267
Thongor Series (Carter, L.), 43
Three Immortals (Viereck), 223
3000 Sequence (Greenberg & Waugh), 258
Through the Ages (Evans), 256
Thunderbirds (Theydon), 212
Thunderbolt (Ohlson), 164
Ti-Coyo (Richer), 180
Time (Cummins), 57
Time Agents (Norton, A.), 159
Time Machine (Monroe), 150
Time Machine (Wells), 229
Time Sequence (Barrett), 17
Time Trilogy (Anderson, M.), 5
Time Trilogy (Ball), 14
Time Tunnel (Leinster), 130
Time War Series (Hawke), 237, 283
Timeliner Trilogy (Meridith), 148
Timequest (Tedford), 211
Timeways Trilogy (Bartholomew), 18
Titus Crow Series (Lumley), 139
Tlen (Lambert), 124
To the Stars (Harrison, H.), 102
Tom Corbett, Space Cadet (Rockewll), 185
Tom Swift (Appleton), 8, 9
Tom Swift Jr. (Appleton II), 9, 10
Tomoe Gozen (Salmonson), 191
Tomorrow People (Price), 174
Tomorrow Testament (Longyear), 134

Topper (Smith, T.), 199
Torin Series (Wilder), 231
Trail Sequence (Verrill), 223
Transformations (Roselle), 268
Trantorian Empire (Asimov), 11
Trauma 2020 (Beere), 21
Traveler (Drumm), 69
Trio For Lute (MacAvoy), 140
Tripods (Christopher), 48
Tristan (Dexter, S.), 63
Tros of Samothrace (Mundy), 155
Trovo (Lory), 135
Troyana (Meek), 147
True Game Trilogy (Tepper), 212
Tschai: Planet of Adventure (Vance), 219
Turning Page Sequence (Karl), 118
II Galaxy (Jakes), 114
2000 A.D. (Reynolds), 179
2069 (Townsend), 214
Tycho Bass (Cameron, E.), 41
Tyrnos (Mayhar), 147

UFO (Burke), 35
UNSA (Greenleaf), 95
Ugglians (Fallaw), 78
U.N.C.L.E., 217, 218
Uncle Paul (Blackwood), 24
Uncle Remus (Harris, J.), 101
Ungruwarkh Trilogy (Gotleib), 278
Universe (Carr), 250
University of Cosmopoli (Blayre), 26
Unknown (Bensen), 246
Unto the Altar (Tigges), 213
Untuswa (Mitford), 149

V, 218, 282

Valentine Flynn (Tralins), 214
Vampirella (Goulart), 92
Vanguard Science Fiction Series (Conklin), 252
Vansittart (Tracy), 214
Vathek (Beckford), 21
Veltakin (Cristabel), 56
Venturer Twelve Series (Kippax), 120
Venus Series (Burroughs, E.), 37
Venus Series (Fraser), 84
Venus Trilogy (Berry, B.), 23
Vernon Templeton (Luigi), 138
Veta (Goll), 91
Vikings (Langholm), 125
Viriconium (Harrison, M.), 102
Vision of Beasts (Lovejoy), 138
Visitor From Venus series (Lach-Szyrma), 123
Vlad Taltos (Brust), 32
Voyage to the Bottom of the Sea, 224

Wandering Jew (Sue), 209
Wandering Stars (Dann), 252
Wandor (Green, R.), 94
War Against the Chtorr (Gerrold), 89
War for Eternity (Rowley), 189
War of 1938 (Wright), 238
War of the Gods on Earth (Offutt), 163
War of the Powers (Vardeman), 221
War of the Wizards (Offutt), 163
Warlord (Frost), 85
Warrior of Vengeance (Coe), 49
Wars of Vis (Lee, T.), 128
Wasteworld (Barton), 18
Weird (Margulies), 262

Weird Heroes (Preiss), 267
Weird Tales (Carter), 251
Well of Souls (Chalker), 45
What If? (Lupoff), 261
Whispers (Schiff), 269
Wilderness of Four (Hancock, N.), 100
Willoughby Chase (Aiken), 3
Windhover Tapes (Norwood, W.), 161
Wintersol (Earnshaw, A. & Thacker), 72
Witch Mountain (Key, A.), 120
Witch World (Norton, A.), 160
Wizard Sequence (Duane), 70
Wolfshead (Bulmer), 34
Women of Wonder (Sargent), 269
Wonderful Farm (Ayme), 13
Wondermakers (Hoskins), 260
World Below (Wright), 235
World Fantasy Awards, 274
World of Tiers (Farmer, P.J.), 79
World Without Men (Maine), 144
World's Best (Wollheim & Carr), 274
World's End Series (Carter, L.), 44
Worlds (Collins), 251
Worlds of If (Quinn & Wulff), 268

Xuma (Lake), 123

Ye Headless Lady Inn (Dryasdust), 70
Year's Best Fantasy Stories, 274, 275
Year's Best Horror Stories, 275
Year's Best Series (Merril), 262
Year's Finest Fantasy (Carr), 251
Yngling (Dalmas), 59

Zacherley, 275
Zalim (Phylos the Tibetan), 171
Zanthar (Williams, R.M.), 232
Zanzibar (Brunner), 32
Zarathustra Refugee Planets (Brunner), 32
Zarkon, Lord of the Unknown (Carter, L.), 44
Ziak II (Morressy), 280
Zimiamvian Trilogy (Eddison), 72
Zip-Zip (Schaeler), 192
Zulu Nation (Haggard), 97

Book Title Index

A For Andromeda, 110
Aardvark Affair, The, 30
Abandon Galaxy!, 83
Abbey of Kilkhampton; or, Monumental Records for the Year 1980, The, 57
Abdallah and the Donkey, 68
Abode of Life, The, 204
Ace of the White Death, 106
Across the Far Mountain, 100
Across the Sea of Suns, 22
Across the Top of the World, 2
Action: Division Three, 169
Adam and the Serpent, 81
Adam Link in the Past, 24
Adam Link--Robot, 24
Addams Family, The, 3
Addams Family Strikes Back, The, 3
Adonis, 123
Adonis at Actum, 123
Adonis at Bomasa, 123
Ads Infinitum, 227
Adventures of Baron Munchausen, The, 17
Adventures of Captain Kettle, 112
Adventures of Jules deGrandin, The, 176
Adventures of Teebo, The, 206
Adventures of the Stainless Steel Rat, The, 102
Adventures of Una Persson and Catherine Cornelius in the Twentieth Century, The, 151
Adventures on Other Planets, 273

Adventuress, The, 178
Adversary, The, 147
Advise and Consent, 70
Affair in Araby, 155
African Mercenary, The, 191
Afrit Affair, The, 13
After Dark, 228
After the End, 243
After World's End, 233
After Worlds Collide, 236
Afterglow, The, 75
Aftermath, 18
Again: Atlan!, 168
Again Dangerous Visions, 255
Against the Prince of Hell, 197
Agency, The, 147
Agent, The, 147
Agent of the Terran Empire, 6
Agents of Destruction, 170
Airplane Boys at Belize, 55
Airplane Boys at Cap Rock, 55
Airplane Boys at Platinum River, 55
Airplane Boys Discover the Secrets of Cuzco, 55
Airplane Boys Flying to Amy-Ran Fastness, 55
Airplane Boys in the Black Woods, 55
Airplane Boys on the Border Line, 55
Airplane Boys with the Revolutionists in Bolivia, 55
Airship Boys, The, 192
Airship Boys Adrift, The, 192
Airship Boys Due North, The, 192

Airship Boys in Finance, The, 192
Airship Boys in the Barren Lands, The, 192
Airship Boys' Ocean Flyer, The, 192
Alanna, 171
Alchemy Deception, The, 106
Aldair: Across the Misty Sea, 18
Aldair: The Legion of Beasts, 18
Aldair in Albion, 18
Aldair, Master of Ships, 18
Alerial; or, A Voyage to Other Worlds, 123
Alf's Button, 60
Alf's Carpet, 60
Alf's New Button, 60
Alias Man, The, 55
Alice in Wonderland, 43
Alice Through the Looking-Glass, 43
Alice's Adventures in Wonderland, 43
Alien Citadel, 105
Alien Debt, 38
Alien Heat, An, 152
Alien Island, 281
Alien Main, 281
Alien Minds, 76
Alien Missle Threat, 113
Alien Seed, 200
Alien Swordmaster, The, 218
Alien Trace, The, 144
Alien Virus, 171
Alien Worlds (Brown), 249
Alien Worlds (Collins), 251
Aliens Among Us, The, 229
Aliens From Analog, 270
All Around the Moon, 222
All Darkness Met, 52
All-Purpose Bodies, The, 141
All Our Yesterdays, 205

All Screwed Up, 52
All the Colors of Darkness, 23
All the Gods of Eisernon, 125
Allan and the Ice Gods, 97
Allan Quartermain, 97
Allan the Hunter, 97
Allan's Wife, 97
Allies of Antares, 33
Alph, 144
Alpha, 1, 271
Alpha, 2, 271
Alpha, 3, 271
Alpha, 4, 271
Alpha, 5, 271
Alpha, 6, 271
Alpha, 7, 271
Alpha, 8, 271
Alpha 9, 271
Alraune, 76
Altar of Evil, 207
Alter Evil, 114
Alternate Orbits, 46
Always on Sunday, 84
Alyx, 189
Amateurs in Alchemy, 61
Amazing Spider-Man: Crime Campaign, 146
Amazing Spider-Man: Mayhem in Manhatten, 145
Amazon Planet, 179
Amazon Strikes Again, The, 80
Amazon's Diamond Quest, The, 80
Amazons!, 269
Amazons II, 269
Ambassadors From Aureigal, 168
Ambulence Ship, 230
Ambush of Shadows, An, 232
American Emperor, An, 214
American Government Through Science Fiction, 268
American Gun Club, The, 222
American Rebellion, 202

America's Last Declaration, 202
Amityville Horror, The, 5
Amityville Horror II, The, 5
Amityville: The Final Chapter, 5
Amok Time, 205
Amphibians, The, 235
Anackire, 128
Analog 1, 249
Analog 2, 249
Analog 3, 249
Analog 4, 249
Analog 5, 249
Analog 6, 249
Analog 7, 249
Analog 8, 249
Analog 9, 249
Analog Anthology #1, The, 270
Analog: Reader's Choice, 270
Analog: Writer's Choice, 270
Analog: Writer's Choice Volume II, 270
Analog Yearbook, 242
Analog Yearbook II, 242
Analog's Children of the Future, 270
Analog's Lighter Side, 270
Anamalous Phenomena, 222
Anarch Lords, The, 46
Ancient Allan, The, 97
And All Between, 200
And Loving It!, 116
And Then There'll Be Fireworks, 74
Android Avenger, 230
Android Planet, 200
Andromeda 1, 273
Andromeda 2, 273
Andromeda 3, 273
Andromeda Breakthrough, 110
Angado, 215
Angel of the Revolution, The, 95

Angry Ghost, The, 183
Angry Planet; An Authentic First-Hand Account of a Journey to Mars in the Spaceship "Albatross," The, 57
Animal People, The, 49
Anjani the Mighty, 80
Annihilist, The, 182
Anome, The, 219
Another Fine Myth, 12
Antarctic Mystery, An, 173
Anthropol, 215
Anthropology Through Science Fiction, 268
Antro, the Life-Giver, 61
Anytime Rings, The, 78
Apollo Legacy, The, 15
Appointment at Bloodstar, 199
Arbor House Celebrity Book of Horror Stories, The, 242
Arbor House Necropolis, The, 268
Arbor House Treasury of Great Science Fiction Short Novels, The, 242
Arbor House Treasury of Horror and the Supernatural, The, 242
Arbor House Treasury of Modern Science Fiction, The, 242
Arbor House Treasury of Science Fiction Masterpieces, The, 242
Archipelago, 123
Archives of Haven, 191
Ardath, The Story of a Dead Self, 54
Arena of Antares, 33
Ariel, A Fantasy Magazine, 255
Ariel, the Book of Fantasy, Volume 2, 255
Ariel, the Book of Fantasy, Volume 3, 255
Ariel, the Book of

Fantasy, Volume 4, 255
Arm of the Starfish, The, 130
Armada of Antares, 33
Armada Sci-Fi One, 253
Armada Sci-Fi Two, 253
Armageddon 2419, A.D., 32
Armata: A Fragment, 75
Armies of Daylight, The, 98
Army of Darkness, 225
Army of the Dead, The, 207
Army of the Undead, 113
Around the Moon, 222
Arthur Gordon Pym; or, Shipwreck..., 173
As On a Darkling Plain, 27
As the Green Star Rises, 43
Ash Staff, The, 81
Ashes and Stars, 238
Asleep in the Afternoon, 125
Asmodeus; or, The Devil on Two Sticks, 130
Assassin, The, 191
Assassin of Gor, 159
Assassination Affair, The, 217
Assassins, The, 77
Assassins From Tomorrow, 103
Asses in Clover, 163
Assignment: Hellhole, 164
Assignment in Nowhere, 126
Astounding Adventures Among the Comets, 222
Astounding-Analog Reader Volume One, The, 259
Astounding-Analog Reader Volume Two, The, 259
Astral Quest, 200
Astronauts & Androids, 270
Asutra, The, 219
At Any Price, 69
At Platinum River, 55
At the Back of the North Wind, 141
At the Defense of Pittsburgh, 100
At the Earth's Core, 36
At the Mountains of Madness, 138
At the Narrow Passage, 148
At the Seventh Level, 74
Atavar, 178
Athalie, 45
Atlan, 88
Atlan #1: Spider Desert, 170
Atlan #2: Flight From Tarkihl, 170
Atlan #3: Pale Country, 170
Atlan #4: The Crystal Prince, 170
Atlan #5: War of the Ghosts, 170
Atlan in Danger, 169
Atom Fire on Mechanica, 170
Atom Hell of Grautier, The, 168
Atoms in Action, 42
Attack From the Unseen, 168
Attar's Revenge, 98
Autumn Accelerator, The, 113
Avenger of Antares, 33
Avengers, The: The Man Who Stole Tomorrow, 146
Avengers Battle the Earth-Wrecker, The, 145
Avengers of Carrig, The, 32
Avenging Liafail, 155
Avon Fantasy Reader, The, 274
Awakening, The, 3
Awful Egg, The, 183
Axe in Miklagard, An, 34
Ayesha: The Return of She, 97

Back to the Stone Age, 37
Backflash, 114
Badland, 85

Balance of Power, 202
Balsamo the Magician, 70
Balthazar the Magus, 220
Baltimore Gun Club, The, 222
Bambi, A Life in the Woods, 191
Bambi's Children, 191
Bamboo Bloodbath, The, 7
Bamboo Demons, The, 195
Bane of Nightmares, 50
Bane of the Black Sword, The, 152
Bantan and the Mermaids, 87
Bantan Fearless, 87
Bantan Incredible, 87
Bantan Primeval, 87
Barbarian, The, 190
Barbarian of World's End, The, 44
Barbarians of Mars, 151
Bard, 211
Bard II, 211
Barnabas Collins, 188
Barnabas Collins and the Gypsy Witch, 188
Barnabas Collins and the Mysterious Ghost, 188
Barnabas Collins and the Quentin's Dream, 188
Barnabas Collins Versus the Warlock, 188
Barnabas, Quentin, and Dr. Jekyll's Son, 188
Barnabas, Quentin, and the Avenging Ghost, 188
Barnabas, Quentin, and the Body Snatchers, 188
Barnabas, Quentin, and the Crystal Coffin, 188
Barnabas, Quentin, and the Frightened Bride, 188
Barnabas, Quentin, and the Grave Robbers, 188
Barnabas, Quentin, and the Haunted Cave, 188
Barnabas, Quentin, and the Hidden Tomb, 188
Barnabas, Quentin, and the Mad Magician, 188
Barnabas, Quentin, and the Magic Potion, 188
Barnabas, Quentin, and the Mummy's Curse, 188
Barnabas, Quentin, and the Nightmare Assassin, 188
Barnabas, Quentin, and the Scorpio Curse, 188
Barnabas, Quentin, and the Sea Ghost, 188
Barnabas, Quentin, and the Serpent, 188
Barnabas, Quentin, and the Vampire Beauty, 188
Barnabas, Quentin, and the Witch's Curse, 188
Barnaby, 116
Barnaby and Mrs. O'Malley, 116
Barnstormer in Oz, A, 20
Baron Munchausen's Miraculous Adventures on Land, 17
Baron Munchausen's Narrative of His Marvellous Travels and Campaigns in Russia, 15
Baron Orgaz, 127
Baron Trump's Marvelous Underground Journey, 133
Baseball 3000, 258
Bat Staffel, 106
Bat-Wing, 187
Bats in the Belfry, 199
Battle For the Planet of the Apes, 172
Battlestar Galactica, 125
Bay City Burnout, 100
Bearing an Hourglass, 8
Beast, The, 203
Beast Master, the, 160
Beasts Below, The, 170
Beasts of Antares, 33
Beasts of Gor, 159

Beasts of Hades, The, 64
Beasts of Tarzan, The, 35
Become the Hunted, 282
Beelzebub Business, The, 30
Behind the Walls of Terra, 79
Behind the Wind, 236
Behold the Man, 151
Beloved Exile, 90
Below the Root, 200
Ben, 89
Beneath an Opal Moon, 220
Beneath the Planet of the Apes, 172
Benita's Platter Pollution, 209
Benny and the Dolphin, 111
Benny and the Space Boy, 111
Berbora, 196
Berbora #2, 196
Berkley Showcase Vol. 1, The, 270
Berkley Showcase Vol. 2, The, 270
Berkley Showcase Vol. 3, The, 270
Berkley Showcase Vol. 4, The, 270
Berkley Showcase Vol. 5, The, 270
Bernard into Battle, 194
Bernard the Brave 194
Berserker, 190
Berserker Base, 190
Berserker Man, 190
Berserker Throne, The, 190
Berserker Wars, 190
Berserker's Planet, 190
Best Fantasy of the 19th Century, The, 244
Best From Fantasy and Science Fiction, Volume 1, 246
Best From Fantasy and Science Fiction, Volume 2, 246
Best From Fantasy and Science Fiction, Volume 3, 246
Best From Fantasy and Science Fiction, Volume 4, 246
Best From Fantasy and Science Fiction, Volume 5, 246
Best From Fantasy and Science Fiction, Volume 6, 246
Best From Fantasy and Science Fiction, Volume 7, 246
Best From Fantasy and Science Fiction, Volume 8, 246
Best From Fantasy and Science Fiction, Volume 9, 246
Best From Fantasy and Science Fiction, Volume 10, 246
Best From Fantasy and Science Fiction, Volume 11, 246
Best From Fantasy and Science Fiction, Volume 12, 246
Best From Fantasy and Science Fiction, Volume 13, 246
Best From Fantasy and Science Fiction, Volume 14, 246
Best From Fantasy and Science Fiction, Volume 15, 246
Best From Fantasy and Science Fiction, Volume 16, 247
Best From Fantasy and Science Fiction, Volume 17, 247
Best From Fantasy and Science Fiction, Volume 18, 247
Best From Fantasy and Science Fiction,

Volume 19, 247
Best From Fantasy and
  Science Fiction,
  Volume 20, 247
Best From Fantasy and
  Science Fiction: 25th
  Anniversary, 247
Best From Fantasy and
  Science Fiction: 22nd
  Series, 247
Best From Fantasy and
  Science Fiction: 23rd
  Series, 247
Best From Fantasy and
  Science Fiction: 24th
  Series, 247
Best From Galaxy, Volume
  I, The, 255
Best From Galaxy, Volume
  II, The, 255
Best From Galaxy, Volume
  III, The, 255
Best From Galaxy, Volume
  IV, The, 255
Best From If, Volume I,
  The, 255
Best From If, Volume II,
  The, 255
Best From If, Volume III,
  The, 255
Best From Orbit, 261
Best Horror and the
  Supernatural of the
  19th Century, The, 244
Best Horror Stories, 252
Best Horror Stories 2, 252
Best Laid Plans, The, 52
Best of British SF 1,
  The, 242
Best of British SF 2,
  The, 242
Best of C.L. Moore, The,
  245
Best of C.M. Kornbluth,
  The, 245
Best of Cordwainer Smith,
  The, 245
Best of Damon Knight,
  The, 245

Best of Destinies, The,
  245
Best of Edmond Hamilton,
  The, 245
Best of Eric Frank
  Russell, The, 245
Best of Frederic Brown,
  the, 245
Best of Frederik Pohl,
  The, 245
Best of Fritz Leiber,
  The, 245
Best of Hal Clement, The,
  245
Best of Henry Kuttner,
  The, 245
Best of Jack Williamson,
  The, 245
Best of James Blish, The,
  245
Best of John W. Campbell,
  Jr., The, 245
Best of L. Sprague De
  Camp, The, 245
Best of Leigh Brackett,
  The, 245
Best of Lester Del Rey,
  The, 245
Best of Murray Leinster,
  The, 245
Best of New Dimensions,
  The, 271
Best of Omni Science
  Fiction, The, 248
Best of Omni Science
  Fiction, No. 2, The, 248
Best of Omni Science
  Fiction, No. 3, The, 248
Best of Omni Science
  Fiction, No. 4, The, 248
Best of Omni Science
  Fiction, No. 5, The, 248
Best of Omni Science
  Fiction, No. 6, The, 248
Best of Philip K. Dick,
  The, 245
Best of Raymond Z.
  Gallun, The, 245
Best of Robert Bloch,

The, 245
Best of Stanley G.
  Weinbaum, The, 245
Best of Trek #1, The, 209
Best of Trek #2, The, 209
Best of Trek #3, The, 209
Best of Trek #4, The, 209
Best of Trek #5, The, 209
Best of Trek #6, The, 209
Best of Trek #7, The, 209
Best of Trek #8, The, 209
Best Rootin' Tootin'
  Shootin' Gunslinger in
  the Whole Damned
  Galaxy, 178
Best SF, 252
Best SF 2, 252
Best SF 3, 252
Best SF 4, 252
Best SF 5, 252
Best SF 6, 252
Best SF 7, 252
Best SF From New Worlds
  4, 263
Best SF From New Worlds
  5, 263
Best SF From New Worlds
  6, 263
Best SF From New Worlds
  7, 263
Best SF From New Worlds
  8, 263
Best SF: 1967, 259
Best SF: 1968, 259
Best SF: 1969, 259
Best SF: 1970, 259
Best SF: 1971, 259
Best SF: 1972, 259
Best SF: 1973, 259
Best SF: 1974, 259
Best SF: 1975, The Ninth
  Annual, 259
Best SF Stories From New
  Worlds No. 1, 263
Best SF Stories From New
  Worlds No. 2, 263
Best SF Stories From New
  Worlds No. 3, 263
Best Science Fiction for
  1972, 266
Best Science Fiction for
  1973, 266
Best Science Fiction
  Novellas of the Year
  #1, The, 251
Best Science Fiction
  Novellas of the Year #2,
  The, 251
Best Science Fiction of
  the 19th Century, The,
  244
Best Science Fiction of
  the Year, The, 250
Best Science Fiction of
  the Year No. 2, The, 250
Best Science Fiction of
  the Year No. 3, The, 250
Best Science Fiction of
  the Year No. 4, The, 250
Best Science Fiction of
  the Year No. 5, The, 250
Best Science Fiction of
  the Year No. 6, The, 250
Best Science Fiction of
  the Year No. 7, The, 250
Best Science Fiction of
  the Year No. 8, The, 250
Best Science Fiction of
  the Year No. 9, The, 250
Best Science Fiction of
  the Year No. 10, The,
  250
Best Science Fiction of
  the Year No. 11, The,
  250
Best Science Fiction of
  the Year No. 12, The,
  250
Best Science Fiction of
  the Year No. 13, The,
  251
Best Science Fiction
  Stories of the Year
  (1971), 254
Best Science Fiction
  Stories of the Year
  (1972), 254
Best Science Fiction

Stories of the Year (1973), 254
Best Science Fiction Stories of the Year (1974), 254
Best Science Fiction Stories of the Year (1975), 254
Best Science Fiction Stories of the Year (1976), 254
Best Science Fiction Stories of the Year (1977), 254
Best Science Fiction Stories of the Year (1978), 254
Best Science Fiction Stories of the Year (1979), 254
Best Science Fiction Stories of the Year (1980), 254
Best Science-Fiction Stories: 1949, The, 247
Best Science-Fiction Stories: 1950, The, 247
Best Science-Fiction Stories: 1951, The, 247
Best Science-Fiction Stories: 1952, The, 247
Best Science-Fiction Stories: 1953, The, 247
Best Science-Fiction Stories: 1954, The, 247
Best Science-Fiction Stories and Novels: 1955, The, 248
Best Science-Fiction Stories and Novels: 1956, The, 248
Best Science-Fiction Stories and Novels: 9th Series, The, 248
Best Tales of Terror, 252
Best Tales of Terror 2, 252
Best Ye Breed, The, 179
Between the Galaxies, 169
Beware More Beasts, 256
Beware of the Mouse, 231
Beware the Beasts, 256
Beware the Microbots, 168
Bewitched, 23
Bewitched Caverns, The, 180
Bewitched: The Opposite Uncle, 23
Beyond Lands of Never, 260
Beyond Life, 40
Beyond Sanctuary, 12
Beyond the Black Enigma, 83
Beyond the Blue Event Horizon, 173, 233
Beyond the Burning Lands, 48
Beyond the Fourth Door, 62
Beyond the Galactic Lens, 216
Beyond the Galactic Rim, 46
Beyond the Great Oblivion, 75
Beyond the Imperium, 126
Beyond the Moon, 99
Beyond the Outer Mirr, 191
Beyond the Tomorrow Mountains, 75
Beyond the Wall of Sleep, 137
Bid for Fortune, A, 27
Big Bankroll, The, 84
Big Black Mark, The, 46
Big Broad Jump, The, 52
Big Snatch, The, 83
Big Time, The, 129
Bili the Axe, 2
Billion Dollar Snatch, The, 52
Billion For Boris, A, 186
Birds-of-a-Feather Affair, The, 218
Birth of a Nation, The, 65
Birth of Flux and Anchor, The, 277
Birthgrave, The, 128
Bishop's Heir, The, 122

Bishop's Wife, The, 157
Black Beast, The, 201
Black, Black Witch, The, 183
Black Castle, the, 59
Black Cauldron, The, 4
Black Chariots, 184
Black Colossus, 109
Black Company, The, 53
Black Death, The, 184
Black Easter, 26
Black Emperor, 103
Black Fire, 204
Black Flame, The, 1
Black Gold, 119
Black Hand, The, 177
Black Hearts in Battersea, 3
Black Holes & Bug-Eyed Monsters, 270
Black Invaders Vs. The Battle Birds, 28
Black Knight of the Iron Sphere, 73
Black Legion of Callisto, 44
Black Lightning, 28
Black Master, The, 93
Black Moon, The, 71
Black Mountains, The, 190
Black Pope, The, 176
Black Spot, The, 183
Black Star Passes, The, 42
Blackbeard's Ghost, 203
Blackman's Burden, 179
Blackship, The, 189
Blades of Mars, 151
Bladesmen of Antares, 33
Blast Off at Woomera, 226
Blast-Off at 0300, 226
Blazing Affair, The, 218
Blazing Sun, 169
Blessing Unbounded, 25
Blight, The, 56
Blind Spot, The, 98
Blitzkrieg Galactica, 170
Blockade: Lepso, 169
Blockade Runners, The, 222
Blood and Dreams, 150

Blood and Iron, 174
Blood and Iron: There Will Be War Volume III, 174, 267
Blood Brothers of Gor, 159
Blood Countess, The, 184
Blood Fountain, 221
Blood Games, 237
Blood Highway, 100
Blood of My Blood, 127
Blood on the Moon, 50
Blood on the Sun, 125
Blood Reign of the Dictator, 207
Blood Ring, The, 184
Blood Sacrifice, 125
Blood Wedding, 92
Bloodcurdling Tales of Horror and the Macabre, 138
Bloodhype, 82
Bloodstalk, 92
Bloodstone, 225
Bloodstone (Moore), The, 153
Bloodstone (Eulo), The, 75
Bloodwind, The, 278
Bloody America, 202
Bloody Cross, The, 176
Bloody Sun, The, 28
Blow My Mind, 83
Blow-Your-Mind Job, The, 52
Blown, 79
Blue Adept, 8
Blue Aura, The, 226
Blue Dwarfs, The, 168
Blue-Eyed Buddha, 89
Blue Ghost Mystery, 25
Blue Grotto Terror, The, 48
Blue Steel, 201
Blue Sword, The, 143
Blue System, 169
Bluebolt One, 141
Bluesong, 220
Bodyguard and 4 Other Short SF Novels From Galaxy, 257

Bolts, a Robot Dog, 120
Bomba the Jungle Boy Among the Slaves, 185
Bomba the Jungle Boy Among the Pygmies, 186
Bomba the Jungle Boy and the Lost Explorers, 185
Bomba the Jungle Boy and the Cannibals, 186
Bomba the Jungle Boy and the Painted Hunters, 186
Bomba the Jungle Boy and the River Demons, 186
Bomba the Jungle Boy and the Hostile Chieftain, 186
Bomba the Jungle Boy at the Moving Mountain, 185
Bomba the Jungle Boy at the Great Cataract, 185
Bomba the Jungle Boy in a Strange Land, 186
Bomba the Jungle Boy in the Abandoned City, 185
Bomba the Jungle Boy in the Swamp of Death, 185
Bomba the Jungle Boy in the Land of Burning Lava, 186
Bomba the Jungle Boy in the Perilous Kingdom, 186
Bomba the Jungle Boy in the Steaming Grotto, 186
Bomba the Jungle Boy on Jaguar Island, 185
Bomba the Jungle Boy on Terror Trail, 185
Bomba the Jungle Boy on the Underground River, 185
Bomba the Jungle Boy; or, The Old Naturalist's Secret, 185
Bomba the Jungle Boy Trapped by the Cyclone, 186
Bombs From the Murder Wolves, 106
Bonds of Eternity, The, 168
Bones of Zora, The, 61
Bonfires and Broomsticks, 161
Book of Andre Norton, The, 253
Book of Being, The, 227
Book of Brian Aldiss, The, 253
Book of Dreams, The, 219
Book of Frank Herbert, The, 253
Book of Fritz Leiber, The, 253
Book of Gordon R. Dickson, The, 253
Book of John Brunner, The, 253
Book of Lost Tales, Part I, The, 213
Book of Lost Tales, Part II, The, 213
Book of Merlyn, The, 230
Book of Philip Jose Farmer, The, 253
Book of Philip K. Dick, The, 253
Book of Poul Anderson, The, 253
Book of Saberhagen, The, 253
Book of Shai, The, 226
Book of Silence, The, 227
Book of Sorrows, The, 227
Book of Suns, The, 201
Book of the Dun Cow, The, 227
Book of the River, The, 227
Book of the Stars, The, 227
Book of Three, The, 4
Book of Vale, The, 201
Book of Van Vogt, The, 253
Boosted Man, The, 34
Border, Breed Nor Birth, 179
Border War, 69

Borribles, 62
Borribles Go for Broke, The, 62
Borrowers, The, 161
Borrowers Afield, The, 161
Borrowers Afloat, The, 161
Borrowers Aloft, The, 161
Borrowers Avenged, The, 161
Borrowers Omnibus, The, 161
Boss of Terror, The, 183
Box of Delights, or When the Wolves Were Running, The, 146
Boy Adventurers in the Forbidden Land, The, 223
Boy Adventurers in the Land of El Dorado, The, 223
Boy Adventurers in the Land of the Monkey Men, The, 223
Boy Adventurers in the Unknown Land, The, 223
Boy Astronaut, 226
Boy Inventors and the Vanishing Gun, The, 27
Boy Inventors' Diving Torpedo Boat, The, 27
Boy Inventors' Electric Hydroaeroplane, The, 27
Boy Inventors' Flying Ship, The, 27
Boy Inventors' Radio-Telephone, The, 27
Boy Inventors' Wireless Triumph, The, 27
Boy Scouts' Craig Kennedy, The, 178
Bra-Burner's Brigade, The, 111
Brain Twister, 87
Brain Twister, 115
Brainz, Inc., 92
Brak: When the Idols Walked, 114
Brak the Barbarian, 114
Brak the Barbarian Versus the Mark of the Demon, 114
Brak the Barbarian Versus the Sorceress, 114
Bran Mak Morn, 110
Brand of the Metal Maiden, 193
Brand of the Werewolf, 181
Brave Free Men, the, 219
Breakaway, 200
Breakfast in the Ruins, 151
Breaking of Northwall, The, 232
Bride of Fu Manchu, The, 186
Bridle the Wind, 3
Brief Candles, 50
Brigands of the Moon, 58
Bright and Morning Star, The, 101
Bright Messenger, The, 25
Bright Red Businessmen, The, 141
Broad Jump, 84
Broken Citadel, The, 95
Broken Cycle, The, 46
Broken Fang, and Other Experiences of a Specialist in Spooks, The, 120
Broken Lands, The, 190
Broken Stone, 150
Bromius Phenomenon, The, 177
Bronwyn's Bane, 192
Bronze Axe, The, 134
Bronze of Eddarta, The, 88
Brother Assassin, 190
Brotherhood of D'ablo, The, 138
Brownstone, The, 75
Buck Rogers in the 25th Century, 33
Bug Awful, 244
Bugaloos and the Vile Vibes, 209
Builders of the Black Empire, 201

Built to Kill, 100
Bull and the Spear, The, 152
Bull Chief, The, 106
Buried Country, The, 101
Burn, Witch, Burn!, 148
Burrowers Beneath, The, 139
Busted, 84
Butterfly Kid, The, 5
By Air Express to Venus, 185
By Space Ship to Saturn, 185
By the Light of the Green Star, 43
Byzantium Endures, 152

C.I.D., 155
Cabal, The, 71
Cage a Man, 37
Calcutta Affair, The, 218
Calix Stay, 100
Call of the Savage, The, 121
Callahan's Crosstime Saloon, 185
Caller From Eternity, 169
Calling Captain Future, 99
Calling Thunderbirds, 212
Camber of Culdi, 122
Camber the Heretic, 122
Camelot in Orbit, 124
Capable of Honor, 70
Captain America: Holocaust for Hire, 145
Captain America: The Great Gold Seal, 145
Captain Black, 167
Captain Future and the Space Emperor, 99
Captain Future's Challenge, 99
Captain Kettle, Ambassador, 112
Captain Kettle, K.C.B., 112
Captain Kettle on the War-Path, 112
Captain Kettle's Bit, 112
Captain of the Guidara, The, 223
Captain Salt in Oz, 19
Captain Scarlet and Mysterons, 212
Captain Scarlet and the Silent Saboteur, 212
Captive, The, 203
Captive of Gor, 159
Captive Scorpio, 33
Captives in Space, 95
Captives of the Flame, 62
Captives of the Savage Empire, 135
Carbonel, 196
Carbonel, the King of the Cats, 196
Cargo Unknown, 183
Carnadyne Hoard, 164
Carnellian Throne, The, 154
Carson of Venus, 37
Cart and Cwidder, 117
Cartoon Crimes, The, 184
Case of Charles Dexter Ward The, 137
Case of Conscience, A, 26
Case of the Disappearing Doctor, The, 95
Case of the Missing Airmen, The, 74
Casebook of Jules DeGrandin, The, 176
Casebook of Lucius Leffing, The, 31
Cassilee, 53
Castaway's World, 32
Castaways in Time, 2
Castaways of the Flag, 223
Castel del Monte; A Romance of the Fall of the Hohenstaufen Dynasty in Italy, 86
Castle Crespin, 7
Castle of Hape, The, 156
Castle of Iron, The, 61
Castle of Llyr, The, 4
Castle of the Otter, The,

234
Castle of Wizardry, 72
Castle Roogna, 8
Castledoom, 127
Castledown, 95
Cat of Silvery Hue, A, 2
Cat Who Walks Through Walls, The, 104
Catseye, 160
Caught in the Organ Draft: Biology in Science Fiction, 244
Caught in the Spider's Web, 106
Cavern of Destiny, 10
Cavern of the Damned, 207
Caverns, 163
Caverns of the Moon, 153
Caves of Death, 161
Caves of Drach, The, 226
Caves of Fear, The, 25
Caves of Fire and Ice, 156
Caves of Klydor, The, 105
Caves of Madness, 153
Caves of Reglathium, The, 196
Caves of Steel, The, 11
Caves of Terror, The, 155
Caves of the Druufs, 168
Celestial Omnibus, The, 30
Celestial Steam Locomotive, The, 51
Cenotaph Road, 221
Centaur Aisle, 8
Centaurians, The, 39
Centre Holds, The, 209
Century of Science Fiction, A, 260
Cerberus: A Wolf in the Fold, 45
Certain Hour, The, 40
Chaining the Lady, 7
Chalet Diabolique, 50
Challenge of the Unknown, 168
Chameleon Corps and Other Shape Changers, The, 91
Champion of Garathorm, 152
Champion of the Gods, 135

Champion of the Last Battle, 2
Champion of the Sidhe, 81
Change War, The, 129
Changeling, 238
Changeling, The, 142
Changeling Earth, 190
Changer's Moon, 49
Changewar, 129
Changing Land, The, 238
Channel's Destiny, 132
Chanur's Venture, 47
Chaos in Lagrangia, 179
Chaos Weapon, The, 118
Chapterhouse: Dune, 104
Charge, Monster, 93
Chariots of Ra, The, 33
Charlie and the Chocolate Factory, 59
Charlie and the Great Glass Elevator, 59
Charlotte Sometimes, 79
Charmed Life, 117
Charon: A Dragon at the Gate, 45
Chattering Gods, 55
Checkmate: Universe, 168
Cheetah-Girl, the, 26
Chessboard Queen, The, 158
Chessmen of Mars, The, 36
Chic Chick Spy, The, 214
Chicago Conversion, The, 218
Child of Storm, 97
Child of Tomorrow, 18
Childermass, The, 132
Children of Despair, The, 56
Children of Dune, 104
Children of Green Knowe, The, 27
Children of Hate, The, 56
Children of Llyr, The, 227
Children of the Future, 244
Children of the Lens, 198
Children of the Night, 122
Children of the Sun, The, 119

Children of the Void, 63
Children of the Wind, The, 101
Chill, 195
Chimneys of Green Knowe, The, 27
Chinese Agent, The, 151
Chivalry, 40
Chiy-Une, 53
Chosen of Mida, 94
Christening Quest, The, 192
Christopher Columbus, 115
Chronicles of Lucius Leffing, the, 31
Chrysalis, 272
Chrysalis 2, 272
Chrysalis 3, 272
Chrysalis 4, 272
Chrysalis 5, 272
Chrysalis 6, 272
Chrysalis 7, 272
Chrysalis 8, 272
Chrysalis 9, 272
Chrysalis 10, 272
Chthon, 7
Chuck You, Farley!, 84
Cimbrians, The, 115
Cingulum, The, 181
Circle, Crescent, Star, 64
Circus of Hells, A, 6
Circus World, 134
Citadel of the Autarch, The, 234
Citizen Vampire, 59
City, The, 88
City Beyond the Clouds, The, 185
City Destroyer, 201
City in the Glacier, The, 221
City in the Sahara, 223
City of a Million Legends, 132
City of a Thousand Suns, 62
City of Baraboo, 134
City of Brass and Other Simon Ark Stories, 105
City of Flaming Shadows, 201
City of Gold and Lead, The, 48
City of Illusions, 129
City of Sorcery, 29
City of the Beast, 151
City of the Chasch, 219
City of the Living Dead, 135
City of the Sun, 85
City of the Sun, The, 202
City on the Edge of Forever, 205
City on the Moon, 129
City Under the Sea, 224
Clan Ground, 21
Clan of the Cave Bear, The, 12
Clansman, The, 65
Clara in Blunderland, 132
Clarion, 273
Clarion II, 273
Clarion III, 273
Clash of Cymbals, A, 26
Claudius the Bee, 128
Claw of the Conciliator, The, 234
Clipper of the Clouds, The, 223
Cloak of Illusion, 181
Clock of Dreams, The, 139
Clocks of Iraz, The, 61
Clockwork Traitor, The, 198
Close to Critical, 49
Closed Worlds, The 99
Cluster, 7
Clutching Hand, The, 178
Cockeyed Cuties, The, 52
Code Duello, 179
Codeword—Golden Fleece, 229
Cold Death, 181
Cold Print, 137
Cold Victory, 6
Cold War in a Country Garden, 96
Cold War in Hell, 25

Colin, 22
Colin II, 22
Coll and His White Pig, 4
Collision Course, 200
Colonel Markesan and Less
 Pleasant People, 137
Colonists of Space, 42
Color Out of Time, The,
 137
Colossus, 117
Colossus and the Crab, 117
Colour Out of Space, The,
 138
Colsec Rebellion, 105
Columbus Affair, 169
Come and Go, 50
Come Ninevah, Come Tyre;
 the Presidency of
 Edward M. Jason, 70
Come One, Come All, 52
Comet in Moominland, 279
Comet Kings, The, 99
Cometeers, The, 233
Comets & Computers, 270
Coming Event, The, 215
Coming of Conan, The, 108
Coming of Morikand, The,
 199
Coming of the Horseclans,
 The, 2
Coming of the Monster; a
 Take of the Masterful
 Monk, The, 70
Commune 2000 A.D., 179
Communipath Worlds, 74
Communipaths, The, 73
Compleat Enchanter, The,
 61
"Complete Original Edi-
 tion" of the Surprising
 Travels and Adventures
 of Baron Munchausen...
 to which is Added, A
 Sequel, Containing His
 Expedition into Africa,
 16
Complete Book of Swords,
 The, 190
Complex Man, 78

Computer Eye, 282
Comrade Don Camillo, 96
Conan, 108
Conan and the Sorcerer,
 109
Conan and the Spider God,
 109
Conan of Aquilonia, 109
Conan of Cimmeria, 108
Conan of the Isles, 108
Conan the Adventurer, 108
Conan the Avenger, 108
Conan the Barbarian, 108
Conan the Buccaneer, 108
Conan the Conqueror, 108
Conan the Conqurer, 108
Conan the Defender, 109
Conan the Destroyer, 109
Conan! The Flame Knife,
 109
Conan the Freebooter, 108
Conan the Invincible, 109
Conan the Liberator, 109
Conan the Magnificent, 109
Conan the Mercenary, 109
Conan the Rebel, 109
Conan the Swordsman, 109
Conan the Triumphant, 109
Conan the Unconquered, 109
Conan the Usurper, 108
Conan the Valorous, 109
Conan the Victorious, 109
Conan the Wanderer, 108
Conan the Warrior, 108
Conception, The, 199
Condition of Muzak, The,
 151
Conflict Center: Naator,
 169
Conqueror of Reglathium,
 The, 196
Conquest of the Amazon, 80
Conquest of the Planet of
 the Apes, 172
Conquistador, The, 191
Contact Lost, 55
Continent in the Sky, 22
Continuum 1, 256
Continuum 2, 256

Continuum 3, 256
Continuum 4, 256
Contraband From Otherspace, 46
Conversations With a Corpse, 63
Copenhagen Affair, The, 217
Copulation Explosion, The, 83
Cords of Vanity, The, 40
Corfu Affair, The, 218
Cornish Pixie Affair, The, 218
Corona, 204
Corpse, 141
Corridors of Time, 62
Corundum's Woman, 163
Cosmic Carnage, 114
Cosmic Decoy, The, 167
Cosmic Echelon, 41
Cosmic Knights, 244
Cosmic Manhunt, 61
Cosmic Traitor, 167
Cosmicomics, 41
Cosmium Raiders, The, 38
Count Brass, 152
Count Zero, 89
Country of the Mind, The, 153
Court Intrigues in a Collection of Original Letters from the Island of the New Atalantis, 145
Court of Lucifer; A Tale of the Renaissance, The, 86
Courts of Chaos, The, 238
Covenant of the Crown, The, 204
Cowardly Lion of Oz, The, 19
Crack Shot, 84
Craghold Creatures, The, 13
Craghold Crypt, The, 13
Craghold Curse, The, 13
Craghold Legacy, The, 13

Craig Kennedy, Detective, 177
Craig Kennedy Listens In, 178
Craig Kennedy on the Farm, 178
Crashing Suns, 99
Crater of Fear, 153
Cream of the Jest, The, 40
Creation Descending, 138
Creature!, 267
Creep, Shadow!, 148
Creeping Death, The, 93
Creeping Unknown, The, 121
Crewel Lye, 8
Crime Cult, The, 93
Crime Oracle, The, 93
Criminal Justice Through Science Fiction, 265
Crimson Capsule, The, 49
Crimson Doom, 28
Crimson Serpent, The, 183
Crimson Universe, 168
Critical Threshold, 202
Crivit Experiment, the, 218
Cross of Gold Affair, The, 217
Cross the Stars, 69
Cross-Currents, 12, 244
Crossroads of Time, The, 159
Croyd, 255
Cruachen and the Killane, The, 56
Crucification Squad, The, 21
Cruise of the Conqueror, Being the Further Adventures of the Motor Pirate, The, 166
Cruise of the "Flying Fish," the Airship-Submarine, The, 51
Cruise of the Snowbird, The, 202
Cruiser Dreams, 154
Cry of the Beast, 161
Cry Shadow!, 94

Cry Silver Bells, 210
Crystal Cave, The, 208
Crystal Clouds, The, 221
Crystal Crown, The, 277
Crystal Gryphon, The, 160
Crystal Seas, The, 135
Crystal Singer, 279
Crystals of Mida, The, 94
Cuckoo Tree, The, 3
Cugel's Saga, 219
Cunning Linguist, The, 52
Cure For Cancer, A, 151
Curious and Entertaining Adventures... of the Renowned Baron Munchausen, Including a Tour Through the United States in the Year MDCCCIII, The, 17
Curious Lobster, The, 102
Curious Lobster's Island, The, 102
Currents of Space, The, 11
Curse of Collinwood, The, 188
Curse of Rathlaw, The, 192
Curse of the Blue Figurine, The, 21
Curse of the Mandarin's Fan, 193
Curse of the Mummy, 138
Curse of the Two-Headed Bull, The, 77
Cutthroat, The, 85
Cyborg, 41
Cyborg IV, 41
Cylon Death Machine, The, 125
Czar of Fear, The, 181

Daddy Jake the Runaway, and Short Stories Told After Dark by "Uncle Remus," 101
Dagger Affair, The, 217
Dagger in the Sky, The, 182
Dagon and Other Macabre Tales, 138

Dai-San, 220
Damiano, 140
Damiano's Lute, 140
Damien: Omen II, 164
Damned, The, 191
Dance of Genghis Cohn, The, 88
Dance of the Hag, 129
Dancer of Gor, 280
Dancer's Illusion, 146
Dancer's Luck, 146
Dancers of Arun, The, 139
Danger in Deep Space, 185
Danger Planet, 99
Dangerous Games, 176
Dangerous Inheritance, 229
Dangerous Quest, 55
Dangerous Visions, 255
Danny Dunn and the Anti-Gravity Paint, 231
Danny Dunn and the Automatic House, 231
Danny Dunn and the Fossil Cave, 231
Danny Dunn and the Heat Ray, 231
Danny Dunn and the Homework Machine, 231
Danny Dunn and the Smallifying Machine, 232
Danny Dunn and the Swamp Monster, 232
Danny Dunn and the Universal Glue, 232
Danny Dunn and the Voice From Space, 232
Danny Dunn and the Weather Machine, 231
Danny Dunn, Invisible Boy, 232
Danny Dunn on a Desert Island, 231
Danny Dunn on the Ocean Floor, 231
Danny Dunn, Scientific Detective, 232
Danny Dunn, Time Traveller, 231
Daring Trip to the Moon,

The, 158
Dark Bright Water, The, 236
Dark Crusade, 225
Dark Design, The, 79
Dark Dimensions, The, 46
Dark Harvest, 56
Dark Man and Others, The, 110
Dark is Rising, The, 53
Dark Pool, The, 180
Dark Return, The, 125
Dark Satanic, 29
Dark Shadows, 188
Dark Stars & Dragons, 270
Dark Straits of Reglathium, 196
Dark Tide, The, 142
Dark Triangle, The, 226
Darkangel, The, 171
Darkchild, 220
Darkest Day, The, 142
Darkling Wind, The, 281
Darkness and Dawn, 75
Darkness and the Deep, 81
Darkness at Sethanon, 80
Darkness Upon the Ice, A, 82
Darkness Weaves, 225
Darkness Weaves with Many Shades, 225
Darkover Landfall, 28
Darya of the Bronze Age, 44
Daughter of Fu Manchu, 186
Daughter of the Bright Moon, 1
Daughters of the Dolphin, 148
Daughters of the Sunstone, 220
David Blaize, 22
David Blaize and the Blue Door, 22
David Starr, Space Ranger, 11
Dawn, 236
Dawn of Darkness, The, 56
Dawn of the Dead, 187

Dawning Light, The, 195
Dawning Light, The, 87
Dawnman Planet, 179
Day After Judgement, The, 26
Day for Damnation, A, 89
Day in the Life, A, 175
Day It Rained Forever, The, 128
Day New York Trembled, The, 132
Day of the Dissonance, The, 82
Day of the Dove, 205
Day of the Dragonstar, 24
Day of the Klesh, The, 83
Day of the Minotaur, The, 210
Day of the Tyrant, 174
Day of the Tyrant: There Will Be War Volume IV, 267
Day of Their Return, The, 6
Day of Wrath, 202
Day the Spaceship Landed, The, 134
Day the World Ended, The, 187
Day They Invaded New York, The, 132
Daybreakers, The, 58
Days of Glory, 202
Dead Astronaut: 10 Stories of Space Flight, The, 266
Dead Duck, 13
Dead Kingdom, The, 101
Dead Line, The, 141
Dead Live, The, 168
Dead of Winter, The, 12
Deadliest Show in Town, The, 143
Deadline, 13
Deadly Dutchman, The, 25
Deadly Dwarf, The, 182
Deadly Years, The, 205
Deadmen Shouldn't Die, 170
Deadwalk, 92

Death and the Spider, 201
Death-Angel, 232
Death Angel's Shadow, 225
Death Box, The, 127
Death-Coach, 232
Death-Doctor, 232
Death Giver, The, 93
Death Had Yellow Eyes, 183
Death in Silver, 181
Death in Slow Motion, 184
Death in the Rising Sun, 56
Death Is a Ruby Light, 119
Death Machine, The, 184
Death of a Legend, The, 2
Death of the Raven, 147
Death Rays of Ardilla, The, 115
Death Reign of the Vampire King, 201
Death-School, 232
Death Tide, 218
Death Torch Terror, 193
Death Tower, 93
Death Waits in Semispace, 168
Death's Angel, 232
Death's Demand, 169
Death's Master, 128
Deathgame, 92
Deathless Amazon, The, 80
Deathstar Voyage, 226
Deathstone, The, 75
Deathwind of Vedun, 189
Deathworld, 102
Deathworld 2, 102
Deathworld 3, 102
Deathworms of Kratos, The, 53
Decade the 1940s, 241, 259
Decade the 1950s, 241, 259
Decade the 1960s, 241, 259
Deep Wizardry, 70
Deeper Than the Darkness, 22
Defiant Agents, The, 159
Delia of Vallia, 34
Delphic Echo, 133
Deluge, 236

Delusion's Master, 128
Demon, 221
Demon Breed, 193
Demon in the Mirror, 163
Demon Island, 184
Demon Night, 197
Demon of Barnabas Collins, The, 188
Demon of Cawnpore, The, 222
Demon of the Dark Ages, 221
Demon's Coronation, 124
Demon's Stalk, 124
Demons of the Dancing Gods, 45
Demons of Zammar, The, 196
Depths, The, 56
Derai, 215
Derrick Devil, The, 182
Deryni Checkmate, 122
Deryni Rising, 122
Desdemona Affair, The, 4
Desert Damsels, The, 4
Desert of Death, 169
Desert of Ice, The, 222
Destination Mars, 226
Destination Moon, 94
Destination: Saturn, 235
Destinies, Vol. 1, no. 1, 245
Destinies, Vol. 1, no. 2, 245
Destinies, Vol. 1, no. 3, 245
Destinies, Vol. 1, no. 4, 245
Destinies, Vol. 1, no. 5, 245
Destinies, Vol. 2, no. 1, 245
Destinies, Vol. 2, no. 2, 245
Destinies, Vol. 2, no. 3, 245
Destinies, Vol. 2, no. 4, 245
Destinies, Vol. 3, no. 1, 245

Destinies, Vol. 3, no. 2, 245
Destiny and the Dolphins, 148
Destiny Dice, The, 24
Destiny Stone, The, 221
Destiny Times Three, 247
Destiny's Orbit, 235
Devil and Ben Camden, The, 92
Devil Doctor, The, 186
Devil Genghis, The, 183
Devil in Iron, The, 109
Devil in the Dark, The, 205
Devil Is Dead, The, 123
Devil On Two Sticks, The, 130
Devil on the Moon, 182
Devil Rides Out, The, 229
Devil to Pay, The, 84
Devil-Tree of El Dorado, The, 12
Devil Upon Crutches, The, 130
Devil Upon Two Sticks, The, 130
Devil Upon Two Sticks in England, The, 130
Devil World, 204
Devil's Bride, The, 176
Devil's Children, The, 64
Devil's Doorbell, The, 107
Devil's Guard, The, 155
Devil's Heart, The, 116
Devil's Horns, The, 184
Devil's Hunting-Grounds; A Fantasy, The, 25
Devil's Kiss, The, 116
Devil's Mistress, The, 50
Devil's Own Dear Son, The, 40
Devil's Playground, The, 181
Devil's Touch, The, 116
Devil's Virgin, The, 50
Devilday, 98
Devils of the Deep, 183
Devils' Drums, The, 147

Diadem From the Stars, 48
Diamond Queen, The, 177
Diamonds Are For Dying, 119
Dilvish, the Damned, 238
Dimension of Dreams, 135
Dimension of Horror, 135
Dimension Search, 168
Dinosaur Planet, 140
Dinosaur Planet Survivors, 140
Dirdir, The, 219
Dirty Rotten Depriving Ray, The, 111
Disappearing Dwarf, The, 25
Dispossessed, The, 129
Distant Worlds, 251
Divine Passion, The, 81
Divine Queen, The, 54
Diving Dames Affair, The, 217
Doctor Doolittle, 134
Doctor Doolittle and the Green Canary, 134
Doctor Doolittle and the Pirates, 134
Doctor Doolittle and the Secret Lake, 134
Doctor Doolittle in the Moon, 134
Doctor Doolittle's Caravan, 134
Doctor Doolittle's Circus, 134
Doctor Doolittle's Garden, 134
Doctor Doolittle's Post Office, 134
Doctor Doolittle's Puddleby Adventure, 134
Doctor Doolittle's Return, 134
Doctor Doolittle's Zoo, 134
Dr. Mirabilis, 26
Doctor Nikola, 27
Dr. Nikola's Experiment, 27

Dr. Nikola's Vendetta, 27
Doctor Orient, 127
Dr. Orpheus, 225
Dr. Phibes, 91
Dr. Phibes Rises Again, 91
Dr. Scarlett: A Narrative of His Mysterious Behavior in the East, 123
Dr. Scofflaw, 247
Doctor Strange: Nightmare, 146
Dr. Time, 184
Doctor to the Stars, 130
Doctor Who and an Unearthly Child, 67
Doctor Who and the Abominable Snowmen, 66
Doctor Who and the Android Invasion, 66
Doctor Who and the Android Invasion, 68
Doctor Who and the Androids of Tara, 67
Doctor Who and the Armageddon Factor, 67
Doctor Who and the Auton Invasion, 66
Doctor Who and the Aztecs, 67
Doctor Who and the Brain of Morbius, 66
Doctor Who and the Carnival Monsters, 66
Doctor Who and the Cave Monsters, 66
Doctor Who and the Claws of Axos, 66
Doctor Who and the Creature From the Pit, 67
Doctor Who and the Crusaders, 66
Doctor Who and the Curse of Peladon, 66
Doctor Who and the Cybermen, 66
Doctor Who and the Daemons, 66

Doctor Who and the Dalek Invasion of Earth, 66
Doctor Who and the Daleks, 67
Doctor Who and the Day of the Daleks, 66
Doctor Who and the Day of the Daleks, 67
Doctor Who and the Deadly Assassin, 66
Doctor Who and the Death to the Daleks, 66
Doctor Who and the Destiny of the Daleks, 67
Doctor Who and the Dinosaur Invasion, 66
Doctor Who and the Dinosaur Invasion, 67
Doctor Who and the Dominators, 67
Doctor Who and the Doomsday Weapon, 66, 68
Doctor Who and the Enemy of the World, 67
Doctor Who and the Face of Evil, 66
Doctor Who and the Five Doctors, 67
Doctor Who and the Full Circle, 67
Doctor Who and the Genesis of the Daleks, 66
Doctor Who and the Giant Robot, 66
Doctor Who and the Green Death, 66
Doctor Who and the Hand of Fear, 66
Doctor Who and the Highlanders, 67
Doctor Who and the Horns of Nimon, 67
Doctor Who and the Horror of Fang Rock, 66
Doctor Who and the Ice Warriors, 66
Doctor Who and the Image

of the Fendahl, 67
Doctor Who and the
Invasion of Time, 67
Doctor Who and the
Invisible Enemy, 67
Doctor Who and the Keeper
of Traken, 67
Doctor Who and the Keys
of Marinus, 67
Doctor Who and the
Leisure Hive, 67
Doctor Who and the Loch
Ness Monster, 66, 68
Doctor Who and the Masque
of Mandragora, 66, 68
Doctor Who and the
Monster of Peladon, 67
Doctor Who and the
Mutants, 58
Doctor Who and the
Nightmare of Eden, 67
Doctor Who and the Power
of Kroll, 67
Doctor Who and the
Pyramids of Mars, 66
Doctor Who and the
Revenge of the
Cybermen, 66, 68
Doctor Who and the Ribos
Operation, 67
Doctor Who and the Robots
of Death, 67
Doctor Who and the Sea
Devils, 66
Doctor Who and the Seeds
of Doom, 66
Doctor Who and the Seeds
of Doom, 68
Doctor Who and the
Sontaran Experiment, 66
Doctor Who and the Space
War, 66
Doctor Who and the State
of Decay, 67
Doctor Who and the Stones
of Blood, 67
Doctor Who and the
Sunmakers, 67
Doctor Who and the Talons
of Weng-Chiang, 66, 68
Doctor Who and the Tenth
Planet, 66
Doctor Who and the Terror
of the Autons, 66
Doctor Who and the Three
Doctors, 66
Doctor Who and the Time
Warrior, 66
Doctor Who and the Tomb
of the Cybermen, 66
Doctor Who and the
Underworld, 67
Doctor Who and the
Visitation, 67
Doctor Who and the War
Games, 67
Doctor Who and the
Warriors' Gate, 67
Doctor Who and the Web of
Fear, 66
Doctor Who and the Zarbi,
66
Doctor Who in an Exciting
Adventure with the
Daleks, 65
Doctor Who on the Planet
of Evil, 66
Doctor Who on the Planet
of Spiders, 66
Doctor Who on the Planet
of the Daleks, 66
Doctor Who, Arc of
Infinity, 67
Doctor Who, Castrovalva,
67
Doctor Who, Earthshock, 67
Doctor Who, Enlighten-
ment, 67
Doctor Who, Four to
Doomsday, 67
Doctor Who, Inferno, 67
Doctor Who, Kinda, 67
Doctor Who, Logopolis, 67
Doctor Who, Mawdryn
Undead, 67
Doctor Who, Meglos, 67
Doctor Who, Snakedance, 67
Doctor Who, Terminus, 67

Doctor Who, Time Flight, 67
Doctor Who, Warriors of the Deep, 67
Documents Relating to the Sentimental Agents in the Volyen Empire, 131
Dolphin Boy, 148
Dolphin Rider, 148
Dome in the Forest, The, 232
Domes of Mars, The, 153
Domes of Pico, The, 226
Domnei, 40
Don Camillo and His Flock, 96
Don Camillo and the Devil, 96
Don Camillo and the Prodigal Son, 96
Don Camillo Meets Hell's Angels, 96
Don Camillo Meets the Flower Children, 96
Don Camillo Takes the Devil By the Tail, 96
Don Camillo's Dilemma, 96
Don Sturdy Across the North Pole, 10
Don Sturdy Captured by Headhunters, 10
Don Sturdy in Lion Land, 10
Don Sturdy in the Land of the Giants, 10
Don Sturdy in the Land of Volcanoes, 10
Don Sturdy in the Temples of Fear, 10
Don Sturdy in the Tombs of Gold, 10
Don Sturdy on the Desert of Mystery, 10
Don Sturdy on the Ocean Bottom, 10
Don Sturdy Trapped in the Flaming Wilderness, 10
Don Sturdy With the Big Snake Hunters, 10

Don Sturdy with the Harpoon Hunters, 10
Donovan's Brain, 195
Don't Bite Off More Than You Can Chew, 52
Don't Bite the Sun, 128
Doom of the Green Planet, 170
Doom That Came to Sarnath and Other Stories, The, 138
Doomed Demons, 2
Doomfarers of Coramonde, The, 59
Doomsayer, The, 3
Doomsday Affair, The, 217
Doomsday Brain, The, 211
Doomsday on Ajait, 117
Doomsday Warrior, 202
Doomstalker, 277
Doomstar, 280
Door Into Fire, The, 70
Door Into Shadow, The, 70
Door to Enigma, 225
Dorothy and the Wizard of Oz, 19
Dorsai!, 65
Dosadi Experiment, The, 104
Double "Z," 93
Down to Earth (Elder), 73
Down to Earth (Capon), 42
Downbelow Station, 47
Dozen Deadly Dragons of Joy, The, 111
Dracula, 208
Dracula Returns, 136
Dracula Tapes, The, 190
Dracula's Brother, 136
Dracula's Curse, 208
Dracula's Disciple, 136
Dracula's Gold, 136
Dracula's Guest, and Other Weird Stories, 208
Dracula's Lost World, 136
Dragon, The, 88
Dragon Lensman, The, 198
Dragon Lord of the Savage Empire, 135

Dragon of Mishbil, The, 277
Dragon of the Lost Sea, The, 237
Dragon on a Pedestal, 8
Dragon Steel, 237
Dragon Winter, 100
Dragon's Blood, 237
Dragon's Egg, 278
Dragondrums, 140
Dragonfall 5 and the Empty Planet, 72
Dragonfall 5 and the Haunted World, 72
Dragonfall 5 and the Hijackers, 72
Dragonfall 5 and the Master Mind, 72
Dragonfall 5 and the Royal Beast, 72
Dragonfall 5 and the Space Cowboys, 72
Dragonfall 5 and the Super Horse, 72
Dragonflight, 140
Dragonquest, 140
Dragonrouge, 44
Dragons of Autumn Twilight, 228
Dragons of Darkness, 249
Dragons of Englor, The, 135
Dragons of Light, 249
Dragons of Spring Dawning, 282
Dragons of Winter Night, 228
Dragonsinger, 140
Dragonsong, 140
Dream Chariots, 34
Dream Dancer, 154
Dream Doctor, The, 177
Dream; or, The Simian Maid, 236
Dreaming Jewels, The, 152
Dreamstone, The, 47
Drinking Sapphire Wine, 128
Drought, The, 56

Drought of Ziak II, The, 280
Drowned Ammet, 117
Drowned Queen, The, 13
Druid's World, 199
Drums of Dracula, 136
Drums of Fu Manchu, The, 186
Drums of Tapajos, The, 147
Dry Spell, 56
Duel Under the Double Sun, 169
Dune, 104
Dune Messiah, 104
Dungeons of Kuba, 64
Dunwich Horror, The, 138
Dushau, 132
Dust of Death, 182
Dustland, 99
Dweller on Two Planets, A, 171
Dwellers, The, 235
Dwellers in the Cruicible, 204
Dwellers in Vale Sunrise, The, 133
Dying Earth, The, 219

E.T.--The Book of the Green Planet, 122
E.T. the Extra-Terrestrial in His Adventure on Earth, 122
Eager Beaver, 52
Eagle's Nest, The, 13
Eagle's Shadow, The, 40
Ear in the Wall, The, 177
Early Asimov, The, 255
Early Del Rey, The, 255
Early Long, The, 255
Early Pohl, The, 255
Early Williamson, The, 255
Earth, 78
Earth Book of Stormgate, The, 6
Earth Dies, The, 168
Earth Dreams, 154
Earth Dweller's Return, An, 171

Earth Enslaved, 216
Earth Fire, 3
Earth Invaded, 243
Earth is Heaven, 215
Earth Lies Sleeping, 114
Earth War, The, 179
Earth Will Shake, The, 234
Earthchild, 228
Earthfall, 201
Earthman, Come Home, 26
Earthman, Go Home, 6
Earthman on Venus, An, 78
Earthman's Burden, 6, 64
Earthsong, 228
Easy Ride, 83
Eater of Worlds, The, 216
Eclipsing Binaries, 199
Ecstasy Connection, The, 119
Edge of Beyond, The, 115
Education of Uncle Paul, The, 24
Egyptian Cat Mystery, The, 25
Eight Stories From the Rest of the Robots, 11
8th Annual of the Year's Best S-F, 262
Eighth Galaxy Reader, The, 257
Electronic Mind Reader, The, 25
Elephant God, The, 44
Elephant Song, 134
11th Annual of the Year's Best S-F, 262
Eleventh Galaxy Reader, The, 257
Elfin Ship, The, 25
Elfstones of Shannara, The, 31
Elixir of Life, The, 71
Elluvon Gift, The, 125
Eloise, 215
Elric at the End of Time, 152
Elric of Melnibone, 152
Elric, the Return to Melnibone, 152

Elsewhere, 273
Elsewhere Vol. II, 273
Elsewhere Vol. III, 273
Emerald City of Oz, The 19
Emerald Elephant Gambit, The, 144
Emma in Winter, 79
Emperor, The, 39
Emperor and the Monster, The, 169
Emperor Fu Manchu, 187
Emperor of Eridanus, 14
Emperor of Mars, 80
Emperor, Swords, Pentacles, 91
Empire of Blood, 135
Empire of the Atom, 220
Empire of the East, 190
Empire Strikes Back, The, 206
Empires of Flux and Anchor, 45
Empress of Outer Space, 46
Enchanted Island of Oz, The, 20
Enchanted Type-Writer, The, 14
Enchanter's End Game, 72
Enchantress From the Stars, 75
Enchantress of World's End, The, 44
End is Coming, The, 3
End of All Songs, The, 152
End of Exile, 27
End of the Line, 38
End of the Matter, The, 82
Endithor's Daughter, 197
Endless Frontier, The, 267
Endless Frontier Vol. II, The, 267
Endless Orgy, The, 88
Ends of the Circle, 232
Enemies From Beyond, 113
Enemy at Green Knowe, An, 27
Enemy From Space, 121
Enemy in the Dark, 169
"Enemy Mine," 134

Enemy Within the Skull, 216
Energy Zero, 30
English Assassin, The, 151
English at the North Pole, The, 222
Enormous Egg, The, 38
Ensign Flandry, 6
Enter Craig Kennedy, 178
Enterprise Stardust, 167
Entropy Effect, The, 204
Envisaged Worlds, 251
Envoy to New Worlds, 126
Epidemic Center: Aralon, 168
Epiphany, 237
Episodes of Vathek, The, 21
Equality, 22
Equality: in the Year 2000, 179
Erewhon; or, Over the Range, 38
Erewhon Revisited Twenty Years Later, 38
Eric Brighteyes, 97
Eric Brighteyes #2: A Witch's Welcome, 97
Eric of Zanthodon, 44
Ernst Ellert Returns, 169
Eros Ascending, 178
Eros at Zenith, 178
Eros Descending, 281
Escape Agents, The, 112
Escape From Macho, 163
Escape From Terror Lagoon, 172
Escape From the Crater, 23
Escape From the Planet of the Apes, 172
Escape on Venus, 37
Escape to Tomorrow, 172
Escape to Venus, 167
Escape to Witch Mountain, 120
Escape Velocity, 206
Eternal Champion, The, 151
Eternal Echo, The, 54
Eternal Lover, The, 35, 37

Eternal Mercenary, The, 190
Ethical Engineer, The, 102
Evangelist, The, 71
Every Boy's Book of Science Fiction, 254
Every Boy's Book of Space Stories, 254
Evil Gnome, The, 183
Executive, 276
Exile of Time, The, 57
Exile's Guest, 147
Exiled From Earth, 27
Exiles at the Well of Souls, 45
Exiles in Time, 62
Exiles of Colsec, 105
Exiles of the Rynth, 69
Exiles of the Stars, 160
Expedition Venus, 226
Experiment in Terra, 126
Exploits of Moominpappa, 279
Exploits of Elaine, The, 177
Explorers of Gor, 159
Extracurricular Activities, 136
Extraordinary Exploits and Experiences of Munchausen, M.D., The, 17
Extraterrestrials & Eclipses, 270
Eye in the Pyramid, The, 234
Eye of the Vulture, 92
Eye of the Zodiac, 215
Eyes of Bolsk, the, 135
Eyes of Horus, 92
Eyes of Sarsis, 163
Eyes of the Overworld, The 219
Eyes of the Shadow, The, 93

Fabulous Riverboat, The, 79
Face, The, 219

Face of Chaos, The, 12, 244
Faceless Man, The, 219
Faces in the Flames, 211
Faith of Tarot, 8
Falcon Strikes, The, 176
Falcons of Eden, The, 64
Falkland and Zicci, 34
Fall of a Nation; a Sequel to the Birth of a Nation, The, 65
Fall of Colossus, The, 117
Fall of the Shell, The, 232
Fall of Worlds, The, 149
Fallen Ones, The, 221
Fallible Fiend, The, 61
False Fatherland, 46
False Front, 169
Famine, The, 56
Fangs of the Sky Leopard, 106
Fantasia Mathematica, 256
Fantastic Four: Doomsday, 145
Fantastic Island, The, 181
Fantasy: The Literature of the Marvelous, 260
Fantasy Annual III, 251
Fantasy Annual IV, 251
Fantasy Annual V, 251
Fantazius Mallare, 103
Far Frontiers, 267
Far Frontiers 2, 267
Far Side of Evil, The, 75
Far Traveller, The, 46
Far Travellers, 249
Faragon Fairingay, 100
"Farewell, Nikola!", 27
Farfetch, 132
Farthest Shore, The, 128
Farthest Star, 173, 233
Fat Camel of Bagdad, The, 68
Fate of the Phoenix, 203
Fear Cay, 181
Fears, 258
Feast Unknown, A, 79
Feathered Octopus, The, 182
Fellowship of the HAND, The, 105
Fellowship of the Ring, The, 213
Fenris Device, The, 202
Field of Ice, 222
Fields of Sleep, 224
Fiend, The, 266
Fiery Menace, The, 183
5th Annual of the Year's Best S-F, 262
Fifth Galaxy Reader, The, 257
Fighting Man of Mars, A, 36
Fighting Men, 13
Fighting Slave of Gor, 159
Figures of Earth, 40
Film Mystery, The, 178
Final Command, 161
Final Encyclopedia, The, 65
Final Programme, The, 151
Final Quest, The, 150
Final Reflection, The, 204
Finger in the Sky Affair, The, 218
Fingers of Death, 93
Finished, 97
Finn Family Moomintroll, 279
Fire and Fog, 100
Fire and Ice (Harding), 100
Fire and Ice (Jensen), 115
Fire Dancer, 146
Fire-Eater, The, 91
Fire Goddess, The, 187
Fire in His Hands, The, 52
Fire in the Ashes, 116
Fire-Tongue, 187
Firelord, 90
Fires of Azeroth, 47
Fires of Scorpio, 34
Fires of Windameir, the, 100
First Battle, 280
First Book of Omni

Science Fiction, The, 252
First Book of Swords, The, 190
First Channel, 132
First Contact?, 226
First Gentleman of America, The, 40
First Lensman, 198
First on the Moon, 226
First World Fantasy Awards, 274
First World of If, The, 268
First, You Fight, 69
Fish Dinner in Memison, A, 72
5 Beds to Mecca, 83
Five Children and It, The, 157
5 Galaxy Short Novellas, 257
Five in the Hole, 84
Five Million Years to Earth, 121
Five Roads to Tlen, 124
Five Thousand Miles Underground, 185
Five Way Secret Agent, The, 179
Fize of the Gabriel Ratchets, 161
Flame Breathers, The, 184
Flame in the Fens, A, 34
Flame Upon the Ice, The, 82
Flame Winds, 165
Flaming Falcons, The, 182
Flaming Mountain, The, 25
Flandry of Terra, 6
Flash Gordon in the Caverns of Mongo, 177
Flashing Swords! #1, 251
Flashing Swords! #2, 251
Flashing Swords! #3, 251
Flashing Swords! #4, 251
Flashing Swords! #5: Demons and Daggers, 251
Flatland; A Romance of Many Dimensions, 1
Fleet of the Springers, 167
Flexing the Warp, 161
Flicker of Doom, 119
Fliers of Antares, 33
Flight From Neveryon, 62
Flight From the Grave, 106
Flight of Exiles, 27
Flight of Fear, , 124, 130
Flight of Honor, 141
Flight of Mavin Manyshaped, The, 212
Flight of Opar, 79
Flight of the Starfire, 154
Flight to Terror, 73
Floating City, A, 222
Floating Continent, The, 61
Floating Game, The, 13
Floating Gods, The, 102
Flood, The, 56
Florians, The, 202
Florida Project, The, 202
Flux, 91
Flying Goblin, The, 183
Flying Nun: Miracle at San Tanco, The, 116
Flying Saucer Gambit, The, 143
Flying Stingaree, The, 25
Flying Sub, The, 199
Flying to Amy-Ran Fastness, 55
Flying Windmill, The, 1
Flying Yorkshireman, The, 121
Foe of Barnabas Collins, The, 188
Follow the Whales; Hydronauts Meet the Otter-People, 23
For Love of Mother-Not, 82
For Your Sighs Only, 4
Forbidden Fountain of Oz, The, 20
Forbidden Territory, The, 229

Forbidden Tower, The, 28
Forerunner, 160
Forerunner: The Second Venture, 160
Forerunner Foray, 160
Forest of Forever, The, 210
Forests of Gleor, The, 135
Forgotten Sea of Mars, The, 36
Forgotten Star, The, 95
Former King, The, 54
Fortress Atlantis, 168
Fortress in Time, 170
Fortress of Solitude, 181
Fortress of the Six Moons, 167
Fortune for Kregen, A, 33
Fortunes of Brak, The, 114
Foundation, 11
Foundation and Empire, 11
Foundation Trilogy, The, 11
Foundation's Edge, 11
Foundling, and Other Tales of Prydain, The, 4
Four Days War, 236
Fourteen Points, The, 178
Fourth Book of Jorkens, The, 71
Fourth Flight of the Starfire, The, 154
Fourth Galaxy Reader, The, 257
Francis, 207
Francis Goes to Washington, 207
Francis... the Army Mule, 207
Frankenstein Factory, The, 105
Fratricide is a Gas, 96
Freak Show Murders & A Quarter of Eight, The, 93
Freaky Friday, 186
Freckled Shark, The, 182
Freddy and Mr. Camphor, 31
Freddy and Simon the Dictator, 31
Freddy and the Baseball Team From Mars, 31
Freddy and the Bean Home News, 31
Freddy and the Dragon, 31
Freddy and the Flying Saucer Plans, 31
Freddy and the Ignoramus, 31
Freddy and the Men From Mars, 31
Freddy and the Perilous Adventure, 31
Freddy and the Pied Piper, 31
Freddy and the Popinjay, 31
Freddy and the Space Ship, 31
Freddy Goes Camping, 31
Freddy Goes to Florida, 31
Freddy Goes to the North Pole, 31
Freddy Plays Football, 31
Freddy Rides Again, 31
Freddy the Cowboy, 31
Freddy the Detective, 31
Freddy the Magician, 31
Freddy the Pilot, 31
Freddy the Politician, 31
Freddy's Cousin Weedly, 31
Freddy's First Adventure, 31
Free Amazons of Darkover, 276
Friend to Mankind, 169
From Earth to Moon, 222
From Gilgamesh to Wells, #1:, 258
From Heinlein to Here, #3:, 258
From Here to Forever, #4:, 258
From Mind to Mind: Tales of Communication From Analog, 270
From Outer Space, 49
From Rapture With Love, 4

From Satan, With Love, 50
From the Earth to The
  Moon, 222
From the Hidden Way, 40
From the "S" File, 266
From Wells to Heinlein,
  #2:, 258
Frontiers 1; Tomorrow's
  Alternatives, 256
Frontiers 2; The New
  Mind, 256
Frosted Death, The, 184
Frostflower and Thorn, 118
Frostflower and
  Windbourne, 118
Frozen God, The, 121
Frozen Waves, The, 221
Fu Manchu's Bride, 186
Fully Automated Love Life
  of Henry Keanridge,
  The, 266
Further Adventures of
  Captain Kettle, 112
Furthest, 74,
Future at War Vol. 1:
  Thor's Hammer, The, 249
Future at War Vol 2: The
  Spear of Mars, The, 249
Future at War Vol 3:
  Orion's Sword, The, 249
Future Commonwealth; or,
  What Samuel Blacom Saw
  in Socioland, The, 47
Future Perfect, 257
Future Perfect, Revised
  Edition, 257
Futures Past, 230
Futurological Congress,
  The, 130
Fuzzies and Other People,
  172
Fuzzy Bones, 172
Fuzzy Sapiens, 172

Gaian Expedient, The, 69
Galactic Alarm, 167
Galactic Derelict, 159
Galactic Diplomat, 126
Galactic Empires, Volume
  One, 241
Galactic Empires, Volume
  Two, 241
Galactic Patrol, 198
Galactic Riddle, The, 167
Galactic Sybil Sue Blue,
  32
Galactic Warriors, 24
Galactic Whirlpool, The,
  204
Galactica Discovers
  Earth, 126
Galaxy Builder, The, 127
Galaxy Mission, 99
Galaxy of the Lost, 216
Galaxy Reader of Science
  Fiction, 257
Galileo 7, The, 205
Gallantry, 40
Gambling Ghost, and Other
  Tales, The, 208
Game of Empire, The, 6
Gamefinger, 4
Gameplayers of Zan, The,
  82
Gammage Cup, The, 119
Gangdom's Doom, 93
Gate of Ivrel, 47
Gates of Creation, The, 79
Gates of Time, The, 17
Gateway, 173, 233
Gateway to Hell, 229
Gateway to Never, The, 46
Gateway to Remembrance, 54
Gateway to Tomorrow, 250
Gateway to the Stars, 250
Gateway to Xanadu, 278
Gathering, The, 99
Gathering of Gargoyles,
  A, 171
Gees' First Case, 224
Genetic Buccaneer, The,
  216
Genetic General, The, 65
Genial Dinosaur, The, 80
Gentle Giants of
  Ganymede, The, 105
Gentleman Solomon, 21
Gentlemen in Hades; The

Story of a Damned Debutante, 122
Gerfalcon, 18
Get Smart!, 116
Get Smart Once Again!, 116
Getaway World, 198
Gholan Gate, The, 216
Ghost Makers, The, 93
Ghost Who Walks, The, 77
Ghosthunt, 49
Ghosts of Epidoris, The, 216
Ghosts of Gol, The, 167
Ghoul!, 268
Giant Horse of Oz, The, 19
Giant of World's End, 44
Giants, 276
Giant's Partner, The, 168
Giants' Star, 105
Gibralter Road, 141
Gift From Berlin, 15
Gift From Earth, A, 158
Giggling Ghosts, The, 182
Ginger Star, The, 28
Girl From B.U.S.T., The, 42
Girl in the Golden Atom, The, 57
Gladiators of Hapanu, 135
Glass Man, The, 184
Glass Mountain, The, 184
Glass of Dyskornis, The, 88
Glass Too Many, The, 224
Glinda of Oz, 19
Global Globules Affair, The, 218
Glue Factory, 148
Gnome King of Oz, The, 19
Go-Go SADISTO, 4
Go Home, Unicorn, 143
Go Saddle the Sea, 3
Goblin Tower, The, 61
Goblins, The, 184
God Emperor of Dune, 104
God of Death, 190
God of Tarot, 8
God of the Labyrinth, The, 233

Goddess of Ganymede, The, 178
Goddess of Mars, 80
Gods Look Down, The, 110
Gods of Mars, The, 36
Gods of Pegana, The, 71
Gods of Riverworld, 79
Gods of the Greataway, 51
Gods of Tlen, The, 124
Gods of Xuma, or Barsoom Revisited, The, 123
Godwhale, The, 18
Goggle-Eyed Pirates, The, 77
Gold Bomb, The, 13
Gold Ogre, The, 182
Gold of Akada, The, 80
Gold of the Gods, The, 177
Golden Amazon, The, 80
Golden Amazon Returns, The, 80
Golden Amazon's Triumph, The, 80
Golden Apple, The, 234
Golden Ax, The, 157
Golden Boats of Taradata Affair, The, 218
Golden Circle, The, 77
Golden Dream: A Fuzzy Odyssey, 172
Golden Goddess Gambit, The, 143
Golden Horn, The, 6, 282
Golden Man, The, 183
Golden Naginata, The, 191
Golden Peril, The, 182
Golden Rooms, The, 81
Golden Scorpio, 33
Golden Scorpion, The, 186, 187
Golden Skull, The, 25
Golden Spaniard, The, 229
Golden Steed, The, 135
Golden Swan, The, 201
Golden Sword, The, 154
Golden Torc, The, 147
Golem in the Gears, 276
Good Peace, A, 52
Gor Omnibus, 159

Gormenghast, 166
Grail War, The, 150
Grampa in Oz, 19
Grand Jubilee, The, 74
Grave, The, 278
Gray Creatures, The, 239
Gray Lensman, 198
Great Dune Trilogy, The, 104
Great Kings' War, 172
Great Ones, The, 61
Great SF Stories 1 (1939), The, 243
Great SF Stories 2 (1940), The, 243
Great SF Stories 3 (1941), The, 243
Great SF Stories 4 (1942), The, 243
Great SF Stories 5 (1943), The, 243
Great SF Stories 6 (1944), The, 243
Great SF Stories 7 (1945), The, 243
Great SF Stories 8 (1946), The, 243
Great SF Stories 9 (1947), The, 243
Great SF Stories 10 (1948), The, 243
Great SF Stories 11 (1949), The, 243
Great SF Stories 12 (1950), The, 243
Great SF Stories 13 (1954) The, 276
Great Science Fiction By Scientists, 252
Great Science Fiction By Doctors, 252
Great Science Fiction Stories About Mars, 255
Great Science Fiction Stories About the Moon, 255
Greek Fire, 84
Green Death, The, 182
Green Eagle, The, 181

Green Eyes, 93
Green Hills of Earth, The, 104
Green Hornet in the Infernal Light, The, 94
Green Killer, The, 184
Green Phoenix, 210
Greenwitch, 53
Greetings From Earth, 126
Grey Fist, 93
Grey King, The, 53
Grey Mane of Morning, The, 47
Grey Shapes, 224
Greyfax Grimwald, 100
Greymantle, 154
Grim Caretaker, The, 10
Grove of Doom, The, 93
Gryphon in Glory, 160
Gryphon's Eyrie, 160
Guardians, The (Mahr), 168
Guardians, The (Baker), 192
Guardians, The (Austin), 12
Guardians 1: The Killing Bone, 192
Guardians 2: Dark Ways to Death, 192
Guardians 3: The (Haunting of Alan Mais, 192
Guardians 4: The Vampires of Finisterre, 192
Guardians of Time, 7
Guardians of the Coral Throne, 135
Guardians of the Singreale, 149
Guardsman of Gor, 159
Gub-Gub's Book: An Encyclopedia of Food, 134
Guilty Head, the, 88
Guinevere, 158
Guinevere Evermore, 158
Gulliver Redivious; or, The Celebrated &

Entertaining Travels...
  of Baron Munchausen,
  Including a Tour to the
  United States of
  America in the Year
  1803, 16
Gulliver Revived,
  Containing Singular
  Travels, Campaigns,
  Voyages, and Adventures
  in Russia, Iceland,
  Turkey, Egypt, Gibral-
  ter, and on the
  Atlantic Ocean; also,
  an Account of a Voyage
  into the Moon, 15
Gulliver Revived, or, The
  Singular Travels,
  Campaigns, Voyages, and
  Adventures of Baron
  Munikouson, Commonly
  Called Munchausen, 15
Gulliver Revived... Baron
  Munchausen, Including a
  Tour of the United
  States of America in
  1803, and the First Two
  Chapters of a Second
  Tour in 1810, 16
Gulliver Revived...
  Russia, Caspian
  Sea, Ireland,
  Turkey,Egypt,
  Gibralter, up the
  Mediterranean...
  Atlantic Ocean...
  Through the Centre
  of Mount Etna... the
  South Sea... to the
  Moon and Dog Star..., 15
Gulliver Revived; or, The
  Vice of Lying Properly
  Exposed..., 16
Gunga Sahib, The, 155
Gunpowder God, 172
Guns of Avalon, The, 238
Guns of Everblack, The, 170
Guns of the Gods, 155

Haakon's Iron Hand, 157
Had Any Lately?, 52
Hadon of Ancient Opar, 79
Halcyon Drift, 202
Half Magic, 72
Half Past Human, 18
Halfling, and Other
  Stories, The, 28
Halloween, 98
Halloween II, 98
Halloween III: Season of
  the Witch, 98
Hallucination Orbit:
  Psychology in Science
  Fiction, 244
Halo Highway, The, 113
Hamlet Had an Uncle, 40
Hammer Home, 51
Hammer's Slammers, 69
Han Solo and the Lost
  Legacy, 206
Han Solo at Stars' End, 206
Han Solo's Revenge, 206
Hand of Dracula, The, 136
Hand of Fu-Manchu, The, 186
Hand of Kane, The, 110
Hand of Oberon, The, 238
Hand of Zei, The, 61
Hands in the Dark, 93
Hands of Glory, 118
Handy Mandy in Oz, 19
Hang Loose, 84
Hanging Stones, The, 228
Happy Killers, the, 184
Happy Returns, 50
Hard Act to Follow, A, 52
Hard Man is Good to Find, A, 52
Hard Way Up, The, 46
Hard-Core Murder, 119
Harder you Try, The
  Harder It Gets, The, 52
Harding's Luck, 157
Harilek, 86
Harp of Imach Thyssel,
  The, 235
Harper Hall of Pern, The,

Harpist in the Wind, 142
Harpy's Flight, 133
Hartinger's Mouse, 141
Hate Genius, The, 183
Hate Master, The, 184
Haunted Ocean, 182
Haunter of the Dark, The, 138
Hauser's Memory, 195
Haven, The, 64
Haven of Darkness, 215
Hawk of May, 29
Hawk of the Wilderness, 48
Hawkmistress!, 29
Hawks of Fellheath, The, 81
He, a Companion to She, Being a History of the Adventures of J. Theodosius Aristaphano on the Island of Rapa Nue in Search of His Immortal Ancestor, 63
He Could Stop the World, 182
Headless Men, The, 183
Healer, 148
Heart's Blood, 237
Heartsease, 64
Hector Servadac, 222
Hedonists, The, 233
Heechee Rendezvous, 173, 233
Heil Harris!, 13
Heir of Sea and Fire, 142
Helene, 155
Hell Below, 183
Heller's Leap, 225, 226
Hellfire Files of Jules deGrandin, The, 176
Helliconia Spring, 4
Helliconia Summer, 4
Helliconia Winter, 4
Helma, 155
Hendra's Book, 175
Her Ways are Death, 224
Her-Bak, "Chick-Pea"; the Living Face of Ancient Egypt, 62
Her-Bak, Egyptian Initiate, 62
Herbert, 234
Herbert's Space Trip, 234
Herbie Rides Again, 45
Heretics of Dune, 104
Heritage of Hastur, The, 28
Heritage of the Lizard People, 169
Heritage of the Star, 75
Hero and the Crown, The, 143
Heroes of Smokeover, The, 113
Heu-Heu; or, The Monster, 97
Hex, 182
Hidden Death, 93
Hidden People; The Story of a Search for Incan Treasure, The, 149
Hidden Valley of Oz, The, 20
Hiero's Journey, 125
High Couch of Silistra, 154
High Crystal, 41
High Deryni, 122
High Hex, The, 115
High King, The, 4
High Place, The, 40
High Queen, The, 29
High Requiem, 54
High Water at Catfish Bend, 35
Highway to Heaven, 25
Hills of the Dead, The, 110
Hira Singh's Tale, 155
History of the Caliph Vathek, The, 21
History of the Science Fiction Magazine Part 1, 1926-1935, The, 242
History of the Science Fiction Magazine Part 2, 1936-1945, The, 242

History of the Science Fiction Magazine Part 3, 1946-1955, The, 242
History of the Science Fiction Magazine Part 4, 1956-1965, The, 242
Hit or Myth, 12
Hitchhiker's Guide to the Galaxy, 1
Hitchhiker's Trilogy; The Omnibus Edition, 1
Hobbit, The, 213
Hoka!, 6, 64
Hollow Crown Affair, The, 217
Hollow Hills, The, 208
Hollow Lands, The, 152
Holmes-Dracula File, 190
Holy Flower, The, 97
Home--To Avalon, 124
Homecoming, The, 59
Homeward Bound, 222
Homework Machine, The, 231
Homeworld, 102
Homing Pigeons, The, 234
Honour of Thieves, 111
Hordes of the Red Butcher, 201
Horn: Green, 169
Horror, The, 168
Horror Chamber of Jules deGrandin, The, 176
Horror in the Museum and Other Revisions, The, 137
Horrors, 258
Horrorscope; Gemini Smile, Gemini Kill, 136
Horrorscope; The Curse of Leo, 136
Horrorscope; The Green Flames of Aries, 136
Horrorscope; The Revenge of Taurus, 136
Horse and His Boy, The, 131
Horseclans Odyssey, 2
Horses of the North, 2
Hospital Station, 229
Hostage, 13
Hostage of Zir, The, 61
Hosts of the Flaming Death, 207
Hot Mahatma, The, 83
Hot Rocks, 84
Hot Spot, The, 124, 130
Hot Time in Old Town, 143
Hotel Transylvania, 237
Hounds of Skaith, The, 28
Hounds of Vengeance, The, 55
Hour of the Dragon, The, 109
Hour of the Gate, The, 82
Hour of the Oxrun Dead, The, 92
House Mother, The, 165
House of Arden, the, 157
House of Cards, 13
House of Dark Shadows, 188
House of Dawn, The, 193
House of Death, 184
House of Entropy, 42
House of Fulfillment: The Romance of a Soul, The, 21
House of Many Worlds, The, 148
House of Scorpions, 195
House of Stranger, 14
House of the Bears, The, 56
House of the Wolf, 235
House of Zeor, 132
House-Boat on the Styx, A, 14
Housenapper, The, 58
How Many Blocks in the Pile?, 147
Howling, The, 30
Howling II, The, 30
Howling III, The, 277
Hubbles and the Robot, 107
Hubbles' Bubble, 107
Hubbles' Treasure Hunt, The, 107
Hugo Winners (vol. 1), The, 243

Hugo Winners (vol. 2), The, 243
Hugo Winners (vol. 3), The, 243
Hugo Winners (vol. 4), The, 243
Hulk and Spider-Man: Murdermoon, 146
Human Bat Vs. The Robot Gangster, The, 106
Humanoid Touch, The, 233
Humanoids, The, 233
Humans of Ziak II, The, 280
Humans Keep Out!, 170
Hundred and One Dalmations, The, 198
Hundred Days, The, 155
Hungry Tiger of Oz, The, 19
Hunt Down the Prize, 150
Hunter Quartermain's Story, 97
Hunters of Gor, 159
Hunters of Jundagai, The, 33
Hunters of Space, 119
Hunters of the Red Moon, 29, 238
Hurok of the Stone Age, 44
Hydra Monster, The, 77
Hydrabyss Red, 211
Hydronauts, The, 23

I Can't Believe I Ate the Whole Thing, 52
I Married a Witch, 199
I, Robot, 11
I'd Rather Fight Than Swish, 52
I'm Cherry, Fly Me!, 84
Ice Desert, The, 222
Ice Dragon, 135
Ice is Coming, The, 236
Ice Maiden, The, 4
Ice Prophet, 82
Icerigger, 82
Iceworld Connection, The, 164

Idol From Passa, 169
Iduna's Universe, 215
Illearth War, The, 68
Ill-Made Knight, The, 230
Image of the Beast, The, 79
Image of Voices, An, 161
Imaro, 191
Immortal of World's End, The, 44
Immortal Unknown, The, 167
Immortals, The (Asimov), 244
Immortals, The, (Berry) 23
Imperator Plot, The, 202
Imperial Stars, 198
Impossibles, The, 87, 115
In a Bind, 84
In a Pinch, 84
In Brighter Climes; or, Life in Socioland, 47
In Search of the Unknown, 45
In the Battle for New York, 100
In the Circle of Time, 5
In the Green Star's Glow, 43
In the Keep of Time, 5
In the Kingdom of Beasts, 202
In the Moons of Borea, 139
In the Ocean of Night, 22
In the Sanctuary, 220
In the Shadow of Omizantrim, 221
In the Tiger's Lair, 149
In Viriconium, 102
In Winter's Shadow, 29
Incident on Ath, 215
Incomplete Enchanter, The, 61
Incredible Hulk, The: Cry of the Beast, 145
Incredible Planet, The, 42
Indestructible, The, 23
Indiana Jones and the Temple of Doom, 113

Inferno, The, 56
Infinite Battle, The, 24
Infinity 1, 259
Infinity 2, 259
Infinity 3, 259
Infinity 4, 259
Infinity 5, 259
Infinity Flight, 167
Inhabitant of the Lake and Less Welcome Tenants, The, 137
Inherit the Stars, 105
Inheritor, The, 29
Inheritors, The, 46
Insidious Dr. Fu-Manchu, The, 186
Instrumentality of Mankind, The, 197
Insulators, The, 56
Interface, 3
Intergalactic Empires, 244
Interlude on Siliko 5, 168
International Incidents, 41
International Relations Through Science Fiction, 265
Interstellar Mutineers, 38
Interstellar Two-Five, 176
Interview with the Vampire, 281
Intimations of Eve, 81
Into the Alternate Universe, 46
Into the Niger Bend, 223
Into the Unknown: A Romance of South Africa, 81
Introductory Psychology Through Science Fiction, 268
Introductory Psychology Through Science Fiction--2, 268
Intruders, The, 78
Invader From Space, 153
Invaders, The, 113
Invaders From the Infinite, 42
Invasion From Space, 167
Invasion of the Nymphomaniacs, 214
Invasion of the United States, The, 100
Invasion of the Yellow Warlords, 207
Investigations and Experience of M. Shawtinbach at Saar Soong, Sumatra, 1972
Invincible Adam, The, 223
Invisibility Affair, The, 217
Invisible Death, 44
Invisible Empire, 207
Invisible Eye, The, 211
Invisibles, The, 111
Ireta Adventure, The, 279
Iron Arm of Michael Glenn, The, 128
Iron Lords, The, 163
Iron Man: And Call My Killer...Modok!, 145
Iron Pirate, The, 167
Iron Skull, The, 184
Iron Tongue, 221
Ironbark Bill, 208
Ironbrand, 154
Irsud, 49
Isaac Asimov Double, An, 11
Isaac Asimov Omnbius, An, 11
Isaac Asimov Second Omnibus, An, 11
Isaac Asimov's Adventures of Science Fiction, 270
Isaac Asimov's Aliens & Outworlders, 270
Isaac Asimov's Marvels of Science Fiction, 270
Isaac Asimov's Masters of Science Fiction, 270
Isaac Asimov's Near Futures and Far, 270
Isaac Asimov's Space of Her Own, 270
Isaac Asimov's Wonders of

the World, 270
Isaac Asimov's Worlds of Science Fiction, 270
Ishmael, 204
Island in the Mist, The, 119
Island of Creeping Death, The, 161
Island of Dogs, The, 77
Island of Evil, 59
Island of Fear, The, 153
Island of Fu Manchu, The, 186
Island of the Mighty, The, 227
Island People, The, 49
Island Snatchers, The, 199
Island Sonata, 133
Islands of Space, 42
Isle of Glass, The, 282
Isle of the Dead, 238
Isotope Man, The, 144
"It"; a Wild, Weird History of Marvelous, Miraculous, Phantasmagorical Adventures in Search of He, She, and Jess, and Leading to the Finding of "It"; a Haggard Conclusion, 63
It's Getting Harder All the Time, 52
It's Not How Long You Make It, 52
It's What's Up Front That Counts, 52
Italian Connection, The, 83
Ivanhoe Gambit, The, 237
Ivory Child, The, 97
Ivory Valley; An Adventure of Captain Kettle, 112

Jack Anderson Against Dr. Tek!, 179
Jack of Swords, 215
Jack Pumpkinhead of Oz, 19
Jade Warrior, The, 134

Jan in India, 121
Jan of the Jungle, 121
Jandar of Callisto, 44
Janissaries, 174
Janissaries: Clan and Crown, 174
Janus Equation, the, 247
Jargoon Pard, The, 160
Jason, Son of Jason, 89
Jaws, 115
Jaws 2, 115
Jehad, 237
Jersey Bounce, The, 84
Jester at Scar, The, 215
Jewel in the Skull, The, 151
Jesus Incident, The, 104
Jewel Merchants, The, 40
Jewel of Arwen, The, 29
Jewel of Jarhen, 216
Jewel of Tharn, 134
Jewel Sowers, 5
Jewels of Gwahlur, 109
Jhereg, 32
Jim Dunlap and the Long Lunar Walk, 166
Jim Dunlap and the Mysterious Orbiting Rocket, 166
Jim Dunlap and the Mysterious Spy, 166
Jim Dunlap and the Secret Rocket Formula, 165
Jim Dunlap and the Strange Dr. Brockton, 165
Jim Dunlap and the Wingless Plane, 165
Jimgrim, 155
Jimgrim and Allah's Peace, 155
Jimgrim Sahib, 155
Jinian Footseer, 212
Jinx on a Terran Inheritance, 277
Jiu San, 183
John Carter and the Giant of Mars, 36
John Carter of Mars, 36

John W. Campbell
  Anthology, 42
John W. Campbell Awards,
  Volume 5, The, 262
Johnny Ludlow, 235
Johnny Ludlow, Fifth
  Series, 235
Johnny Ludlow, Fourth
  Series, 235
Johnny Ludlow, Second
  Series, 235
Johnny Ludlow, Sixth
  Series, 235
Johnny Ludlow, Third
  Series, 235
Joining of the Stone,
  The, 156
Jondelle, 215
Jongor Fights Back, 232
Jongor of the Lost Land,
  232
Jonuta Rising!, 164
Joris of the Rock, 18
Jorkens Borrows Another
  Whiskey, 71
Jorkens Has a Large
  Whiskey, 71
Jorkens Remembers Africa,
  71
Joseph Balsamo, 70
Joseph Balsamo, Vol. II,
  71
Journey, 176
Journey Behind the Wind,
  236
Journey into Space, 48
Journey Into Terror, 172
Journey of Tapiola, 157
Journey to Jupiter
  (Greene), 95
Journey to Jupiter
  (Walters), 226
Journey to Mesharra, 196
Journey to the Flame, 278
Journey to the North
  Pole, A, 222
Journey to the
  Underground World, 44
Jovial Ghosts, The, 199

Joy Ride, 42
Judas Mandate, The, 73
Judgement of Dragons, A,
  91
Judgement on Janus, 160
Judges of Hades and Other
  Simon Ark Stories, The,
  105
Jules LeVallon, 25
Jungle Book, The, 120
Jungle Fever, 88
Jungle Girl, The, 44
Jungle Jest, 155
Jungle Tales of Tarzan, 35
Jupiter Equilateral, 171
Jupiter in the Chair, 85
Jurgen, 40
Just a Silly Millimeter
  Longer, 52
Justice and Her Brothers,
  99
Justice, Inc., 184
Juxtaposition, 8

Kabumpo in Oz, 19
Kai Lung: Six, 30
Kai Lung Beneath the
  Mulberry Tree, 30
Kai Lung Omnibus, The, 30
Kai Lung Unrolls His Mat,
  30
Kai Lung's Golden Hours,
  30
Kajira of Gor, 159
Kak-Abdullah Conspiracy,
  The, 140
Kalin, 215
Kar Karballa, King of the
  Gogs, 199
Kar-Chee Reign, The, 60
Kaspa, the Lion Man, 208
Kavin's World, 146
Keep It Up, Rod!, 52
Keeper's Price, The, 29
Kemlo and the Craters of
  the Moon, 74
Kemlo and the Crazy
  Planet, 74
Kemlo and the End of

Time, 74
Kemlo and the Gravity Rays, 74
Kemlo and the Martian Ghosts, 74
Kemlo and the Masters of Space, 74
Kemlo and the Purple Dawn, 74
Kemlo and the Satellite Builders, 74
Kemlo and the Sky Horse, 74
Kemlo and the Space Invaders, 74
Kemlo and the Space Lanes, 74
Kemlo and the Space Men, 74
Kemlo and the Star Men, 74
Kemlo and the Zombie Men, 74
Kemlo and the Zones of Silence, 74
Kensho, 192
Kesrick, 44
Kesrith, 47
Key Out of Time, 159
Key to Irunium, The, 33
Key to Venudine, The, 33
Kiai!, 7
Kidnap Club, The, 178
Kif Strike Back, The, 47
Killashandra, 279
Killer Pine, 96
Killer Planets of Binaark, 135
Killer's Town, The, 77
Killers From Hyperspace, 169
Killers of Innocence, The, 56
Killing Machine, The, 219
Killing Time, 204
King Chondo's Ride, 238
King Cobra, 46
King Conan, 108
King David's Spaceship, 174

King Goshawk and the Birds, 163
King Hunters, 88
King in Check, The, 155
King Kobold, 206
King Kobold Revived, 206
King Kull, 110
King Maker, The, 183
King of No Man's Land, The, 85
King of Terror, The, 183
King of the Dead, 12
King of the Jungle, 208
King--of the Khyber Rifles, 155
King--of the Khybers, 155
King of the Slavers, 164
King of the Swords, The, 152
King of the World's Edge, 156
King of Zunga, 135
King Solomon's Mines, 97
King Solomon's Treasures, 63
King Solomon's Wives, 63
King Stag, The, 29
King Was in His Counting House, The, 40
King's Assegai, The, 149
King's Blood Four, 212
King's Death, The, 34
King's Justice, The, 122
Kingdom Come (Comstock), 51
Kingdom Come (Drumm), 69
Kingdom of Carbonel, The, 196
Kingdom of Evil, The, 103
Kingdom of Royth, 135
Kingdom of Summer, 29
Kingdom of the Cats, 91
Kingdom That Was, The, 124
Kings of Crime, 93
Kings of Space; a Story of Interplanetary Adventure, 115
Kingsbane, 154
Kioga of the Unknown

Land, 48
Kioga of the Wilderness, 48
Kirlian Quest, 7
Kiss My Assassin, 83
Kiss Not the Child, 213
Kleinert Case, The, 224
Klingon Gambit, The, 204
Knave in Hand, 115
Knee-Deep in Thunder, 150
Knight of Ghosts and Shadows, A, 6
Knight of the Swords, The, 152
Knight's Castle, 72
Koren, 139
Kothar--Barbarian Swordsman, 83
Kothar and the Conjurer's Curse, 83
Kothar and the Demon Queen, 83
Kothar and the Wizard Slayer, 83
Kothar of the Magic Sword, 83
Koyama's Diamond, 23
Krozair Cycle, The, 34
Krozair of Kregen, 33
Kull, 110
Kutath, 47
Kutnar, Son of Pic, 125
Kyric: Warlock Warrior, 84
Kyric and the Lost Queen, 84
Kyric and the Wizard's Sword, 84
Kyric Fights the Demon World, 84

Labyrinth of Lies, 23
Ladies in Hades; A Story of Hell's Smart Set, 122
Lady From L.U.S.T., 83
Lady in Heat, 83
Lady of Darkness, 166
Lady of Light, 166
Lady of the Bees, 210

Lady of the Haven, 64
Lady of the Snowmist, The, 163
Lady Penelope: The Albanian Affair, 212
Lady Sativa, 127
Lady Takes It All Off, The, 83
Lagrange Five, 179
Lagrangists, The, 179
Laid in the Future, 83
Lallia, 215
Lamarchos, 49
Lame Devil, The, 130
Land Beyond the Map, 33
Land Leviathan, The, 152
Land of Always-Night, 181
Land of Darkness, with Some Further Chapters in the Experiences of The Little Pilgrim, 164
Land of Fear, 182
Land of Long Juju, 182
Land of Mist, The, 69
Land of No Shadow, The, 48
Land of Oz, The, 19
Land of Terror, 37
Land of Terror, The, 181
Land of the Giants, 124, 130
Land That Time Forgot, The, 37
Lando Calrissian and the Flamewind of Oseon, 206
Lando Calrissian and the Mindharp of Sharu, 206
Lando Calrissian and the Starcave of Thonboka, 206
Lands of Never, 260
Lankar of Callisto, 44
Last Amazon, The, 46
Last American, The, 202
Last and First Men, 203
Last Battle: A Story For Children, The, 131
Last Call of Mourning, The, 92
Last Communion, 237

Last Days of Atlantis, The, 168
Last Days of Man on Earth, The, 151
Last Disaster, The, 226
Last Enchantment, The, 208
Last Legend of Smokeover, The, 113
Last Licks, 52
Last Men in London, 203
Last of the Cybernauts, 13
Last Post For a Partisan, 73
Last Resort, The, 156
Last Son of Krypton, 144
Last Train to Limbo, 266
Laugh of Death, The, 183
Laugh Was on Lazarus, The, 13
Laughing Dragon of Oz, The, 20
Laughter of Carthage, The, 152
Lava, 163
Lavalite World, The, 79
Lay Me Odds, 83
Lay of the Land, The, 77
Lays of Beleriand, The, 282
Lazarus Effect, The, 104
Le Diable Boiteaux; or, The Devil Upon Two Sticks, 130
League of Light, The, 56
Leaves of Time, The, 17
Left Hand of Darkness, The, 129
Legacy, 247
Legends From the End of Time, 152
Legends of Angria, 31
Legion of Space, 232
Legion of the Lost, The, 55
Legion of Time, The, 233
Legionnaire, The, 191
Legions of Antares, 33
Legions of the Death Master, 207

Lensman From Rigel, 198
Lerios Mecca, The, 124
Let the Spacemen Beware, 6
Leviathan, 234
Liafail, 155
Liberator of Jedd, 134
Life for Kregen, A, 33
Life for the Stars, A, 26
Life Hunt, 168
Life Probe, 279
Life, the Universe, and Everything, 1
Light in the West, A, 34
Light on the Sound, 209
Lights! Action! Murder!, 84
Lights of Zetar, The, 153
Lilith: A Snake in the Grass, 45
Limanora: The Island of Progress, 210
Limbreth Gate, the, 133
Line of Love, The, 40
Lineage of Lichfield, The, 40
Liners of Time, 80
Lion Game, The, 193
Lion Men of Mongo, The, 177
Lion of Petra, The, 155
Lion, the Witch, and the Wardrobe, The, 131
Lion's Way; a Story of Men and Lions, The, 208
Little Fuzzy, 172
Little Green Men, The, 116
Little Men, The, 119
Little Monsters, The, 256
Little Myth Marker, 276
Little Pilgrim, A, 164
Little Red Captain: An Early Adventure of Captain Kettle, The, 111
Little White Bird; or, Adventures in Kensington Gardens, The, 18
Little Wizard Stories of Oz, 20
Little World of Don

Camillo, The, 96
Littlest Rebels, The, 116
Lives and Times of Jerry Cornelius, The, 151
Living Fire Menace, The, 182
Living Legend, The, 126
Living Shadow, The, 93
Llana of Gathol, 36
Log of the "Flying Fish," a Story of Aerial and Submarine Peril and Adventure, The, 51
Logan's Run, 158
Logan's Search, 158
Logan's World, 158
Lonely Astronomer, The, 80
Long ARM of Gil Hamilton, The, 158
Long Night, The, 6
"Long Odds" in: Allan's Wife and Other Tales, 97
Long Patrol, The, 126
Long Shot for Rosinante, 90
Long View, The, 38
Look Out For Space, 158
Looking Backward From the Year 2000, 179
Looking Backward, 2000-1887, 22
Looters of Tharn, 135
Lord Darcy Investigates, 87
Lord Foul's Bane, 68
Lord Kalvan of Otherwhen, 172
Lord of Blood, 219
Lord of Nightmares, 50
Lord of Terror, 107
Lord of Thunder, 160
Lord of the Apes, 172
Lord of the Green Planet, 170
Lord of the Horizon, 92
Lord of the Spiders, The, 151
Lord of the Trees, 79
Lord Tedric, 73

Lord Valentine's Castle, 195
Lords of the Crimson River, The, 135
Lords of the Serpent Land, 51
Lords of the Shadows, 121
Lords of the Starship, 89
Lore of the Witch World, 160
Lost and the Lurking, The, 228
Lost Bomb, The, 4
Lost City, The (Blaine), 25
Lost City (Garron), The, 88
Lost City of Uranus, 95
Lost Dorsai, 65
Lost Farm, The, 58
Lost Giant, The, 183
Lost in Blunderland, 132
Lost in the Milky Way, 39
Lost King of Oz, The, 19
Lost Oasis, The, 181
Lost on Jupiter, 36
Lost on the Moon, 185
Lost on Venus, 37
Lost Planet, The, 143
Lost Prince, The, 238
Lost Princess of Oz, The, 19
Lost Provinces, The, 214
Lost Road, 193
Lost Tribe, The, 10
Lost Trooper, The, 155
Lost Valley, The, 103
Lost Valley of Iskander, The, 110
Lost World, The, 69
Lost Worlds of Cronus, The, 118
Love Bug, The, 45
Love Machine, The, 51
Love 3000, 258
Lovely, 148
Loxfinger; a Thrilling Adventure of Hebrew Secret Agent Oy-Oy-7,

Israel Bond, 228
Luck of Brin's Five, The, 231
Lucky Bucky in Oz, 20
Lucky Starr and the Big Sun of Mercury, 11
Lucky Starr and the Moons of Jupiter, 11
Lucky Starr and the Oceans of Venus, 11
Lucky Starr and the Pirates of the Asteroids, 11
Lucky Starr and the Rings of Saturn, 11
Lud of Lunden, 155
Lunar Attack, 200
Lure of the Basilisk, The, 227
Lurker at the Threshold, The, 137
Lurking Fear and Other Stories, The, 138
Lust of Hate, The, 27
Lyonesse, 219
Lyonesse II: The Green Pearl, 219

Macabre Ones, The, 78
Mad Empress of Callisto, 44
Mad Eyes, 182
Mad Goblin, The, 79
Mad God's Amulet, The, 151
Mad King, The, 37
Mad Mesa, 182
Mad Scientist Affair, The, 217
Mad Scientists, 243
Madame Trinh, 14
Made in Japan, 84
Madwand, 238
Maeve, 49
Magazine of Fantasy and Science Fiction: A Thirty Year Retrospective, The, 247
Magic Ball From Mars, The, 23
Magic Bed-Knob, The, 161
Magic By the Lake, 72
Magic Goes Away, The, 265
Magic in Ithkar 2, 280
Magic Island, The, 183
Magic Labyrinth, The, 79
Magic May Return, The, 265
Magic of Oz, The, 19
Magic Pictures; More About the Wonderful Farm, The, 13
Magic Tale of Harvanger and Yolande, The, 15
Magical Mimics in Oz, The, 20
Magician, 80
Magician of Mars, The, 99
Magician's Gambit, 72
Magician's Nephew, The, 131
Magicians of Caprona, The, 117
Magick of Camelot, The, 124
Magnetic Man, The, 13
Mahogany Trimrose, 132
Maia, 2
Maiwa's Revenge, 97
Majii, The, 182
Majipoor Chronicles, 195
Major Operation, 229
Maker of Shadows, 224
Maker of Universes, The, 79
Making of the Representative for Planet 8, The, 131
Making the Stand for Old Glory, 100
Malign Fiesta, 132
Malignant Metaphysical Menace, The, 111
Mama Liz Drinks Deep, 179
Mama Liz Tastes Flesh, 179
Mammoth Hunters, The, 276
Mammoth Man, 42
Man and Monster, 168
Man From Atlantis, The, 184

Man From Moscow, The, 141
Man From S.T.U.D. in the Solid Gold Screw, The, 77
Man From S.T.U.D. Vs. the Mafia, 77
Man From U.N.C.L.E., The, 217
Man From U.N.C.L.E. and the Affair of the Gentle Saboteur, The, 218
Man of Bronze, The, 181
Man of Many Minds, 76
Man the Fugitive, 172
Man the Hunted Animal, 172
Man Who Captivated New York, The, 132
Man Who Counts, The, 6
Man Who Fell Up, 183
Man Who Mastered Time, The, 57
Man Who Rocked the Earth, The, 214
Man Who Shook the Earth, The, 182
Man Who Shook the World, The, 56
Man Who Smiled No More, The, 182
Man Who Sold Christmas, The, 132
Man Who Sold the Moon, The, 104
Man Who Upset the Universe, The, 11
Man Who Vanished Into Space; Another Adventure of the Spacecraft "Tavona" in the Great Unknown, The, 115
Man Who Was God, The, 84
Man Who Was Scared, The, 183
Man With Two Faces, The, 169
Man Without a Planet, The, 43
Man Without a Shadow, 233

Manatitlans; or, A Record of Recent Scientific Explorations in the Andean La Plata, S.A., 197
Man-Eater, The, 52
Manhounds of Antares, 33
Manhuntress, The, 164
Manifest Destiny, 134
Manitou, The, 279
Many Dimensions, 231
Many-Colored Land, The, 147
Maracot Deep, and Other Stories, The, 69
Marauders of Gor, 159
March of the Flame Marauders, 207
Marie, 97
Marigold, 5
Mark of the Red Hyena, The, 36
Mark of the Shadow, 94
Mark of the Vulture (Hogan), 106
Mark of the Vulture (Macao), 140
Marriage and the Family Through Science Fiction, 269
Marriage of Captain Kettle, The, 112
Marriage of Kettle, The, 112
Marriages Between Zones Three, Four, and Five, The, 131
Martin Magnus on Mars, 211
Martin Magnus on Venus, 211
Martin Magnus, Planet Rover, 211
Marune: Alastor 933, 219
Marvelous Land of Oz, The, 19
Mary Poppins, 214
Mary Poppins Comes Back, 214
Mary Poppins From A to Z,

214
Mary Poppins Opens the Door, 214
Mary Poppins in Cherry Tree Lane, 214
Mary Poppins in the Kitchen: A Cookery Book with a Story, 214
Mary Poppins in the Park, 214
Mask of Cthulhu, The, 137
Mask of Fu Manchu, The, 186
Mask of Mephisto & Murder by Magic, The, 93
Masked Invasion, The, 207
Masks of Scorpio, 34
Masque of Satan, 50
Masque World, 166
Master Baiter, The, 52
Master Mind of Mars, The, 36
Master Must Die, The, 80
Master of Borango, 196
Master of Broken Men, 207
Master of Evil, 198
Master of Fortune, A, 112
Master of Misfit, 164
Master of the Dark Gate, 114
Master of the Death Madness, 201
Master of the Etrax, 135
Master of the Five Magics, 100
Master of the Hashomi, 135
Master of the Moon, The, 153
Master of the Sidhe, 81
Master of the World, 223
Master Weed, The, 171
Masterful Monk, The, 70
Masters of Flux and Anchor, 45
Masters of Solitude, 90
Masters of the Lamp, 136
Masters of the Pit, The, 151
Masters of the Vortex, 198

Mathematical Magpie, The, 256
Matilda's Stepchildren, 46
Matter for Men, A, 89
Matthew Looney and the Space Pirates, 20
Matthew Looney in the Outback, 20
Matthew Looney's Invasion of the Earth, 20
Matthew Looney's Voyage to Earth, 20
Matzohball; A New Adventure of Hebrew Secret Agent Oy-Oy-7, Israel Bond, 228
Max Smart and the Ghastly Ghost Affair, 116
Max Smart and the Perilous Pellets, 116
Max Smart Loses Control, 116
Max Smart--The Spy Who Went Out to the Cold, 116
May Fair, 10
Mayday Orbit, 6
Mayenne, 215
Mayhars of Pellucidar, 37
Mazes of Scorpio, 34
Mean City, The, 124, 130
Med Series, The, 130
Medusa: A Tiger by the Tail, 45
Meet Simon Black, 200
Megiddo's Ridge, 236
Melome, 215
Memoirs of a Physician, 70, 71
Memoirs of Alcheringia, The, 69
Memoirs of Europe, Towards the Close of the Eighteenth Century, 145
Men Are Like Animals, 143
Men of War, 174
Men of War: There Will Be War Volume II, 267

Men Who Die Twice, 103
Menace of the Mutant
  Monster, 167
Menace of the Saucers, 24
Menalacor of Veltakin, 56
Mental Wizard, The, 182
Mercenaries of Gor, 159
Mercenary, 8
Mercenary, The, 174
Mercenary From Tomorrow,
  179
Merchant's War, The, 173
Merchanter's Luck, 47
Merchants of Disaster, 182
Merciless Mermaids, The, 4
Merlin's Godson, 156
Merlin's Mistake, 157
Merlin's Ring, 156
Merry Go Round in Oz, 20
Message Ends, 55
Messengers of Darkness,
  225
Messiah at the End of
  Time, A, 152
Metal Monster, The
  (Merritt), 148
Metal Monster, The
  (Robeson), 182
Metamorphosis, 205
Meteor Men, The, 113
Meteor Menace, 181
Methods of Dr. Scarlett,
  The, 123
Methuselah's Children, 104
Mexican Standoff, 84
Mezenthian Gate, The, 72
Michael. A Tale of the
  Masterful Monk, 70
Microcolony, The, 231
Micronauts, 231
Micro-Techs, The, 168
Midas Man, The, 182
Midnight at the Well of
  Souls, 45
Midnight Folk, The, 146
Midnight Murder, 184
Midsummer Tempest, 6
Midway Between, 161
Midworld, 82

Mightiest Machine, The, 42
Mighty Barbarians, The,
  269
Mighty Swordsmen, The, 269
Mike Mars and the Mystery
  Satellite, 234
Mike Mars Around the
  Moon, 234
Mike Mars, Astronaut, 234
Mike Mars at Cape
  Canaveral, 234
Mike Mars Flies the
  Dyna-Soar, 234
Mike Mars Flies the X-15,
  234
Mike Mars in Orbit, 234
Mike Mars, South Pole
  Spaceman, 234
Million Missing Maidens,
  The, 111
Mimics of Dephene, 216
Mind Brothers, The, 103
Mind Guest, 278
Mind Master, The, 111
Mind Partner and 8 Other
  Novelets From Galaxy,
  257
Mind Trap, 153
Mind Wizards of Callisto,
  44
Mind-Breaks of Space, 201
Mindshadow, 281
Mind-Twisters Affair,
  The, 217
Mindy's Mysterious
  Miniature, 58
Minnipens, The, 119
Minos of the Sardanes, 208
Miracle Monday, 144
Mirkheim, 6
Mirror of Dionysos, The,
  51
Mirror of Minds, 238
Miss Bianca, 194
Miss Bianca and the
  Bridesmaid, 194
Miss Bianca in the
  Antarctic, 194
Miss Bianca in the

Orient, 194
Miss Bianca in the Salt Mines, 194
Miss From S.I.S., The, 214
Miss Pickerell and the Geiger Counter, 142
Miss Pickerell and the Supertanker, 142
Miss Pickerell and the Weather Satellite, 142
Miss Pickerell Goes on a Dig, 142
Miss Pickerell Goes to Mars, 142
Miss Pickerell Goes to the Arctic, 142
Miss Pickerell Goes Undersea, 142
Miss Pickerell Harvests the Sea, 142
Miss Pickerell Meets Mr. H.U.M., 142
Miss Pickerell on the Moon, 142
Miss Pickerell Tackles the Energy Crisis, 142
Miss Pickerell Takes the Bull By the Horns, 142
Miss Pickerell to the Earthquake Rescue, 142
Missed it By That Much!, 116
Missing Safari, The, 88
Mission of Gravity, 49
Mission to Mars, 153
Mission to Mercury, 226
Mission to Moulokin, 82
Mission to the Moon, 62
Mistress of Death, 7
Mistress of Devil's Manor, 207
Mistress of Magic, 29
Mistress of Mistresses, 72
Mists of Doom, The, 163
Mists of Fear, The, 56
Mists of Time, The, 5
Mobsmen on the Spot, The, 93
Modern Atalantis; or, the Devil in an Air Balloon, The, 145
Mohole Menace, The, 226
Mohole Mystery, the, 226
Molt Brother, 132
Moment of the Magician, The, 82
Mondo SADISTO, 4
Monster of Metelaze, 216
Monster of the Maze, 134
Monster Wheel Affair, The, 217
Monsters, The, 181
Monstre Gai, 132
Mont Cant Gold, 81
Moominland Midwinter, 279
Moominpappa at Sea, 279
Moominsummer Madness, 279
Moominvalley in November, 279
Moon Base One, 226
Moon Express, 13
Moon in the Cloud, The, 101
Moon Magic, 82
Moon Maid, The, 37
Moon Maker, The, 214
Moon Men, The, 37
Moon Odyssey, 200
Moon of Gomrath, The, 87
Moon of Much Gladness, The, 30
Moon of Mutiny, 62
Moon of Skulls, The, 110
Moon of Three Rings, 160
Moon on an Iron Meadow, 211
Moon People, The, 49
Moon Pool, The, 148
Moon-Voyage, The, 222
Moonchild, The, 142
Moongather, 49
Moonrock, 229
Moonscatter, 49
Moorland Monster, The, 84
Mordred, 32
More Adventures of Captain Kettle, K.C.B., 112

More Adventures on Other Plants, 273
More Little Monsters, 256
More Magic, 265
More Penguin Science Fiction, 241
More Science Fiction Tales, 256
More Soviet Science Fiction, 272
More Than Melchisedech, 123
More To and Again, 31
More Wandering Stars, 252
More Women of Wonder, 269
Moreta, Dragonlady of Pern, 140
Morphodite, The, 83
Moscow Coach, 141
Mote in God's Eye, The, 174
Mother Earth, 143
Mother Goose Murders & Crime Over Casco, 93
Mother of Invention, 116
Motherlines, 47
Motion Menace, The, 182
Motor Pirate, The, 166
Mountain Monster, The, 183
Mountain of Brega, 135
Mountains of Mystery, 85
Mouse on the Moon, The, 231
Mouse on Wall St., The, 231
Mouse That Roared, The, 231
Mouse That Saved the West, The, 231
Mouthpiece of Zitu, The, 89
Mox, 93
Mr. Bass's Planetoid, 41
Mr. Kettle--Third Mate, 112
Mr. Munchausen, Being a True Account of Some of the Recent Adventures Beyond the Styx..., 17
Mr. Tompkins Explores the Atom, 86
Mr. Tompkins in Wonderland; or, Stories of C, G, & H, 86
Mr. Tompkins Inside Himself; Adventures in the New Biology, 86
Mr. Tompkins Learns the Facts of Life, 86
Mr. Wicker's Window, 60
Mudd's Angels, 203
Multiface, 3
Mummy!, 267
Mummy, The Will, and The Crypt, The, 21
Mummy Walks, The, 138
Munchausen XX, by the Baron, Being the Wondrous but Veracious Happenings Which Befell My Ancestors..., 17
Munchausen at Walcheron ... Exploits at Walcheron, the Dardanelles, Talavera, Cintra, etc., 16
Munchausen at the Pole... Together with a Correct List of the Curiosities Brought Home and Deposited in the Museum and Tower of London, 16
Munitions Master, The, 182
Munsters, The, 156
Munsters and the Great Camera Caper, The, 156
Murder and Magic, 87
Murder Melody, 181
Murder Mirage, 182
Murder on Mars, 226
Murder on Wheels, 184
Murder Trail, 93
Murgunstrumm and Others, 137
Music From Behind the Moon, 40
Musrum, 72
Mutant Weapon, The, 130

Mutants, 243
Mutants Vs. Mutants, 167
Muted Strings, 133
Mutiny in the Time
   Machine, 150
Mutiny on the Enterprise,
   204
My Enemy, My Ally, 204
My First Two Thousand
   Years, 223
My Own Fairy Book, 125
Mysterious Ambassador,
   The, 77
Mysterious Island, the,
   222
Mysterious Monoplane,
   The, 2
Mystery The, 230
Mystery at Collinwood,
   The, 188
Mystery For Mr. Bass, A,
   41
Mystery Men of Mars, The,
   48
Mystery of Arthur Gordon
   Pym, The, 173
Mystery of Dr. Fu Manchu,
   The, 186
Mystery of Khufu's Tomb,
   The, 155
Mystery of No. 1, The, 107
Mystery of the Anti, 169
Mystery of the Missing
   Corpses, The, 74
Mystery of the Sea Horse,
   The, 77
Mystery of the Snow, The,
   182
Mystery on Happy Bones,
   183
Mystery Under the Sea,
   The, 181
Mystic Mullah, The, 181
Myth Conceptions, 12
Myth Directions, 12
Myth-ing Persons, 12

Nada the Lily, 97
Nail Down the Stars, 153

Naked Sun, The, 11
Napoleons of Eridanus,
   The, 14
Narrative of Arthur
   Gordon Pym of Nan-
   tucket..., The, 173
Narrow Passage, The, 38
Natural Man; A Romance of
   the Golden Age, The, 133
Nature of the Catastro-
   phe, The, 151
Nautilus Sanction, The,
   283
Nautipuss, 4
Navigator of Rhada, The,
   90
Nearest Fire, The, 231
Nearly Neptune, 226
Nebula Alert, 46
Nebula Award Stories 10,
   263
Nebula Award Stories 11,
   263
Nebula Award Stories 16,
   264
Nebula Award Stories 17,
   264
Nebula Award Stories 18,
   264
Nebula Award Stories 19,
   264
Nebula Award Stories 8,
   263
Nebula Award Stories 9,
   263
Nebula Award Stories No.
   2, 263
Nebula Award Stories No.
   3, 263
Nebula Award Stories No.
   4, 263
Nebula Award Stories No.
   5, 263
Nebula Award Stories No.
   6, 263
Nebula Award Stories No.
   7, 263
Nebula Award Stories, 263
Nebula Winners, 12, 263

Nebula Winners, 13, 263
Nebula Winners, 14, 263
Nebula Winners, 15, 263
Necromancer, 65
Necromancer Nine, 212
Nectar of Heaven, 215
Needle, 49
Nemesis, 78
Nemesis of Evil, The, 44
Nemydia Deep, 211
Neptune One is Missing, 226
Neq the Sword, 7
Neural Atrocity, 79
Neuromancer, 89
Neutral Stars, The, 120
Neutron Star, 158
Never let Up, 144
Neveryona, or: The Tale of Signs and Cities, 62
Nevlo, 184
New Decameron; Further Tales From the Sarogossa Manuscript, The, 174
New Dimensions 1, 271
New Dimensions 2, 271
New Dimensions 3, 271
New Dimensions 4, 271
New Dimensions 5, 271
New Dimensions 6, 271
New Dimensions 7, 271
New Dimensions 8, 271
New Dimensions 9, 271
New Dimensions 10, 271
New Dimensions 11, 271
New Dimensions 12, 271
New England Resistance, The, 218
New Life For Old, 114
New Minds, The, 153
New Tales of the Cthulhu Mythos, 137
New Terrors 1, 249
New Terrors 2, 249
New Voices II, 262
New Voices III, 262
New Voices IV: The John W. Campbell Award Nominees, 262
New Voices in Science Fiction, 262
New Wizard of Oz, The, 19
New Women of Wonder, The, 269
New Worlds of Fantasy, 250
New Worlds of Fantasy No. 2, 250
New Worlds of Fantasy No. 3, 250
New Worlds Quarterly No. 1, 263
New Worlds Quarterly No. 2, 263
New Worlds Quarterly No. 3, 263
New Worlds Quarterly No. 4, 263
New Worlds Quarterly No. 5, 263
New Writings In Horror and the Supernatural #1, 272
New Writings In Horror and the Supernatural #2, 272
New Writings in SF 1, 264
New Writings in SF 2, 264
New Writings in SF 3, 264
New Writings in SF 4, 264
New Writings in SF 5, 264
New Writings in SF 6, 264
New Writings in SF 7, 264
New Writings in SF 8, 264
New Writings in SF 9, 264
New Writings in SF 10, 264
New Writings in SF 11, 264
New Writings in SF 12, 264
New Writings in SF 13, 264
New Writings in SF 14, 264
New Writings in SF 15, 264
New Writings in SF 16, 264
New Writings in SF 17, 264
New Writings in SF 18, 264
New Writings in SF 19, 264
New Writings in SF 20, 264
New Writings in SF 21, 264

New Writings in SF 22, 264
New Writings in SF 23, 264
New Writings in SF 24, 264
New Writings in SF 25, 264
New Writings in SF 26, 264
New Writings in SF 27, 264
New Writings in SF 28, 264
New Writings in SF 29, 264
New Writings in SF 30, 264
New York Necromancy, 140
Nice Day for Screaming,
   A, 193
Night Face, The, 6
Night Mare, 8
Night of the Dragonstar,
   24
Night of the Living Dead,
   The, 187
Night of the Saucers, 24
Night of the Scorpion,
   The, 107
Night of the Shadow, The,
   94
Night of the Trilobites,
   The, 113
Night Stalker, The, 180
Night Strangler, The, 180
Night Winds, 225
Night's Master, 128
Nightbirds on Nantucket, 3
Nightflyers, 247
Nightmare Begins, The, 3
Nightmare Farm, 224
Nightmare Machine, The,
   279
Nightmare on Vega 3, 111
Nightmares, 258
Nights of the Round
   Table; A Book of
   Strange Tales, 127
Nights With Uncle Remus;
   Myths and Legends of
   the Old Plantation, 101
Nightwitch Devil, The, 184
Nine Lives, 46
Nine Princes in Amber, 238
Nine Unknown, The, 155
1972 Annual World's Best
   SF, The, 274

1973 Annual World's Best
   SF, The, 274
1974 Annual World's Best
   SF, The, 274
1975 Annual World's Best
   SF, The, 274
1976 Annual World's Best
   SF, The, 274
1977 Annual World's Best
   SF, The, 274
1978 Annual World's Best
   SF, The, 273
1979 Annual World's Best
   SF, The, 273
1980 Annual World's Best
   SF, The, 273
1981 Annual World's Best
   SF, The, 273
1982 Annual World's Best
   SF, The, 273
1983 Annual World's Best
   SF, The, 273
1984, 165
1984 Annual World's Best
   SF, The, 273
1985, 165
1985 Annual World's Best
   SF, The, 273
9th Annual of the Year's
   Best S-F, 262
Ninth Galaxy Reader, The,
   257
Ninth Life, The, 224
Ninth Vibration and Other
   Stories, The, 21
No Brother, No Friend, 148
No Earthly Shore, 149
No Room for Man, 65
Noblest Experiment in the
   Galaxy, The, 215
Nomads of Gor, 159
Nonborn King, The, 147
Nor Crystal Tears, 82
Norgil the Magician, 94
Norgil: More Tales of
   Prestidigitation, 94
Norstrilia, 197
Northern Girl, The, 139
Not in Our Stars, 282

Notched Hairpin, 103
Nova 1, 259
Nova 2, 259
Nova 3, 259
Nova 4, 259
Nova Express, 37
Now To the Stars, 115
Nowhere Hunt, The, 49
Nowhere on Earth, 73
Nude in Mink, 187
Null-A Three, 220
Number Two, 175
Nunquam, 71
Nymph Island Affair, The, 214

Oak and the Ram, The, 152
Oasis, The, 56
Oath of Blood, 34
Oath of the Renunciates, 29
Oath to Mida, An, 94
October's Baby, 52
Octopus of Crime, 193
Odd Job No. 101, 92
Odds Are Murder, The, 143
Of Alien Bondage, 163
Off On a Comet!, 222
Og of the Cave People, 57
Og, Son of Og, 57
Og--Boy of Battle, 57
Og--Son of Fire, 57
Ogre, Ogre, 8
Ojo in Oz, 19
Old Friend of the Family, An, 190
Old Gods Waken, The, 228
Old Ugly Face, 155
Olga Romanoff, 95
Om: The Secret of Ahbor Valley, 155
Omega Point, The, 238
Omen, The, 164
Omen III: The Final Conflict, 164
Omen IV: Armageddon 2000, 164
Omen V: The Abomination, 164

Omens of Kregen, 277
Omicron Invasion, The, 199
Omina Uncharted, 189
Ominous Orgy, The, 111
Omnivore, 7
On a Lark to the Planets, 150
On a Pale Horse, 8
On a Torn-Away World, 185
On Alien Wings, 92
On the Boundaries of Bleakness, 100
On the Edge of the Infinite, 201
On the Heights of Himilay, 220
On the Trail of Space Pirates, 185
On the Wings of Flame, 1
One Against a Wilderness, 48
One Against Eternity, 220
One Against the Legion, 233
100 Fathoms Under, 25
100 Great Fantasy Short Short Stories, 243
100 Great Science Fiction Short Short Stories, 243
One Hundred Years of Science Fiction, 260
One is One, 176
One Tree, The, 68
One-Eye, 91
One-Eyes Mystic, 183
1,000 Year Plan, The, 11
Opener of the Way, The, 137
Operation Boudoir, 214
Operation Columbus, 226
Operation Doomsday, 119
Operation Nuke, 41
Operation Omina, 189
Operator 5 #2: The Invisible Empire, 207
Opium General, The, 151
Orbit, 260
Orbit 2, 260
Orbit 3, 260

Orbit 4, 260
Orbit 5, 260
Orbit 6, 260
Orbit 7, 260
Orbit 8, 260
Orbit 9, 260
Orbit 10, 260
Orbit 11, 260
Orbit 12, 260
Orbit 13, 260
Orbit 14, 260
Orbit 15, 260
Orbit 16, 260
Orbit 17, 261
Orbit 18, 261
Orbit 19, 261
Orbit 20, 261
Orbit 21, 261
Orbitsville, 194
Orbitsville Departure, 194
Ordeal in Otherwhere, 160
Order of the Octopus, The, 107
Orgy at Madame Dracula's, The, 77
Original Travels and Surprising Adventures of Baron Munchausen, 17
Original Travels of Baron Munchausen, The, 17
Orion, 27
Orn, 7
Oron, 197
Oron: Mosutha's Magic, 197
Oron: The Ghost Army, 197
Orphan, The, 203
Orphan Star, 82
Orphans in the Sky, 104
Other Half of the Planet, The, 42
Other Human Race, The, 172
Other Side of Time, The, 126
Other Side of the Sun, The, 42
Other World, The, 182
Other Worlds, 251
Other Worlds 1, 272

Other Worlds 2, 272
Our Girl From MEPHISTO, 4
Our Man From SADISTO, 4
Out, 148
Out of This World 1, 273
Out of This World 2, 273
Out of This World 3, 273
Out of This World 4, 273
Out of This World 5, 273
Out of This World 6, 273
Out of This World 7, 273
Out of Time's Abyss, 37
Out of the Abyss, 75
Out of the Ashes, 116
Out of the Dead City, 62
Out of the Mouth of the Dragon, 89
Out of the Silent Planet, 131
Outerworld, 247
Outlaw of Gor, 159
Outlaw World, 99
Outlaws of Mars, The, 121
Outlaws of the Moon, 99
Outpost on the Moon, 226
Outreach, 279
Outrider, The, 100
Outside the Universe, 99
Outsider and Others, The, 137
Outward Bound, 54
Outworlder, 43
Over Sea, Under Stone, 53
Over the Hump, 84
Over the Polar Ice, 1
Over the Sea's Edge, 58
Overlord of the Damned, 201
Owl Hoots Twice at Catfish Bend, The, 35
Ox, 7
Ozma of Oz, 19
Ozoplaning with the Wizard of Oz, 20

Pacific Book of Australian Science Fiction, 246
Pageant of Life, 70

Palace, The, 237
Palace of Love, The, 219
Palos of the Dog Pack, 89
Pan Sagittarius, 225
Panama Plot, The, 178
Pandora, 178
Pandora Stone, The, 95
Panzer Soldier, 190
"Paradise" Coal-Boat, and Other Stories, The, 112
Paradise Game, The, 202
Paralyzing Ray Vs. The Nuclears, The, 158
Paratime, 172
Parsival, or A Knight's Tale, 150
Parting of Arwen, The, 29
Passage to Pluto, 226
Passing of Gloria Mundy, The, 13
Passing of the Gods, The, 198
Passionate Witch, The, 199
Past Through Tomorrow, The, 104
Pastel City, The, 102
Pat Collins and the Captive Scientist, 165
Pat Collins and the Hidden Treasure, 165
Pat Collins and the Mysterious Orbiting Rocket, 165
Pat Collins and the Peculiar Dr. Brockton, 165
Pat Collins and the Secret Engine, 165
Pat Collins and the Wingless Plane, 165
Patchwork Girl of Oz, The, 19
Path of Exoterra, The, 140
Path of the Eclipse, 237
Path to Conquest, 282
Pathless Trail, The, 85
Paths of the Perambulator, The, 278
Patrimony, The, 2

Patterns of Chaos, 118
Pawn of Prophecy, 72
Pawns and Symbols, 281
Pawns of Null-A, The, 220
Pearl of Patmos, 135
Pebble in the Sky, 11
Peking Pornographer, The, 111
Pellucidar, 36
Penelope, 7
Penelope, the Damp Detective, 7
Penetrator, The, 52
Penguin Science Fiction, 241
Penultimate Adventure, The, 60
People of the Abyss, The, 75
People of the Black Circle, The, 108, 109
People of the Darkness, 224
People of the Talisman, 28
People of the Wind, The, 6
People: No Different Flash, The, 104
People That Time Forgot, The, 37
Percy, 105
Percy's Progress, 105
Peregrine: Primus, 60
Peregrine: Secundus, 60
Perelandra, 131
Perfumed Planet, The, 73
Peril in the North, 183
Peril of Barnabas Collins, The, 188
Peril of the Ice Planet, 167
Peril on Mars, 153
Peril on the Lost Planet, 143
Peril Unlimited, 170
Perilous Country, The, 55
Perry Rhodan #1: The Wasp Men Attack, 170
Perry Rhodan #2: Menace of Atomigeddon, 170

Perry Rhodan #3: Robot Threat: New York, 170
Perry Rhodan #4: In the Center of the Galaxy, 170
Perry's Planet, 204
Persian, The, 191
Persimmon Sequence, The, 85
Peter and the Atomic Valley, 150
Peter and the Flying Saucers, 150
Peter and the Moon Bomb, 150
Peter and Wendy, 18
Peter Pan and Wendy, 18
Peter Pan in Kensington Gardens, 18
Peter Pan; or, The Boy Who Would Not Grow Up, 18
Phantom and Barnabas Collins, The, 188
Phantom City, The, 181
Phantom Fighter, The, 176
Phantom Fleet, 169
Phantom Horde, 170
Phantom Shark, The, 25
Pharaoh's Ghost, The, 183
Phoenix, The, 191
Phoenix and the Carpet, The, 157
Phoenix in Obsidian, 151
Phoenix Man, The, 195
Phoenix of Megaron, 200
Phoenix Prime, 230
Phthor, 7
Pic, the Weapon-Maker, 125
Picnic on Paradise, 189
Pictures of Death, 184
Piece of Resistance, A, 73
Piece of the Action, A, 205
Pig Plantagenet, The, 7
Pilgrim of a Smile, The, 60
Pilgrimage: The Book of the People, 104

Pillar of Night, 221
Pilot Error, 41
Pimpernal Plot, The, 237
Pirate, The, 281
Pirate of the Pacific, 181
Pirate of World's End, The, 44
Pirate's Ghost, The, 182
Pirates in Oz, 19
Pirates of Gohar, 135
Pirates of Rosinante, The, 90
Pirates of Shan, The, 25
Pirates of the Air, 2
Pirates of Venus, 37
Place of Demons, The, 92
Plague of Nightmares, A, 50
Plague of Oblivion, The, 168
Plague of Silence, The, 56
Plague of Sound, The, 177
Plague Ship, 159
Plains of the Sea, The, 100
Plane Without a Pilot, The, 2
Planet Buyer, The, 197
Planet Called Krishna, A, 61
Planet Mechanica, 169
Planet Murderer, The, 164
Planet of Dread, 216
Planet of Exile, 129
Planet of Flowers, The, 161
Planet of Judgement, 203
Planet of Light, 117
Planet of No Return, 102
Planet of Peril, The, 121
Planet of Tears, The, 280
Planet of the Apes, 172
Planet of the Blind, 114
Planet of the Damned, 102
Planet of the Double Sun, The, 117
Planet of the Dying Sun, 167

Planet of the Gods, 167
Planet of Treachery, 199
Planet Poachers, The, 133
Planet Probability, 14
Planet Savers, The, 28
Planet Topside, Please Reply, 168
Planet Wizard, The, 114
Planetary Agent X, 179
Planets in Peril, 99
Planets of Peril, 201
Planned Parenthood Caper, The, 77
Plantos Affair, The, 177
Plasma Monster, 169
Platypussy, 4
Playboy Book of Horror and the Supernatural, The, 266
Playboy Book of Science Fiction and Fantasy, The, 266
Playboy Book of the Sinister and Strange, The, 266
Players of Gor, 159
Players of Hell, the, 219
Players of Null-A, The, 220
Pnume, The, 219
Poison Island, 182
Poisoned Belt, The, 69
Poisoned Mountain, The, 46
Poisoned Pen, The, 177
Poisoned Pussy, The, 83
Polar Fleet, 161
Polar Treasure, The, 181
Polaris and the Immortals, 208
Polaris of the Snows, 208
Police Patrol: 2000 A.D., 179
Police!!!, 45
Politician, 8
Polymath, 32
Pool of Fire, The, 48
Port of Peril, The, 121
Postmarked the Stars, 159
Power and the Prophet, The, 111
Power Cube Affair, The, 218
Power Key, 169
Power of the Serpent, The, 213
Power of the White Wolf, 280
Power That Preserves, The, 68
Power's Price, 169
Praetor's Dungeon, the, 155
Prelude in Prague: A Story of the War of 1938 236
Preserve and Ptotect, 70
President Fu Manchu, 186
President Kettle, 112
Pride of Chanur, The, 47
Pride of Monsters, A, 193
Pride of the Phoenix, The, 203
Priest-Kings of Gor, 159
Priestess of the Damned, 50
Prince Caspian: The Return of Narnia, 131
Prince in Waiting, The, 48
Prince of Annwn, 227
Prince of Peril, The, 121
Prince of Scorpio, 33
Prince of the Godborn, 101
Prince Prigio, 124
Prince Ricardo of Pantouflia, 125
Princess and Curdie, The, 141
Princess and the Goblin, The, 141
Princess and the Thorn, The, 81
Princess of Mars, A, 36
Princess of the Atom, The, 57
Princess of the Chamelin, A, 231
Printer's Devil, 151
Prison of Night, 215

Prisoner, The, 175
Prisoner in Fairyland, A, 24
Prisoner in the Mask, The, 229
Prisoner in the Oak, The, 29
Prisoner of Reglathium, The, 196
Prisoner of Time, 168
Prisoner of Zhamanak, The, 61
Prisoners and Pawns, 218
Prisoners in Serpent Land, 51
Prisoners of the Clouds, 2
Prisonland, 85
Private Cosmos, A, 79
Private Isle, 183
Probability Man, The, 14
Probability Pad, The, 5
Procyon's Promise, 279
Professor Challenger Stories, The, 69
Project: Earthsave, 168
Prologue to Analog, 249
Prometheus Design, the, 204
Promised Land, 202
Propeller Island, 222
Prophet, The, 3
Prophet of Fire, The, 56
Prophet of Lamath, The, 111
Protector, 158
Proud Enemy, The, 38
Prowlers of the Deep, The, 119
Pseudo One, The, 168
Psychic Detective: The Unicorn, 106
Psycho Duel, The, 169
Psychomorph, The, 201
Psychopath Plague, The, 202
Psychotechnic League, The, 6
Puck of Pook's Hill, 120
Pucky's Greatest Hour, 169

Pulsar 1, 259
Pulsar 2, 259
Pure Blood, 143
Purity Plot, The, 199
Purloined Planet, The, 43
Purloined Prince, The, 226
Purple Aces, 106
Purple Dragon, The, 183
Purple Pirate, The, 155
Purple Prince of Oz, The, 19
Purple Sapphire, The, 26
Purple Tornado, 28
Purple Zombie, The, 184
Purrfect Plunder, 164
Pursuit of Diana, The, 218
Pursuit of the House-Boat, The, 14
Pursuit of the Screamer, 64
Pursuit on Ganymede, 178

Quaking Lands, The, 221
Quark/1, 253
Quark/2, 253
Quark/3, 253
Quark/4, 253
Quartermass II, 121
Quartermass and the Pit, 121
Quartermass Experiment, The, 121
Queen Cleopatra, 155
Queen of Atlantis, A, 12
Queen of Sorcery, 72
Queen of the Black Coast, 109
Queen of the Legion, The, 233
Queen of the Secret City, The, 68
Queen of the Swords, The, 152
Queen of Zamba, The, 61
Queen's Necklace, The, 71
Quest, 247
Quest, The, 3
Quest Beyond the Stars, 99
Quest Crosstime, 159

Quest for Cush, The, 191
Quest for Simbilis, A, 219
Quest for Tanelorn, 152
Quest for the Perfect Planet, The, 115
Quest for the Well of Souls, 45
Quest for the White Witch, 128
Quest of Qalara, The, 164
Quest of Qui, 181
Quest of the DNA Cowboys, The, 79
Quest of the Dawnstar, 140
Quest of the Gypsy, 92
Quest of the Spaceways, 153
Quest of the Spider, 181, 182
Quest of the Three Worlds, 197
Quest Through Space and Time, 167
Quick Action, 45
Quiet of Stone, A, 129
Quillian Sector, The, 215

Race Across the Stars, A, 164
Racing Around the World, 1
Radiant Dome, The, 167
Radio Beasts, The, 78
Radio Boys on Secret Service Duty, 30
Radio Boys on the Mexican Border, 30
Radio Boys Search for the Incas Treasure, 30
Radio Boys Seek the Lost Atlantis, 30
Radio Boys with the Border Patrol, 30
Radio Boys with the Revenue Guards, 30
Radio Detective, The, 178
Radio Detectives, The, 223
Radio Detectives in the Jungle, The, 223
Radio Detectives Southward Bound, The, 223
Radio Detectives Under the Sea, The, 223
Radio Man, The, 78
Radio Planet, The, 78
Radioactive Camel Affair, The, 217
Raga Six, 127
Rahne, 53
Raiders of Gor, 159
Raiders of Mars, 153
Raiders of Noomas, 162
Raiders of the Lost Ark, 113
Rainbow Affair, The, 217
Rajan, 139
Ramsden, 155
Ramsong, 228
Rangers of the Universe, 127
Rape is a No-No, 77
Rape of Sun Lee Fong, The, 140
Raphael, 140
Rare Earth, 165
Rashanyn Dark, 211
Ratha's Creature, 21
Ratman's Notebooks, 89
Raxl, Voodoo Priestess, 59
RE: Colonised Planet 5: Shikasta, 131
Re-Enter Fu Manchu, 187
Real Munchausen, The, 17
Realm of the Tri-Planets, 168
Reavers of Skaith, The, 28
Rebel of Antares, 33
Rebel of Rhada, The, 90
Rebel Worlds, The, 6
Rebel's Quest, 38
Rebels of Tuglan, 167
Recruits for Arkon, 169
Rector, The, 209
Red America, 202
Red Chindvit Conspiracy, The, 106
Red Eye of Betelgeuse, The, 168
Red Fire on the Lost

Planet, 143
Red Flame Burning, 278
Red Flame of Erinpura, The, 155
Red Journey Back; A First-Hand Account of the Second and Third Martian Expeditions by the Space-Ships "Albatross" and "Comet," The, 57
Red Limit Freeway, 61
Red Men of Mars, 80
Red Menace, 93
Red Moon, 184
Red Moon and Black Mountain, 47
Red Nails, 109
Red Plague in Bolivia, 140
Red Planet, The, 48
Red Skull, The, 181
Red Snow, 182
Red Spider, The, 183
Red Terrors, The, 183
Redcap, 141
Reefs, 163
Reefs of Space, The, 173, 233
Refugee, 8
Reluctant King, The, 61
Rendezvous on a Lost World, 46
Renegade of Callisto, 44
Renegades of Kregen, 33
Renegades of the Future, 168
Rensime, 132
Repairmen of Cyclops, The, 32
Reply Paid, 103
Requiem for a Ruler of Worlds, 277
Rescue of Athena One, The, 41
Rescuers, The, 194
Rest of the Robots, The, 11
Restaurant at the End of the Universe, 1

Resurgent Dust, 23
Resurrection, 18
Resurrection Day, 182
Reteif and the Warlords, 126
Retief: Ambassador to Space, 126
Retief at Large, 126
Retief: Diplomat at Arms, 126
Retief: Emissary to the Stars, 126
Retief of the CDT, 126
Retief to the Rescue, 126
Retief Unbound, 126
Retief's Ransom, 126
Retief's War, 126
Return From Omina, 189
Return From the Dead, 114
Return From the Void, 168
Return From Witch Mountain, 120
Return of Conan, The, 108
Return of Dr. Fu-Manchu, 186
Return of Fursey, The, 225
Return of Jongor, The, 232
Return of Kai Lung, The, 30
Return of Kavin, The, 146
Return of Nathan Brazil, The, 45
Return of Star Man, The, 39
Return of Sumuru, 187
Return of Tarzan, The, 35
Return of Tharn, The, 32
Return of the Jedi, 206
Return of the King, The, 213
Return of the Living Dead, The, 187
Return of the Opium Wars, 140
Return of the Shadow, 93
Return of the Time Machine, The, 229
Return to Doomstar, 280
Return to Eddarta, 88

Return to Kaldac, 135
Return to Mars, 115
Return to Oz, 20
Return to the Lost
  Planet, 143
Return to the Stars, 99
Return to the Wonderful
  Farm, 13
Returning Creation, 154
Rev. Captain Kettle, The,
  112
Revenge of Increase
  Sewell, The, 92
Revenge of the
  Horseclans, 2
Revenge of the Manitou,
  279
Revenge of the Wizard's
  Ghost, 22
Revolt in 2100, 104
Revolt of the Galaxy, 199
Revolt of the Micronauts,
  231
Revolt On Venus, The, 185
Revolution From
  Rosinante, The, 90
Rewards and Fairies, 120
Rhapsody in Black, 202
Rhialto the Marvelous, 219
Riallaro: The Archi-
  pelago of Exiles, 210
Riddle-Master of Hed,
  The, 142
Riders of the Sidhe, The,
  81
Riding the Torch, 247
Right Hand of Extra, The,
  123
Rim Gods, The, 46
Rim of Space, The, 46
Ring of Allaire, The, 63
Ring of Fire, The, 156
Ring of Garamas, The, 177
Ring of Ikribu, The, 197
Ring-A-Ding UFOs, The, 214
Rings of Tantalus, The, 53
Ringworld, 158
Ringworld Engineers, 158
Rinkitink in Oz, 19

Rissa and Tregare, 38
Rissa Kerguelen, 38
Ritual in the Dark, 233
Rival Rigelians, The, 179
River at Green Knowe,
  The, 27
River of Eternity, 79
River of Ice, 184
River of the Dancing
  Gods, 45
Rivet in Grandfather's
  Neck, The, 40
Rivets and Sprockets, 120
Road of Kings, The, 109
Road of the Sea Horse,
  The, 6
Road to Oz, The, 19
Road to the Middle
  Islands, The, 100
Road to the Rim, The, 46
Road War, 69
Roar Devil, The, 183
Robot Invitation, The, 170
Robot Rocket, The, 185
Robots and Empire, 11
Robots, Bombs, and
  Mutants, 170
Robots of Dawn, The, 11
Robots of Saturn, 95
Robur the Conqueror, 223
Roburta the Conqueress, 4
Rocannon's World, 129
Rock City Rebels, 209
Rock of Three Planets,
  The, 133
Rocket Jumper, The, 25
Rocket Riders Across the
  Ice, 87
Rocket Riders in Stormy
  Seas, 87
Rocket Riders in the Air,
  87
Rocket Riders Over the
  Desert, 87
Rocket's Shadow, The, 25
Rogers' Rangers, 32
Rogue Dragon, 60
Rogue of Gor, 159
Rogue Planet, 200

Rogue Star, 1173 233
Rogues in the House, 109
Roman Candle, 84
Romance of Elaine, The, 177
Romance of Palombris and Pallogris, The, 15
Romance of Two Worlds, A, 54
Romanoff Jewels, The, 93
Round the Moon, 222
Round Trip Space Ship, 196
Royal Book of Oz, The, 19
Ruby Ray Mystery, The, 25
Ruins of Kaldac, The, 135
Runaway Airship, The, 2
Runes, 150
Runes of the Lyre, 147
Runestaff, The, 151
Russian Intelligence, The, 151
Russian Science Fiction, 261
Russian Science Fiction, 1968, 261
Russian Science Fiction, 1969, 261

SADISTO Royale, 4
SF 57: The Year's Greatest Science Fiction and Fantasy, 262
SF 58: The Year's Greatest Science Fiction and Fantasy, 262
SF 59: The Year's Greatest Science Fiction and Fantasy, 262
SF: 12, 262
SF: Author's Choice, 258
SF: Author's Choice 2, 259
SF: Author's Choice 3, 259
SF: Author's Choice 4, 259
SF: The Best of the Best, 262
SF: The Year's Greatest Science Fiction and Fantasy, 262
Sable Moon, The, 201
Sabotage in Space, 185
Saboteurs in A-1, 169
Saga of the Lost Earths, 170
Sailor on the Seas of Fate, The, 152
Saint Camber, 122
Saint-Germain Chronicles, The, 237
Sal's Book, 175
Salamander War, 42
Salome: The Wandering Jewess, 223
Salome: 2000 Years of Love, 223
Salute to Bazarada and Other Stories, 187
Sam Small Flies Again; The Amazing Adventures of the Flying Yorkshireman, 121
Samarkind, 64
Samarkind Dawn, 64
Samax, the Gladiator, 78
Samurai Combat, 189
Samurai Steel, 189
Sand and Satin, 187
Saragossa Manuscript; A Collection of Weird Tales, The, 173
Sargasso of Space, 159
Sargasso Ogre, The, 181
Satan Black, 183
Satan's Seed, 195
Satan's World, 6
Satana Enslaved, 163
Satanist, The, 229
Satellite City, 179
Satori, 192
Savage Empire, 135
Savage Horde, The, 3
Savage Mountains, The, 2
Savage Pellucidar, 37
Savage Scorpio, 33
Savages of Gor, 159
Savior of the Empire, 169

Scalawagons of Oz, The, 20
Scales of Justice, 51
Scarecrow of Oz, The, 19
Scarlet Lake Mystery, The, 25
Scarpante the Spy, 223
School and Society Through Science Fiction, 268
School on the Moon, 226
Science Fiction 1, 263
Science Fiction 2, 263
Science Fiction 3, 263
Science Fiction Adventures in Dimension, 252
Science Fiction Adventures in Mutation, 252
Science Fiction Hall of Fame Volume 1, 271
Science Fiction Hall of Fame Volume 2A, 271
Science Fiction Hall of Fame Volume 2B, 271
Science Fiction Hall of Fame Volume III, 271
Science Fiction of the 30s, 245
Science Fiction of the 40s, 245
Science Fiction of the 50s, 245
Science Fiction Tales, 256
Science Fiction Thinking Machines, 252
Science Fiction Through the Ages 1, 256
Science Fiction Through the Ages 2, 256
Science Fiction: The Future, 241
Science Fiction: The Future, Second Edition, 241
Science Fiction: The Great Years, 267
Science Fiction: The Great Years Vol. II, 267
Science Fictional Olympics, The, 244

Science Metropolis, 80
Scorpia Menace, 77
Screaming Dead Balloons, The, 141
Screaming Man, The, 183
Screwtape Letters, The, 131
Screwtape Proposes a Toast, and Other Pieces, 131
Sea Angel, The, 182
Sea Gold, 25
Sea Magician, The, 182
Sea Priestess, The, 82
Seagoing Tank, The, 199
Seal of John Solomon, The, 21
Search, 229
Search for Ka, The, 88
Search For the Sun, 118
Search for Zei, The, 61
Search of Mavin Manyshaped, The, 212
Second Avon Fantasy Reader, The, 274
Second Book of Fritz Leiber, the, 253
Second Book of Omni Science Fiction, The, 253
Second Book of Swords, The, 190
Second Flight of the Starfire, The, 154
Second Foundation, 11
Second Galaxy Reader of Science Fiction, 257
Second Isaac Asimov Double, A, 11
Second Jungle Book, The, 120
Second Kingdom, The, 138
Second Leopard, The, 124
Second Nature, 231
Second Pacific Book of Science Fiction, The, 246
Second Part of Armata, The, 75

Second Part of the Abbey of Kilkhampton, The, 57
Second Seal, the, 229
Second Stage Lensman, 198
Second War of the Worlds, The, 199
Second World of If, The, 268
Secret Agent of Terra, 32
Secret Barrier X, 167
Secret City: A Romance of the Karroo, the, 68
Secret Memoirs and Manners of Several Persons of Quality of Both Sexes From the New Atalantis, an Island in the Mediterranean, 144
Secret Mission: Moluk, 169
Secret of Barnabas Collins, The, 188
Secret of Bigfoot Pass, The, 41
Secret of Red Skull, The, 203
Secret of Sinharat, The, 28
Secret of the Lost Planet, 143
Secret of the Runestaff, The, 151
Secret of the Sixth Magic, 100
Secret of the Sky, The, 181
Secret of the Su, The, 184
Secret of the Time Vault, 167
Secret Scorpio, 33
Secret Sisterhood, 179
Secret Under Antarctica, 64
Secret Under the Caribbean, 64
Secret Under the Sea, 64
Section G: United Planets, 179
Sector General, 230

Seed of Stars, 120
Seedbearers, The, 213
Seeds of Frenzy, The, 73
Seeds of Ruin, 169
Seeking Sword, The, 118
Seeking the Mythical Future, 110
Seetee Alert!, 216
Seetee Ship, 233
Seetee Shock, 233
Seg the Bowman, 34
Sentenced to Prism, 278
Sentinel, The, 191
Sentinels of Solitude, 170
Sequel to the Adventures of Baron Munchausen..., 16
Serpent, The, 88
Servants of the Skull, 193
Servants of the Wankh, 219
Seth Papers, The, 127
Seven Agate Devils, The, 182
Seven Alters of Dusarra, The, 227
7 Cardinal Virtues of Science Fiction, The, 243
7 Deadly Sins of Science Fiction, The, 243
Seven Magical Jewels of Ireland, The, 2
Seven Sins, 187
Seven Stars for Catfish Bend, 35
Seventeen Thieves of El-Kalil, The, 155
7th Annual of the Year's Best S-F, 262
Seventh Galaxy Reader, The, 257
Seventh Gate, The, 101
Several Minds, The, 153
Severed Hand, The, 127
Sex Diary of Gerard Sorme, The, 233
Sex Machine, The (Conway), 52
Sex Machine (Geis), The,

88
Sex-Ray, The, 4
Sgt. Robot, 169
Shaara's Exile, 29
Shade of Difference, A, 70
Shadow and the Golden Master, The, 93
Shadow and the Voice of Murder, The, 93
Shadow Beware, 94
Shadow Girl, The, 57
Shadow Go Mad, 94
Shadow Laughs!, The 93
Shadow Lord, 204
Shadow Magic, 235
Shadow of All Night Falling, A, 52
Shadow of Doom, 56
Shadow of Fu Manchu, The, 186
Shadow of the Mutant Master, 168
Shadow of the Swan, 235
Shadow of the Torturer, The, 234
Shadow of the Wolf, 106
Shadow on the Earth, The, 70
Shadow on the Sea, The, 167
Shadow on the Stones, 138
Shadow on the Sun, The, 101
Shadow Out of Time and Other Tales of Horror, The, 138
Shadow Over Innsmouth, The, 137
Shadow Singer, 22
Shadow Strikes, The, 93
Shadow's Revenge, The, 94
Shadow's Shadow, The, 93
Shadowed Millions, 93
Shadowline, 53
Shadows (Sherman), 195
Shadows (Grant), 257
Shadows, 2, 257
Shadows, 3, 257
Shadows, 4, 257

Shadows, 5, 258
Shadows, 6, 258
Shadows, 7, 258
Shadows Attack, The, 169
Shadows Linger, 53
Shadows of Doom, 142
Shadows of Sanctuary, 12, 244
Shadows Out of Hell, 163
Shaggy Man of Oz, The, 20
Shaggy Planet, 91
Shai's Destiny, 226
Shallows of Night, 220
Shape Changer, The, 127
Shape of Terror, The, 183
Shapechangers, 180
Shardik, 2
Shattered Chain, The, 28
Shattered Stars, 141
Shawl of Solomon, The, 21
She, 97
She and Allan, 97
Sheep Look Up, 32
Ship From Atlantis, The, 156
Ship From Outside, The, 46
Ship That Sailed the Time Stream, The, 73
Ships of Durostorum, The, 33
Ships of Tarshish, Being a Sequel to the "Wandering Jew," The, 209
Shon'Jir, 47
Shriveling Murders, The, 239
Shrouded Planet, The, 87, 195
Shrouded Walls of Borango, The, 196
Shuna and the Lost Tribe, 120
Shuna, White Queen of the Jungle, 120
Shuttered Room and Other Pieces, The, 137
Shy Leopardess, 18
Si-Fan Mysteries, The, 186
Sibyl Sue Blue, 32

Sideshow, 178
Siege of Earth, 80
Sign at Six, The, 230
Sign of the Moonbow, 163
Sign of the Mute Medusa, The, 226
Sign of the Raven, The, 6
Sign of the Seven Seas, The, 60
Sign of the Unicorn, The, 238
Silence is Deadly, 23
Silence of Gom, The, 168
Silent Bullet, The, 177
Silent Death, The, 93
Silent Seven, 93
Silent Watcher, The, 207
Silmarillion, The, 213
Silver Chair, The, 131
Silver Crown, The, 187
Silver on the Tree, 53
Silver Princess in Oz, The, 20
Silver Skull, The, 59
Silver Stallion, The, 40
Silver Sun, The, 201
Silver Warriors, The, 151
Silverfinger, 84
Silverthorn, 80
Simon Black and the Spacemen, 200
Simon Black at Sea, 200
Simon Black in China, 200
Simon Black in Coastal Command, 200
Simon Black in Peril, 200
Simon Black in Space, 200
Simon Black in the Antarctic, 200
Simon Black Takes Over, 200
Sin Funnel, The, 4
Sing For Your Supper, 84
Singular Adventures of Baron Munchausen, The, 17
Singular Adventures of Baron Munbchausen, The, 17

Singular Travels, Campaigns, Voyages, and Sporting Adventures of Baron Munnikhouson, Commonly Pronounced Munchausen, 15
Singular Travels, Campaigns, and Adventures of Baron Munchausen, 17
Sinister Madonna, 187
Sinister Power, The, 170
Sinister Scourge, 193
Sins of Sumuru, 187
Sirian Experiments: Report By Ambien II of the Five, The, 131
Six of Swords, The, 69
6th Annual of the Year's Best S-F, 262
Sixth Galaxy Reader, The, 257
69 Pleasures, The, 83
Skeleton Closet of Jules deGrandin, The, 176
Skin Game Dame, 83
Skinner, 141
Skirmish, 280
Skull-Face and Others, 137
Skull of Kanaima, The, 161
Skulls in the Stars, 110
Sky Buddies, The, 55
Sky Pirates of Callisto, 44
Sky Walker, The, 184
Skylark DuQuesne, 198
Skylark of Space, 198
Skylark of Valeron, 198
Skylark Three, 198
Skyprobe, 141
Slave Girl of Gor, 159
Slave Market of Mucar, The, 77
Slave of Sarma, 134
Slave Ship From Sergan, 216
Slaves of Reglathium, The, 196
Slaves of Sumuru, 187

Slaves of the Lamp, 84
Slaves of Venus, The, 39
Sleep, The, 56
Sleepers, The, 169
Sleeping Dragon, The, 187
Sleeping Sorceress, The, 152
Slow Fall to Dawn, 129
Smiling Dogs, The, 184
Smire, 40
Smirt, 40
Smith, 40
Smith Minor on the Moon, 101
Smog, The, 56
Smuggler's Reef, 25
Snakegod, 92
Snares of Ibex, The, 49
Snarkout Boys and the Avocado of Death, The, 171
Snarkout Boys and the Baconburg Horror, The, 171
Snow Queen, 224
Snowman in Flames, 167
So Long, and Thanks For All the Fish, 1
So You Want to Be a Wizard?, 70
Social Gangster, The, 177
Social Problems Through Science Fiction, 269
Sociology Through Science Fiction, 269
Sock It To Me, Zombie!, 77
Soft Whisper of the Oxrun Dead, The, 278
Softly By Moonlight, 78
Solar Assassins, 168
Solar Invasion, The, 99
Soldier, Ask Not, 65
Soldier of Fortune, 191
Solid Gold Kidnapping, The, 41
Solomon Kane, 110
Solomon's Quest, 21
Some Summer Lands, 88
Some Women of the University, 26
Something About Eve, 40
Something Near, 137
Somewhere in the Night, 151
Somewhere Out There, 78
Son of a Witch, 52
Son of Tarzan, The, 35
Son of the Flying Tiger, 140
Son of the Stars, 117
Son of the White Wolf, 110
Son of Ti-Coyo, 180
Song of Homana, The, 180
Song of Mavin Manyshaped, The, 212
Song of Rhiannon, The, 227
Song of Sorcery, 192
Song of the Axe, The, 232
Sonic Slave, 119
Sons of Satan, 56
Sons of the Bear-God, 165
Sorak and the Clouded Tiger, 180
Sorak and the Sultan's Ankus, 180
Sorak and the Tree-Men, 180
Sorak of the Malay Jungle, 180
Sorcerer of the Castle, The, 207
Sorcerer's Amulet, 151
Sorcerer's Apprentice, The, 76
Sorcerer's Blood, 49
Sorcerer's Shadow, The, 197
Sorcerer's Skull, The, 221
Sorceress of Qar, The, 230
Sorceress of Rome, The, 86
Sorceress of the Witch World, 160
Sorcery 1: The Shamutanti Hills, 113
Sorcery 2: Khare--City-port of Traps, 113
Sorcery 3: The Seven Serpents, 114

Sorcery 4: The Crown
    Kings, 114
Sorrowing Vengeance, 198
Sorry, Chief..., 116
SOS From Mars, 57
S.O.S. From Three Worlds,
    129
SOS: Spaceship Titan, 168
Sos the Rope, 7
Soul of Melicent, The, 40
Soul of the City, 276
Soul Scar, The, 178
Soul-Singer of Tyrnos, 147
Soul Stealers, The, 111
Sound of Midnight, The, 92
Source of Magic, The, 8
South of the Bordello, 83
South Pole Terror, The,
    183
Soviet Science Fiction,
    272
Space 1, 253
Space 2, 253
Space Agent and the
    Ancient Peril, 143
Space Agent and the Isles
    of Fire, 143
Space Agent From the Lost
    Planet, 143
Space Ark, The, 133
Space Barbarians, The, 90
Space Cat, 213
Space Cat and the
    Kittens, 213
Space Cat Meets Mars, 213
Space Cat Visits Venus,
    213
Space Circus, The, 177
Space Eagle; Operation
    Doomsday, 166
Space Eagle; Operation
    Star Voyage, The, 166
Space For Hire, 158
Space Guardians, The, 200
Space Lords, 197
Space Mail, 243
Space Mail Vol. II, 243
Space Mavericks, The, 122
Space Mercenaries, 46

Space Merchants, The, 173
Space Pioneers, 265
Space Pioneers, The, 185
Space Pirates, 73
Space Platform, 129
Space Police, 265
Space Prison, 90
Space Puppet, 171
Space Service, 265
Space Ship in the Park,
    The, 196
Space Ship Returns to the
    Apple Tree, The, 196
Space Ship Under the
    Apple Tree, The, 196
Space Tug, 129
Space War, 117
Space-Jackers, The, 201
Spacehawk, Inc., 91
Spacepaw, 64
Spaceship For the King,
    A, 174
Spaceship of Ancestors,
    168
Spaceship Returns, The,
    134
Spaceship to Planet Veta,
    91
Spaceship to Saturn, 226
Spacial Delivery, 64
Spacious Adventures of
    the Man in the Street,
    The, 163
Spartan Planet, 46
Spawn of Laban, 216
Spawn of the Death
    Machine, The, 230
Spawn of the Winds, 139
Speaking Stone, The, 183
Specter!, 268
Spectrum, 241
Spectrum 2, 241
Spectrum 3, 241
Spectrum 4, 241
Spectrum 5, 241
Spectrum of a Forgotten
    Sun, 215
Speedy in Oz, 19
Spell for Chameleon, A, 8

Spell of the Sorcerer's Skull, 22
Spell of the Witch World, 160
Spell Sword, The, 28
Spellcoats, The, 117
Spells, 244
Spellsinger, 82
Sphereland; A Fantasy About Curved Spaces, 1
Spider Strikes, The, 201
Spiders' War, 236
Spirit of Dorsai, The, 65
Spirits of Flux and Anchor, 45
Splinter of the Mind's Eye, 206
Splintered Sunglasses Affair, The, 217
Split Infinity, 8
Spock, Messiah!, 203
Spock Must Die!, 203
Spook Hole, 182
Spook Legion, The, 181
Spoor of the Antis, 169
Spot of Life, The, 98
Spotted Men, The, 183
Sprockets, a Little Robot, 120
Spy Who Came in From the Copa, The, 41
Spy With the Blue Kazoo, The, 41
Spybot!, 168
Squaring the Circle, 100
Squeaking Goblin, The, 182
Stainless Steel Rat, The, 102
Stainless Steel Rat for President, The, 102
Stainless Steel Rat is Born, A, 102
Stainless Steel Rat Saves the World, The, 102
Stainless Steel Rat Wants You!, 102
Stainless Steel Rat's Revenge, The, 102
Stairway to Danger, 25

Stalkers, The, 69
Stand By For Mars!, 185
Stand on Zanzibar, 32
Star Ancored, Star Angered, 74
Star Barbarian, 219
Star Born, 159
Star City, 34
Star Courier, 46
Star Diaries, The, 130
Star Fighters, 149
Star Force, 149
Star Healer, 230
Star Hunters, 49
Star Ka'at, 161
Star Ka'at World, 161
Star Ka'ats and the Planet People, 161
Star Ka'ats and the Winged Invaders, 161
Star King, 219
Star Kings, The, 99
Star Light, 49
Star Maker, 203
Star Mill, The, 170
Star of Danger, 28
Star of Doom, 197
Star of Stars, 266
Star Prince Charlie, 6, 64
Star Quest, 149
Star Rebel, 38
Star Riders of Ren, 149
Star Rogue, 43
Star Science Fiction Stories, 266
Star Science Fiction Stories, No. 2, 266
Star Science Fiction Stories, No. 3, 266
Star Science Fiction Stories, No. 4, 266
Star Science Fiction Stories, No. 5, 266
Star Science Fiction Stories, No. 6, 266
Star Search, 118
Star Short Novels, 266
Star Slaver, 164
Star Surgeon, 229

Star Trek, 204
Star Trek 2, 204
Star Trek 3, 204
Star Trek 4, 204
Star Trek 5, 204
Star Trek 6, 205
Star Trek 7, 205
Star Trek 8, 205
Star Trek 9, 205
Star Trek 10, 205
Star Trek 11, 205
Star Trek 12, 205
Star Trek II: The Wrath of Khan, 204
Star Trek III: The Search For Spock, 204
Star Trek Log Eight, 205
Star Trek Log Five, 205
Star Trek Log Four, 205
Star Trek Log Nine, 205
Star Trek Log One, 205
Star Trek Log Seven, 205
Star Trek Log Six, 205
Star Trek Log Ten, 205
Star Trek Log Three, 205
Star Trek Log Two, 205
Star Trek: Mission to Horatius, 203
Star Trek: The Motion Picture, 204
Star Trek: The New Voyages, 205
Star Trek: The New Voyages, vol. 2, 205
Star Wars, 206
Star Well, 166
Star Wolf!, 230
Starboy, 23
Starbrat, 153
Starchild, 173, 233
Starcross, 117
Stardreamer, 197
Stardrift, 153
Starfishers, 53
Starfollowers of Coramonde, The, 59
Starkhan of Rhada, The, 90
Starless Realm, The, 169
Starless World, The, 203

Starlight Barking, The, 198
Starquake, 278
Starrigger, 61
Stars Are Ours!, The, 159
Stars' End, 53
Stars in Shroud, The, 22
Stars, Like Dust, The, 11
Stars Scream Murder, The, 178
Starship, 6
Starship Sapphire, 164
Starsilk, 220
Starworld, 102
Station of the Invisibles, 170
Stealer of Souls, and Other Stories, The, 152
Steel Tsar, The, 152
Steel of Rathskar, The, 88
Stellar #1, 254
Stellar #2, 254
Stellar #3, 254
Stellar #4, 254
Stellar #5, 254
Stellar #6, 254
Stellar #7, 254
Stellar Short Novels, 254
Sten, 50
Step to the Stars, 62
Stiff Proposition, A, 52
Stingray, 212
Stingray and the Monster, 212
Stockholders in Death, 184
Stolen Continent, The, 195
Stolen Lake, The, 3
Stolen Planet, The, 146
Stolen Spacefleet, The, 169
Stolen Sun, The, 170
Stone in Heaven, A, 6
Stone Man, The, 183
Stone-Cold Dead in the Market Affair, The, 218
Stories from Doctor Death, 239
Storm Lord, The, 128
Storm of Wings, A, 102

Storm Over Vallia, 34
Storm Over Warlock, 160
Storm Season, 12, 244
Stormbringer, 152
Stormqueen, 28
Story of Doctor Doolittle, The, 134
Story of the Amulet, The, 157
Stowaway to the Mushroom Planet, 41
Strange Conflict, 229
Strange Conflict, A, 19
Strange Discovery, A, 173
Strange Encounters, 247
Strange Papers of Dr. Blayre, The, 26
Strange Paradise, 59
Strange People, A, 19
Strange Tomorrow, 118
Stranger at Green Knowe, A, 27
Strangers at Collins House, 188
Strangler's Moon, 198
Straws and Prayer-Books, 40
Submarine Mystery, The, 182
Subspace Encounter, 198
Subspace Explorers, 198
Subterfuge, 144
Sugar in the Air, 125
Summer Birds, The, 78
Summerfair, 64
Sumuru, 187
Sunburst, 54
Sundered Realm, The, 221
Sunless World, The, 117
Suns of Scorpio, The, 33
Sunset Warrior, The, 220
Sunstrike, 141
'Super Nova' and the Frozen Man, 143
'Super Nova' and the Rogue Satellite, 143
Supermen, 244
Supermen of Alpha, 38
Supermind, 87, 115

Surprising Adventures... Miraculous Escapes, and Wonderful Voyages... of the Renowned Baron Munchausen..., The, 16
Surprising Adventures of Baron Munchausen, The, 16
Surprising Adventures of Baron Munchausen, The, 17
Surprising Adventures of Baron Munchausen, The, 17
Surprising Adventures of the Renowned Baron Munchausen Abridged..., The, 16
Surprising Travels and Adventures of Baron Munchausen..., The, 16
Survivor, 115
Survivor and Others, The, 137
Survivors, The (Bradley & Zimmer), 29, 238
Survivors (Godwin), The, 90
Survivors, The (Sibson), 195
Suspension, 78
Swamp Rats, The, 77
Swan Song, 202
Sweat of Fear, The, 63
Swiftly Tilting Planet, A, 130
Sword and Sorceress I, 248
Sword and Sorceress II, 248
Sword and the Chain, the, 187
Sword and the Stallion, The, 152
Sword for Kregen, A, 33
Sword For the Empire, 124
Sword in the Stone, The, 230
Sword of Aldones, The, 28
Sword of Calandra, The, 63

378

Sword of Chaos, 29
Sword of Conan, The, 108
Sword of Fire, 278
Sword of Forebearance, 282
Sword of Morning Star, The, 147
Sword of Poyana, 14
Sword of Shannara, The, 31
Sword of Skelos, The, 109
Sword of the Bheleu, The, 227
Sword of the Dawn, The, 151
Sword of the Gael, 163
Sword of the Horseclans, The, 2
Sword of the Lamb, 235
Sword of the Lictor, The, 234
Sword of the Nurlingas, 14
Sword of the Spirits, The, 48
Sword Swallower, The, 91
Swords Against Darkness, 265
Swords Against Darkness II, 265
Swords Against Darkness III, 265
Swords Against Darkness IV, 265
Swords Against Darkness V, 265
Swords Against Death, 129
Swords Against Wizardry, 129
Swords and Deviltry, 129
Swords and Ice Magic, 129
Swords in the Mist, 129
Swords of Lankhmar, The, 129
Swords of Mars, 36
Swordships of Scorpio, 33
Swordsman of Mars, The, 121
Swordsmistress of Chaos, 121
Symbol of Terra, 215
Synoptic Manhunt, 79

Synthetic Men of Mars, 36

T Zero, 41
Tactics of Mistake, 65
Tahara Among African Tribes, 194
Tahara, Boy King of the Desert, 194
Tahara, Boy Mystic of India, 194
Tahara in the Land of Yucatan, 194
Taking of Satcon Station, The, 50
Tale of Three Lions, A, 97
Tale of Two Clocks, A, 193
Tales From Moominvalley, 279
Tales From the Travels of Baron Munchausen, 17
Tales From the Vulgar Unicorn, 12, 244
Tales of Chinatown, 187
Tales of Conan, 108
Tales of East and West, 187
Tales of Known Space, 158
Tales of Neveryon, 62
Tales of the Cthulhu Mythos, 137
Tales of the Horseclans, 2
Tales of the Werewolf Clan I: In the Tomb of the Bishop, The, 156
Tales of the Werewolf Clan II: The Master Goes Home, 156
Tales of the Wonder Club, 70
Tales of the Wonder Club, Volume 2, 70
Talking Devil, The, 183
Tall Stories, The, 277
Talons of Scorpio, 34
Tama of the Light Country, 58
Tama, Princess of Mercury, 58
Taming Power; The First

Qhe Adventure, The, 26
Tanar of Pellucidar, 36
Tapiola's Brave Regiment, 157
Tar-Aiym Krang, The, 82
Tar-Baby, and Other Rhymes of Uncle Remus, The, 101
Taran Wanderer, 4
Target Star, 169
Target: Terra, 115
Tarnsman of Gor, 159
Tartarus Incident, The, 95
Tarzan and the Abominable Snowman, 36
Tarzan and the Ant Men, 35
Tarzan and the Castaways, 36
Tarzan and the Cave City, 36
Tarzan and the City of Gold, 35
Tarzan and the Forbidden City, 36
Tarzan and the Foreign Legion, 36
Tarzan and the Golden Lion, 35
Tarzan and the Jewels of Opar, 35
Tarzan and the Leopard Men, 36
Tarzan and the Lightning Man, 36
Tarzan and the Lion Man, 35
Tarzan and the Lost Empire, 35
Tarzan and the Lost Safari, 36
Tarzan and the Madman, 36
Tarzan and the Silver Globe, 36
Tarzan and the Snake People, 36
Tarzan and the Tarzan Twins with Jad-Bal-Ja, the Golden Lion, 35
Tarzan and the Valley of Gold, 36
Tarzan and the Winged Invaders, 36
Tarzan at the Earth's Core, 35, 37
Tarzan, Lord of the Jungle, 35
Tarzan of the Apes, 35
Tarzan the Invincible, 35
Tarzan the Magnificent, 36
Tarzan the Terrible, 35
Tarzan the Untamed, 35
Tarzan Triumphant, 35
Tarzan Twins, The, 35
Tarzan's Quest, 36
Tas and the Postal Rocket, 74
Tas and the Space Machine, 74
Taste for Honey, A, 103
Taste for Murder, A, 103
Taste of Armageddon, A, 205
Tears of the Singers, The, 204
Technos, 215
Teen-Age Outer Space Stories, 257
Teen-Age Science Fiction Stories, 257
Teen-Age Space Adventures, 257
Teeth of the Dragon, 93
Telsa Raiders, The, 28
Telzey Toy, The, 193
Temple of the Dead, The, 161
Temple of the Sun, The, 277
Temple of Truth, The, 215
Temples of Ayocan, The, 135
Tempting Fate, 237
Ten Ton Snakes, The, 183
10th Annual of the Year's Best S-F, 262
Tenth Galaxy Reader, The, 257
Tenth Planet, The, 99

Terra Data, The, 215
Terra SF, 265
Terra SF II, 265
Terraces of Night, Being Further Chronicles of the "Club of the Round Table," The, 127
Terrible Ten, The, 111
Terridae, The, 215
Terror, The, 56
Terror By Satellite, 226
Terror in the Navy, The, 182
Terrors, 258
Tery, The, 247
Testing of Tertius, The, 157
Texas Run, The, 218
Thanks to Claudius, 128
That Hideous Strength, 131
That Man on Beta, 33
Their Island Home, 223
Themes in Science Fiction, 260
Thendara House, 29
There is Another Heaven, 157
There Were No Asper Ladies, 11
There Were Two Pirates, 40
There Will Be War, 174, 267
These Charming People, 10
They Died Twice, 183
They Shall Have Stars, 26
Thief of Llarn, 83
Thief of Thoth, The, 43
Thieves' World, 12, 244
Thing of the Past, A, 80
Thinking Machine Affair, The, 218
Thinking Machines, 243
Thinking Seat, The, 211
Third Book of Swords, The, 190
Third Flight of the Starfire, The, 154
Third Galaxy Reader, The, 257

Third Isaac Asimov Double, The, 11
Third Omni Book of Science Fiction, The, 253
This Darkening Universe, 23
This Drakotny, 141
This Star Shall Abide, 75
This World is Taboo, 130
Thongor Against the Gods, 43
Thongor and the Dragon City, 43
Thongor and the Wizard of Lemuria, 43
Thongor at the End of Time, 43
Thongor Fights the Pirates of Tarakus, 43
Thongor in the City of Magicians, 43
Thongor of Lemuria, 43
Thora's Sacrifice, 168
Thorn, 190
Thousand Coffins Affair, The, 217
Thousand-Headed Man, The, 181
Thousand Shrine Warrior, 191
Thousand Years a Minute, A, 48
Thousandstar, 7
Thrall of Hypno, The, 167
Three Against the Witch World, 160
Three-Bladed Doom, 110
Three-Eyes, 91
Three Faces of Time, 148
Three Gold Crowns, 184
Three Hainish Novels, 129
Three Hearts and Three Lions, 6
Three Inquisitive People, 229
Three-Legged Hootch Dancer, The, 178
Three-Seated Space Ship,

The, 196
Three to Dorsai!, 65
Three Wild Men, The, 183
Threshold of the Stars, 22
Throne of Madness, The, 209
Through Space to Mars, 185
Through Space to the Planets, 127
Through the Air to the North Pole, 185
Through the Dark Curatin, 192
Through the Eye of the Needle (Clement), 49
Through the Eye of the Needle (Howells), 110
Through the Eyes of Time, 110
Through the Looking-Glass, and What Alice Found There, 43
Through the Sun in an Airship, 146
Thunder Dragon Gate, the, 155
Thunder of Hell, 276
Thunder of Stars, A, 120
Thunderbirds, 212
Thunderbirds Are Go, 212
Thunderbirds Ring of Fire, 212
Thunderbolt and the Rebel Planet, 164
Thunderbolt of the Spaceways, 164
Thurb Revolution, The, 166
Thuvia, Maid of Mars, 36
Ti-Coyo and His Shark; An Immoral Fable, 180
Ticket That Exploded, The, 37
Tides of Kregen, The, 33
Tiger River, 85
Tigerman of Terrahpur, The, 127
Tigers and Traitors, 222
Tigris leaps, The, 168
Tik-Tok of Oz, 19

Time and Mr. Bass, 41
Time and Space, 41
Time and the Gods, 71
Time and the Hunter, 41
Time Bender, The, 126
Time Bomb, 216
Time Enough For Love, 104
Time Factor, 189
Time Fighters, The, 201
Time for Dying, A, 121
Time Garden, The, 72
Time Gladiator, 179
Time Machine, The, 229
Time Machine II, The, 229
Time Machine to the Rescue, 150
Time Masters, The, 216
Time of Ghosts, A, 121
Time of the Annihilator, The, 154
Time of the Dark, The, 98
Time Patrolman, 7
Time Slip, 130
Time Terror, The, 183
Time Traders, The, 159
Time Trap, 39
Time Trap Gambit, The, 144
Time Trap of Ming XIII, The, 177
Time Travelers Strictly Cash, 185
Time Tunnel, The, 130
Time Twister, The, 144
Time Warps, 244
Time Window, 38
Time's Dark Laughter, 118
Time's Last Gift, 79
Time's Lonely One, 168
Timekeeper, The, 18
Timekeeper Conspiracy, The, 237
Timepiece, 14
Timepit, 14
Timepivot, 14
Tin Woodman of Oz, The, 19
Titan, 221
Titus Alone, 166
Titus Groan, 166
To and Again, 31

To Arkon!, 168
To Catch a Rat, 13
To Control the Stars, 107
To Demons Bound, 221
To Die in Italbar, 238
To Dream of Evil, 51
To Escape the Stars, 107
To Keep the Ship, 46
To Kill a Corpse, 11
To Kill a Shadow, 69
To Outer Space, 115
To Play the Devil, 98
To Prime the Pump, 46
To Russia with L.U.S.T., 83
To Sail the Century Sea, 73
To the Devil--A Daughter, 229
To the Sun? A Journey Through Planetary Space, 222
To Worlds Unknown, 115
To Your Scattered Bodies Go, 79
Told by Uncle Remus: New Stories of the Old Plantation, 101
Tom Hale, Space Detective, 226
Tom Swift (Jr.) and His Aquatomic Tracker, 9
Tom Swift (Jr.) and His Atomic Earth Blaster, 9
Tom Swift (Jr.) and His Cosmotron Express, 10
Tom Swift (Jr.) and His Deep-Sea Hydrodome, 9
Tom Swift (Jr.) and His Diving Seacopter, 9
Tom Swift (Jr.) and His Dyna-4 Capsule, 10
Tom Swift (Jr.) and His Electronic Retroscope, 9
Tom Swift (Jr.) and His Flying Lab, 9
Tom Swift (Jr.) and His Giant Robot, 9
Tom Swift (Jr.) and His G-Force Inverter, 10
Tom Swift (Jr.) and His Jetmarine, 9
Tom Swift (Jr.) and His Megascope Space Prober, 9
Tom Swift (Jr.) and His Outpost in Space, 9
Tom Swift (Jr.) and His Polar-Ray Dynasphere, 10
Tom Swift (Jr.) and His Repelatron Skyway, 9
Tom Swift (Jr.) and His Rocket Ship, 9
Tom Swift (Jr.) and His Sonic Boom Trap, 10
Tom Swift (Jr.) and His Spectromarine Selector, 9
Tom Swift (Jr.) and His Subocean Geotron, 10
Tom Swift (Jr.) and His 3-D Telejector, 10
Tom Swift (Jr.) and His Triphibian Atomicar, 9
Tom Swift (Jr.) and His Ultrasonic Cycloplane, 9
Tom Swift (Jr.) and the Asteroid Pirates, 9
Tom Swift (Jr.) and the Captive Planetoid, 10
Tom Swift (Jr.) and the Cosmic Astronauts, 9
Tom Swift (Jr.) and the Electronic Hydrolung, 9
Tom Swift (Jr.) and the Galaxy Ghosts, 10
Tom Swift (Jr.) and the Mystery Comet, 10
Tom Swift (Jr.) and the Visitor From Planet X, 9
Tom Swift (Jr.) in His Space Solartron, 9
Tom Swift (Jr.) in the Caves of Nuclear Fire, 9
Tom Swift (Jr.) in the Race to the Moon, 9
Tom Swift (Jr.) on the Phantom Satellite, 9

Tom Swift Among the
 Diamond Makers, 8
Tom Swift Among the Fire
 Fighters, 9
Tom Swift and His Aerial
 Warship, 9
Tom Swift and His Air
 Glider, 8
Tom Swift and His Air
 Scout, 9
Tom Swift and His Airline
 Express, 9
Tom Swift and His
 Airship, 8
Tom Swift and His Big
 Dirigible, 9
Tom Swift and His Big
 Tunnel, 9
Tom Swift and His Chest
 of Secrets, 9
Tom Swift and His
 Electric Locomotive, 98
Tom Swift and His
 Electric Rifle, 8
Tom Swift and His
 Electric Runabout, 8
Tom Swift and His Flying
 Boat, 9
Tom Swift and His Giant
 Cannon, 9
Tom Swift and His Giant
 Magnet, 9
Tom Swift and His Giant
 Oil Gusher, 9
Tom Swift and His Great
 Searchlight, 9
Tom Swift and His House
 on Wheels, 9
Tom Swift and His
 Motor-Boat, 8
Tom Swift and His
 Motor-Cycle, 8
Tom Swift and His Ocean
 Airport, 9
Tom Swift and His Photo
 Telephone, 9
Tom Swift and His Planet
 Stone, 9
Tom Swift and His Sky
 Train, 9
Tom Swift and His
 Submarine-Boat, 8
Tom Swift and His Talking
 Pictures, 9
Tom Swift and His
 Television Detector, 9
Tom Swift and His
 Undersea Search, 9
Tom Swift and His War
 Tank, 9
Tom Swift and His
 Wireless Message, 8
Tom Swift and His Wizard
 Camera, 8
Tom Swift Circling the
 Globe, 9
Tom Swift in Captivity, 8
Tom Swift in His Sky
 Racer, 8
Tom Swift in the Caves of
 Ice, 8
Tom Swift in the City of
 Gold, 8
Tom Swift in the Land of
 Wonders, 9
Tomb and Other Tales,
 The, 138
Tombs of Atuan, the, 128
Tombs of Kobol, The, 126
Tomoe Gozen, 191
Tomorrow People in "The
 Visitor," The, 174
Tomorrow People in "Three
 in Three," The, 174
Tomorrow Plus X, 216
Tomorrow Testament, The,
 134
Tomorrow's Heritage, 54
Tomorrow's TV, 243
Tong in Cheek, 83
Tonight We Steal the
 Stars, 114
Too Many Magicians, 87
Topper: An Impossible
 Adventure, 199
Topper Takes a Trip, 199
Torian Pearls, The, 135
Torture Machine, The, 211

Torture Trust, 193
Tortured Planet, The, 131
Total War, 3
Touch of Death, The, 56
Touch of Eternity, A, 168
Tour of the Moon, A, 222
Tower of Darkness, 103
Tower of Death, The, 163
Tower of the Elephant, The, 109
Tower of Zanid, The, 61
Towers of Melnon, The, 135
Towers of Toron, The, 62
Towers of Utopia, The, 179
Toyman, 215
Trader to the Stars, 6
Trail of Blood, 125
Trail of Bohu, The, 281
Trail of Cthulhu, The, 137
Trail of Fu Manchu, The 186
Trail of the Cloven Foot, The, 223
Trail of the White Indians, The, 223
Trails of Peril, 49
Traitor to the Living, 79
Traitors' Doom, 55
Tramontane, 170
Transformation of Miss Mavis Ming, The, 152
Transformations, 268
Transformations II, 268
Transformer, 83
Transit of Earth, 266
Transit to Scorpio, 33
Transition of Titus Crow, The, 139
Transmutation of Ling, The, 30
Transvection Machine, The, 105
Trappers of Venus, 95
Travel Tales of Mr. Joseph Jorkens, The, 71
Traveler From Altruria, A, 110
Travels and Adventures by Sea and Land of Baron Munchausen, The, 17
Travels and Adventures of Little Baron Trump and His Wonderful Dog Bulger, 133
Travels and Suprising Adventures of Baron Munchausen, The, 17
Travels and Surprsing Adventures of Baron Munchausen, The, 17
Travels by Sea and Land of the Renowned Baron Munchausen, Including a Tour Through the United States in the Year 1803, The, 16
Travels of Baron Munchausen, The, 17
Travels Through Time, 243
Treachery in Outer Space, 185
Treasure Chest, 84
Treasure of Green Knowe, The, 27
Treasure of the Lake, The, 97
Treasure of the Stars, 135
Treasure of Tranicos, The, 109
Treasure of Wonderwhat, The, 203
Treasure-Train, The, 178
Treasury of Great Science Fiction Volume 1, A, 248
Treasury of Great Science Fiction Volume 2, A, 248
Tree of Swords and Jewels, The, 47
Trek to Madworld, 203
Trellisane Confrontation, The, 204
Tremaynes and the Masterful Monk, The, 70
Trey of Swords, The, 160
Trial by Fire, 12
Triangle, 204
Triangle (Asimov), 11
Tribal War, 88

Tribesmen of Gor, 159
Trick Top Hat, The, 234
Trip Around the World in a Flying Machine, A, 223
Trip To the Moon, Containing an Account of the Island of Noibla, Its Inhabitants, Religious and Political Customs, Etc., The, 139
Trip To the Moon, Containing an Account of the island of Noibla, Its Inhabitants, Religious and Political Customs, Etc., Volume II, The, 139
Triplanetary, 198
Triumph of Elaine, The, 178
Triumph of Time, The, 26
Tros, 155
Tros of Samothrace, 155
Trouble Twisters, The, 6
Trouble With Tribbles, The, 205
Trout's Testament, 85
Troyana, 147
True Names, 247
Trullion: Alastor 2262, 219
Trumps of Doom, 238
Truthful Harp, The, 4
Tsimmis in Tangier, 111
Tunc, 71
Tuned for Murder, 184
Tunnel Terror, 183
Turn the Other Sheik, 52
Turned on to L.U.S.T., 83
Turning Page, The, 118
Turret, The, 194
Twelve Adventurers, and Other Stories, The, 31
12 Adventures of the Celebrated Baron Munchausen, 17
Twelve Fair Kingdoms, 74
12 Must Die, 239

Twenty Thousand Leagues Under the Sea, 222
Twilight at the Well of Souls: The Legacy of Nathan Brazil, 45
Twilight of the Serpent, 213
Twilight River, The, 247
Twin of the Amazon, 80
Twin Worlds, 117
Two Days of Terror, 42
Two Sought Adventure, 129
Two to Conquer, 29
Two Towers, The, 213
Two-Eyes, 91
2001: A Space Odyssey, 48
2010: Odyssey Two, 48
2069, 214
2069+1, 214
2069+2, 214
Tyrant of Hades, The, 118

U.F.O. 517, 78
UFO, 35
UFO 2, 35
UFO-1; Flesh Hunters, 35
UFO-2; Sporting Blood, 35
Ugglians, The, 78
Ugglians at Large: Second Book of Ugg, The, 78
Uhura's Song, 204
Ultimate Enemy, The, 190
Unbegotten, The, 56
Unbeheaded King, The, 61
Uncharted Stars, 160
Uncle Remus and Brer Rabbit, 101
Uncle Remus and His Friends; Old Plantation Stories, Songs, and Ballads, 101
Uncle Remus and the Little Boy, 101
Uncle Remus, His Songs and His Sayings: Folklore of the Old Plantation, 101
Uncle Remus Returns, 101

Under a Calculating Star, 153
Under Old Earth, and Other Explorations, 197
Under Other Conditions, 123
Under the Green Star, 43
Under the Ocean to the South Pole, 185
Under the Stars of Druufon, 168
Under Twin Suns, 164
Underground Picnic, The, 116
Underpeople, The, 197
Undersea, 103
Undersea City, 173, 233
Undersea Fleet, 173, 233
Undersea Quest, 173, 233
Undying Wizard, The, 163
Undying World, 135
Unfair Fare Affair, The, 217
Unfinished Tales of Numenor and Middle-Earth, 213
Unforsaken Hiero, The, 125
Unfortunate Fursey, The, 225
Unicorn Creed, The, 192
Unicorn Girl, The, 5
Universal Prey, The, 282
Universe, 104
Universe 1, 250
Universe 2, 250
Universe 3, 250
Universe 4, 250
Universe 5, 250
Universe 6, 250
Universe 7, 250
Universe 8, 250
Universe 9, 250
Universe 10, 250
Universe 11, 250
Universe 12, 250
Universe 13, 250
Universe 14, 250
Universe 15, 250
Universe Against Her, The, 193
Universe Next Door, The, 234
Unkindness of Ravens, An, 147
Unknown, The, 246
Unknown 5, The, 246
Unknown Danger, 124, 130
Unknown Destiny, 78
Unknown Sector: Milky Way, 168
Unleased Powers, 169
Unless She Burn, 149
Untamed, The, 161
Until the Celebration, 200
Unto the Altar, 213
Unto Zeor, Forever, 132
Up and Coming, 52
Up Your Ante, 84
Urban Prey, 21
Utopia Affair, The, 217
Utopia Hunters, 209

V, 218
V: East Coast Crisis, 218
Vagabond of Space, 169
Valentine Pontifex, 195
Valley of Creeping Men, The, 55
Valley of Fear, The, 55
Valley of Horses, The, 12
Valley of Ogrum, The, 197
Vampire, 195
Vampire Affair, 217
Vampire Lestat, The, 281
Vampires and the Witch, The, 77
Vanisher, The, 182
Vanishing Tower, The, 152
Var the Stick, 7
Vathek: An Arabian Tale, 21
Vazkor, Son of Vazkor, 128
Vega Sector, The, 167
Vegas Vampire, 195
Veiled Lady, The, 77
Veiled Raiders, The, 25
Veiled World, The, 136
Veils of Fear, 147

Vendetta in Spain, 229
Vengeance of the Dancing
    Gods, 45
Venom of Argus, The, 53
Venus in Danger, 167
Venus, Inc., 280
Venus Trap, The, 167
Veruchia, 215
Vestiges of Time, 148
Victor, The, 158
Victoria Winters, 188
Victory for Kregen, A, 33
Victory on Janus, 160
Viking Slaughter, 34
Viking's Revenge, The, 157
Virgin, The, 53
Virgin and the Swine,
    The, 227
Virgin in Flames, 187
Virgin of Zesh, The, 61
Viriconium Nights, 102
Virility Gene, The, 34
Virus X, 107
Viscous Circle, 7
Vision of Tarot, 8
Visions of Nowhere, 172
Visit From Venus, A, 84
Visitors From Oz, The, 20
Visitors From Planet
    Veta, The, 91
Voice From Another World,
    A, 123
Voice of the Mountain,
    The, 228
Voiceless Ones, The, 56
Voices of Mars, The, 153
Volcano Ogre, The, 44
Volteface, 3
Volunteers For Frago, 170
Voodoo!, 267
Voodoo Planet, 159
Vortex Blaster, The, 198
Voyage of the Dawn
    Treader, the, 131
Voyage of the Starfire to
    Atlantis, The, 154
Voyage to Dari, A, 225
Voyage to the Bottom of
    the Sea (Jones), 224

Voyage to the Bottom of
    the Sea (Sturgeon), 224
Voyage to the City of the
    Dead, 82
Voyage to the Moon, A, 222
Voyages of Doctor
    Doolittle, 134
Vulcan!, 203
Vulcan Academy Murders,
    The, 204
Vultures of the White
    Death, 106

Wagered World, The, 115
Wailing Octopus, The, 25
Waiters on the Dance, 191
Walk to the End of the
    World, 47
Wall Around a Star, 173,
    233
Wall of Serpents, The, 61
Wallet of Kai Lung, The,
    30
Walls of Air, 98
Wanderer, 192
Wanderer in Space, 153
Wandering Jew, The, 209
Wandering Stars, 252
Wandl the Invader, 58
Wandor's Battle, 94
Wandor's Flight, 94
Wandor's Journey, 94
Wandor's Ride, 94
Wandor's Voyage, 94
War Against the Chtorr:
    Invasion, the, 89
War and Peace, 270
War for Eternity, The, 189
War Gamers' World, 225
War Games of Zelos,
    The, 53
War God, The, 157
War in Heaven, 231
War Machines of Kalinth,
    The, 124
War of Nerves, 98
War of the Cybernauts,
    The, 177
War of the Gods, 126

War of the Gurus, 179
War of the Moonrhymes, 149
War of the Wing Men, 6
War on Aleph, 114
War Terror, The, 177
War Wings, 2
Ware Hawk, 160
Warlock, 206
Warlock Enraged, 281
Warlock In Spite of
  Himself, The, 206
Warlock of Rhada, The, 90
Warlock of the Witch
  World, 160
Warlock Unlocked, The, 206
Warlord, The (Frost), 85
Warlord, The (Sadler), 190
Warlord of Mars, The, 36
Warlord of the Air, The,
  152
Warlords of Gaiken, 135
Warlords of Xuma, 123
Warmaster, 141
Warrior Enchained, The, 94
Warrior of Llarn, 83
Warrior of Mars, 80
Warrior of Scorpio, 33
Warrior of the Dawn, 32
Warrior of World's End,
  The, 44
Warrior Rearmed, the, 94
Warrior Within, The, 94
Warrior's World, 32
Warriors of Dawn, The, 83
Warriors of Laittan, 135
Warriors of Mars, 151
Warriors of Noomas, 162
Warriors of Serpent Land,
  51
Warriors of Terra, The, 80
Watchers of the Dark, 23
Watchers Out of Time and
  Others, The, 138
Watchtower, 139
Waters of Centaurus, The,
  32
Way Back, The, 46
Way-Farer, The, 192
Way of Ecben, The, 40

Way to Dawnworld, The, 203
We Claim These Stars!, 6
Wealth Seeker, The, 93
Weapon Makers, The, 220
Weapon Shops of Isher,
  The, 220
Weapons From Beyond, The,
  99
Weathermonger, 64
Web, The, 3
Web of Darkness, 29
Web of Easter Island,
  The, 137
Web of Sand, 215
Web of Light, 29
Web of the Romulans, 204
Web of the Spider, 163
Web of the Witch World,
  160
Weird Adventures of the
  Shadow, The, 93
Weird Adventures of the
  Shadow: Grove of Doom,
  The, 93
Weird Heroes Volume 1, 267
Weird Heroes Volume 2, 267
Weird Heroes Volume 3, 267
Weird Heroes Volume 4, 267
Weird of the White Wolf,
  152
Weird Show, 266
Weird Tales, 262
Weird Tales #1, 251
Weird Tales #2, 251
Weird Tales #3, 251
Weird Tales #4, 251
Weirdstone, The, 87
Weirdstone of Brisin-
  gamen, The, 87
Welcome Home, Jaime, 136
Well of Darkness, The, 88
Well of Shiuan, 47
Wereblood, 113
Werenight, 113
Werewolf!, 267
Werewolf of Ponkert, The,
  155
Werewolves of Kregen, 34
West of Honor, 174

Wham! Bam! Thank, You, Ma'am Affair, The, 52
What If? Volume 1: Stories That Should Have Won The Hugo, 261
What If? Volume 2: Stories That Should Have Won The Hugo, 261
What If? Volume 3: Stories That Should Have Won The Hugo, 261
What a Way to Go (Fox), 84
What a Way to Go! (Tralins), 214
Whatever Goes Up, 52
Wheel of Death, 201
Wheelworld, 102
When Death Birds Fly, 163
When Dreamers Cease to Dream, 18
When Hell Laughs, 197
When the Green Star Calls, 43
When the Star Kings Die, 114
When Trouble Beckons, 143
When Voiha Wakes, 47
When Wendy Grew Up: An Afterthought, 18
When Worlds Collide, 236
Where No Man Has Gone Before, 205
Where No Stars Guide, 120
Where Satan Dwells, 207
Where the Action Is, 84
Where the Ni-Lach, 22
Whetted Bronze, 34
Whiff of Madness, A, 91
Whipping Star, 104
Whirlpool of Stars, 34
Whisker of Hercules, The, 183
Whisper of Glocken, The, 119
Whispering Box Mystery, The, 25
Whispering Mountain, The, 3
Whispers, 269

Whispers II, 269
Whispers III, 269
Whispers IV, 269
Whispers V, 269
White Dragon, The, 140
White Fangs, 88
White Fire, 26
White Fire, The, 282
White Gold Wielder, 68
White Hart, The, 201
White Mountains, The, 48
White Python, 46
White Robe, The, 40
White Rose, The, 53
White Shield, The, 149
Who Fears the Devil?, 228
...Who Needs Enemies, 82
Wicked Day, The, 208
Wiggins for President, 31
Wild Adventures Round the Pole, 202
Wild Alien Tamer, The, 178
Wild Inventions, 243
Wild Ones, The, 46
Wildeblood's Empire, 202
Wilder Curse, The, 184
Wilderness of Ice, The, 222
Wildings of Westron, The, 123
Will Men Be Like Gods?, 70
Will of the Gods, The, 94
Will the Real Rod Please Stand Up?, 52
Willard, 89
Win With Sin, 214
Wind From the Abyss, 154
Wind in the Door, A, 130
Winds of Darkover, 28
Winds of Gath, The, 215
Winds of the Heliopolis, 85
Winds of the World, The, 155
Windsingers, The, 133
Wine, Women and Wars, 41
Wings of Adventure, 2
Wings of Omen, 12, 244
Wings of Peace, The, 56

Wings of the Black Death, 201
Wings of the Navy, 2
Winnowing Winds, 14
Winterking, 103
Wintermind, 90
Wintersol, 72
Wisdom's Daughter, 97
Wishing Horse of Oz, The, 19
Wishsong of Shannara, The, 31
Witch Goddess, The, 2
Witch in the Wood, The, 230
Witch of the Dark Gate, 114
Witch Queen of Lochlann, 199
Witch Queen of Mongo, The, 177
Witch Shall Be Born, A, 108
Witch Wolf: An Uncle Remus Story, The, 101
Witch World, 160
Witches, 244
Witches of Kregen, 34
Witchfinders, The, 51
Witching Hour, The, 207
Witching of Dracula, The, 136
With a Tangled Skein, 276
With Airship and Submarine; a Tale of Adventure, 51
With Friends Like These ..., 82
With Mercy Toward None, 52
With the Revolutionists in Bolivia, 55
Wizard, 221
Wizard in Waiting, The, 111
Wizard of Earthsea, A, 128
Wizard of Lemuria, The, 43
Wizard of Linn, The, 220
Wizard of Oz, The, 19
Wizard of Rentoro, 135

Wizard of Storms, 219
Wizard of Venus, The, 37
Wizard's Eleven, 212
Wizards of Senuchria, The, 33
Wizards, 244
Woggle-Bug Book, The, 20
Wolf Bell, The, 156
Wolf Worlds, The, 50
Wolves of Willoughby Chase, The, 3
Woman Ayisha, The, 155
Woman of the Horseclans, A, 2
Women of Wonder, 269
Wonder City of Oz, The, 20
Wonderflower of Utik, 169
Wonderful Adventures of Arthur Gordon Pym, The, 173
Wonderful Electric Elephant, The, 150
Wonderful Farm, The, 13
Wonderful Flight to the Mushroom Planet, The, 41
Wonderful Wizard of Oz, The, 19
Wondermakers, 260
Word for World is Forest, The, 129
Word of the Sorceress, The, 149
World Aflame, A, 216
World Assunder, The, 225
World Below, The, 235
World Called Camelot, A, 124
World Changer, The, 38
World Enough, and Time, 118
World Fantasy Awards Volume Two, The, 274
World Gone Mad, A, 168
World in Eclipse, 63
World in Peril, The, 48
World of A, The, 220
World of Mazes, 221
World of Mists, 153
World of Null-A, 220

World of Promise, 215
World of Ptavvs, 158
World of the Sleeper, 227
World of the Starwolves, The, 99
World Shuffler, The, 127
World That Couldn't and 8 Other SF Novelets, 257
World Without End, 203
World Without Men, 144
World Without Mercy, 170
World Wreckers, The, 28
World's Best Science Fiction: 1965, 274
World's Best Science Fiction: 1966, 274
World's Best Science Fiction: 1967, 274
World's Best Science Fiction: 1968, 274
World's Best Science Fiction: 1969, 274
World's Best Science Fiction: 1970, 274
World's Best Science Fiction: 1971, 274
World's End, 224
World's Fair Goblin, 182
Worlds, 98
Worlds Apart (Lach-Szyrma), 123
Worlds Apart (Haldeman), 98
Worlds of the Imperium, 126
Worlds of Weird, 262
Worlds of Wonder, 115
Worm Ouroboros, The, 72
Worms of the Earth, 110
Worse Things Waiting, 137, 228
Worst Man in the World, The, 107
Wounded Land, The, 68
Wounded Sky, The, 204
Wraith Board, 24
Wrath of Fu Manchu and Other Stories, The, 187
Wrath of Grapes, The, 231

Wreck of Westminister Abbey, Alias the Year Two Thousand, Alias the Ordeal of Sepulchral Candour, The, 57
Wrexham's Romance, 86
Wrinkle in Time, A, 130
Wyst: Alastor 1716, 219

Yankee in Oz, 20
Year 2018!, 26
Year of the Unicorn, 160
Year's Best Fantasy Stories, The, 274
Year's Best Fantasy Stories: 2, The, 274
Year's Best Fantasy Stories: 3, The, 274
Year's Best Fantasy Stories: 4, The, 274
Year's Best Fantasy Stories: 5, The, 274
Year's Best Fantasy Stories: 6, The, 274
Year's Best Fantasy Stories: 7, The, 275
Year's Best Fantasy Stories: 8, The, 275
Year's Best Fantasy Stories: 9, The, 275
Year's Best Fantasy Stories: 10, The, 275
Year's Best Horror Stories, The, 237
Year's Best Horror Stories: Series II, The, 275
Year's Best Horror Stories: Series III, The, 275
Year's Best Horror Stories: Series IV, The, 275
Year's Best Horror Stories: Series V, The, 275
Year's Best Horror Stories: Series VI, The, 275

Year's Best Horror Stories: Series VII, The, 275
Year's Best Horror Stories: Series VIII, The, 275
Year's Best Horror Stories: Series IX, The, 275
Year's Best Horror Stories: Series X, The, 275
Year's Best Horror Stories: Series XI, The, 275
Year's Best Horror Stories: Series XII, The, 275
Year's Finest Fantasy, 251
Year's Finest Fantasy Volume 2, 251
Yearwood, 103
Yellow Claw, The, 187
Yellow Cloud, The, 182
Yellow Death; a Tale of Occult Mysteries, 120
Yellow Hoard, The, 184
Yellow Knight of Oz, The, 19
Yellow Scourge, The, 207
Yendi, 32
Yesterday's Son, 204
Yet More Penguin Science Fiction, 241
Ylana of Callisto, 44
Yngling, The, 59
Yoke of Magic, A, 221
Yoke of Shen, The, 164
Yorath the Wolf, 231
You Will Never Be the Same, 197
Young Rissa, 38
Young Unicorns, The, 130
Young Warriors, The, 126

Z-Lensman, 198
Z-Sting, 225
Zacherley's Midnight Snacks, 275
Zacherley's Vulture Stew, 275
Zagribud, 80
Zanoni, 34
Zanthar at Moon's Madness, 232
Zanthar at the Edge of Never, 232
Zanthar at Trip's End, 232
Zanthar of the Many Worlds, 232
Zanthodon, 44
Zarsthor's Bane, 160
Zemba, 93
Zenda Vendetta, the, 237
Zenya, 215
Zero Stone, The, 160
Zero the Slaver: a Romance of Equatorial Africa, 81
008 Meets Gnatman, 4
008 Meets Modesta Blaze, 4
Zip-Zip and His Flying Saucer, 192
Zip-Zip and the Red Planet, 192
Zip-Zip Goes to Venus, 192
Zombie, 127

BIBLIOGRAPHY

REFERENCE TEXTS

AMERICAN BOOK PUBLISHING RECORD, CUMULATIVE 1965-1969, VOL. V: FICTION. NY: R.R. Bowker Co., 1970.

AMERICAN BOOK PUBLISHING RECORD 1982. NY: R.R. Bowker Co., 1983.

AMERICAN BOOK PUBLISHING RECORD 1983. NY: R.R. Bowker Co., 1984.

BARRON, NEIL, ed. Anatomy of Wonder: A Critical Guide to Science Fiction. 2nd ed. NY: R.R. Bowker Company, 1981.

BENET, WILLIAM ROSE, ed. The Reader's Encyclopedia. 2nd ed. NY: Crowell, 1965.

BLEILER, E.F. The Checklist of Science-Fiction and Supernatural Fiction. Glen Rock: Firebell Books, 1978.

BLEILER, E.F., ed. The Guide to Supernatural Fiction. Kent, OH: Kent State University Press, 1983.

BLEILER, E.F., ed. Science Fiction Writers. NY: Charles Scribners Sons, 1982.

BOOKS IN PRINT. NY: Bowker, 1981-1983.

BRITISH MUSEUM GENERAL CATALOGUE OF PRINTED BOOKS TO 1955, COMPACT EDITION. 27 Volumes. NY: Readex Microprint Corporation, 1967.

BRITISH MUSEUM GENERAL CATALOGUE TO PRINTED BOOKS, TEN-YEAR SUPPLEMENT, 1956-1965. 50 Volumes. London: Trustees of the British Museum, 1968.

BURNHAM, MARY et.al., eds. The Cumulative Book Index, July 1924-June 1925. NY: H.W. Wilson Company, 1925.

CASEBEER, LANCE, ed. "Collecting Paperbacks?" Vol.2 #3; Vol.3 #s 1,3,4,5. Portland, Ore., nd (c.1980).

COMMIRE, ANNE, ed. Something About the Author. 37 Volumes. Detroit: Gale Research Co., 1971-1985.

COMMIRE, ANNE, ed. Yesterday's Authors of Books For Children. 2 Volumes. Detroit: Gale Research Co., 1977.

CONTEMPORARY AUTHORS FIRST REVISION (112 Volumes) and CONTEMPORARY AUTHORS NEW REVISION SERIES (13 Volumes). Detroit: Gale Research Co., 1967-85.

CURREY, L.W. Science Fiction and Fantasy Authors: A Bibliography of First Printings of Their Fiction. Boston: G.K. Hall & Co., 1979.

DAVIS, JOE LEE. James Branch Cabell. NY: Twayne Publishers, Inc., 1962.

EVANS, I.O. Jules Verne and His Work. NY: Twayne Publishers, Inc., 1966.

GREENE, DAVID L. & DICK MARTIN. The Oz Scrapbook. NY: Random House, 1977.

HAWKINS, ELEANOR E. et.al., eds. The United States Catalog Supplement, January 1918-June 1921. NY: H.W. Wilson Company, 1921.

HAWKINS, ELEANOR E. et.al., eds. The United States Catalog Supplement, July 1921-June 1924. NY: H.W. Wilson Company, 1924.

HEINS, HENRY HARDY. A Golden Anniversary Bibliography of Edgar Rice Burroughs. Revised Ed. West Kingston, RI: Donald M. Grant, 1964.

HUBIN, ALLEN J. The Bibliography of Crime Fiction: 1749-1975. San Diego: University of California/Del Mar, Publisher's Inc., 1979.

HUBIN, ALLEN J. Crime Fiction 1749-1980: A Comprehensive Bibliography. NY & London: Garland Publishers, Inc., 1984.

HUSBAND, JANET. Sequels: An Annotated Guide to Novels in Series. Chicago: American Library Association, 1982.

KERR, ELIZABETH MARGARET. Bibliography of the Sequence Novel. NY: Octagon Books/Farrar, Straus and Giroux, 1973. Reprinted from University of Minnesota Press, 1950.

KIRKPATRICK, D.L., ed. Twentieth-Century Children's Writers. NY: St. Martin's Press, 1978.

"LOCUS: THE NEWSPAPER OF THE SCIENCE FICTION FIELD"
Oakland, CA: Locus Publications, issues 1984-85.

LYNN, RUTH NADELMAN. Fantasy For Children: An Annotated Checklist. NY: Bowker, 1979.

McKENZIE, ALAN, ed. "Doctor Who Summer Special" London: Marvel Comics, Ltd., 1984.

NICHOLS, PETER, ed. The Science Fiction Encyclopedia. NY: Dolphin/Doubleday & Co., 1979.

REGINALD, R. Science Fiction and Fantasy Literature, A Checklist 1700-1974. Detroit: Gale Research Co., 1979.

REILLY, JOHN M., ed. Twentieth-Century Crime and Mystery Writers. NY: St. Martin's Press, 1980.

ROCK, JAMES A. Who Goes There: A Bibliographic Dictionary of Pseudonymous Literature. Bloomington: James A. Rock & Co., 1979.

"THE SCIENCE-FICTION COLLECTOR #4". Calgary, Alberta: Pandora's Books Ltd., 1977.

SEARLS, BAIRD, BETH MEACHAM, & MICHAEL FRANKLIN. A Reader's Guide to Fantasy. NY: Avon Books, 1982.

SEARLS, BAIRD, MARTIN LAST, BETH MEACHAM, & MICHAEL FRANKLIN. A Reader's Guide to Science Fiction. NY: Avon Books, 1979.

SMITH, CURTIS C. Twentieth-Century Science-Fiction Writers. NY: St. Martin's Press, 1981.

TUCK, DONALD H. The Encyclopedia of Science Fiction and Fantasy Through 1968. Chicago: Advent, 1978.

TYMM, MARSHALL B., ed. Horror Literature. NY: R.R. Bowker Company, 1981.

WELLS, STUART W. III. The Science Fiction and Heroic Fantasy Author Index. Duluth, MN: Purple Unicorn Books, 1978.

DEALERS' CATALOGS

CURREY, L.W. "Catalogue #68: Fantasy & Science Fiction". Elizabethtown, NY: L.W. Currey, Inc., 1982.

CURREY, L.W. "Catalogue #77: Into the Unknown: Fantasy & Science Fiction Literature". Elizabethtown, NY: L.W. Currey, Inc., 1984.

THE GHENT BOOKWORM. "Catalogue of Sci-Fi & Fantasy". Norfolk, 1980.

LAWRENCE, J. STEPHEN. "Rare Books Catalogue #40: Science Fiction and Fantasy". Chicago: J.S. Lawrence, nd.

STEPHENS, CHRISTOPHER P. "Catalogue #60: Modern Firsts". New York, 1984.

WEINBERG, ROBERT & PHYLLIS. "November '84 Catalogue". Oak Forest, IL: 1984.

----. "April '85 Catalogue". Oak Forest, IL: 1985.

PUBLISHERS PROMOTIONS AND CATALOGS

Ace/Charter/Berkley Paperbacks
Avon Books
Ballantine/Del Rey Publishing
Bantam Books
New American Library (DAW/Signet)
Pinnacle/Tor Science Fiction
Pocket Books/Baen Books

JUL 29 1987